RACE : NATION : PERSON

SOCIAL ASPECTS OF THE RACE PROBLEM—
A SYMPOSIUM

RACE : NATION : PERSON
Social Aspects of the Race Problem

A SYMPOSIUM

By

JOSEPH T. DELOS, O.P.
L'Université Catholique de Lille

ANTON C. PEGIS, Ph.D.
Fordham University

YVES DE LA BRIÈRE, S.J.
L'Université Catholique de Paris

ANDREW J. KRZESINSKI, Ph.D., S.T.D.
The Jagellonian University of Cracow

LUIGI STURZO, Ph.D., S.T.D.

GEORGE BARRY O'TOOLE, Ph.D., S.T.D.
The Catholic University of America

And Three European Scholars Whose Names
May Not Be Disclosed

———

With a Preface by His Excellency
BISHOP JOSEPH W. CORRIGAN
Late Rector of The Catholic University of America

New York
BARNES & NOBLE, INC.

1944

Nihil obstat:

ARTHUR J. SCANLAN, S.T.D.
Censor Librorum

Imprimatur:

✠FRANCIS J. SPELLMAN, D.D.
Archbishop, New York

July 15, 1943

PREFACE

This symposium of monographs by internationally known savants, both European and American, turns upon three pivotal ideas: race, nation and person.

Race from the standpoint of the natural sciences was the subject of a previous symposium.[1] In the present one, the same theme is discussed from the standpoint of history, philosophy, ethics, jurisprudence and the social sciences generally.

Here, however, besides race, the cognate concept of nation had to be taken into account; for the word "race" is unfortunately equivocal, being used in an ethnic, no less than a biological sense. In its biological acceptation, the term signifies a sub-species or variety—one of several heritable biotypes within a single organic species. Used in its ethnic sense, however, it is roughly synonymous with nation.

To interchange these two distinct concepts in the same discourse simply because both happen to bear an identical name is equivocation, a fatal fallacy, particularly in the domain of political theory where all inconsequential reasoning leads inevitably to disastrous social consequences.

Indeed, the whole political ideology of National Socialism—especially its inhuman applications exemplified in so-called eugenic and discriminatory legislation—rests upon this fundamental fallacy of unwarranted transition from race in the biological, to race in the ethnic sense.

By dint of such sophistry a pretext is found for enacting into law enforced sterilization and various forms of racial discrimination which, whatever else they may be, are above all so many disavowals of the supreme human value—the personal dignity of man. For "person," to quote the words of St. Thomas Aquinas, "signifies that which is most perfect in the whole of nature." [2]

Every human individual is a person, that is to say, normally a free agent, the originator of his own conduct, for which he is in

[1] *Scientific Aspects of the Race Problem.* The Catholic University of America Press, Washington, D. C. (Longmans, Green and Co., New York), 1941.
[2] *Summa Theologica,* P. I, q. 29, a. 3.

consequence fully responsible. As God is the absolutely First Cause of the universe, so man is in a certain, if limited, sense, the first cause of his own actions. It is, therefore, in so far as he is a person that he is said to be "made to the image and likeness of God."

Before the advent of Christianity, human knowledge did not reach full recognition of the dignity of human personality. It was through faith in the Christian mystery of the Incarnation—in a Divine personality replacing human personality in Christ—that men came to know that they were, as persons, capable of elevation to the sonship of God.

What makes the democratic conception of government peculiarly Christian is its basic principle of respect for person—for the conscience and God-given rights of the human individual. It is, on the contrary, the degradation of person, the supervaluation of the collectivity of race, nation or State at the expense of the personal dignity of the individual, that stamps the totalitarian ideologies of government as not only unchristian but inhuman.

Early in 1938, the Holy See[3] passed censure on eight propositions, covering the range of these errors, prefacing its condemnation with this memorable exhortation addressed to the rectors and faculties of Catholic universities throughout the world:

"On Christmas Eve of the year just past (1937), the August Pontiff, happily reigning, in profound sorrow delivered to their Eminences, the Cardinals, and to the Prelates of the Roman Curia an address on the dire persecution which, as all are aware, afflicts the Catholic Church in Germany.

"But what weighs most heavily upon the Holy Father's mind is the fact that in order to excuse the enormity of such injustice, shameless men interpose a smoke screen of calumny and seek to corrupt minds and uproot the true religion by disseminating far and wide the most pernicious doctrines masked under the false name of science.

"That being so, this Sacred Congregation calls upon Catholic universities and faculties to spare no pains or effort to defend the truth against the errors that are springing up.

"Wherefore, let the professors, each in his own field, be it

---

[3] See the *Letter of the S. Congr. of Seminaries and Universities,* April 13, 1938, to the rectors of "Catholic Universities and Faculties"—among others to the late Most Rev. Bishop Joseph M. Corrigan, Rector of The Catholic University of America. (Note of the editor.)

biology, history, apologetics, or the juridico-moral sciences, diligently forge the intellectual weapons required validly and scientifically to refute as utterly absurd the following dogmas."

The dogmas which the Sacred Congregation thereupon condemned were:

" (1) The races of mankind differ so greatly from one another, by virtue of their innate and inalterable character, that the lowest of them is farther removed from the highest than it is from the highest species of brutes.

" (2) It is imperative at all costs to preserve and promote racial vigor and the purity of the blood; whatever is conducive to this end is by that very fact honorable and permissible.

' (3) From the blood, in which the genius of the race resides, spring all the intellectual and moral qualities of man, as from their principal source.

' (4) The chief purpose of education is to develop racial characteristics and to kindle in the soul a burning love for one's own race as the highest good.

" (5) Religion is subordinate to the law of race and must needs conform thereto.

" (6) The primary source and supreme norm of the whole juridical order is the racial instinct.

" (7) Only the KOSMOS or Universe exists; all things, including man himself, are but different forms of the *Living Universe*, developing in the long course of ages.

" (8) Individual men exist only through the State and for the sake of the State; whatever rights they have originate exclusively from a concession on the part of the State."

After listing these eight propositions, the *Letter* concludes as follows:

"To these most odious opinions anyone might easily add others.
"Our Most Holy Father, Prefect of this S. Congregation, takes it for granted that You, Most Reverend Sir, will leave no stone unturned to carry out fully what, by these presents, the Sacred Congregation has enjoined."

Responding at once to the foregoing call to action, The Catholic University of America undertook, in connection with its Semicentennial Celebration, the arduous task of assembling this symposium—of soliciting, collecting and translating the various monographs.

Providentially, this work of mobilizing the best minds of Europe and America against the racist and nationalist errors was begun nearly four years ago—on November 23, 1938. Germany's invasion of Poland on September 1, 1939, kindled the spark of the Second World War. After that date the monographs could scarcely have been written, much less forwarded to the editors.

Even so, three of them have had to be published anonymously. To disclose their names might mean death or imprisonment for the European authors in question. This fact alone bears eloquent testimony to the need of the present publication. Expedient though it be to withhold their identity, there must be no suppression of the truth to which they bear witness. This, however, is but a provisional shift, pending the advent of freer times in which, without danger to any of the writers, it will be possible to publish a future edition giving all of them credit for their respective contributions, as was done in the case of the first symposium.

Washington, D. C.

JOSEPH M. CORRIGAN
Bishop of Bilta
Rector of The Catholic University
of America

EDITOR'S FOREWORD

We had hoped to publish this international symposium at an earlier date, but insurmountable obstacles intervened to defeat our intention. Before it could see the light, the two leaders, to whom the work owed its inception, had died: Pope Pius XI on February 10, 1939, and Bishop Corrigan, late Rector of The Catholic University of America, on June 9, 1942.

It is, however, none the less timely for the delay. The need of the hour is for an antidote to secularist thought which by its denial of the personal dignity of man saps the foundation of American democracy, making for the triumph at home of the very totalitarianism we are fighting abroad. And such an antidote the Christian personalism expounded in this volume provides.

American democracy is founded on the personalist principle that all men are rational subjects of God-given rights—"all men . . . are endowed by their Creator with certain unalienable rights" (*The Declaration of Independence*). In a word, man is a *person,* not a *thing.* An irrational thing may be an *individual,* like a horse or a tree, but only a rational being can be a person. Man is an individual by his body; he is a person by his reason. Individuality is a divisive factor that keeps men distinct and apart; reason is a unifying force that enables men to agree on what is for the common good. Hence, personalism is not to be confounded with selfish individualism which, under the qualification "rugged," has deservedly come in for opprobrium in our day. Personalism, however, which is free from this reproach, is the only sound basis for democracy. In the words[1] of Étienne Gilson: "Individualism always breeds tyranny, but personalism always breeds liberty, for a group of individuals is but a herd, whereas a group of persons is a people." It is only by returning to Christian personalism that America can hope to avoid State socialism, the despotic extreme to which reaction against the abuses of an unreasonably antisocial individualism will inevitably lead.

By secularizing on principle the education of youth, American educators have precipitated the present decay of our democratic

[1] *Cf.* Gilson's Address at the Harvard Tercentenary Conference of 1936.

institutions. For materialistic secularism, as Mortimer Adler points out,[2] cuts all ground of logical justification from under the democratic ideal. We quote:

> "They (the majority of American educators) talk a great deal about natural rights and the dignity of man, but this is loose and irresponsible talk in which they lightly indulge because they do not mind contradicting themselves. There are no natural rights if there is no natural moral law, which is binding upon all men everywhere in the same way. Man has no dignity if he is not a rational animal, essentially distinct from the brutes by reason of the spiritual dimension of his being . . .
>
> 'For all these reasons I say we have more to fear from our professors than trom Hitler. It is they who have made American education what it is both in content and in method. . . .'"

Editing this symposium has been no easy task. Competent authors had to be found who were willing to contribute the projected articles. Of those who accepted our invitation some were subsequently snatched away by the war or incapacitated for other reasons; these had to be replaced by other writers. Ultimately, however, we were able to assemble these ten monographs, five of which had then to be translated into English. By May 28, 1942, the work was complete, and Bishop Corrigan (who had associated me with himself in the editorship of this volume) wrote the foregoing Preface, less than two weeks before he died.

We are conscious that the work still has imperfections which careful revision might remove, but we feel that, in view of past delay, further postponement of its publication would be inadvisable.

In conclusion, this editor wishes to express his appreciation of the help received from his colleagues. Acknowledgements are due not only to the Editorial Committee, who planned the present volume, but also to those who assisted in the work of translation. Among the latter, Dr. Herbert Wright, Professor of International Law, and Dr. Anthony De Vito, Instructor in Romance Languages —both of The Catholic University of America, Washington, D. C. —and Dr. Ignatius Kelly, formerly Professor of Romance Languages in De Sales College, Toledo, Ohio, are deserving of special mention.

Washington, D.C.   G. BARRY O'TOOLE
                                               Assistant Editor

[2] See his paper on "God and the Professors," *Science, Philosophy and Religion: A Symposium*, New York, 1941, pp. 136, 137.

CONTENTS

xi

I

RACISM, LAW AND RELIGION

By ———————

RACISM, LAW AND RELIGION

I

For a long time the racist theory remained quite unscientific and assumed many different forms. Today we begin to be thoroughly familiar with it, for it has given rise to the appearance of numerous works in Germany and abroad.[1]

It would be inexact to believe that we are dealing here with an entirely new theory. Rather must we see herein the culmination of a movement begun many centuries ago, as far back as Martin Luther, who placed the truly German way of thought and the truly German sentiments in opposition to those of the Latins. Then came Kant, who reversed the natural order of things and derived the good from duty and no longer, as heretofore, duty from the good. With Hegel, Fichte, Herder and their disciples, we establish the glorification and at times almost the deification of the State, the nation, the people, and, even at this time, the intention, which is very clear in all and evident in Fichte, of placing

[1] See particularly Grete Stoffel, *La dictature du facisme allemand* (Paris, 1936); Roger Bonnard, *Le droit et l'État dans la doctrine nationale-socialiste* (Paris, 1936; 2d ed. rev., 1939); Marcel Cot, *La conception hitlérienne du droit* (Paris, 1938); Hassan Chahid Nouraï, *Recherches sur la conception nationale-socialiste du droit des gens* (1938); Jacques Fournier, *La conception nationale-socialiste du droit des gens* (Paris, 1939). These last two works contain very carefully prepared bibliographies of German works on the question up to 1938.

Among the articles in periodicals, I shall cite especially Lawrence Preuss, "La conception racial nationale-socialiste du droit international," in *Revue générale de droit international public*, vol. 42 (1935), p. 668; Eduard Bristler, "La doctrine nationale-socialiste du droit des gens," in *Revue internationale de la théorie du droit*, vol. 12 (1938), p. 116, a very condensed article in which will be found the gist of his work, *Die Völkerrechtslehre des Nationalsozialismus* (Zürich, 1938); Mircea Djuvara, "Le nouvel essai de philosophie politique et juridique en Allemagne," in *Revista de Drept public*, Bucarest, vol. 14 (1939), no. 1-2; in this last article will be found references to the most important German works on the question which have appeared in these last months. The citations which I shall hereafter make of the foregoing authors by their last name alone will refer to the works mentioned above.

Finally, let me point out a review devoted particularly to this question, *Races et racisme*, which began in Paris in 1938 and in which there have already appeared many well-documented articles.

3

the German State, nation or people in the first rank, a veritable
Kulturvolk, and even the only *Vollkulturvolk,* when compared
with the other peoples, which have remained more or less in the
state of nature *(Naturvölker)* .

But there had not yet been found the scientific criterion which
would permit the distinction of the Germans from the rest of
humanity and the constitution of them as a group of a superior
nature and therefore having superior rights to those of the other
peoples. At least the attempt of Fichte in this direction, with the
Ursprache of the *Urvolk,* had pitiably failed, since no one could
take seriously his assertions about the original language of the
primitive people, who come directly from God and alone have
the right to the name of people, and that the German people
alone have the right to this primitive and divine character that
confers upon a race the status of nation.[2]

It is only in comparatively recent times that the Germans, profit-
ing from the works of two foreigners, Count Arthur Joseph de
Gobineau[3] and Houston Stewart Chamberlain,[4] have sought to
substitute the idea of race for that of nation or people. The first
efforts towards the application of the new theory immediately
disclosed its virulence and the grave dangers which it presents
in Germany itself with the Jewish persecution and abroad with
the conquest of Austria and of Czechoslovakia. Since 1938 its
principal assertions have been condemned by the Holy See,
especially the following: "The primary source and supreme rule
of the entire juridical order is the racial instinct." [5]

After a critical exposé of this theory, it will be our task to probe
to the bottom of the matter and to show its radical opposition not
only to Christianity, but also to humanism and that which may be
termed the common morality of the nations.

---

[2] See J. Gottlieb Fichte, *Die Reden an die deutsche Nation,* in his *Sämmtliche
Werke* (Berlin, 1846), vol. 8, p. 392, and the study thereon of J. Declareuil, "Les
discours à la nation allemand," in *Revue de droit public et des sciences politiques,*
vol. 24 (1917), pp. 361 ff. See also Louis Le Fur, *Races, Nationalités, États* (Paris,
1922), pp. 28 ff.

[3] *Essai sur l'inégalité des races humaines* (Paris, 1856).

[4] *Die Grundlagen des XIX. Jahrhunderts* (Leipzig, 1907). Chamberlain was a naturalized German.

[5] Letter of the Sacred Congregation of Seminaries and Universities to His Emi-
nence Cardinal Baudrillart, under date of April 13, 1938, proposition VI. His Exc.
Bishop Corrigan, Rector of The Catholic University of America, also received this
Letter of the S. Congr., which was addressed to all rectors of Pontifical Catholic
universities throughout the world.

So far as the exposé of the racist theory is concerned, it will be possible to be rather brief, because the essential points of this doctrine are now sufficiently well known. As Marcel Cot very justly remarked, it is reduced to these four fundamental principles:

1. The observation of the human *milieu* proves the existence of distinct races.
2. These races are of unequal value.
3. The first of all is the Nordic race, the purity of which must be protected.
4. It is the Nordic race which constitutes the superior element of the German symbiosis and gives it its value.[6]

The chief point of the new doctrine is the importance attached to the idea of race. In several passages, Hitler insists on this point:

Then the basic realization is *that the State represents not an end, but a means. It is indeed the presumption for the formation of a higher human culture, but not its cause. On the contrary, the latter lies exclusively in the existence of a race capable of culture. . . .* It is not the State in itself that creates a definite cultural level, it can only preserve the race which conditions the latter. . . . *Thus the presumption for the existence of a higher humanity is not the State, but the nationality which possesses the essential ability.*[7]

Thus, jurists and publicists, historians and philosophers have been mistaken heretofore in showing preference for the State, the nation or the people. The people *(Volk)* must be considered not as a juridical notion, as the object of the possessor of power, but rather as an ethnic notion resting upon the idea of race. The new Germany is communitarian; its essential characteristic is that of being a *Gemeinschaft.* Law as well as morality, language as well as art, all this is the function of the national soul, the *Volksgeist.* In the *Volksgemeinschaft,* in the National-Socialist sense—

the co-ordination of the popular collectivity results from the fact that all the members of this collectivity are each permeated with the objective spirit of

[6] Cot, p. 144.

[7] *Mein Kampf* (auth. Eng. trans., compl. and unabr., fully annotated, New York, Reynal & Hitchcock, 1939), pp. 592-94. Italics in the original. The State is always "based on the instinct of the preservation of the species"; it is "a means to an end. Its end is the preservation and the promotion of a community of physically and psychologically equal living beings." *Ibid.*

The only complete French translation is that by J. Gaudefroy-Demombynes and A. Calmettes (Paris, 1934); the *Führer* refused to authorize it, preferring to have circulated in France expurgated editions, in which the most violent passages disappeared, whereas they were carefully retained in the new German editions.

the people and thus present themselves as the supporters of the *Volksgeist*.
They think socially and not individually.[8]

The first racist conception, as it was developed by Hitler in
Mein Kampf, rested upon the idea of unity of race in the biological
sense, hence upon the community of blood. Then, when face to
face with the twofold impossibility of finding a criterion of the
Aryan race (language, somatic characteristics, physical type or
moral qualities) and of justifying the application of this criterion
to the German people, it was necessary to fall back on another conception, that of the plurality of races, the only exact one in fact
for Europe. But Germany would present this peculiarity, that, in
this mixture of races of very unequal value, the proportion of the
superior elements would be very much higher in them than in
any other people. It is this predominance of the superior race
that must be maintained at any cost—hence the necessity of the
expulsion of the Jews—and this predominance suffices to justify
the German claim for presenting itself as the *Vollkulturvolk*.

Not only are there races which are distinct and of very different
value—the inferior races being more allied to the animal than the
superior races—but each race has its own law and morality, its own
religion, its own arts. The popular will, for law especially, but to
some extent in all matters, is expressed by the Führer. This is how
the National-Socialist doctrine explains the origin of law, with
which, for reasons readily understood, it is more occupied than
with morality, religion or the arts, all matters which are subject
to the control of the Führer, but which do not present as direct a
political interest.

Law originates from the people, it appears as a sort of secretion
of the *Volksgemeinschaft*, which cannot live without law. Its primary origin is in the *Volksgeist* (spirit of the people), but the
people is not capable of governing itself. The *Volksgemeinschaft*
is therefore necessarily subject to a leadership (*Führung*); that
is, it is led, directed by a *Führer*—*Führer* and *Duce* are equivalent
terms—who, for the purpose of carrying on this direction of all
the people to its welfare, is aided in the first place by the National-
Socialist Party, which has caused him to reach power, and then
by the State, which is simply the means for their attaining the
public welfare. The *Führer* is not the elect of a majority, he is the

[8] R. Bonnard, p. 35.

very expression of the people, which has recognized in him its true head and has bestowed upon him its complete confidence.[9]

The *Führer* exercises a personal, original and unique power. A personal power, for it is to him that the power has been entrusted, because he is permeated to the highest degree by the *Volksgeist*, the spirit of the people. An original power, because this capacity can be conferred by no one, not even by the people; it belongs to such a person by reason of his natural qualities. A unique power, not that he may not make use of aides, counselors or *Unterführer*, but they exercise their power only in conformity with the wishes of the *Führer*, otherwise it would be in contradiction of the fact that the spirit of the people resides to the highest degree in the latter. It might be said in the ancient terminology that the *Führer* is an absolute sovereign, but the ancient sovereigns claimed to hold their power from God or from their sword, whereas the *Führer* is closely united to the community from which he arises. On the other hand, the latter owes him obedience:

> The laws of the *Führer* and the manifestations of his will have a sacred character and the orders of the *Führer* are manifestations of the central and vital organ of the people.[10]

Thus, practically, all the powers of the *Volksgemeinschaft*, that is, of the people established by unity of race, and those of the State, simply a necessary means, are combined in the hands of the *Führer*, who directs, that is, practically commands without any superior control.

II

Such are the fundamental principles of National Socialism, as they appear from the declarations of its founders, beginning with the *Führer* himself in *Mein Kampf*, and as they have in fact been applied by him in the Germany of today. Let us now try to make a critical examination of them.

The most important of all these notions is that of race, the foundation of the entire system. The races are relatively of quite different values and Germany belongs to the superior race. This

[9] On the *Führung* and the *Führer*, see Bonnard, pp. 8 and 51, and Cot, pp. 43 ff.
[10] Roland Freisler, Secretary of State for Justice of the Reich, *Deutsche Justiz* (month?, 1936), p. 155.

presupposes a twofold criterion, the first a criterion of the idea of races which permits the making of a distinction of one from the other and the second a criterion of the element of superiority. These two points are most often combined in Germany under the concept of the superior race.

Do different human races exist and how are they to be distinguished one from the other? The assertion, which is often repeated in Germany, that there is a much greater difference between the men of the superior races and those of the inferior races than between the latter and the higher animals, is contrary not only to all religious and sociological notions (there is no Black, Yellow or Red race, from which may not spring individuals superior in intelligence and in morality to many Whites), but also to all scientific notions. The experience of thousands of years shows that all the human races without distinction are interfertile with one another, whereas such is not the case with the great apes which are closest to man.

Clearly that is by no means the same as saying that in the human species there may not be and are not different races. In fact, it is clear that, apart from the difficulty of borderline cases found in all classifications, certain races exist which cannot fail to be recognized as different from one another, beginning with the three great races, the White, the Yellow and the Black. Nor can it be doubted that there are subdivisions within this first classification. But today, especially in Europe and more particularly in Germany, the grand highway of the invasions from the East to the West, can one still speak of a pure race in this great country, after the mixture of people resulting from the wars, the invasions, the unions between distinct races? There is not a scholar who can sustain this. In fact, there is lacking the primary condition for such a differentiation—the existence of a precise criterion of race —and, in spite of all their efforts, the Germans have never succeeded in finding one.

It suffices here to run briefly over these efforts. The very variety of the attempts shows their vanity. Each ends, sooner or later, in the same improbabilities as Fichte's theory about the *Ursprache,* the only original and primitive German language. There may be Aryan languages and, on this score, the Hindus and the Iranians would be as Aryan as the Germans, but there is no Aryan race.

The sociologists then turned to the physical and somatic characteristics, at first the form of the skull. Gobineau had already thought to remark that the superior races—the Nordic races—are dolichocephalic, that is, with elongated skull, whereas the southern races are brachycephalic, with short skull. Unfortunately, the German scholars themselves had to admit that certain races which have left a brilliant record in history are brachycephalic, whereas, among those races which they despised the most, some are dolichocephalic. Many Jews are dolichocephalic and there are also dolichocephalic negro races.

It became necessary therefore to cast about for another feature. Even adding to the elongated form of the skull, as did Günther, Wilser, Woltmann and other German raciologists, a tall stature, blue eyes, blond hair, blue blood and transparent veins, and, as did Günther, "the noble, tranquil and assured gait," [11] it was still necessary to recognize the insufficiency of these morphological theories. The great majority of Germans are brachycephalic and do not answer to this description, beginning with the *Führer* himself.

Continuing their researches, the German scholars launched upon a new tack, the examination of the blood. The principal theorist of National Socialism, Dr. Rosenberg, in his great work, *Der Mythus des XX. Jahrhunderts,* put forth what he himself termed the myth of blood:

Today we see a new faith revealed to life, the myth of the blood. It is the religion of the blood that . . . will replace wonderfully well the old sacraments, which it has already succeeded largely in supplanting.

This was the theory which the *Führer* adopted. Some specialists, notably Bernstein, asserted quite at the start that the serological indices of the blood constituted a much more reliable criterion of the race than the measurement of the skull or the color of the hair or eyes, but once more the Germans were destined to be deceived. Observation proved that the serological composition of the blood, its genotypic index, varied as high as double in Germany itself, and it is precisely among the Germans of the east, who are most Slavicised, that it is the weakest.[12]

[11] Hans Günther, *Rassenkunde des deutschen Volkes* (Munich, 1930), p. 22.

[12] On the results of this experimentation, see the article of Dr. J. Brutzkus, "Le Mythe du sang allemand," in *Races et racisme,* vol. 1 (janvier-mars 1938), p. 1; Georges Lakhovsky, *La civilisation et la folie raciste,* pp. 110 ff., and appendix (*Recherches et travaux sur les groups sanguins*), pp. 126-140.

In despair of their cause, it became necessary to turn to moral and psychological qualities, the "heroic virtues" which Hitler considers characteristic of the pure Aryan and of which Günther was destined to give a long list: courage, fidelity, devotion, honor, justice, realism, critical sense, discipline, etc. Even the German racists had to acknowledge that this lacked somewhat of precision, unless one subverted the meaning of the terms, as certain National Socialists did, and declared that every true German possesses these qualities by nature. Others, more honest, abandoned this last criterion and Theodor Fritsch,[13] after having referred to these various criteria, reached the conclusion, somewhat over-simplified and pessimistic, that the surest way to recognize a Jew is by his name.

Moreover, many biologists today do not hesitate to assert that purity of race, if pushed too far, is a cause of degeneration, as has happened with the Samaritans, who are today reduced to a few dozens, and that the best human types result, on the contrary, from felicitous crossbreedings, as is the case with all Europe and a great part of America.

It is necessary therefore to abandon the theory of the superiority of a race which has remained for a long time without mixture, and the superiority of the German race, which, for that matter, is not at all a pure race, is in contradiction with the data of science, whether it is made to rest on dolichocephaly or on the constants of the blood. In clinging to this in spite of all the proofs to the contrary, official German science only proves once more that it does not have for its object the investigation of scientific truth, but rather the justification of a theory which *a priori* is favorable to Germany. Indeed, this is openly acknowledged by the most famous exponent of National Socialism, Alfred Rosenberg, when he asserts that there is no science independent of race, and that "what we today call science is the most outstanding creation of the German race." [14] And it has also been indirectly acknowledged by the *Führer,* when he declares that National Socialism "tends to the creation of a new human type *(Menschentyp)* ." [15] There is question then of a race which does not yet exist, even in Germany, of a race to be created, which it is easy to endow, in dreaming, with all the qualities.

[13] *Handbuch der Judenfrage* (Leipzig, 1934).
[14] Rosenberg, *Der Mythus des XX. Jahrhunderts* (4th ed., Munich, 1932), p. 121.
[15] Speech of 1937, reproduced in the *Völkischer Beobachter,* July 19, 1937.

It would remain to prove that not the present German "race," which does not exist, but the present German individuals are, from the threefold point of view, physical, intellectual and moral, superior to all the others. Such an assertion would doubtless arouse vigorous denials from many quarters, which would not seem to be without some foundation, when one reflects on the way of conduct in Germany with regard to certain nationals or certain foreign peoples.

After race, the fundamental point of the National-Socialist system is the notion of the *Führung* and the possessor of this power, the *Führer*. The *Führung*, in the proper sense of the word, is a "leading." The people is led (*geführt*) by the *Führer*, whom it follows, forming thus his *Gefolgschaft*.[16] The power of the *Führer* is, as we know, a personal and original power. It is possible, with more or less subtlety, to declare that the *Führer* is neither a dictator, nor a representative of the nation, nor an organ of the State. Practically, he is all that at one and the same time, since he concentrates in himself all the functions of the State, legislative, executive and even judicial. National Socialism does not admit the separation of the powers. If the *Führer* exercises only in exceptional cases the function of judge, he must be able to do so, should occasion arise. The summary executions of June 30, 1934, are a proof of this, and their legality has been defended by many German jurists, notably Karl Schmidt. Professor Ulrich Scheuner[17] explains that the *Volksgeist*—considered by some as pure myth— is the spirit of the people, the sentiment of justice living in the heart of the people; but the people has only a vague idea of law (*droit*), which must be directed and stated precisely. This will be the rôle of the *Führer*, who, by his varied acts—statutes (*lois*), regulations, judgments—creates law. It is his way of forming the *Volksgeist*. Popular sentiment can never place limits upon the initiative of the *Führer*.

As Nouraï points out, this involves a complete vicious circle:

On the one hand, the *Führer* presents himself as the emanation and most authorized representative of the spirit of the people, and, on the other hand, he contributes to its formation by dictating to it its proper initiative and what it must will.[18]

[16] See Bonnard, pp. 44-95; Cot, pp. 43-62.

[17] "L'État et le droit dans la doctrine national-socialiste," in *Revue de droit public et de la science politique en France et à l'étranger*, vol. 44 (1937), p. 18.

[18] Nouraï, p. 37.

Scheuner avoids the difficulty by declaring that the National-Socialist theories "present difficulties of comprehension to foreigners"; this is but natural, since, in this doctrine, law (*droit*) is a question of races and varies with them.

In fact, the personal power of the *Führer* goes far beyond that of a Louis XIV or a Wilhelm II. It is the revival of the old Caesaro-Papism. The *Führer* is at once the infallible pope of a new religion and the sole master of a great disciplined country which deserves a better fate and which, in a word, to satisfy his *amour propre* or a need for prestige, its master may send to war without consulting it.

The consequences of these two fundamental notions of the National-Socialist system, the inequality of the races and the omnipotence of the *Führer*—consequences which are at the same time the end intended, since German science has ceased to be objective in order to labor always for the greatness of Germany—are of immense significance in all that concerns law and its different branches, morality and religion itself. I shall insist here especially on law. We shall see that, in the new German theories, there is a negation of law in the customary sense of the word and the substitution of a new law, the tendencies of which may be easily shown from the way in which it is presented not only by the German jurists, but also by the administrative authorities, ministers and secretaries of State and the *Führer* himself. What, therefore, does such a law comprise?

The answer is to be found in the concordant assertions of the highest official personages and of the jurists who enjoy the greatest authority in Germany, assertions corroborated by the facts, which show that the theory has not remained a dead letter and that it has speedily established the present law of the Third Reich.

For the National Socialists, the sovereignty of the law does not exist. There is no longer the universal law as the basis of justice and morality. Law is henceforth a *Volksrecht,* that is, a law of the people, made by and for it (in fact, by the *Führer*) , and no longer, as previously, a *Justizrecht.* All non-political (*unpolitisch*) law is but a fiction. Law is born with the people and dies with the people. The *Volk* is its sole support. The security of the people, therefore, is its great objective. "Justice and injustice," says Rosenberg, quoting an old adage of Indian law, "do not walk up and down proclaiming: 'Here we are!' No, Law is that which Aryan men consider to be just." [19]

[19] *Der Mythus des XX. Jahrhunderts,* p. 571.

The jurist Hans Frank lays down the following principles:

Law is not an end in itself. . . . The racial community is the basis and the source of all law. . . . Neither the State nor law are ends in themselves. They are in reality only the means for attaining an end (*Mittel zum Zweck*), the *Volk*. . . . All law must serve the race and the *Volk*. . . . That which is useful to the people is just, that which damages the people is unjust.[20]

This definition of "just" was given likewise by Dr. Wilhelm Frick, Minister of the Interior of the Reich, before the Congress of German Jurists, October 14, 1935, a fact which in some fashion endows it with official value.[21]

As a consequence of this conception of law, there is no longer, for certain categories of persons, notably the Jews and to a less extent all enemies of the regime, the right of family. A marriage may be dissolved, if one of the two parties has a Jewish ancestor. There is no longer the right of property nor of succession nor even the right to life. As the sequel to a murder committed in Paris by a Jew upon the person of a German diplomat, many Jews were slaughtered, all the Jewish stores in Berlin were plundered and, by way of reparations, the proprietors were fined and obliged to repair all damage at their own expense.

The entire penal law has been warped in a monstrous fashion and this has occurred while proceeding from principles which appeared very beautiful in theory. The new German penal law rests entirely on the notion of honor—social and individual honor.[22] But from this it is immediately concluded that the essential rule is the fidelity due to the *Führer*. Every form of opposition is therefore proscribed. The same is true in the case of private conversations.[23] Every member of the party, and for that matter every German, has the duty of being a spy and informer, even with regard to the members of his own family, as in Bolshevist Russia.

The two principles which have been considered for more than a century as the fundamental principles of penal law, namely, *nullum crimen sine lege* and *nulla poena sine lege*, have been

---

[20] *Nationalsozialistischen Handbuch für Recht und Gesetzgebung* (Munich, 1935), pp. vii, xiii and xxiv.

[21] Numerous other citations in this sense will be found in the works listed in note 1, *ante*, especially those of Bonnard, Nouraï and Cot.

[22] Memorandum of the Prussian Minister of Justice on the project of a new Penal Code. See also Hans Frank and the authors cited by Cot, pp. 93 ff.

[23] Law of December 1, 1934.

replaced by the principle of free incrimination and the principle
of arbitrary penalties.

Whoever commits an act which the law regards as liable to a penalty or
which merits punishment according to the principle of a law or the good
sense of the people is punished.[24]

The judges may thus create out of whole cloth and punish crimes
for which the law has made no provision simply on the invocation of the good sense of the people or, more simply still, on the
instructions of the Minister of Justice. Moreover, the judges are no
longer irremovable or independent and there exist many special
tribunals composed of Nazis. Under such conditions it is understandable that the prisons, even when enlarged, might have been
found to be insufficient in Germany and that it became necessary
to establish numerous concentration camps, in which the Gestapo
crams its prisoners and submits them, without any judicial or administrative control, to a regime so harsh that many never return therefrom.

On all these points, the German law has taken a stand diametri-
cally opposed to all civilized legislation. The dignity of man, his
freedom and his equality of nature are equally violated. It is the
abandonment of the conquests of civilization, which it had been
hoped were definitive. By its fruits is the tree judged.

To be sure, it will still occur to some German authors to speak
of natural law and even to write volumes on the subject. But what
is the natural law of which they treat? For there are two natures in
man, his spiritual nature, that which makes him man, and his
physical nature which he shares with the animals. Now when force
is stressed, when no more is made of law than a question of constraint—a general tendency in Germany since Kant—then we
have the triumph of the inferior nature, a return to the law of
the jungle.

There is nothing sadder than these tactics of perversion, this
art of distorting the meaning of words, which is found so often in
National-Socialist Germany. It is not only that the natural law
is taken in a sense directly contrary to the traditional sense, but
that, in the name of honor, the dignity of man is trampled under
foot; in the name of freedom, those who do not think as you do
are interned in a concentration camp; in the name of loyalty, the

[24] Law of January 28, 1935.

observance of a cramping treaty is refused; in the name of truth, an unjust attack is made in the guise of self-defense.

III

The very same principles, whose consequences we have just seen in domestic law, because well understood, have likewise been applied to international law. But here there have been some modifications. Some years after the war (in 1933), Ludwig Schecher, suppressing the very term *Völkerrecht* (international law or law of nations), published a book entitled *Deutches Aussensstaatsrecht* (German External Public Law), with a cover (later suppressed) announcing "the study of the international consequences of the National-Socialist doctrine." In this book he asserted that, since the State alone can create law, there exists but one law, the national law, which regulates the life of individuals inside and outside the State. In reality, therefore, there is no international law emanating from any source other than the State and capable of being in opposition to the national law.[25] The State is sovereign, the supreme value of the racist State is the notion of honor, the so-called "general international" law is law in Germany only if it has been "received" by the German law and only in the measure in which it is in conformity therewith.

This denial of international law seemed premature. Germany in 1933 could not appeal to a force superior to the other States; she still had need of the general principles of international law, the equality of States, the right of the free movement of peoples, the respect for treaties freely concluded, including above all the Fourteen Points of President Wilson. Schecher's theory was criticized in Germany as a simple reproduction of the primitive theory of Hans Kelsen, a monistic theory which made all law originate from the State, and erroneous, because it is the *Volk* which is the origin of law and not the State. This was the time when Chancellor Hitler was delivering great pacifistic speeches wherein he asserted Germany's will to peace and the recognition of the solidarity of nations. All that Germany claimed then was the equality of rights (*Gleichberechtigung*). The Chancellor condemned war from the point of view of right and morality, and even also from the point of view of politics:

[25] On the theory of Schecher, cf. Nouraï, pp. 134-155.

Neither from the point of view of politics nor from the point of view of economics could the use of any violence whatsoever create in Europe a more favorable situation than the present situation.

The disarmament of Germany was already a *fait accompli.*

The National-Socialist Government could not have any other task than to secure the peace of the world.[26]

And the Chancellor offered to renounce offensive arms, especially aerial arms, which Germany did not have at that time.

But Germany succeeded very quickly in rearming herself. After having done her best to wreck the Disarmament Conference, a thing which she definitely achieved, Germany, on her own authority, freed herself successively from all the clauses of the Treaty of Versailles which had limited her military power. Contrary to the Treaty of Peace, she re-established compulsory military service in May 1935. Contrary not only to the Treaty of Peace, but also to the Agreements of Locarno, which she had freely signed and which she had solemnly promised to respect forever, she reoccupied the Rhineland with military forces in March 1936, an action which had been expressly declared equivalent to an act of aggression by those agreements and which consequently should have immediately brought about the intervention of the two guarantor States, namely, Great Britain and Italy. For different reasons, neither of the two budged and France made the great mistake of following suit, in spite of the offer of action by Poland and Czechoslovakia, the only two States which at that time had clear vision of what the immediate future held in store. It is because she was unwilling to follow their lead that Europe found herself condemned to suffer, in the course of the three ensuing years, the disappearance of several independent States and to ruin herself with costly armaments for the sake of preventing a new war unloosed by Germany with a view to securing her own supremacy in Europe.

Twice did the Powers condemn in the most solemn manner this inexcusable violation of treaties by Germany. On April 17, 1935, at the time of the re-establishment of compulsory military service by Germany, the Council of the League of Nations, after having

[26] Speech of May 17, 1933, *Die Reden für Gleichberechtigung und Frieden,* in *Die Reden Hitlers als Kanzler* (month?, 1933). An analysis of this speech will be found in Nouraï, pp. 75-96.

affirmed the duty of scrupulously respecting all the obligations of treaties and having stated that the German Government, by its unilateral action, had been unable to create any right—

declares that Germany has failed in the duty which lies upon all the members of the international community to respect undertakings which they have contracted and condemns any unilateral repudiation of international obligations.

Another condemnation in equally solemn terms was pronounced by the Powers signatory to the Treaty of Locarno on March 17, 1936, after the reoccupation by Germany of the demilitarized zone of the Rhineland. But both times it was a matter of mere condemnation in words with no action following. From this day on the die was cast. Right exists only as long as there is a decision to cause it to be respected. Germany, seeing that no action had been taken in that direction, visualized the possibility of resuming her interrupted dream of world hegemony and threw herself into the arms of Hitler, who pointed out to her the means to that end.

After the revindication of equality (*Gleichberechtigung*), came the affirmation that a strong people, belonging to a superior race, has rights not possessed by weak peoples or inferior races. After the annexation of Austria (in which the *Führer* was violently opposed to the plebiscite of Chancellor Schuschnigg, which he knew was bound to be unfavorable to him) and the annexation of Sudetenland in the name of the right of the free disposition of peoples, came the brutal annexation of the Czechs and Moravians under a disguised protectorate, achieved this time in the name of "living space" (*Lebensraum*), against the will of practically the entire population. Then came the annexation of Memel, the annexation of Albania by Italy, and the turning over of Danzig and the Polish Corridor was about to come, with Hungary, Rumania, the Ukraine and other countries still on the list, when finally a sudden act of will of the two great democratic Powers began to interpose a barrier to the rising tide of annexations.

Very often these violations of law followed closely on the heels of recent promises to respect the treaty in question. First, after the return of the Saar to the Reich, Hitler had at this early date asserted that he had nothing more to claim.[27] After the re-estab-

---

[27] Speech broadcasted on January 15, 1935.

lishment of compulsory military service, he declared that
Germany—

> had freed herself from the articles of the Treaty which constituted a uni-
> lateral burden upon and a discrimination against the German nation. . . .
> On the other hand, she is herself convinced that the other articles concern-
> ing international life, including the territorial clauses, cannot be denounced
> unilaterally by any Power and that consequently they are respected by Ger-
> many.[28]

The same speech affirms the obligation of respect for treaties. The
Reich has freed itself, on its own authority, from certain articles
of the Treaty which constituted a unilateral burden on and a
discrimination against the German nation; but if—

> the Government of the Reich will sign no treaty which appears to it to be
> impossible of execution, on the other hand it will observe every treaty freely
> concluded, even if it has been signed before its own accession to power. Conse-
> quently, it will respect all the obligations resulting from the Pact of Locarno
> as long as the other signatories of the Pact adhere to the Pact.

The *Führer* even specified that this respect for treaties would extend to the demilitarized zone; whereupon, less than ten months
later, the Rhineland was reoccupied with military forces.

To lull the disquietude which such acts engendered, Hitler, in
a great speech delivered before the Reichstag on January 30, 1937,
recalled his agreements with Austria and Poland, with a view to
removing the old tensions; whereupon, on March 13, 1938, Austria was annexed.

Once more the *Führer* declared himself fully satisfied. In a great
speech delivered in the Sportspalast on September 26, 1938, he
stated, with regard to the Sudeten, that he asked only to labor in
collaboration with Great Britain and France.

> One last problem faces us. It must be solved. It is solely our revindication
> in Europe, but it is the only one which I do not renounce.

Neville Chamberlain, in his speech at Birmingham on March 18,
1939, declared that Hitler had told him that he had no further
territorial ambitions in Europe and that he did not desire to include within the frontiers of the Reich peoples who were not of
the German race.

[28] Speech to the Reichstag, May 21, 1935.

I have assured Mr. Chamberlain and I repeat now that, with this problem solved, Germany will have no further territorial problems in Europe. I shall never have further occasion to take interest in the Czech State and I guarantee it. We do not wish Czechs within our frontiers.

Germany then annexed Sudetenland by virtue of the Convention of Munich, together with the entire line of Czechoslovak defenses. But, less than six months after, in March 1939, Hitler, invoking imaginary "wild excesses" committed against the Germans, ordered the brutal invasion of Bohemia and Moravia and imposed upon them a protectorate which actually deprives them of all autonomy.[29]

Each of these violent annexations constituted the flagrant violation of a formal promise only a few months old. It is the policy of the "scrap of paper" erected into a rule, by always asserting each time contrary action for the future, with a view to restoring the confidence of the other States, which, after each new experience, seem to ask only to be allowed to be deceived once more.[30]

Herein is not a single isolated fact, but an entire series of facts, which prove that Germany, since becoming powerful again, has reverted to her true tendency, the cult of force, which is characterized as *Kultur* when it is exercised by Germany to her own profit. It is this cult which is celebrated in a score of passages in *Mein Kampf,* especially throughout the part devoted to international policy.

The point of departure is always the distinction between superior and inferior races. Hitler distinguishes three categories among them: those which create civilization, a rôle reserved to the Aryans alone; those which preserve the deposit of civilization; and finally those which destroy civilization.

There follow a number of passages which seem to affirm in a general way the principle of autarchy and the right of a people to spread out with the increase of its population; but this principle may be applied only to Germany and perhaps to her allies, since otherwise nearly all peoples and States would clash in competitions incapable of solution. According to Hitler—

only that relationship can ever be regarded as *healthy* which assures the nourishment of a people from its own soil and territory. Every other situation,

[29] See the text of the Draconian statute imposed on these countries by a decree of the *Führer,* signed at Prague, March 16, 1939, in *Revue de droit international,* vol. 17 (1939), pp. 95 ff.

[30] Cf. Edmond Vermeil, *Le racisme allemand,* pp. 46 ff.

though it may last centuries and even millennia, is nevertheless unhealthy, and will sooner or later lead to the injuring if not the destruction of the people concerned.

Only a sufficiently extensive area on this globe guarantees a nation freedom of existence.

It is necessary—

To bring the land into consonance with the population. . . . we must undertake the setting of objectives for our political work in two directions: *Soil and territory as the goal of our foreign policy, and a new unified foundation, solid in its view of life, as the goal of our domestic work.*

. . . The demand for the re-establishment of the frontiers of the year 1914 is political nonsense of such a degree and consequences as to look like a crime; this quite apart from the fact that the frontiers in the year 1914 were anything but logical. For they were, in reality, neither complete with respect to the inclusion of people of German nationality, nor intelligent with respect to geo-military appropriateness.

Notice to the Hungarians, the Rumanians, the Ukrainians and all the other States in which are found men of German nationality!
A little farther on, Hitler continues:

Never tolerate the establishment of two continental powers in Europe. See an attack on Germany in any such attempt to organize a military power on the frontiers of Germany, be it only in the form of the creation of a State capable of becoming a military power, and, in that case, regard it not only a right, but a duty, to prevent the establishment of such a State by all means including the application of armed force, or, in the event that such a one be already founded, to repress it.[31]

This has in view at once Great Britain, Poland and Russia, but even more directly France, whose destruction is presented as a necessity for Germany, since she is "the mortal enemy of our nation."[32]

This then is the way in which Germany understands equality, the famous *Gleichberechtigung:* there must be in Europe no other military power besides herself, no other State capable of resisting her! And it is she who has branded with the name of infamous dictation the Treaty of Versailles, which had sought to put an end to her will for domination. One might gather from *Mein Kampf* several other passages which show how Hitler understands equality, as, for example:

[31] *Mein Kampf, ed. cit.,* pp. 935, 944, 944-45.
[32] *Ibid.,* p. 964.

It must be a greater honor to be a citizen of this Reich as a street cleaner, than to be a king in a foreign State.[33]

It is easy to understand that encouragement from so high a source given to autarchy, to the preponderance of military force, to the superiority of Germany was received with enthusiasm in that country. Following their *Führer,* the great mass of German authors, jurists, publicists and historians vied with one another in insisting on Germany's right of "self-preservation," the right of the State (read "of Germany," since this right, if applied to all States, would lead directly to frightful confusions) "to safeguard its vital interests," to "do everything which is necessitated by the concrete situation without regard to its international obligations," the "right of free self-development," the necessity of considering equality as a "relative" notion based on the "intrinsic value" of the different nations, divided into superior and inferior races.[34]

The program of the National-Socialist Party, adopted on February 25, 1920, gave as its first Point:

We demand the union of all Germans by the right of self-determination of peoples, in one great Germany.

Point IV reads:

Only a member of our own people (*Volksgenosse*) may be a citizen (*Staatsbürger*). Our own people are *only* those of German blood without reference to confession. Therefore, no Jew may be a member of our people.[35]

This excludes the Jews, but includes, on the other hand, even against their formal will, the people of Alsace-Lorraine, the Austrians, the *Sudeten* and the Germans of Rumania, the Ukraine and

---

[33] *Ibid.,* p. 659.

[34] Wolgast, Kraus, Lehmann, Bilfinger, and others, cited by E. Bristler, "La doctrine nationalsocialiste du droit des gens," in *Revue internationale de la théorie du droit,* vol. 12 (1938), p. 122.

See also L. Preuss, *op. cit.,* notes 28 and 35; he is among the German authors who do not hesitate to declare that every territory in which the German population represents 10 per cent of the entire population is German territory, because the German inhabitants, thanks to their cultural superiority, are bound to have a qualitative majority.

Thus the way is paved for future annexations like that of Czechoslovakia, where today a majority of several million Czechs is entirely under German domination.

[35] English translation from Vera Michels Dean *et al., New Governments in Europe* (New York, 1935), pp. 140-41.

North and South America.[36] If the same rule be applied in thought to all peoples which have swarmed abroad, in France, England, Spain and Italy, the frightful imbroglio which will result therefrom will become immediately evident. If it be recalled also that this right of self-determination of peoples claimed by Germany (which, by the way, has just renounced it for the Tyrol to the profit of Italy) is at the same time presented by her as one of the great mistakes of the French and Anglo-Saxons, since it encouraged everywhere the right of secession and anarchy, it will be seen with what degree of good faith an unrestricted claim is made for the application to oneself of principles the benefit of which is denied to other States.

Preoccupations of this sort by no means stop the German jurists. Otto Köllreuter declares that, so far as the observance of the rules of international law commonly followed are concerned, "policy alone decides thereon" and that—

[36] Herein lies the tremendous danger, not always apparent at first sight, which results from the substitution of the notion of *Volk* (people) for that of nation. The nation either forms a State (a national State is the end towards which all strong collectivities tend) or, within a great State like the British Empire, a secondary collectivity, more or less decentralized, but remaining dependent on the sovereign State. (I leave aside the case of the great Dominions with responsible government, which are today true States.) Even groups too small to form a nation are in principle protected today by the law of nations under the name of racial, linguistic or religious minorities. There is therefore an agreement possible between State and Nation. It is evidently necessary that there be harmony between the two essential elements, population and territory, which, together with the third, social authority, form the State. Otherwise the millenary notion of the State would be destroyed in favor of the new Utopian entity, race, which scientifically does not exist. This is precisely what is produced with the notion of *Volk*. The Germans, who in various periods of their history have been induced to establish themselves in more or less compact groups in certain countries of Europe, or of America in the nineteenth century, now claim, by virtue of this theory, to continue to belong to the German *Volk*. For them it would be a right and a duty, as soon as they can do so, to claim their reattachment to the whole of the *Volk*, that is, in reality to the German State, for it is vain, under the notion of *Volk* as well as that of nation, nay, it is impossible for anyone to dispense with that sovereign juridical organization which in our time everywhere bears the name of State. This is what has just been done successfully, first, by the Nazis of Austria, then by the Sudeten (less than three million of them have been sufficient to cause the loss of independence to nine million Slavs), then by the people of Memel. This is what the people of Danzig are attempting to do at this very moment, at the risk of unchaining a general war. After this it would be the turn of the German groups inhabiting the Ukraine, then certain States of South America, which happily have sensed the danger and have already begun to combat it. As the national State evidently cannot tolerate on its territory the organization of a group belonging directly to another, perhaps hostile, State, it is easy to see all the germs of future war which, with a race convinced of its right to special treatment as a superior race, would be sown by the substitution in the law of nations of the notion of *Volk* for that of nation.

it is universally recognized that the national interest takes precedence over the international interest and that the *Volk* comes well before humanity.

Norbert Gierke likewise asserts that "the science of law is a political science"; the foundation of law is found in the material interests of each people, and every transcendental or humanitarian idea tending towards the restoration of an universal order must be systematically rejected.

According to Adolf Walz, author of a theory of intercorporative international law, all vital questions are of a political nature and therefore removed from the jurisdiction of international tribunals. In case of disagreement between national law and international law—

the maintenance and the revision of international obligations belong solely within the domain of the head of the German State, the *Führer* and Chancellor, who is solely responsible for the Reich.

Under this conception, therefore, in case of international conflict, it is the *Führer* who takes the place of the international jurisdictions whose establishment was attempted after the Hague Conferences and during the post-war period!

Hermann Held admits, not a Society of States, but a juridical community of nations resting on the right of each nation to existence and equality. But he adds that this right of the nations demands the representation of ethnic minorities by the mother-nation. So that, in all the countries where a German minority exists, this minority depends for its protection on the German State and not on the State wherein it resides.[37]

Even the jurists who in Germany still defend the theory of the natural law, such as Herbert Kraus and Hans Keller, do so in such a way and with such reservations—fundamental rights to honor, to existence, excuse of necessity and the clause *rebus sic stantibus* extended beyond all measure—that this alleged natural or objective law may be easily twisted to suit all national subjective positions and places not the slightest barrier in the way of an aggressor government. Hans Keller states expressly that recourse to force

[37] Not to pad this study, I have reduced the citations for each of these authors to one essential point of their theory and I have not given bibliographical references. They will be found, with many more details on each of these theories, in the work of Nouraï. See especially, with regard to the passages cited above, pp. 163, 169, 226 and 249.

must be considered as a source of right; the revolutionary is the one who has the "better right" on his side, since he is aiding in the triumph of the law of tomorrow. In his dream of a dynamism which is always victorious, he neglects to add that he envisages only the revolutions which have succeeded, and such is not always the case. Thus it is that, in Italy, in Germany and in still other countries, it is the extreme-left parties which, by their excesses and their defeat, have contributed most to the triumph of the totalitarian States. The alleged natural law of Hans Keller finally comes down to the very German theory of the success which proves the right, that is, of the fact creating the right. In point of natural law, this means always the rejection of a right proper to man and the acceptance for him of the law of animal or vegetable nature, the law of the struggle for life.

It would be possible to multiply these citations from the German jurists, but this has already been done more than once, notably in the works which I have already pointed out. Even those of the foreign jurists, ever decreasing in numbers, who have recently participated in scientific congresses in Germany[38] and who still would like to be able to believe in the scientific objectivity of Germany, cannot help making the most explicit reservations on this subject.[39] And in fact a telling remark may be made on this point of view. Still more important than the considerable number of jurists and publicists who defend the National-Socialist theories is the fact that, among the rest, there is not a single one who dares to raise his voice in favor of common morality or general principles of right, even when they are openly trampled under foot. For the past five years the German Government has multiplied violations of treaties, breaches of solemn promises, in a manner to arouse general reproof and to achieve the record of eliciting within a few months two official protests from the Council of the League of Nations and from the Powers. But not a single German jurist has protested against the annexation by force of Austria, then of Czechoslovakia, nor against the arbitrary actions of every

[38] For example, the congress of April 1939 for the twenty-fifth anniversary of the Institut·für Staatswissenschaft und internationales Recht of the University of Kiel, which was attended by representatives of the German Government and of all the local authorities, but by only four foreign professors.

[39] This is the case, for example, with Djuvara, in his study already cited, "Le nouvel essai de philosophie juridique et politique en Allemagne." See particularly the long note on pages 43-48 and its conclusion on pages 52 ff.

sort which followed these annexations. Likewise with regard to the unspeakable injustices and the degrading humiliations inflicted upon the Jews, all the plundering, the forced suicides and the murders committed in the course of pogroms during these last years, not a single protest has been heard in Germany. It is impossible that all Germans have been at the same time deprived of all sense of justice on this matter, but, if they may say nothing against the most reprehensible actions without fear for their freedom or for their very life, it may be seen what remains of freedom of thought in Germany and in what measure it is still possible to believe in the objectivity of German science!

There is no doubt but that, in National Socialism, one is confronted with a new attempt in favor of the establishment of a law on the basis of force, which corresponds with the old German tendencies.[40] There is question here not simply of a denial of law, but of a denial of morality and of religion itself, and this is proof once more of the strict solidarity of these three great disciplines of human life. Following Kant, for whom law rests on restraint (law and restraint, says he, are identical), Hitler manifested his ideas clearly in the same sense:

> . . . No consideration of foreign policy can be guided by any point of view but this: *Does it benefit our nation now or in the future, or will it be harmful to it?*
> This is the sole preconceived opinion permitted in dealing with this question. Partisan, religious, humanitarian, and all other points of view in general are completely beside the point.[41]

This, as he himself expressly admits in other passages, clearly results in the law of force. In fact, it is evident that, to make the interest of a country prevail over every other interest, even if it be more just, such a country can take account only of force. The old "raison d'État" was never of any value unless backed up, not by right reason, but by a good army.

As long as Germany had no such army, she knew well how to moderate her covetousness. Today, when she believes herself to have become the strongest, she no longer needs to dissimulate. Dr.

---

[40] See Le Fur, *Les Grands Problèmes du droit* (Paris, 1937), Chapter XI (Le droit et les doctrines allemandes), pp. 312-388, where the three phases, theological, philosophical and scientific or positive, through which they passed, are successively reviewed, as well as the synthesis achieved by the jurists.

[41] *Mein Kampf, ed. cit.,* p. 888.

Goebbels, in an article in the *Völkischer Beobachter* for March 25, 1939, devoted to England, which he accuses of "moralizing hypocrisy," is not afraid to say that rich peoples, the "have" peoples, whose expansion has come to an end, may afford the luxury of morality; the peoples on the road to fortune may not do so. This is the transfer of the class-struggle within a country into the class-struggle of international politics; it is the struggle between satisfied peoples and famished peoples. But nothing is more fallacious than such slogans of German or Italian politics. As was immediately asked of Dr. Goebbels, would he classify Poland and Turkey perchance among the "capitalist" nations? And how can he represent Germany as a "proletarian" nation, when his own statistics proclaim a national revenue five times greater than that of France for a population scarcely twice as large? But the richest country may ruin itself and cause its population to suffer, if it devotes dozens of billions to unproductive expenditures.

In the face of such conceptions, which the governments of great States would wish to see become the law of the future, must it be declared, as certain publicists, even in the great democracies of the West, discouraged by the actual state of affairs, have done, that international law is the law practised by States and peoples and that consequently, in the face of the rejection by the totalitarian States of the traditional international law, the latter must be abandoned? This would be tantamount to recognizing that, in the relations between States, more than ever policy prevails over right! No, that would constitute an act of treason on the part of the jurists; that would be an abdication on their part, the abandonment of moral and juridical truth to admit nothing more than the law of force. We must defend ourselves at all costs against theories of this sort, but, outside of the defense by arms in case of aggression, the best defense consists in fighting to the end for truth. More than once already, after an eclipse more or less prolonged, as in 1914, we have witnessed the rebirth of international law in greater vigor. Law and morality are normative sciences. They visualize, as the Germans themselves recognize, not the *Sein,* but the *Sollen*—the "should-be," which is not necessarily the present reality.

IV

Before concluding, it is necessary to probe more deeply into this question of racism. Here there is question not merely of divergences of conceptions between a new system and the traditional doctrine on some isolated points, even as important as respect for treaties or the right of the State to have recourse to war in the name of its sovereignty. Going to the bottom of things, it will be perceived that there is at stake here nothing less than a complete reversal of the scale of values, a reversal of the order willed by God and hitherto accepted not only by every Christian, but by every man who believes in a natural morality and a natural religion.

All Christians, and many others besides, believe in a personal God, Creator and Rewarder; they believe in the immortality of the soul, which changes everything for man.[42] This was one of the dogmas of the civil religion of Rousseau, one of the necessary postulates of Kant. It is not the State nor the nation, not the race nor the class that is immortal, but man and man alone. He is, as has been said, the sole bearer of the eternal and unalienable values and it is from this that the primacy of the human person springs. As has been well expressed by Father Antonin D. Sertillanges, O.P.—

Among the reversals of values which were effected by Jesus Christ, the following is essential: the entire worth of human life is evaluated from within, from man's relation to God and to himself, while the pagan and profane spirit derives it from without, from the relation of man to nourishing nature and society. It is from this point that the two sources of morality and religion as envisaged by Bergson take their separate paths.[43]

Thus the racist doctrine raises this fundamental point in the life of societies: which of the two—man or the collectivity (State, *Volk* or social class) —is an end in relation to the other? This point is fundamental, because thereon depends the question of knowing which of the two is only the means to the other. For all spiritualists (non-materialists), social institutions, including the State and even the Church itself, established to lead man to his last end, exist entirely in view of the human person. The political or economic collectivity which encounters no limit always has a tend-

[42] See Jacques Chevalier, "Le problème de la mort et de la survie de l'âme," in *La vie morale et l'au-delà* (Paris, 1938), pp. 138 ff.

[43] *Spiritualité*, p. 36.

ency to become totalitarian, therefore oppressive. And this means a return to the ancient paganism, which Christianity alone was able to destroy, for the sake of providing an advantageous substitute. A collectivity, from the very fact that it has no immortal soul, has no moral superior; it does not possess that other life which is the sole guaranty of the reparation of the injustices so numerous in this life; or, at least, it possesses no morality except insofar as it holds itself bound by that of its members, but then one is thrown back once more on the primacy of the human person. Otherwise, a collectivity considers as moral only its own interest, that is, as we have seen, its own force, which alone is capable of making its interest prevail.

So, on this point of decisive importance for the life of man and of societies, the Church, from the very moment of her first appearance, has not hesitated to take sides, and she has never changed her position in the two thousand years of her existence. Christianity is an open religion, it entails the dissociation of group and religion. Its God is the God of all men, no longer that of such-and-such a tribe or city, hostile to all non-citizens. It is from his very being, from the fact that he was created in the image of God, that man derives his dignity and not from the fact of belonging to such-and-such a national or racial group.

When Kant, starting from his moral postulate, proclaims the principle of the dignity of man, he merely reproduces a Christian truth. This substitution of the primacy of man for the primacy of the collectivity constituted a real revolution, and it is understandable that for centuries the civil powers struggled against a religion which has for its end the liberation of man from the State, the vindication of the rights of the human soul against the temporal authority. Even the Greeks, individualists as they were, did not know how to liberate the human person. Through excess of individualism, they continually fluctuated between anarchy and tyranny, the first always inducing the second within a short time. Christianity alone definitively enfranchises the individual and, at the same time, by the obligation of respect for legitimate authority, removes all fears of disorder and anarchy. City or State, like the individual, must respect the divine law, which makes of the former a necessary means to the latter. This revolution, so profound, so much more important in its results than a violent revolution, was produced slowly, by the force of a reasoned conviction, and its only victims were the Christians themselves, candidates for martyrdom for almost three hundred years.

Now that Germany, under pressure from her governors, tends to return to the old paganism, to that state of affairs so well defined by the expression "totalitarian State," wherein the State, acting in the name of the nation, the *Volk* or the race, is everything and the human person is nothing, the Catholic Church can not help recalling to mind once more her traditional doctrine. This she has done several times of late in the most formal manner. In his December consistory of 1926 and expressly in a recent encyclical, Pius XI declared: "The State exists for man, not man for the State," [44] and the S. Congr. of Seminaries and Universities addressed to Cardinal Baudrillart, Rector of the Catholic Institute of Paris, and to the Rectors and Faculties of other Catholic universities, a letter in which a certain number of condemned propositions appear, notably the following:

> Individual men exist only by the State and for the State; whatever rights they possess come solely from a concession of the State.[45]

The theory of the race, if it were to succeed in establishing itself, would involve the reversal of values to an order exactly opposite to the one brought about by Christianity, and it is for this

---

[44] See the Encyclical *Divini Redemptoris* (On Atheistic Communism) of March 19, 1937 (*Act. Apost. Sed.*, v. 29, p. 79, 31 mart., 1937); also the Encyclical *Mit brennender Sorge*, March 14, 1937 (*Act. Apost. Sed.*, v. 29, pp. 145-167, 10 April., 1937).

[45] Proposition VIII of the letter from the Sacred Congregation of Seminaries and Universities. By reason of the importance of this letter, which bears directly on the question of racism, it is well to reproduce here the eight propositions condemned:

1. The human races, by their natural and immutable characteristics, are so different that the lowest of them is farther from the highest than from the highest species of brutes.

2. It is necessary, by all means, to preserve and cultivate the vigor of the race and the purity of the blood; everything that conduces to this result is by that very fact upright and permissible.

3. It is from the blood, the seat of the characteristics of race, that all the intellectual and moral qualities of man spring as from their principal source.

4. The essential end of education is to develop the characteristics of race and to inflame minds with a burning love of their own race as the highest good.

5. Religion is subject to the law of race and must be adapted thereto.

6. The primary source and supreme rule of the entire juridical order is the racial instinct.

7. Only the Kosmos, or the Universe, exists as a living Being; all things, including man, are only various forms of the Living Universe, multiplied in the course of the ages.

8. Individual men exist only by the State and for the State; whatever rights they possess come solely from a concession of the State.

reason that Brunetière, who, long before the war, had envisaged the first outlines of the new regime, was able to speak, and very justly so, of a return to paganism. In place of the Christian, dualist and transcendent conception, the racist theory substitutes a monistic and immanent morality, immanent not in man but in the race, since it is race that makes man what he is. While the great sociological novelty of Christianity consisted in giving to religious convictions a basis at once personal and rational, breaking through, from the religious point of view, every necessary bond between the human person and the collectivity, family or *gens,* City or State,[46] the racist theory returns to a social morality. It revives the old adage, which the progress of civilization has caused to be regarded as monstrous, *cujus regio, ejus religio.* It is sufficient to substitute for the word "region," which envisaged rather the territory subject to a sovereign, the word "race," to have exactly the racial theory, according to which law, morality and religion are a secretion or, if preferable, an emanation of race and vary with race.

Such a conception, as did the ancient theories of the sovereignty of the people and of the national soul, rests upon a series of fictions. The collectivity does not have either its own soul or its own will. The national soul is a figure expressing with some inexactness of language the very proper idea that life in common under analogous conditions, education, the press, etc. give in each country to the entirety of its nationals certain characteristics that distinguish them from those of other countries. The will of the people and *a fortiori* that of the race, unless they are considered as the will of the majority, are also mere fictions; in fact, this so-called will is immediately appropriated by its alleged representatives, mandataries, the organs of the *Führer.*

Because it has neither its own soul nor its own will, the collectivity can have no morality of its own, unless through the intermediary of its members, whom it must take as they are. It is for this reason that the morality of interest, the *raison d'État,* is the sole rule for a collectivity which is devoid of all belief in a higher moral law and for which consequently there no longer exists any fixed point. That is precisely what we discover in the National-Socialist doctrine, in open conflict with the liberal individualism,

---

[46] On this point, cf. Luigi Sturzo, *Politique et Morale,* p. 112; *Politics and Morality* (London, 1938); *L'Église et l'État* (Paris, 1937), pp. 25 ff; *Church and State* (New York, 1939).

which, in the eighteenth and nineteenth centuries, had in its turn attempted in an excessive manner to combat the regime of the absolute sovereignty of the Prince, exercised in the name of the *raison d'État*. To National Socialism, law and morality are no longer a question of justice and reason, but merely a question of racial feeling.

This is the very negation of the common law and of objective and transcendental morality, both of which impose on the State as well as on man, justice, good faith and the duty of respecting in others that which it is desired to have respected in oneself. The golden rule, "Do unto others that which you would have them do unto you," is replaced among the chosen people—for from this point of view Germany takes the place of the Jews whom she persecutes—by the duty of fidelity towards the Party and the *Führer* alone; with regard to enemies, every means is good for attaining the end. With the Christian, one may say, with every normal moral man, good faith consists in the obligation of respecting the plighted word: *etiam hosti fides servanda est*. With the National Socialists, this obligation exists only with regard to themselves; that is to say, with regard to outsiders, what would otherwise be called bad faith is licit.

In the case of Germany, this danger of the absence of a higher moral law and consequently of any fixed point to guide and—should occasion arise—to arrest social evolution, becomes more aggravated because of the lack of measure which is a characteristic of that country.[47]

With all her great qualities, her love of work and her respect for authority, Germany possesses what might be called the feeling of immoderation;[48] of this she has already given proof in different periods of her history. Therein lies perhaps the best proof of the impossibility of man doing without a religion, true or false, of his need of finding a new absolute when God has been discarded. Hegel deified the State. Fichte made an Absolute of the nation. With the historic materialism of Karl Marx, one proceeds from the mysticism of the nation to the mysticism of the class. Today, with National Socialism, a new Absolutism, the mysticism of race, is substituted for the previous mysticisms.

It is a quite remarkable fact that these four mysticisms, some of

---

[47] Cf. Max Hermant, *Idoles allemandes* (Paris, 1935), *passim*.

[48] [The Germans themselves have a proverb, *Zu wenig und zu viel ist aller Narren Ziel* (Too little and too much is the goal of all fools).—Tr. note.]

which were destined to upset the world, are due, all four of them, to Germans. They have thus manifested in four different ways that feeling of immoderation to which I have just alluded. Forgetting that only power arrests power, they entrust omnipotence to an entity more or less mystical, freed from all obligation to a superior rule, moral law or religion.

From this point of view, the present racist movement has been pushed farther than the previous movements. Now and then a quasi-deification of the *Führer* is witnessed. At the beginning of meals, among certain groups of young Nazis, his name replaces that of God in the *Benedicite*. The *Pater* and the *Credo* have been parodied into a National-Socialist *Pater* and *Credo*, wherein the *Führer* takes the place of the Father or the God of the Christian prayers. In Germany, there is need of having a God of their own— *Führer* or Old German God, the God of the Scandinavian sagas, the God of the true Aryans. Now and then there seems to be among the Germans a violent reaction against what has often formerly been called their inferiority complex, a reaction which is manifested today in a feeling of immoderate pride.

One of the great arguments of the National-Socialist theory is the necessity of combating what is called the individualistic error. It visualized the results, too often disastrous in effect, in which anarchical individualism has culminated, first in ancient Greece, then in Italy of the Renaissance and later in Europe of the eighteenth and nineteenth centuries. Is there not really a logical contradiction between the primacy of man and the duty of obedience to the State, which no one can refuse and which sometimes extends to the obligation of sacrificing oneself for the community? Once more, in such an alleged contradiction, we are confronted with a pure exaggeration of abstract logic. The duty of obedience and the obligation of sacrifice exist only as long as one is confronted with interests of the same order, for example, with economic interests. Then, as is just and reasonable, the whole prevails over the part; no common life is possible without certain necessary sacrifices. But no power can ask of the individual the sacrifice to a material interest of spiritual interests which are of another order, as Pascal says.

Like a twofold hierarchy, there is a state of reciprocal dependence between the person and the State, the former being the true end and the latter the necessary means. We return always to the same point: the necessary recognition of an objective truth, of a moral and juridical good which dominates society as well as the individual. But, as has been very justly said, objectivism is possible only for those who believe in God. The rest, by definition, cannot go beyond man. Therefore, the necessary consequence of agnosticism is moral and juridical subjectivism. Thus and thus only can one solve the paradox between the primacy of the human person and his duty of obedience to social authority, at times even at the cost of the sacrifice of his life. Of the two great forces confronting each other, it is the human person, alone endowed with an immortal soul, which is the last end; but, as society—of which the State is the political and juridical organ—is for man a necessary means, then when its normal functioning and perhaps its very existence are at stake, it is a duty for the individual, who is simply a part of a whole, to sacrifice himself when this is indispensable to ensure the life of that whole which the members of the group cannot do without. On the other hand, it is not only the majority which has rights, nor the race, nor the class, but every man, and each one should respect the right and the dignity of his neighbor as much as his own. But this is just what the racist theory refuses to admit by its very conception of a superior race invested with all rights in relation to allegedly inferior races.

In bringing this study to a conclusion, I could not do better than to quote the judgment on his compatriots put forth by a very talented German writer who has remained impartial. There are several such writers, but of course they can no longer live in their own country.[49] Ernst Erich Noth has interpreted in moving

[49] One might quote also the eminent professor Foerster. In many passages with great courage and loyalty, he has insisted on the fact that the greatest fault of Germany, once she had been vanquished (for it was not so at the beginning of the war, when she hoped for a prompt termination thereof in her own favor), is her persistent unwillingness to recognize her responsibility in the origin of that war which ruined Europe. In the course of the negotiations which preceded the declaration of war, throughout the war itself and afterwards, the German rulers continually did their best to deceive their people, hiding from them the efforts made by the Allies in July 1914 to reach a peaceful solution and allowing them to believe that they had been unjustly attacked. It is from this that all the evil has arisen; Germany, unwilling to believe herself guilty, has considered the Treaty of Versailles as an "infamous *Diktat*." She has resisted with desperation the monstrous injustice of the obligation, imposed upon her yet never fulfilled by her, to repair the enormous ruin which she had wrought. In exactly the same way she represented the Czechs in 1938 as being the aggressors against the Sudeten and, in this summer of 1939, seeks to have Poland considered as the aggressor because the latter requests respect for the treaties that Germany herself, in full peace, had five years ago promised to respect for a period of ten years.

terms the rupture with the civilized world which has been effected in these last years by Germany under the influence of the National-Socialist Party.[50] He points out the categorical refusal with which Germany has resisted all pacific collaboration with other peoples, her complete rejection of all European and world solidarity. The greatness of Germany is the only thing that counts for her, but this is understood to the detriment of other States, and the end, which is the domination of Europe first and then of the rest of the world, may be achieved by any means whatsoever. "Today we possess Germany and tomorrow the entire world," says the battle song of the German Youth, which unfortunately, through the weakness and lack of understanding of the other States, has, in these last days, begun to receive a fulfilment that has served but to heighten Nazi enthusiasm.

In the place of the precepts of Christian morality or even of common human morality, German professors, officials and statesmen have substituted the official maxim: "Everything which is profitable to Germany is just." That which serves the interests of the race constitutes justice and law, but this actually applies only to the German race. To it everything is permitted; crimes, arsons, murders, perjuries become meritorious acts if they are done in the interest of race. In the beginning the young partisans of Hitler were led to believe that they were called to create a new, strong, yet just society. But, states Erich Noth—

far from having been able to create a healthy organic economy. National Socialism assigns to its subjects, to satisfy their hunger and to provide them with a living, the house of their neighbor.

All moral and spiritual values, instead of having been "revaluated," were purely and simply destroyed. The noise of arms, "of boots," says Erich Noth, stifles the voice of conscience. A new language has been created for the National Socialists, unintelligible to those not belonging to the Party, with the result that, for the moment, all understanding between Germany and the non-totalitarian peoples has been rendered impossible. That is "the unpardonable crime committed by the new masters of Germany."

[50] See his fine book, *La voie barrée* (trans. by A. E. Sernin, Paris, 1938), and his article, "A quoi pense la Jeunesse allemande?" in *Nouveaux Cahiers* (July 15, 1939), pp. 2 ff.

Education in the schools and in the universities (the term of which has been considerably reduced . . .) has broken officially with all notion of scientific objectivity, with the most elementary intellectual honesty. Censorship and inquisition lie in wait for whoever is occupied with things of the spirit.

In the last analysis, everything is reduced to a question of faith:

The secret of the indomitable dynamism of the Third Reich resides in the advent of a new religion. . . . Here is involved the brutal and offensive return of a tribal or rather islamic religion, the end of which, openly avowed and proclaimed, is to impose itself on the world and take possession of the world by fire and sword.

I do not care to add anything to words so serious, to this judgment passed with so much sadness by a German upon the new values of life, the new *Weltanschauung* of the country he loves so well.

Summer, 1939.

II

THE RIGHTS OF THE HUMAN PERSON
vis-à-vis of
THE STATE AND THE RACE

By JOSEPH T. DELOS, O. P.

*Professeur à la Faculté de Droit
de
l'Université Catholique de Lille*

THE RIGHTS OF THE HUMAN PERSON
vis-à-vis of
THE STATE AND THE RACE

The development of Racist conceptions has had immediate and telling repercussions on both private and public law. Not only has it modified the institutions, but it has affected the very principles of the juridical and social order. The authors of this development have been fully aware of this influence and have drawn arguments from it in their own favor.

One of the apparent and most serious consequences of the racist doctrines has been the discrimination brought about among the citizens of the State. In place of equality before the law, there has been substituted a juridical regime of inequalities dependent on race, which affects the members of the reputedly inferior races in the sphere of civil, family and economic rights. The distinction between "dependents of the State" and "citizens who enjoy civic rights," the prohibitions relative to *connubium,* the organization of economy and certain forms of *"numerus clausus,"* are but a few examples, among many others, offered by the wholesale racist legislation of recent years. These discriminations are logical consequences of the racist principles; it was through them that the influence of the latter was, in varying degrees, first manifested in German, Italian and Hungarian legislation, to mention no other instances.

Whatever novelty these recent discriminatory laws may exhibit, they are not, nevertheless, to be regarded as an isolated phenomenon. Not only does racism possess old, even if at times tenuous roots in certain theories of American and French origin (we are thinking particularly of Gobineau and Vacher de Lapouge), but in its resultant discrimination between citizen and citizen, it reverts to conclusions deduced from other political or social doctrines completely foreign to biology. The same political, discriminatory solutions present in this way a point of convergence for doctrines that are quite distinct.

39

It is within this rather general framework that we must reinstate the measures of discrimination inspired by racism. Its action affects the general principles of private and public law, and, in the offensive it has undertaken on its own account, it has joined forces with allies. We have, therefore, first to state the problem in general terms: Have men certain basic rights that are anterior and superior to government? Is every person to be regarded as equal in these rights to every other? The reply to these questions will enable us to pass on to the consideration of the question raised by racism. Can the State set up among its subjects a discrimination based upon race?

PART ONE

THE RIGHTS OF THE HUMAN PERSON AND THE STATE

I

GENERAL DATA OF THE PROBLEM

Public law draws a traditional distinction between the Government and the State; or rather, let us say, distinguishes in the State itself, between the Government and the State proper. The first term designates the agencies by which the functions of the State, legislative, judicial and executive, are exercised. The second term designates the body politic which undertakes the work of government. Between the two there is a distinction, but no separation; the governmental agencies give to the State its form and the means of exercising its specific activities; without them the State would be nameless, formless and inert; neither can we conceive of a government without a social body in which it is inherent, and in which, according to Hauriou's declaration, "it develops the enterprise of the commonwealth." [1]

This distinction invokes another, just as classical, and one that is more important for our purpose: that between the State and the body social which it personifies. It may be said that our civiliza-

[1] Hauriou, *Précis de Droit Constitutionnel*, Paris, Sirey, 1929, p. 78. It is well known that the works of this author, even those devoted to positive law, have unusual value for the philosophy of law.

tion rests on this distinction. After having noted that the State, properly so called—our modern State with public power on a territorial basis—is "the preferred form of static civilization," Hauriou seeks the reason for this "eminent value" and believes that he finds it in the fact that the State is a "superstructure." [2] As a matter of fact, different as have been the conceptions of the State, its forms and its principles of government in our modern epoch, everyone is agreed upon not confusing the State with the society or social body that constitutes the human substratum of the State.

Theory and political practice have been able to enthrone despotism, to oppress individual liberties, to disregard the rights of the family, to ignore the needs of a true culture, to rebel against the laws of an economics of free exchange, but they only succeeded in displacing thereby the boundaries separating the domain of private activity from that of the State, without ever abolishing completely the existence of these boundaries.

Hence, they have never ceased to recognize that the social and juridical order was founded on a twofold ground: the individual with his rights, the State with its rights. If the State is a superstructure, it is because there is a substructure, an ensemble of activities that are economic, family, cultural, religious, which have their own laws, their own specific and non-political ends; in these ends man finds a principle of action which is external to the State, independent of it, and which in consequence will impose itself on the State. Of course, conflicts may result; at times, it will be difficult to reconcile the rights of man and those of the State, and many doctrines will fail to effect this reconciliation; the *individualistic* formulas will exaggerate the prerogatives of the individual even to the point of dissolving the State, whereas the *state-ist* solutions will extend unduly the powers of the State in matters which pertain to economics, the family, education and religion; and the *absolutist* conceptions will do the same in political matters; but all of these are errors springing up within the bosom of a common order of civilization whose framework and first principles they in no way modify.

In consequence, the determination to establish among great peoples of high culture a social order which no longer rests upon the dual basis of the rights of man and the rights of the State, or upon the distinction of private life and public life, assumes a his-

[2] Hauriou, *op. cit.*, p. 79.

torical importance. This new departure is all the more serious in that it claims to find justification in a new political philosophy and metaphysics better able than any other to go to the roots of the truth. The authors of this new order declare that with their achievement, an era of altogether unprecedented civilization is dawning—a declaration that would be true enough, provided the results achieved and philosophical reflection permitted retention of the name "civilization."

It is in such consequences that racism ends when left to pursue its natural bent. But, as we have observed in our Introduction, it would be a mistake to believe that it alone leads to this result, for such is the fate of all doctrines which attribute to collective values superiority over personal values.

Such would have been the case with the French sociologism, associated with the name of Durkheim, if it had been able to develop all that was latent in it and we must in fairness acknowledge that the consequences in question would have astonished even that sociologist himself. The Durkheim movement is bound up with the sociological and ethnographical research which marked the end of the XIXth century and which developed simultaneously in different countries. Sociology found in Durkheim and in certain of his disciples minds more taken up with Ethics and Metaphysics than they themselves realized—scientists who would willingly have become reformers through the medium of ideas and national education. They attributed pre-eminence to society, not only over the institutions which pertain to private life and find their origin in the heart itself of the individual man, such as religion or the family, but over the very elements of personality. The sentiments that most directly manifest this personality, such as the verdicts of conscience, as well as the sense of responsibility itself, have a social origin. The human personality is thus dissolved in the social body; it ceases to be an original and irreducible source of energy and thought, true cause of its own acts. Society makes man; it is anterior and superior to man. As a consequence, the juridical order can no longer have for its foundation the inalienable rights of the human person; the social body expresses the necessities or the utilities of the life of society and brings about their triumph through constraints. If it protects the individual and guarantees him the exercise of certain of his activities, it is on account of the social utility of the latter, and not because of an inherent value bound up with man's quality as man. Whatever treatment be accorded him, man is delivered over to society: he belongs to it as the vase belongs to the potter.

It does not seem fair, however, to dwell any further upon this sociological theory. However real its practical influence may have been in the first quarter of the twentieth century, it is far from being perpetuated. The effort to introduce its principles into our public law by the pathway of science has failed; the name of one of our great professors of the science of Law, *Duguit,* the respected Dean of the Faculty of Bordeaux, remains linked with this attempt, but it constitutes the feeble part of his work. Finally and above all, the efficacy this doctrine might have had pales into insignificance when compared with that of the totalitarian and racist conceptions.

It is with the creation of the totalitarian States that the problem of civilization has been raised in its full extent and consequences. The history of their origin reveals in each of them the joining of two features that could easily and really should be contradictory. On the one hand, each one rests upon a general philosophy, upon a metaphysical concept of life. They are all ideological. On the other hand, they are all essentially pragmatic; born of the stimulus of political necessities, issuing out of revolutions, or from movements whose primary objective was the acquisition of power; they are concerned only with action and its result. On this score, they boast of being eminently opportunist and pragmatic.

From the ideological point of view, they are essentially different; different to such a degree that the opinion was current for quite some time that their votaries could not dwell on the same planet and that they would be sure to tear one another to pieces. However, in our opinion, it is Racism alone which can lead to the theory of an integral totalitarianism. It alone, in fact, builds on the foundation of a perfect sociological materialism. Fascist totalitarianism is essentially political. It can always reconcile itself with newly admitted facts in the order of reality, such as the family or the religious sentiment. As for Marxism, it always contains, at least in its latest expression, an individualistic residue.

It is from the pragmatic point of view that they all resemble one another. It is in their results that they coincide. The systems, whether political, juridical or economic to which they tend have analogous characteristics. What is their common feature? The series of identifications which they establish. Men absorbed by their quality of nationality, the nation identified with the State; the State identified with the Government; the Government absorbed in the person of the Leader; the Leader is the Leader precisely because he is who he is, which is to say that his personal qualities coincide exactly or eminently with the qualities of the nation and with the historical aspirations which the nation possesses or ought to possess: such is the series of identifications established by the doctrinaires of Fascism. It is the same with racist totalitarianism; the only modification needed is in a racial sense; the race determines the people and its culture, it incorporates into itself the State and the Law which are its means of expression; it culminates in the person of the Leader, who is the Leader because in him are eminently manifested the qualities and the rights of the race. In the measure that the Marxist State is classed among totalitarian States, the series will be predicated upon class; it is no longer the Nation, nor the Race, but the economic criterion of production which will furnish the standard of values and the principle of social order. Let it be added that this series of identifications is revealed in a new and specific creation—the one-Party. There is but one active political element of the Race, of the Nation, of the Class, of the People, of the State, of the Government; it is the Party, in which the Leader is everything.

From this fact, there follow two consequences, one of which is well understood; the other is less often studied and yet it deserves more serious attention. Together they form a diptych and may not be separated.

The first has given its name to the system: totalitarianism. The State is everything in relation to the individual, who belongs entirely to the State. What gives value to man, as a matter of fact, in the system of the State-Nation, is not his humanity, but his *"nationality,"* his *Italianity,* his quality of Frenchman or Celt; or again, it is the Race's seed of which he is the bearer; Aryan, and among the Aryans, Falic or Nordic. Or finally, what merits attention is man's capacity as proletarian or producer. In every case, the principle of value is put in a collectivity: nation, race, class. It is in living more fully this collective life, in opening one's mind to it even to the point of identifying oneself with the group and becoming a part of the Whole that the individual increases his value and is reunited with the absolute.

Thus, from the philosophical point of view, totalitarianism is the doctrine which ascribes intrinsic anteriority and superiority to the collectivity (race, nationality, class) whose values it rates as above the person and personal values. From the viewpoint of the sociology of the State, it is that doctrine which suppresses the distinction between the State and the Social body that makes up its human substance; from the juridical point of view, it is that doctrine which establishes the juridical order upon the rights of the collectivity and upon them alone, denying or disregarding any rights the individual might possess by reason of his own independent dignity.

But here is the other panel of the diptych. Up to now, totalitarianism has appeared to be an exaltation of the State; the State being everything. But at the same time, totalitarianism sanctions the conquest of the State and its subordination to the Nation, to the Race, to the Class. It entails undue influence over the State. The modern epoch is familiar with the national State, and although it is not the State form necessary for civilization, it is a healthy form. It implies that the body politic which gives itself a government and which "develops within itself the enterprise of the commonwealth," is a national group. The State remains a superstructure and preserves its transcendency. There will indeed be talk of "sovereignty of the nation," but this expression has a historical sense. It means that the concern of the common weal does not belong to a dynasty, nor to a man, but to the collective whole. It by no means prevents the State once established from having its own end, *specifically political* and not purely ethnic or nationalistic. On the other hand, the State-Nation and the State-Race are new facts. The State is now subordinated to the Nation, or to the Race; its end is to realize the purpose ascribed to the Race; it is in its service; it has lost its transcendency; the law which it establishes is an instrument at the service and for the advantage of the ethnic group, for it is this group which is raised up in sovereignty, as the source of right.

The upshot is that such a State will necessarily establish a discrimination among its subjects. In effect, since the State becomes identified with a race, with an ethnic character, they who are of another race are out of the State. Since right has its source in the race, they who live within the boundaries of the State, without belonging to the race, are outside of the juridicial order. Thus discrimination is established automatically; and if there is recognition of some rights in such individuals, it is by way of opportunism, or for reasons of utility, a pure concession of society and of the State, always revocable.

Hence the issue upon which the fate of civilization hangs today is a single one, but has two aspects: On the one hand, it is the transcendency of the human person that is in peril; does man possess fundamental rights anterior and superior to those of the State? On the other hand, the examination of the actual data of the problem reveals the fact that the transcendency of the State is likewise at stake; the State must be delivered from the usurpation of the collectivity which has conquered and enslaved it. Might it not be that in finding again its transcendency, in becoming once more a superstructure, the State would again become capable of respecting the equality of all men? Would not the transcendency of the human person with reference to the collectivity, involve the transcendency of the State with reference to the social body and thus disclose the secret of a regime of equality? This is what we must next consider after examining the data of the problem.

II

THE IRREDUCIBLE HUMAN PERSON AND THE LAW

The problem of the source of right is one whereby the juridical and social sciences are joined with metaphysics. Indeed it is impossible to resolve it without settling the essential problem of Values. It is not enough to speak of "the eminent dignity of the human person" and to establish the social order upon this dignity; we must see in what this "dignity" consists and why it has a juridical import. But this is to resolve the problem of Values.

The dignity of the human person will be known through its operations. No man will find any difficulty in admitting that his characteristic operations are thought and the exercise of free will.

Now, by reason of intelligence and the reflex consciousness he has of himself, man already "possesses himself." To have consciousness of himself, by turning his thoughts inward to observe himself and judge himself, is to have intellectual mastery over his own states of consciousness. It is not without reason that the French language makes current use of the expression *"se rendre maître de . . . saisir"* to designate the act of the human intellect comprehending its object. It is we who are apprehending ourselves when we are conscious of *you*.

It is true that sensation already raises us to the level of conscious life; but it gives us no mastery of ourselves. On the contrary, it might rather be said, sensation is that by which the external world leads and controls us: hunger, cold, pleasure, pain, repel or attract the animal; they are guides to its acts. It is by means of such externals that we lead the animal; even as those men who fail to raise themselves to the plane of thought are likewise led by such sensations. But it is by thought that we turn inwardly upon our sensations and upon our intellectual operations, and this is a first manner, an intellectual way of controlling ourselves.

It is in truth we ourselves who govern ourselves, for the consciousness of our acts and of our states of consciousness gives us knowledge of our nature, our "whatness"—the what we are; the potentialities of our nature, or what it is capable of becoming; the order even of its natural elements, the inter-relation finally of its acts and of what it has a right to be. Appreciating his *being,* man realizes his *right to be;* for the right to be of an individual is inscribed in his being. Thus is the law of our development made known to us, the order of an activity in conformity with our nature, and with the law of our being.

What was heretofore simply possession or purely intellectual mastery of self, is now to declare itself upon the plane of action. For just as man possesses a power of thought and of having consciousness of himself, his nature and his purposes, so too does he possess an original source of spiritual energy, a will that enables him to put himself in motion. This spiritual energy moves well only in the clear light of intelligence. If the intellect presents to the will an object which is indubitably its good, in conformity with its nature and the necessary expansion of its being, the more imperious because the more profound, the will turns to this object spontaneously, with energy, with joy. When the intellect hesitates, because it sees in an object merely a doubtful or a problematic good, the will itself stops on the brink of action, remains suspended in its course. But whatever be its hesitation, it must act, both with regard to reason as well as in virtue of the necessity of attaining the good. The choice must be made in order to act; the mind has this faculty of choosing among the objects which attract it, it determines and governs itself, thus becoming the cause of its own choice and responsible from then on for the course upon which it has freely entered. Thus, it affirms itself master of itself on the plane of action.

The same mastery is exercised *a fortiori* over the surrounding world. This, too, man grasps by knowledge; the sciences deliver it over to man. The intellect comes to know the laws of this surrounding world and henceforth takes command over it; for to know the laws of the universe is to be able to direct its operations and to utilize these in whatever ways accord with any given one of these laws—to make them subservient to the advantage of man.

Such is the human person. Why is it that his qualities and his very nature possess a juridical value? Why do they find their expression in terms of law?

The human person is, in a sense that we propose to explain, an *absolute*. This means that it is, in the etymological sense of this word, *solutus* (detached) with respect to other things. The intellect, in fact, gives person the capacity to grasp things through knowledge, to have authority over them, and by discovering their laws to exercise control over them. In what concerns himself, the person knows the purposes of his life, and moves himself of his own accord to realize them. He bears then within himself the principle of his own action; instead of being "alienated," i.e. instead of depending on another, *alienus,* he finds in himself the *raison d'être* of his own acts. Person knows but one complete dependence, that of its being, with relation to the Creator, but this dependence, far from "alienating it," confirms it in its being, since it binds it to that which communicates to it intelligence and will.

Such a being has value of itself. It has its own worth in the scale of beings, because it dominates them all by its power to know them. It has its value in its relations with the world, because it exercises control over the world. It possesses worth in its relations with other persons, for with regard to them it enjoys a complete independence, and there is not one of them who, *qua* an intelligent being capable of judgment, fails to recognize such a being's value in the hierarchy—his quality of *absolute* or of end in himself.

And this is to recognize in the human person the character of a subject of right. This notion which is fundamental in the social sciences and in the philosophy of law, is linked with the notion of person and that of value. It is in reality one of the first affirmations of reason. As a matter of fact, when two beings who possess consciousness of their personality and of the worth it confers upon them enter into mutual relation, is it possible for reason to proffer any other judgment than that such worth must be respected? Each one of them is independent and therefore does not belong to the other; each one has an absolute value before the bar of reason, and every act which belittles this value or denies it, is a destruction of worth, an injustice, a disturbance wrought in the *"adaequatio rerum,"* in the reciprocal order of values obtaining between them. To affirm of someone that he is a subject of right is to affirm that he has an absolute value, in face of all opposition, a value respect for which is demanded by order.

From this it follows that every man is a subject of right, seeing that this title attaches to his personality as such, to his nature as a free and intelligent being. Like his nature itself, it cannot be lost and it establishes equality among men. Each individual, in fact, constitutes an absolute of value and this value attaches to his spirituality. Indeed, it is to be noted that in searching for the basis of rights, we have never come upon the idea of race, nor of nation, nor of social function, but only upon the quality of person, the dignity of thought and of liberty. Of course, in the exercise of these faculties, the individual will be subject to the effect of the physical or social conditions which are his very own; the differences will appear numerous and will beget differences of rights. But it is not upon the exercise of these faculties, or upon their conditioning that right is established; it is founded on these faculties themselves, independently of their individual conditioning by the race, the social or national milieu and their own functioning; more deeply rooted still, it is based upon man's very being; the equality of men is as incapable of being lost as is their nature, even though it admits, as does their nature too, of individual inequalities.

What place will this equality of persons and these ethnic or social inequalities take in the eyes of the State? This is the question we must now examine; but first of all, let us ask ourselves, in what relation the State stands to the human person.

III

THE STATE, THE PERSON AND RIGHT

If we open a discussion on the duties of the State by affirming, for example: the State is made up of conscious, free citizens, who possess the dignity of human persons; it has for its end the protection of these citizens in the exercise of the rights bound up with their quality of Person; but these rights are equal for all; respect for the equality is a part of the respect for the rights, and, like the latter, is imposed upon the State. To this affirmation there might probably be opposed a refusal to admit its relevancy, and this refusal might be supported by other affirmations as weighty as our own. It might be said, for example: the State is made up of people of the same race; it has for its end the maintenance and the defense of the racial elements which they possess; the rights of its members are based upon the quality of the racial germ they bear; a discrimination on this basis is imposed in the name of the law. Or again, the State is made up of men of a dominant nationality (in the sociological and ethnical sense of the word), it has for its end the safeguarding of the culture and the interests of that nationality. The discussion could then never be fruitful due to the absence of a common ground, for each would start from a definition of the State suggested by a previously established philosophy. It must indeed be observed that the partisans of the racial State or of the Nation-State do not claim that the State is actually made up of people of the same race or of the same nationality; they know well that this is not so; but they judge that it should be so, and it is in the name of "what ought to be," based on a particular conception of the State, that they draw their conclusions.

It is very evident, that, in order to resolve the problem, we shall have to come to a conception of the nature of the State, but we should like to arrive at it by adopting a starting-point common to us and the other side: for example, the analysis of an incontestable fact.

We believe that we find such a starting-point in the fact of sociability, something so well known that it suffices to recall it without further description. Its analysis is simple. Its results show that there is no human need which can be satisfied without some recourse to social assistance. For each of these needs, a collaboration is necessary, that is, relations that call for a certain institutional organization—a veritable society. Thus, groups come into existence—family, economic, cultural, religious—distinguished from one another by their end or the human need which they answer. The similarities of language, manners, ethnic characteristics themselves, give rise to a true community when the feeling of harmony engendered by them awakens a certain common will-to-live and a certain attachment to common manners. These social relations each answer a particular need of human nature; their ensemble embraces all human life, their blossoming is the essential manifestation of civilization.

But their number and their diversity make more apparent a specific need: that of an order. Indeed, there must be assurance for the coexistence of so many individuals, the untrammeled functioning of so many private groups, the effective working of so many heterogeneous relations. The assurance of a peace which includes everyone and which is the result of a general order that none may evade, is a specific and distinct end.

Indeed, this order is at once *public and juridical,* and these two qualities belong to it as properties. Each of the groups we have just mentioned pursues only a partial end; it procures for its members only a fraction of human benefit. The family assures the perpetuation of the species through generation and education; but this task, noble as it is, does not absorb all of human activity. The groupings of economic order procure the subsistence of man; but he has other needs in addition to his daily bread, or his comfort and leisure. The groupings which have for their object culture, art, even religion, make no claim to divert men from other necessary or useful activities. The values produced by nationality—language, manners, religious traditions, etc.—are always themselves limited in number, but there are besides these universal values: truth, science, religion, which are by their nature supranational. In short, in each case, the objective is limited, partial, if it be compared to the totality of human aspirations and human needs.

This is why each of these groupings is "private" and not "public." What does this mean? It means that to have access to them, a title is necessary, distinctive, specific, discriminatory. One must be parent, child or domestic (in the sense of the "domus") to penetrate within the society of the family. One must subscribe to a

Credo to be part of a religious community. One must be interested, by title of shareholder, employer, worker, or the like to belong to an occupational grouping. One must speak a certain language, have certain customs and traditions to be welcomed fraternally by one's "compatriots." These are closed societies which choose their members by requiring a title; they are not public.

It is entirely different with the society which has for its object the assurance of an order which each of the groups or of the private individuals needs and which embraces all. The point in question is, by definition, to effect a peaceful organization of each and all of the human activities that have a social aspect. Nothing therefore pertaining to humankind escapes this order; no condition of occupation, of family, of religion, of language, of race can be required for its enjoyment, since it is a matter of a superstructure organizing all the elements of human life and all its values. Accordingly, one qualification alone is required in order to be a part of this community, namely the qualification of being *man*. For all the particular differentiations, all the activities, all the states consequent upon physical nature, family status, occupation, nationality, culture, are finally referred to one and the same subject, *man,* and it is to man finally that the order itself, of which we speak, is referred. It is in one's capacity as man that one becomes a part of this community and that is why it is "public."

This is the reason, too, it is juridical. For we have shown above that every man in social life necessarily becomes a subject of right. That is a title attached to his value, a quality inherent in his being and not the corollary of a particular determination such as would be that of owner, or workman, of father or child, of unmarried or married, of national or foreigner. Still less is it a prerogative linked with physiological characteristics. And so the order established among such subjects is necessarily an order of right. Among subjects of right, how could the relationships fail to be juridical? As they are economic in the occupational grouping, domestic in the home, so too they are juridical in the State, since the State is an order established among subjects of right.

We see now how the State takes for its starting-point the human person, independently of his individual determinations of class, race, culture, or religion. It has the human person also as its end: its end is to permit the expansion of all human activities, without discrimination, provided they have a human value. The only discrimination permitted the State is that which is made between good and evil, order and disorder, the respect of the rights of the human person and their violation.

We can now examine more closely the problem of discriminations based upon Race.

PART TWO

THE STATE, THE RACE AND RIGHT

The modern epoch may be called the "period of the National-State." The historian of public law sees it gravitating in this direction even at the end of the XIV and in the XV century; in the XVIII century it evolves in the direction of national sovereignty; the XIX century becomes the "century of nationalities." With some peoples, the doctrine emphasizes its ethnical and racial meaning, and in the first quarter of the XX century a veritable current of racial mysticism spreads among two at least of the largest countries of Europe and America, and for the first time, we catch a glimpse of the Racist State. The idea of race lays claim to the absorption of its predecessor, the idea of nationality, and to the domination of the entire field of law and politics.

A history of national, ethnic and racial doctrines, with their repercussions on political institutions and conceptions of the State, is still to be written; and the wish may be expressed that the project of such a history may soon tempt some group of specialists, or arouse the initiative of one or another learned body. We shall rest content with considering the racist doctrines in their actual form, as they are used to support the idea of the State.

However, this examination immediately encounters a difficulty. All authors rightfully note that the word "Race" is accepted in two meanings. Not only the general public, but scientists themselves use the word alternately in these two senses, and even at times pass unconsciously from one meaning to the other. This confusion has been a notable factor in spreading the errors relative to race and the Racial State.

On the one hand, race is accepted as a purely biological fact. It consists in likeness of physical, anatomical or physiological characteristics transmitted by heredity. It is distinguished therefore very definitely, both from linguistic families, which group populations on the basis of affinities of their language, and from cultural cycles, in which ethnography groups men on the basis of their civilization according to criteria borrowed from their tools, their customs, their weapons or their institutions. It would be desirable if we could retain exclusively the biological or anthropological sense of the word *race*.

But it is observed that anthropologists and biologists themselves, upon leaving their laboratory to descend into the political terrain, almost inevitably give another meaning to the word. They then designate by the term *race* populations which present no real homogeneity from the physical point of view, but psychic or social rather than biological similarities. The word race thus takes on an ethnic sense, and the term "Jewish Race" is used, whereas the heterogeneity of our contemporary Jews is, it seems, an established fact. Or again, in certain circles, the terms "Aryan Race" and "non-Aryan" will be defended, even though the "Aryan Race," in the light of the most serious studies, appears to be a creation of armchair scientists, to borrow the expression of Hartmann. There will even be talk of the Latin race, the French race, or the German race, although we know well today that these terms are misnomers.

Regrettable as this confusion is, we cannot set aside a usage that is so widespread. We shall therefore study the problem, using the term race successively in its two different meanings. This will be no mere concession to an ordinary whim, for we shall then proceed to show that if the very people who apologize for the fault slip involuntarily from the biological to the ethnical plane, they are led into this error by a modicum of truth.

A.

RACE IN ITS BIOLOGICAL MEANING AND THE STATE

Race, in the biological meaning of the word, is neither a constitutive element of the political society or State, nor a datum of the juridical order: it is not generative of rights. These two affirmations which can be made boldly, call for an explanation and a justification.

That the race is not a constitutive factor of the State in its specific character of political society, could be demonstrated by historical argument. Never has the map of any well organized

State coincided with a racial frontier. The fact is, in itself, of great importance; however, in the present debate, we recognize that it is not enough to compel conviction. One may indeed, in ascertaining the fact, regret it: true civilization, it will be said, would require an authentically racial State. It is therefore, the racial fact itself that must be analyzed.

Now, it is enough to consider its nature to understand that the biological fact of race does not involve the formation of a natural human society. In contrast to the fact of generation, to that of work, or the organization of public order, race implies neither association nor collaboration of men. Hence the very particular, and to put it exactly, the very conventional nature of the racial group, as compared with the family, the occupational group, the city.

The notion of race, as a matter of fact, is a notion borrowed from Zoology and legitimately applied to man, insofar as he is also an animal. The race is a variation of the species, "collection of organized beings, born one of another, or of common parents, and of those who resemble them as much as they resemble one another," to adopt, for example, Cuvier's definition. But even when it is a question of the species, the problem presents itself of determining whether it be a "reality," a "constant type, defined by permanent characteristics." [3] In practice, the classification of species is based upon morphological resemblances, but as E. Rabaud notes,[4] "the appreciation of resemblances and differences rests on no precise rule" and M. Lester adds pertinently: "it is . . . impossible, when dealing with living beings, to establish specific distinctions corresponding to an *objective* reality: these distinctions are necessary for the classification of organisms, useful for their designation, but the species remains nevertheless a purely *conventional* group whose value varies with the organisms studied." [5] For a much stronger reason, the animal race—"variation of the species more or less determined by heredity"—has limits at once conventional and shifting. "We do not have at our disposal any valid criterion of a general import which would permit affirming that two individuals belong to the same (animal) race or belong, on the contrary, to two distinct races." [6]

[3] P. Lester, in: *Les Races humaines,* Paris, Colin, 1936, p. 12.
[4] E. Rabaud, *Elements de la biologie générale,* Paris, Alcan, 1926, p. 309.
[5] P. Lester, *op. cit.,* p. 13 (italics ours).
[6] P. Lester, *op. cit.,* p. 14.

The absence of an objective criterion makes itself felt even more in Anthropology. It is therefore very natural that scientists accept criteria of their own choice. Some will seek them from morphological anthropology, others from physiological anthropology, or from both simultaneously. At times, they will dwell upon descriptive characters: coloration of the skin, congenital pigmentary stain, texture and color of the hair, development of the pilose system, form of the eyes and pigmentation of the iris, prominence of the face; at other times, they will have recourse to measurements: cephalic index, facial index, length of limbs and their proportion to the total height of the body; again, they will retain the characters of the soft parts; more often still, they will combine the different procedures. Physiological anthropology, for its part, will draw up tables of growth, will study the blood, the metabolism, the sense organs, or again the functioning of the endocrine glands, fecundity and the sex-ratio; it will frequently seek complementary indications from pathology.

To the multiplicity of criteria is joined the incertitude and the vagueness of the definitions of race. Let us take, for example, the definition of A. Pittard: "a grouping together of similar individuals sprung from parents of the same blood." [7] It is evident that this definition brings no decisive light to general sociology or to social philosophy. The difficulty is precisely to furnish an objective criterion of resemblance. As for the common origin, it is practically incapable of verification. On the other hand, it may theoretically lead to the unity of race, since men of all races and their hybrids are interfertile with one another.

The statement has recently been made: "In this research, where a preponderant part rests on personal appraisal" (choice of criteria) "and on hypothesis" (indication of causes), "the anthropologist, by a profound study of populations, forces himself to make a *sorting* of the individuals presenting like physical characteristics, which he then regroups on paper. It is the groups thus arrived at which constitute the human races; they are necessarily artificial, provisional to a certain degree, and they vary according to the relative importance given by anthropologists to the various anatomical characteristics." [8] These groupings of population, "pa-

---

[7] Pittard, *Les Races et l'histoire*, Paris, 1924, P.h.

[8] P. Lester, Sous-Directeur de Laboratoire au Muséum d'Histoire naturelle, and J. Millot, professor in the Faculty of Sciences of Paris—*Les Races humaines—op. cit.*, p. 18.

per groupings," leave outside their boundaries numerous fractions
of the population whose classification is uncertain; this necessitates
the creation of sub-groups and sub-races.

A concrete example will illustrate these conclusions from the
studies made by anthropology. If we consider a State with a political and national unity as advanced as that of France, we shall distinguish in its population a section of Nordic type, which occupies
two departments of the north, grouped perhaps along the Channel,
and which is quite like analogous populations of Sweden, Den-
mark, Norway, Friesland, Northern Germany and Flanders; a
section of Galatian (or sub-Adriatic) type, which dwells in the zone
between the Somme and the Loire, extends towards the East, and
as far south as Savoy; it is again found in Luxembourg, Zeeland,
the Rhineland, Bavaria and German Austria; another section of
Celtic type; and finally another of Mediterranean type, whose
geographical area we shall not describe. We thus see how Anthropology, in order to fix racial limits, takes for a starting-point
real characteristics, objective similarities; but race is a principle of
grouping only on paper, in the laboratory of the scientist. Whereas
the family, professional work, civic life, reveal a natural society,
the race, by contrast, creates no association, nor real collaboration.
It has never escaped anyone that generation, education, work involve the formation of associative bonds, but we do not observe
any such bonds that are the result of skeletal likenesses, or pigmentary similarities; these resemblances are not a principle of association among men.

The reasons which explain this fact are of primary importance
in political science and in the philosophy of public law. If the race
does not create among men any social bond in the proper sense of
the term, it is because it does not propose to them any common
end, any common good. This is a fact of observation which may be
raised to a sociological law: no group or human society is formed
except when a unique object or end furnishes an idea and a program of action, implicit or explicit. It is in appreciation of the end
that social functions are given their hierarchy and that an organization is effected: the education of children, economic profit,
the security of refined life are the ends common to the members
of the family, of economic enterprise, of the State; the authority,
the functions, the organization proper to each of these societies
is in relation to their end.

Now, the fact of possession of the same cephalic index or the same pigmentation is not creative of any common need among men requiring their collaboration, or constraining them to organize for its attainment.

In the absence of society, does not the race produce a classification, a grouping among men? Not at all. Since the race is perpetuated by the transmission of hereditary characteristics, there would in that case have to be no interfertility except among people of the same race; then, we should see humanity break up in groups whose line of demarcation no generation could cross. Each group would have at one and the same time a community of origin and the exclusive ownership of its hereditary characteristics.

But the interfertility of the members of all races with one another, coupled with the unimpaired fertility of their hybrids, is precisely the definitive mark of mankind. This is not only the cause of a continual mixing of all races, it is a testimony to the homogeneity of the human stock. From it we must conclude to the unity of the human species and seek in consequence the specific character of this species in a truly permanent trait of its nature; in an activity of the brain that no other animal brain knows. "The morphological character that dominates man in his 'thinking' brain (sic), which enabled the most diminutive hominid we can imagine in the far away of tertiary times, to discipline his strength by arming the fingers of his fore-paws with a stone, to discover the use of fire, to defend himself effectively, in the midst of a hostile nature against innumerable enemies." [9]

Here we are again brought back to *thought,* that is to the spirituality of man, but we emerge from the domain of pure biology. There are no human societies except where there are common representations and consciousness; to find them, we have to go outside the analysis of race; the latter is not a fact generative of human society.

Neither is it, as we have said, a juridical fact and it is now easy to understand why. No one, by reason of his race, enjoys any rights which are his own by virtue of being attached to his biological race, and which would demand a consequent discrimination in his favor.

The errors so widespread in the course of late years have a common cause: the development of the spiritual values of culture, of

---

[9] Lucien Mayet, in charge of the courses of Anthropology and Human Palaeontology in the University of Lyon, *Races humaines préhistoriques et actuelles,* pp. 186-187. Dans: *Hérédité et Races,* Editions de Cerf. 1931.

civilization and of morality has been placed in deterministic and absolute dependence upon race. Their advance is made to depend, as though from a necessary cause, upon the hereditary germ-plasm transmitted by generation. Hence, the distinction of noble and inferior races and the inequality of absolute value of individuals according to their race. This distinction entails an inequality of rights which the juridical order, established by the State, must sanction. They alone enjoy all civil rights, they alone may participate freely in the economic life who belong to the noble race; for them, too, alone is the *connubium* with the plenitude of its prerogatives.

In reality, this determinism is only a new form of materialism. It is biological and racial. In the XIX century we were made acquainted with scientific materialism which considered thought a secretion of the brain; this new materialism makes thought dependent on blood and heredity. It is, moreover, sociological: the "values" attributed to the race are collective values; the race is superior to the individual, the group is of higher worth than the person, because the group confers on the person whatever value he possesses.

We have, of course, no intention of denying the different aptitudes of each individual, nor the influence of the physical upon the exercise of the spiritual faculties. But we refuse to confound the *conditions* which happen to give their *mode* to the *exercise* of these faculties with the faculties themselves and the spirit whose power and nature the latter reveal. We refuse even to admit, since it is not a scientifically demonstrated fact, that among these conditions those due to the biological race are the principal ones. Let it be well noted, however, that our thesis would be in no wise impaired if they were. However, they are not; up to now it has been impossible scientifically to establish the existence of a cause-and-effect bond of any importance between racial characteristics (pigmentation, for example, or prognathism) on the one hand and thought or morality on the other, without falling back into a particular case of the much more vast problem of the influence of the physical upon the moral, or of the environment's influence upon the individual.

But, above all—and this is of capital importance in the discussion—we deny that the differences of individual aptitudes warrant a discrimination touching the rights of the human person. From these differences of aptitudes, there will result in a legitimate way differences of function, which can be protected by an appropriate juridical regime. But, just as in each function and in each different activity, it is man who acts, so too, in each juridical regime, whether of manual laborer or of employer, of illiterate or savant, of fool or wise man, of White or Yellow or Black, it is the rights of the human person that are protected and honored. There is distinction of the individual aptitudes, division of the functions, but no discrimination of persons. The justice that presides over social relationships will be a distributive justice, but this justice, in the "proportion" it establishes, takes into account both the hierarchy of functions and the equality of persons. On the ground of differentiation of aptitudes and needs, it will apportion diversely official positions and social advantages; in the name of equality of persons, which is also one of the principles of distributive justice, the social order will assure to each man the conditions of a life truly human, conforming with his dignity and his destiny as a human person.

Hence, in the name of the dignity of the human person, we reject every discrimination based on race. But it is in the very name of the dignity of the human person that certain individuals think they can admit, at least by way of expediency, some rights founded on race. Without lapsing into the materialism and the determinism which we have just condemned, they contend that purity of blood is helpful for the vigor of the population and that the consideration *"mens sana in corpore sano"* cannot leave the State unconcerned. It is natural, so they think, for the State to establish a discrimination of persons on the score of their social utility; even the individual will profit thereby.

We find ourselves here in the presence of one of the numerous fallacies arising from the unpreciseness of the term *race*. What is meant by purity of race and purity of blood? Are they synonomous? To begin with, it has to be proved that mixture of blood constitutes in itself a blemish, that it causes a moral or physical weakening of individuals. All we can say is that at the present time there is no proof that this is so at all; blood relationship, with the sameness of blood that it implies, is on the contrary a frequent cause of physical degeneration. But even if it were proved, the problem of right would be in no wise changed. Marriage and procreation are faculties attaching to the very nature of the human person; they are part of his physical and moral nature and constitute rights. The exercise of these rights, as well as of all those inherent in man's nature, are dependent on the judgment of his reason, of his conscience, of his prudence. In all times, natural morality, as well as the morality of Christianity, has recognized that the exercise of the right to transmit life involved a responsibility and that respect for certain conditions, even physical ones, may be imposed on conscience, lest the offspring and society have to bear the burden of certain defects. The intervention of the State, to facilitate the accomplishment of these duties of prudence, is no more than legitimate; but its action finds a basis, not in the rights of the race, but in the rights of the person; and the intervention of the State is merely a particular aspect of a policy of public welfare destined to assure the human person the blessing of a sound heredity and a vigorous physique. This basis will suffice to preserve it from exaggerations that might lead to a repetition of the errors of racism. Indeed, if physical vigor is a blessing, it is because this physical strength ordinarily makes possible a more perfect human life. But a sickly Pascal, inventor and immortal philosopher, whose thought still nourishes us today, has a much greater human value, both individual and social, than a robust but illiterate Pascal would have had.

Thus, the myth of race, in the biological sense, vanishes from the field of law, and it is the human person that juridical philosophy finds once more at the end of its analysis. Does the same thing hold true if we take race in its ethnical sense?

B.

Race in the Ethnical Sense and the State

We have already voiced our opposition to the use of the word *race* in any sense other than the purely anthropological and zoological one. True, we may likewise give it an ethnic meaning, provided we make clear in each case the meaning we attach. The abuse consists in changing from one sense to the other without even adverting to the fact, or taking the trouble to give due notice of it. If we yield provisionally to a general usage which makes race synonomous with ethnic group, it is because not to do so would leave a number of problems raised by political racism unanswered. It is also because said general usage finds a certain justification even in science.

The variability of races is indeed a truth affirmed by many

anthropologists. "The day is long past since we believed in the fixity of human races," wrote Mr. J. Millot only a short time ago, ". . . Far from having an absolute value, races like species and even more so than species, are only momentary realizations . . . capable of undergoing the most profound and sometimes the most rapid transformations." [10] This affirmation is by no means incompatible with the immutability of hereditary characteristics, where such immutability has been definitely ascertained; it simply proves there are other factors than heredity in the strict sense that intervene in the formation of races.

What are these factors? Leaving aside the problem of "brusk variations," which has hardly any interest for us here, let us confine ourselves exclusively to such variations as are due to *mesological causes*. It is not our concern to know whether the influences of the environment are fixed by the heredity of acquired characters, whether they act directly through the play of external factors, or whether, on the contrary, they are exercised by means of the metabolism or chemism of the organism. These are questions whose solution we can leave to specialists. But however reserved we may wish to be as regards the explanation of the fact, the fact itself is something we cannot but assert.

It is because it undergoes the influence of environment that we are justified in considering race as belonging to the "perpetuated and fixated sociological" order.

At the same time, all the complex elements which constitute the environment, become proportional factors of change in the race: physical, climatic, geographical conditions, nourishment, work, social institutions themselves in a certain measure, etc. And let us note it well: among these causes, there are institutional and social factors, and consequently, factors which come into direct dependence upon the spiritual.

Thus considered, the race creates among its members a truly social bond. How could it be otherwise, since ethnic characters are, at least in part, "of perpetuated and fixated sociological" nature? The race, or to use a handy term, the "ethnos," is a natural grouping, real, differentiated, which manifests itself by traits of temperament, by tastes, often by a language, by aptitudes, by a mentality and a turn of mind. It is in this sense that we find such expressions as "Jewish," "Latin," "Slav," or "Germanic" race constantly recurring.

[10] Millot, *op. cit.*, p. 179.

What, then, will be the State's rôle in relation to the "ethnos"? Will it be possible for the State to establish among its dependents a discrimination based on difference of race understood in this sense?

To answer this question, we must consider the *ethnos,* the nature of the characteristics it imprints upon its members and the rôle such characteristics play in human life. A thorough analysis would reveal that ethnic likenesses are "determinations"—forms, which characterize the individual in his physical and psychic being; they condition the exercise of his faculties, confer upon him certain manners of thinking and feeling, and accustom him to certain manners of acting. They reveal themselves by a certain bent, tastes and corresponding emotions; they confer a "potential" analogous to the national genius, that is, an ensemble of aptitudes linked with temperament. Hence, generations that follow one another in their ethnic line carry preformations which affect the human composite, which impart a certain character and certain common tendencies to sensitiveness and temperament, and, through them, to the whole of life and culture.

We are here faced with a new fact: in opposition to purely biological characters, the ethnic contribution has a real human value. Fruit of the environment, the ethnic characteristics bring the individual into harmony with his mesological conditions of life; they stabilize and fix him. They constitute moreover a sort of inherited contribution which has a human and cultural value. Compared indeed to the abstract nudity of human nature, these preformations, these aptitudes are an embellishment. The real man, the concrete individual is not a pure spirit; he owes to his spiritual soul the fact that he has access to the universal and the infinite, but his personality realizes itself under certain forms. It is a necessity of nature and these forms enrich by the element of humanity they contain. There are, then, ethnico-cultural values, which constitute the common good of the members of the *ethnos;* these members benefit in their mutual relations because of them, they make use of them to fulfill their common destiny, they have the mission of transmitting them to future generations which in their turn will find therein the elements for their own enrichment.

In consequence, the State's attitude with regard to ethnic groups presents a threefold aspect.

The *ethnos* is a formation resting on a natural basis which comprises certain human values. Now, the State is at the service of the human person. It is the guardian of every value that contributes to the expansion of personality. It must assure for cultural institutions and the groups which are the support of these values such protection as they need to fulfill their enriching function. This protection can be demanded in the name of law, for it is the State's duty to give it. If the State, however, protects different ethnic groups within its territory, far from establishing among them a discrimination excluding one or the other from juridical protection and dooming such to disappear, it must on the contrary distinguish in each of them its hidden values and cultivate these for the welfare of all. No antagonism ought to exist between these groups and the State: the principle of their harmony is the service of the human person; it is this which establishes reciprocal rights and duties and a collaboration between the State and the *ethnos* to which each contributes its own means.

However—and this is the second aspect of the problem—if the ethnic groups are always bearers of some cultural value, there is no one of them which contains all the values to which the human person aspires. They enrich, as we have said, but they could also impoverish man, were he not to seek outside of them the complement demanded by a truly human culture with its outlook opened upon the infinite. There are other values which have nothing of the ethnic about them, which, on the contrary, are by their nature intolerant thereof, because they are spiritual in their essence: values of truth and of science, of morality and charity; and much more so, religious values. The "ethnos" would become a spiritual ghetto if it confined man within the limits of its closed society: the State must be watchful to maintain access of minds to the higher and universal values of culture.

May it not come about finally that an ethnic temperament will contribute prejudices unworthy in themselves or aptitudes whose effects, not in themselves condemnable, will be unfortunate in a particular social order on which they are liable to act like a corrosive and a solvent? It is often facts of this kind that, in a given environment, give rise to some "anti-wave," the classic example of which best known in Europe is anti-Semitism. Now, from these ethnic factors and from the State's duty to protect them, many argue in favor of measures of discrimination calculated to affect a race in its political liberties, its economic activity or its family life.

A sound philosophy of State will not deny the duties which the care of the common good imposes upon the latter; but in the discharge of these duties, the State will, on the one hand, avoid all discrimination among persons; on the other hand, it will interest itself in human *acts* to ascertain which are good and which are bad, to encourage the good, to punish the bad. If a deed is contrary to the common good, the State will perform its duty by forbidding and punishing it, no matter who the author of it may be. On the contrary, the State will be recreant to its duty, if, upon the pretext that a certain category of citizens is more frequently guilty of reprehensible actions, it brands the latter with a note of infamy that affects them in their person, even before their personal acts have warranted censure. To do so would be to create a caste of pariahs, excluded from certain rights; it would be tantamount to an assault upon equality of rights and a disregard of its two consequences: the equality of persons before the law and the equal responsibility of each individual for his personal acts and for them alone.

Thus will there be assured, even in repression, the equality of men and the service of the human person, the two landmarks that point the way to juridical progress.

BIBLIOGRAPHICAL DATA

The synthetic character of our study precludes the attachment of a bibliography, which would have to be either unduly long or abbreviated to the point of being useless. We list herewith only certain works singled out and retained because of their conformity or opposition to our point of view.

1—Concerning the State:

Maurice Hauriou, *Précis de Droit Constitutionnel*, Sirey, Paris, 1929.

Maurice Hauriou, *Précis de Droit Administratif et Droit Public*, Sirey, 1927, 2nd vol.

Maurice Hauriou, *Principes de Droit Public*, 1916.

Maurice Hauriou, *Aux Sources du Droit. Le pouvoir, l'Ordre et la liberté.* Paris, Bloud et Gay, 1933.

Léon Duguit, *Traité de Droit Constitutionnel*, 5 vol. de Boccard, Paris, 1921-24. (Principally vol. 1.)

Léon Duguit, *Leçons de Droit public général*, de Boccard, Paris, 1926.

Léon Duguit, *L'État, le Droit objectif, la loi positive*, 1901.

Carré de Malberg, *Contribution à la Théorie générale de l'État*, 2 vol. Sirey, 1921.

Jean Dabin, professor à l'Université de Louvain, *Doctrine générale de l'État,* Paris, Sirey, 1939. 1 vol.

2—Of the works which deal with the juridical conceptions proper to the totalitarian regimes, we shall content ourselves with citing two, both of which give an abundant bibliography:

Marcel Prélot, *L'Empire faciste, les origines, les tendances, et les institutions de la dictature et du corporatisme italiens,* Sirey, 1936, 1 vol.

Roger Bonnard, professeur à Faculté de Droit de Bordeaux, *Le droit et l'État, dans la doctrine nationale-socialiste,* Paris, Librairie générale de Droit et de Jurisprudence, Paris, 1936.

3—Finally, we may be permitted to refer to some other publications in which some of the ideas summarized in the present synthesis are more extensively expounded and justified:

J. T. Delos, *La Société Internationale et les Principes du Droit public,* Paris, Pedone, 1929. (See particularly, chapters 1, 2, 4, 7.)

J. T. Delos, *La Fin propre de la Politique: le Bien Commum temporel* in: *La Société Politique et la Pensée Chrétienne,* (XXV° Session de Semaines Sociales de France, Gabalda, Paris, 1933.)

J. T. Delos, *La Société et Personalité Morale,* Lyon, 16 rue du Plat., 1938.

J. T. Delos, *Les buts du Droit, Bien Commum, Securité, Justice.* Annuaire de l'Institut International de Philosophie du Droit et de Sociologie juridique, Paris, Sirey, 1938.

III

MAN AND THE CHALLENGE OF IRRATIONALISM

By Anton C. Pegis, Ph.D.,

Associate Professor of Philosophy
in
The Graduate School of Fordham University

MAN AND THE CHALLENGE OF IRRATIONALISM

EDITOR'S NOTE: In the pages that follow Professor Pegis explores the meaning and implications of Dewey's *anti-intellectualist* philosophy of education. What bearing, the reader may ask, has anti-intellectualism or irrationalism (as Dr. Pegis calls it) on the problems of *racism* and ultra-nationalism? The answer is, that anti-intellectualism is in the nature of things the main premiss whence all irrational *particularisms,* including racism, are deducible. For just as *intellectualism,* its opposite, is the basis of *universalism:* the doctrine that truth is neither racial nor local, but the same for all races and nations, all times and all places, so anti-intellectualism is the basis of theories like Rosenberg's that truth is the brain-product of a particular race. This, in fact, is what Rosenberg himself expressly states. He says: "The strongly accentuated and capital point expounded in book I, but continuously insisted on, that *universalism* is a twin-brother of individualism, shows itself in this, that said *universalism* suffers from the same disease as its seeming opponent. Both are *intellectualist,* that is, anti-natural." (*Der Mythus des 20. Jahrhunderts,* 66-62 Aufl., München, 1935, S. 695—italics ours.)

Now, one of the first corollaries Rosenberg deduces from his anti-intellectualist philosophy is, that *science* is not universal truth, common to all nations and national cultures, but a special creation of the German race—"What we call science today is pre-eminently the creation of the German Race." (*Op. cit.,* 4 Aufl., München, 1932, S. 121.)

In opposition to this particularism of a purely racial or national truth, *intellectualism* teaches *universalism*—its "conviction that though the various expressions of truth unavoidably bear the mark of their local origins, truth itself, both in the speculative and in the practical order, is not true for a certain civilization, nor for a certain nation, but belongs to mankind as a whole." (Gilson's 1937 Harvard Tercentenary *Address.*)

But *anti-intellectualism,* or, if one prefers, *irrationalism,* is precisely what John Dewey, so-called "Czar of American Education," "has been preaching . . . for half a century out of Chicago and New York." In view, therefore, of the appalling consequences which such anti-intellectualism brought upon German education and the German nation, American educators would do well to re-examine this Deweyite *empiricism* in the light of reason and history. An irrationalistic experimentalism that makes science not universal truth, objective and the same for all, but a system of mental fictions elaborated by human brains and only afterwards applied to reality, is headed in the same general direction as Rosenberg's racial theory which makes *science* a brain-child of the German race. "Every time philosophy yields to the temptation of giving up reason as an organizing power, it regularly brings about the triumph of obscure forces whose self-assertion is their only possible justification." (Gilson, *ibidem.*)

I

That the Christian is called upon to work in the world in which he lives, and to bring to it through his effort the truth and the light of his Faith, is an idea that all Catholics would accept. How to do this work, however, how to assert truths that are at least as old as Christianity so that they may act, at the present moment in history, as the means of transforming the world in which we live, is an issue whose gravity cannot be overestimated. And yet, this is a task that faces the Catholic thinker in general and the Catholic educator in particular. The Catholic educator must know the world in which he lives as well as the perennial truths that it is his mission to teach. There are many senses in which the world is worldly and in which the secular order is not only anti-religious but also anti-natural and anti-rational. These are facts which the Catholic educator cannot deny. These are facts, however, which require him to exercise an extraordinary prudence in order to avoid the errors of secularism and yet do justice to the true autonomy of the secular, avoid the errors of naturalism and yet do justice to the true autonomy of the natural. He cannot preach an anti-worldly Christianity in order to avoid worldliness; he must therefore seek, under the guidance of his Faith, the proper meaning of the natural and of the secular in order to further the temporal mission of Christianity. He cannot run to the cloister, nor can he preach a cloisterly view of Christian education, for he would be doing violence to the analogy of sanctity which is essential to the Catholic conception of salvation.[1] Against the rationalists he must find reason; against the naturalists he must find nature; against those who either dissipate eternity in time or run from time and history to an illusory utopia he must safeguard the temporal order.

This is a serious and noble work in the world to which the Catholic teacher is called. Let us go farther. How can he be an understanding critic of a man such as John Dewey, preach order against Mr. Dewey's scientism, intelligence against Mr. Dewey's empiricism, truth against Mr. Dewey's skepticism, unless he knows these things in himself and unless he is as interested in keeping his own house in order as he is evidently interested in putting Mr.

[1] Cf. the significant book of W. R. O'Connor, *The Layman's Call* (New York: P. J. Kenedy, 1942), *passim*.

Dewey's house in order? The magnitude of Mr. Dewey's errors is not merely that he commits them and has been preaching them for half a century out of Chicago and New York; the magnitude of his errors is rather that they are the overt expression of a long series of calamities in the history of European thought, calamities in which the failures of Catholics are as prominent and as serious as the failures of those who have been their successors and opponents in the modern world. The same history which has produced Mr. Dewey is in part a Catholic history, and for this reason it is at least as important for the Catholic thinker and educator to work for the purification of his own traditions as it is to condemn Mr. Dewey's errors. Seen in the perspective of history, Mr. Dewey is the victim, though the satisfied victim, of a history whose errors have not entirely ceased to disturb much Catholic education both in theory and in practice. It is not, therefore, so much to accuse Mr. Dewey as to call attention to the problems that he concentrates within himself in such an extraordinary way, that the following essay is written.

II

Philosophers find it difficult not to divorce themselves from history in order to preserve the *permanence* of philosophical truths. Let us resist this impulse to fly from history, for it is born of the illusion that *abstraction,* like an Acropolis, freezes into an eternal and closed immobility the ceaseless change of the Athenian marketplace which is the world of history. It remains, however, that Parmenides is not the god of the intellect, any more than Heraclitus is the god of history; it remains that the human intellect does not add to the truth of reality by thinking it, nor does the manifold dynamism of being lose the permanence of truth by transcending the immobility of logic. Let us, therefore, enter not only the world of history but also the history of the world. We need not fear that we shall lose the true universalism of the intellect by being engaged in history: those who know man know him when they see him even in the bypaths of history. Let us even enter history, not as judges who damn with ready rhetoric the errors of the philosophers, but as students who seek enlightenment from the actual course of history itself.

I hasten to add that there is every provocation to resort to rhetoric. Mr. Joseph Ratner, for example, indulged quite recently in a very hysterical effort to make the world safe for the philosophy of John Dewey.[2] One may express genuine astonishment at the idea that the whole history of human thought has been a long enslavement of the human race to a philosophical tyranny, instituted by the Greeks, which has kept man in ignorance of the truth—until the appearance of John Dewey. It is equally astonishing to hear that Deweyism is to be a new liberation of the human race—to the extent that it succeeds in driving out Platonism and Aristotelianism from the world. These are, so we are told, the ultimate cause of the "cultural lag" in our world; and the *lag*, needless to say, is our benighted resistance to scientific instrumentalism in philosophy.[3]

Such astonishment, however, becomes relatively unimportant when we begin to recognize that behind Mr. Ratner's feat of destroying the history of European thought by the mere appeal to the instrumentalist gospel, there lies an indisputable fact. The philosophy which Dewey has been formulating since the 1890's, when the Hegelianism of his Johns Hopkins and Michigan days began to wear thin in the face of James' "flippant" attack upon absolute idealism, is, in his own estimation, a complete historical break with the traditions of European and American thought. Ancient and mediaeval thought were in bondage to the vitiating error of the Platonic metaphysics. The revolt of modern thought during the sixteenth and seventeenth centuries succeeded only in

---

[2] Cf. the long introduction which Mr. Ratner recently contributed to his edition of selections from the works of John Dewey: *Intelligence in the Modern World* (New York: Random House, 1939), pp. 3-241.—This introduction, however, is much less happily inspired than is Mr. Ratner's challenging title. I am referring not only to his caustic polemic against Plato, Aristotle, Christianity and even Whitehead and Russell, but also to the entirely surprising fact that, whereas the success of instrumentalism hinges on its applicability to social facts, Mr. Ratner spends his whole time proving the fundamentally obvious, namely, how the methodism of Dewey, conceived in the spirit of the physical sciences, is in real harmony with the procedures of those sciences, and that a philosophy *so* conceived *should* be in such harmony. The only relieving feature in this curious performance is that it should appear just at the moment when Mr. Dewey, in some telling pages of *Freedom and Culture*, is beginning to see very disturbing shadows on his scientific horizon. It must have been painful for him to say that "a culture which permits science to destroy traditional values but which distrusts its own powers is a culture which is destroying itself" (*Freedom and Culture*, New York: G. P. Putnam's Sons, 1939, p. 154). Mr. Dewey is evidently facing an embarrassing question: what if physical science is incapable of developing moral techniques? *This* is the moment of Mr. Ratner's elaborate *ignoratio elenchi*.

[3] Joseph Ratner, *Intelligence in the Modern World*, pp. 5, 7.

part, since ideas and institutions from the age of bondage were allowed to survive. Mr. Dewey undertook, therefore, what was in his own eyes nothing less than a second Copernican revolution, the effort to be the complete liberator of mankind.[4] We must take both Mr. Dewey's intention and his execution literally. Indeed, there is little excuse for any misunderstanding on this point, since his works have been a progressive statement, developed and refined for almost half a century, of this revolution which he was making.

More than this, however, since the roots of Mr. Dewey's revolt are deep within the traditions of European thought, to misunderstand the significance of the work of this second Copernicus is not to recognize either the meaning of the breakup of European thought at the end of the middle ages or the meaning of its progressive desperation in the modern world. With Mr. Dewey, the sun of European intelligence hangs very low over the western horizon, and it is his hope that he will accomplish its setting. Whether we agree with him or not, it remains that we are in the presence of an enormous decision. Mr. Dewey has devoted himself for half a century to making the blueprints for the complete dissolution of the ideals and the principles of traditional Western thought. I hasten to add that he himself admits this. According to his reading of history, he has reached a philosophical position which embodies the last lesson and preaches the last moral of the decline of modern thought.

I repeat: not only has Mr. Dewey found the last ray of light in a world which has revolted against intelligence and is now sanctifying that revolt with the name of liberty, he has also given an interior history of his revolution which makes the creed of instrumentalism an understandable utopia of light in a world of chaos and illusion. The rains may come, but Mr. Dewey stands fast upon his nothingness. He preaches instrumentalism, and his disciples have been practising it assiduously in the American schools. Perhaps I should add that, of late, they have been practising it defiantly, not to say, belligerently.[5] No doubt, Mr. Hutchins and Mr. Adler, apostles of intelligence that they are, have been too intent and too uncompromising in their attacks upon the rock of the instrumentalist nothingness. Here, however, let me leave aside

---

[4] John Dewey, *The Quest for Certainty* (Gifford Lectures, New York: Minton, Balch and Co., 1929), pp. 287-313.

[5] Cf. *infra*, note 32.

the general spirit of belligerency which seems to be the prevailing
mood among a good many professors of the instrumentalist enlightenment and consider only the interior history of instrumentalism as it can be seen in *Reconstruction in Philosophy;
Experience and Nature; The Quest for Certainty; Individualism,
Old and New; Art as Experience; A Common Faith; Liberalism
and Social Action; Freedom and Culture.*[6]

III

As it is known, the author of these and other books is an
emancipated man. He has parted company not only with Plato,
Aristotle and their mediaeval disciples; not only with Christianity
both Catholic and Protestant; but also with the idealism of the
seventeenth and nineteenth centuries. He has retained one faith
which is, in its most distinctive form, the product of his own
making. For the dividing line between himself and the past, a line
drawn with sharpness but not with suddenness, was the pragmatism
of William James to which Mr. Dewey added the scientific method
that transformed it from an ethical meliorism into an instrumen-

[6] I realize that these titles of books written by Mr. Dewey since 1920 are incomplete even for this period. I realize also that I am not following a suggestion made
by Mr. Dewey himself that *Democracy and Education* (New York: Macmillan and
Co., 1916) was for many years the book in which his philosophy "was most fully
expounded" ("From Absolutism to Experimentalism" in *Contemporary American
Philosophy*, ed. G. P. Adams and W. P. Montague, New York: The Macmillan Co.,
1930, vol. II, p. 23). In the choice I have made, my purpose has been not to give
a direct exposition of Dewey's thought, but rather to see it in the light of its own
conception of its relations to the history of philosophy. From this point of view,
such a work as *The Quest for Certainty* is a central piece in the interpretation of
Dewey.

The works of Dewey which I am using are dated as follows: *Reconstruction in
Philosophy* (New York: Henry Holt and Co., 1920); *Experience and Nature* (Chi-
cago: Open Court Publ. Co., 1925, 2nd ed., 1926); *The Quest for Certainty* (New
York: Minton, Balch and Co., 1929); *Individualism, Old and New* (New York:
Minton, Balch and Co., 1930); *Art as Experience* (New York: Minton, Balch and
Co., 1934); *A Common Faith* (New Haven: Yale University Press, 1934); *Liberalism
and Social Action* (New York: G. P. Putnam's Sons, 1935); *Logic: The Theory of
Inquiry* (New York: Henry Holt and Co., 1938); *Freedom and Culture* (New York:
G. P. Putnam's Sons, 1939).

For recent bibliographies of the works of Dewey, cf. P. A. Schilpp (ed.) *The
Philosophy of John Dewey* (*The Library of Living Philosophers*, I, Evanston and
Chicago: Northwestern University Press, 1939), pp. 611-676; M. H. Thomas, *A
Bibliography of John Dewey*, 1882-1939 (New York: Columbia University Press,
1939).

talism.[7] To Mr. Dewey that dividing line has come to mean the difference between the sinners of metaphysics and theology and the saints of science; as well as the difference between those who believe in the past and those who believe in the future. In the governance of the present, the future is for Mr. Dewey very real, very rich and very open. It is the frontier before which he stands like a courageous and undismayed pioneer. Its vastness dwarfs the history of European thought into an insignificant incident: "Seen in the long perspective of the future, the whole of western European history is a provincial incident." [8] And finally, it is also known that because this provincial episode is still an embarrassing reality for Mr. Dewey, he is striving to organize the present in such a way that the free and limitless future of which he dreams will become a reality. For him, therefore, experimentalism is both a means of destroying the survival of the past and the channel—the only channel—of exploring the limitlessness of the future.

It would be a mistake to minimize the intensity and the thoroughgoing character of this ideal; just as it would be a mistake to minimize the magnitude of its revolutionary intentions. Mr. Dewey has broken many idols, but this is scarcely unique. He has also attacked all the principles in theology, in metaphysics, in morals and in politics which have been dear to Christianity. Yet this too is not exactly unique, for Mr. Dewey is not alone in striking at the universalism of order which is the cornerstone of Christian education. Mr. Dewey's uniqueness lies rather in his conscious translation of this complete attack on Christian thought into a cardinal dogma and principle of his vision of the possibility of the future. Strange as it may seem, for a man whose quest lies so thoroughly in the future, Mr. Dewey is forever facing the past in order to attack it. All his anticipations are, in seed, revulsions; and his prospective freedom is a disguised flight from the past. His quest is fundamentally a protest, and beneath his love of experimentalism and of its work of liberating the future there lies a revolt against the past which is also a despair.

From a history of European thought Mr. Dewey has discovered a lesson which, as he thinks, his predecessors told very badly. To discover that lesson in its completeness, to translate it into

---

[7] John Dewey, "The Development of American Pragmatism" (*Studies in the History of Ideas*, vol. II, 1925, p. 367).
[8] "From Absolutism to Experimentalism," p. 26.

the very meaning of life and of all the institutions of man in society, is not only the very significance of Dewey but also the very significance of being, in his eyes, modern. For so understood, the modern man is, or ought to be, the secularized man. He is, *in his very essence,* anti-theological and anti-metaphysical; he is anti-Greek and anti-Christian; he is anti-idealistic and anti-realistic. These oppositions spell for him the very meaning of his natural-ness and the very meaning of the humanism which he is supposed to have won through philosophical experimentalism. Or almost. When, at last, as he hopes, he comes of age as an integral natural man, he will embody the very perfection of these negations. But so long as the dead past persists, he can discover his essence only in a radical opposition to the past and to its insular provinciality. In practising a radical experimentalism, he can work to eliminate the oppressive past and to achieve the full liberty of his natural-ness. For the moment, he lives in the fortress of his illusion waiting for the day when the world itself will become an illusion; and he can only dream, like another Ulysses, of the future that lies beyond the arch of the present.

There can scarcely be any question that this is Mr. Dewey's philosophical and educational ideal. Mr. Sidney Hook, fervent disciple that he is, has given recently a remarkable intellectual por-trait of his hero which reveals in greater elaboration these very traits.[9] The question, therefore, is not whether Mr. Dewey's philosophy of the modern man contains all these marks of revolt in his nature; the question is rather to recognize what these marks mean and how they are to be understood within the record of his-tory. Let us grant that Mr. Dewey's philosophy is as professionally anarchical, as resolutely relativistic as Mr. Hook has said that it is. Let us even resist the temptation to marvel at men who can wor-ship at the shrine of chaos. We are still left with the problem of understanding the significance of a philosophy which is relativistic even about its relativism.

To Mr. Dewey let us grant that, *in the light of his interpretation of history,* nature and reason are tyrants, and Plato, Aristotle and St. Thomas Aquinas are the most authoritarian of dogmatic philosophers. Unless this be true, Mr. Dewey stands discredited, as he himself has pointed out in his recent passage at arms with Presi-dent Hutchins; which ought to mean also that his decision is not

[9] Sidney Hook, *John Dewey,* An Intellectual Portrait (New York: John Day Co., 1939).

only momentous, but also precarious. Yet the question remains. Is Mr. Dewey's decision an interpretation and criticism of the history on which it depends, or merely a consequence of it? Is it an objective lesson drawn from history, or is it rather a conclusion made in the image of the record from which it proceeds? From exactly what angle of vision can St. Thomas Aquinas be seen as a disciple of what Mr. Dewey supposes to be the unreasoning tyranny of metaphysics? And exactly how free from the history that he is interpreting is Mr. Dewey to see a mark of tyranny in the Thomistic or Aristotelian respect for metaphysics?

For the truth of the matter is that Mr. Dewey's ideas have very old roots, and though he has undertaken to build a new world—a world that is entirely free of the provincial episode of two thousand years of Christian thought—what he has succeeded in doing is nothing more than to rake the ashes of a very old one. Nor is this true because Mr. Dewey preaches old doctrines. On the contrary, Mr. Dewey is intent on living and thinking in the foremost files of time. This is true rather because Mr. Dewey, like a great artist, has been painting his own portrait in all he has written. Now precisely, the more Mr. Dewey builds the new world of science with instruments which are nothing more than protests against the old sinful world of metaphysics and theology, the more he reveals his own location in that same old world against which he protests so much. For what Mr. Dewey ought to see, and what Catholics ought to see with him, is that the *man* from whom a philosophy such as his could come forth is the very product and outcome of the world against which he is protesting. Mr. Dewey has thought that he has been speaking *against* the past; in reality, he has been speaking *for* it; his new world is the *end* of an age, and the radical openness of the future is simply a eulogistic consecration of the equally radical bankruptcy of the immediate past.

IV

This same conclusion may be stated differently by saying that the philosophical and historical opinions of John Dewey proceed on the assumption that nominalism is the natural philosophy of the human intellect and that the principles of nominalism underlie the realms of nature, morals, politics and social action. Whether we follow the line of thought which goes from mediaeval nominalism through Protestant theology to the skepticism of Dewey, or the line of thought which goes from nominalism to Cartesian methodism and idealism, from Cartesian and Kantian idealism through the absolutism of Hegel to the pragmatist revolt of James, the result is fundamentally the same. From a religious point of view, Mr. Dewey has discovered that he is living in a long line of skeptics and ought to call himself a skeptic; from a philosophical point of view, he has been living in a long line of those who have fostered the illusion of a univocist universalism of knowledge and of philosophical method—that false universalism which cuts being and knowing to the measure and the intelligibility of a particular science. From Descartes to Dewey univocism has run a steady and downhill course in modern philosophy. At least in Descartes, the human intellect had the semblance of liberty, for it chose mathematics as the torch of its new enlightenment; but in Mr. Dewey, living as he does in the wake of so many disappointments that Descartes did not know and that the latter's *angelism* (as Maritain has called it) could not withstand, the old univocist universalism has now plunged itself into matter and has completely suffocated the liberty of the human intellect. Skepticism, methodism, a univocism whose register is experimentalism—these are the marks of Mr. Dewey's revolutionism. He has, therefore, sought the repose which is proper to his search; it is the repose of one who hesitates forever upon an ounce of matter.[10]

From *Reconstruction in Philosophy* we know the platform of this descent into matter. From *The Quest for Certainty* we know the essence of Mr. Dewey's new faith, its sources, its procedures, its ideals. From *Experience and Nature* we know the enormous effort Mr. Dewey has made to give a new meaning to *intelligence, nature, art, science, experience, reality.* In his hands, these terms have become the tools of a self-conscious revolutionism. From *Logic: The Theory of Inquiry* we know how Mr. Dewey's radical anti-metaphysicism has translated what was once a science of demonstration into a pure theory of instrumentality and prediction, in order to express in the very method and procedure of his thinking the ideal at which he aims: operational security and control, not truth. From *A Common Faith* we know the meaning of Mr. Dewey's experimentalist gospel, the radical consecration of secularism, the elimination of Christianity and its theology, the revolt against human nature itself as an historical encumbrance.

[10] Cf. Jacques Maritain, *Le songe de Descartes* (Paris: ed. R. A. Corrêa, 1932), ch. III-IV.

Mr. Dewey is nothing if not masterly and thorough as the apostle of revolution. All these ideals are parts of a coherent whole systematically developed and patiently refined. There has been one cardinal sin in human nature in the past, just as there remains one cardinal sin in human nature in the present. This sin is the object of Mr. Dewey's indignation. The sin of classical philosophy was that it believed in metaphysics, that in the name of this science of the "invariant" it could disparage the order of physical nature, and that, finally, in Christian hands it conceived the world of sense as radically corrupt.[11] Mr. Dewey pursues this sin and pretension to metaphysics wherever he finds it. With one stroke, by adopting the method of the physical sciences, he rids philosophy of both the pretension and the problems of Greek and Christian thought. In turning to the method of the physical sciences, therefore, as the true method of philosophy in the modern world, Mr. Dewey's aim is constant and to the point: he sees in this method the tentativeness and the professional search for control rather than for truth, which are the only adequate vehicle of a radical skepticism. In this sense, he has found in experimentalism *the* natural philosophy of skeptics.[12] That is why, when he protests against some of his contemporaries, Mr. Dewey's fundamental concern is to attack their wayward straying in the direction of pretensions to truth. Thus, Mr. Dewey's fundamental objection to Marxism in his *Freedom and Culture* is not that it is wrong, but that it pretends to being absolutely true.[13] Exactly. How dare anyone disturb Mr. Dewey's repose in chaos?

That is why Mr. Dewey himself is so meticulous in his own handling of the meaning and value of scientific method. He weights it with the full burden of his skepticism, and he guards its radical tentativeness, with a brooding intensity, from the least infection from truth. He seeks, not truth, but an operational security which is also a skepticism.[14] He attacks any view, epistemological or logical, political or social, which does not leave his method secure in its skepticism.[15] It is thus exact to say that the effort of Mr. Dewey is aimed exclusively at making the revolt from theol-

---

[11] *The Quest for Certainty*, pp. 14, 16-17, 18, 19, 27, 36, 51, 255; *Experience and Nature*, pp. 48-49, 78-120, 249-252, 354-358, 412-413. Cf. Joseph Ratner, *Intelligence in the Modern World*, pp. 18 ff., 210-212.

[12] *The Quest for Certainty*, pp. 107, 136-137.

[13] *Freedom and Culture*, pp. 74-102.

[14] *The Quest for Certainty*, pp. 136-139, 166-169.

[15] *Ibidem*, pp. 180-181, 181-182, 183, 184, 186, 187, 192-195, 210.

ogy and metaphysics a going concern. Man now has only one life,
servitude to physical nature, because he now knows only one aim,
to extend and to naturalize the philosophy of operational control
over nature in order thus to perpetuate and legalize skepticism.[16]

To translate this new dispensation of skepticism into a faith, a
faith which Mr. Dewey is optimistic enough to call a *Common
Faith,* is to see in the secularization of society *the* accomplishment
of the modern world.[17] It is not surprising, therefore, that every
traditional item of belief is held to be in the balance,[18] that *natural*
now means *scientific* and that experimentalism is a new road to
truth,[19]—though "truth" is scarcely a satisfactory word in such a
context, even for Mr. Dewey. It is still less surprising to hear Mr.
Dewey say of *A Common Faith* that "it was addressed to those who
have abandoned supernaturalism." [20] He goes on to say in the same
reference that this book was not addressed to those for whom
"metaphysical" was substantially identical with "supernatural."

Now, useless as it would be to quarrel with Mr. Dewey at this
point, we must yet say that he betrays a strange ignorance of both
metaphysics and the *supernatural.*[21] For it is a fact that he does not
see far into the past which he criticizes so much. His notion of
Christianity is constantly that of a derationalized theology and of
a dehumanized supernaturalism. Of course, Mr. Dewey is free to
accept or reject whatever doctrines he pleases; but he is surely not
free with respect to the record of history. He is not free, therefore,
to interpret the meaning of metaphysics and theology in the
middle ages in the light of Protestantism. Coming at the end of the
nominalist tradition, Mr. Dewey is in the embarrassing situation
of being engulfed by the very world across which he tries to look
but across which, nevertheless, he cannot see. It is the lesson of
nominalism that man has a bankrupt intellect. That lesson found
a fitting biography in Kant's *Critique of Pure Reason.* But this
lesson was revealed to the world at a cataclysmic moment, a moment of failure within mediaeval thought itself. Conceivably, Mr.
Dewey might believe that Christian supernaturalism means a faith

---

[16] *Ibidem,* pp. 212-215.—On the extension of instrumentalism to morals, cf. same
work, pp. 258, 273-274.

[17] *A Common Faith,* pp. 61-67.

[18] *Ibidem,* pp. 32, 34, 42-43, 50-51, 56.

[19] *Ibidem,* pp. 34, 31-32.

[20] "Experience, Knowledge, Value" (*The Philosophy of John Dewey,* ed. P. A.
Schilpp, p. 597).

[21] Cf. E. Gilson, *L'ésprit de la philosophie médiévale* (Paris: J. Vrin, 1932), 2nd
series, ch. VIII-X; *Christianisme et philosophie* (Paris: J. Vrin, 1936).

and a theology without reason; conceivably, he might believe that man in his true and natural state is an irrational animal. But it is a confusing historical naïveté to suppose that fifteen centuries of patristic and mediaeval thought entertained such notions about Christianity or man; just as it is an equal naïveté to suppose that Mr. Dewey's conceptions of faith and reason, born at the moment when the Christian man finally decided to call his human nature corrupt and his human reason blind, can do justice to the facts of history or see anything in man save a wearied pietism posing as faith and a despairing nominalism posing as true reason. The intellectual nature of man was dropping out of the world at the end of the middle ages. We already know at least the outlines of that story. But here is Mr. Dewey discovering what is to him the true state of man by the method of measuring the whole history of human thought on the Procrustean bed of nominalism.

In a sense, therefore, it remains that man himself is the issue between Mr. Dewey and the Catholic educator. Mr. Dewey's man is intellectually bankrupt; Mr. Dewey, therefore, educates him with the exclusive intention of leaving his bankruptcy intact. This is, in fact, the fundamental issue behind Mr. Dewey's iconoclasm. It is not quite that he has no tradition or lacks any sense of historical culture. Nor yet is it simply that he has no respect for the world of the past. It is rather that he has lost and does not recognize within himself those various marks and characteristics which go to make up the human nature of man such as it has been conceived by centuries of Catholic thought. Indeed, to begin with the Greeks, exactly what is left of man and of human educability after we have eliminated completely the philosophical principles contained in the *Republic* of Plato and in the *Metaphysics,* the *Nicomachean Ethics* and the *Politics* of Aristotle? Here is man without the famous Platonic kingship of reason, as well as without the equally famous educability in Aristotelian virtue. In short, here is man without a permanent intellectual nature. Mr. Dewey's prescription fits his patient, for his theory of education fits what is left of human educability after the separation from man of his nature. What Mr. Dewey has not seen is that he has naturalized what was, in reality, a loss. At least one proof that it was a loss is the fact that, though Mr. Dewey has wanted to be an integral and autonomous man, he has succeeded only in formulating a philosophy of pure flight from metaphysics and theology. In this he has verified in his own way the very essence of what Maritain has called an anthropocentric humanism. To seek liberty and autonomy is an enduring human desire; it is even an indication of the unfailing tendency of man towards a good that he cannot deny, however he may disfigure himself. But Mr. Dewey has wanted to be a free man by not being either a creature of God or a rational being, and by proceeding as though he were not. And this is his contradiction and his mystery, for he cannot have what he wants, he does not know what he has, and he cannot avoid what he does not want.

Mr. Dewey cannot have what he wants. He wants liberty, but a liberty *against* reason; he therefore discovers, not liberty, but chaos. No, Mr. Dewey cannot disembarrass himself of human nature so easily. A liberty against reason is a pure illusion. Hence, though he may want liberty, his sins against human nature drive him to seek peace in chaos, however it may be true that he does not know it. Nor has he succeeded in avoiding what he does not want. If the pretension to metaphysics was the cardinal sin of Greek philosophy, it is clear that Mr. Dewey himself has not departed from it; unless, of course, we are willing to argue that the entirely negative philosophy of one whose whole effort is an attack upon metaphysics is itself a new philosophy. If the logic of Aristotle was one of the shackles that bound the mediaeval mind, it is not at all clear that by changing the Aristotelian doctrine of inference into a theory of scientific prediction and future instrumentality, Mr. Dewey is doing any more than introducing into the old logic an impassioned sentiment of skeptical revolt. It is not clear that Mr. Dewey has solved the problems of his predecessors or improved upon their solutions by the mere act of counseling and professing resignation in their presence. I say it is not at all clear that a philosophy of calculated defeatism is succeeding in doing anything more with old problems than merely to restate them and to leave them unsolved. Assuredly, Mr. Dewey cannot avoid what he does not want, for this conclusion amounts to saying that if we call ourselves dead, we cannot be accused of not living well.

It remains, therefore, that while *The Quest for Certainty* is charged with a liberating message, the *key* which has opened the door upon such a liberty is the elimination of reality, of truth and of reason from knowledge; and the liberty which lies beyond such a door is intent upon making reason the slave of matter in order to save it from the dogmatism of truth. The result, by whatever progressive name Mr. Dewey chooses to call it, is a recognizable historical reality. After all, Mr. Dewey is not such a rebel as he thinks; and his revolution is much more an episode in the *decline* of European thought than he imagines. There is nothing anti-mediaeval in opposing Aristotelian metaphysics. On the contrary, the fourteenth and fifteenth centuries did that long before Mr. Dewey. The fact is, therefore, that instead of eliminating the nominalistic despair which ruined the late mediaeval world, Mr. Dewey is rather bringing to its abysmal fruition the most disastrous aspect of mediaeval thought itself.

V

It might seem academic, not to say doctrinaire, to be concerned at the present moment with Mr. Dewey's educational aims. It might be argued that, however much Mr. Dewey may worship chaos, it still remains a fact that our more immediate problem is to be concerned with winning the war and holding aloft the banner of freedom against the ruthless and barbarian darkness of totalitarianism. Who can deny that? And yet, though the end of the war is not in sight, there are those who are already thinking of winning the peace which is to follow it. There are important public men who, like Vice-President Wallace, are already laying the foundation for what has been called the people's century to come. Now these foundations will not be laid by rhetoric, nor will they be established *against* anyone. The question still remains, therefore: what resources have we within ourselves with which to build a civilization? It is natural to fight against barbarism, but that is not exactly a definition or a plan of civilization; it is natural and noble to fight against tyranny, but that is neither a definition nor a guarantee of liberty. For the real issue is not quite so simple as this, and we should be guilty of a most serious injustice if we thought, even for a moment, that Mr. Dewey does not want liberty or has not been its impassioned defender for over half a century. On the contrary, what we must see is that the problem of liberty at the present moment is not only a problem of defending it against tyranny, but also a problem of defending it against anarchy.

It is at this point, after all, that an academic issue such as that of skepticism assumes a significance that is second to none even for the future of civilization itself. It is an illusion to suppose that our present problems are *immediate* problems in the sense that our aims have not deep roots in history. It is an illusion to suppose that Mr. Dewey's opposition to the Greek ideal of intelligence and to the mediaeval love of this ideal is a quarrel with the past. On the contrary, Mr. Dewey is fighting intelligence in the present, he is seeking to give to this attack upon intelligence a free and unimpeded reign in the modern world by means of the instrumentality of science. It is for the present and future success of anarchy that Mr. Dewey has been opposing Greek intelligence and metaphysics. Our issue lies here. Having done all in our power to save civilization against despotism, indeed, *doing* all in our power to defend the personality and the liberty of man against the barbarians, we must also do all in our power to see to it that what will have been saved from the degradation of slavery is not lost in the wilderness of anarchy.

That is why it is permissible to think that the educational conflict between Mr. Dewey and Mr. Hutchins is not a bookish quarrel to be confined to schools and educators. That is why, too, Mr. Adler's willingness to go over the heads of his fellow professors in the American schools and to appeal to the American public against the positivism and the skepticism of his colleagues is no mere wish to make a public spectacle of an academic quarrel. On the contrary, the very fact that Mr. Hutchins has so often braved being called a pretender to intellectual dictatorship indicates the extreme seriousness with which he views the anti-intellectual disease that has taken hold of American education. The moral of *The Higher Learning in America* is that there seems to be no higher learning; and Mr. Hutchins can only wonder at the intellectual health of a society whose schools have the chaotic unity of encyclopedias.[22] As for Mr. Adler, having recently faced the riotous vocabulary of his colleagues, but having done so willingly and knowingly, he can be said to have an extremely acute awareness of the crisis we are facing.[23]

Mr. Hutchins, as everyone knows, has brought down upon his head a veritable storm by appealing to metaphysics as the science which will give unity to the higher learning of the university. He knows, of course, that he is preaching an unpopular theory of education. Indeed, what he himself has not suspected, he has been told

[22] R. M. Hutchins, *The Higher Learning in America* (New Haven: Yale University Press, 1936), p. 95.

[23] I am referring, of course, to the violent reception given to Mr. Adler's paper, "God and the Professors" (*Science, Philosophy and Religion,* A Symposium, New York: Conference on Science, Philosophy and Religion, 3080 Broadway, 1941, pp. 120-138). For the reactions, cf., for example, *The Daily Maroon* of the University of Chicago (Thursday, Nov. 14, 1940).

by his critics. He defends the human intellect, and he is immediately accused of pretensions to intellectual dictatorship.[24] He appeals to metaphysics, and he is asked: *Whose* metaphysics? [25] He introduces the names of Plato, Aristotle and St. Thomas Aquinas, and he is gently reminded that schools like Harvard, Yale and the University of Chicago cannot return to their original moorings "through Thomas Aquinas, or indeed through any single authoritative theology." In other words, a return "must be found through their own cultural tradition, which is that of historic Protestantism." [26] Precisely. Mr. Hutchins' offenses are many and high. What he is being told with varying degrees of annoyance and criticism comes to this: that he is proposing a theory of education which is, as a matter of historical fact, an impossible one to accept now. If to be modern means for Mr. Dewey and his disciples to be by nature skeptical of all truths, and if to be Christian means for Mr. Brown the elimination of Greek and mediaeval metaphysics,[27] then Mr. Hutchins *is* in serious trouble. *Whom* is he educating, and for whom is he proposing metaphysics as the architectonic science of the modern university? Obviously, he is not writing for Catholics, even though on occasion he has sent some well-aimed criticisms in the direction of Catholic schools. And yet, for whom can he be proposing the Platonic-Aristotelian-Thomistic tradition

[24] H. D. Gideonse, *The Higher Learning in a Democracy* (New York: Farrar and Rinehart, 1937), p. 30.—On this entirely revealing little book, cf. A. C. Pegis, "Higher Education and Irrationalism" *(Thought,* XIV, 52, March, 1939, pp. 113-119).

[25] H. D. Gideonse, *op. cit.,* pp. 5-10. Cp. *infra,* note 32.

[26] W. A. Brown, *The Case for Theology in the University* (Chicago: The University of Chicago Press, 1938), pp. 89-90.

[27] W. A. Brown, *op. cit.,* ch. II.—It would be useless to enter here into a discussion of this interesting chapter. Mr. Brown has not written a polemical book, nor is it his intention to minimize the differences between the Catholic and the Protestant conceptions of the relations between faith and reason. Rather than attribute to him any such extraordinary ignorance of Catholic theology, I find it easier to suppose that he is proposing to Mr. Hutchins, not that he should seek metaphysics in Protestantism rather than in Catholicism, but that he should adopt what Mr. Brown calls *theology* in the place of the metaphysics which Mr. Hutchins had sought in St. Thomas Aquinas. Evidently, Mr. Brown knows that it is *not* true to say that what *he* calls theology Mr. Adler calls *philosophy* and Mr. Hutchins, *metaphysics (op. cit.,* p. 58); just as he undoubtedly knows that no Catholic would agree with him when he writes that "there is nothing, then, in the appeal to faith which differentiates theology from metaphysics" *(op. cit.,* p. 49). Judging by what they have written, I feel obliged to say that such a lack of differentiation would ruin the very reality of metaphysics for Mr. Hutchins and Mr. Adler as well. In brief, and without entering into any details, let us simply observe that Mr. Brown's position would ruin in principle not only the metaphysics of Plato and Aristotle by eliminating the *natural* from Christianity, but also the Catholic ideal of theology as understood, for example, by St. Thomas Aquinas.

as the means of introducing order into the confusion and the chaos
of the modern university?

Considered in the light of Mr. Hutchins' critics, this question
really has no answer. For it is not so much a question as an impasse.
Mr. Hutchins himself will admit, I think, that the case against him
at the hands of his critics can be put somewhat as follows: The man
of today is radically undogmatic and he is by nature untouched in
his faiths by any theological or metaphysical dogmatism. Hence,
Mr. Hutchins' dilemma. Either he is writing for the man of today
—and then nothing is more inapplicable to such a man than
the dogmatism of Mr. Hutchins' metaphysics—or he is not serious about his *philosophical* attachment to the *historical* traditions
of Plato, Aristotle and St. Thomas Aquinas, and then he is raising
a tremendous *historical* storm which fails, however, to carry the
philosophical lightning that it should. In brief, there seems to be
considerable obscurity in the relations between Mr. Hutchins' historical and philosophical attachments.

This dilemma is not entirely the product of Mr. Hutchins'
critics. But in helping to formulate it, these critics focus our attention upon what is surely the most embarrassing problem confronting Mr. Hutchins. He speaks of man, and he cites Plato and
Aristotle. He speaks of the intellectual virtues, and he cites the
Summa Theologica.[28] What relationship is there between the man
of whom he is speaking and these citations? This is an unavoidable
question. It is the point of Mr. Hutchins' critics that *they* could not
talk about man without disparaging and even eliminating these
same citations. How can Mr. Hutchins give to his view of man *such*
historical clothing? Is he prepared to accept the historical loyalties
which his use of metaphysics imposes upon him? Is he prepared to
undo the intellectual traditions of modern history in order to edu-
cate in the twentieth century under the guidance of Plato, Aristotle and St. Thomas Aquinas? *His philosophical decision is necessarily an historical choice.* For Mr. Brown, the Christian man is
anti-metaphysical, and for Mr. Dewey man is both anti-metaphysical and anti-theological. Even if Mr. Hutchins had not seen this
difficulty, as indeed he has, his critics would not allow so crucial a
point to go unnoticed. Not every historical choice will bear Mr.
Hutchins' message. It is the point of his critics that both the
philosophical decisions and the historical choices of Mr. Hutchins
are wrong and unacceptable.

[28] R. M. Hutchins, *The Higher Learning in America*, p. 63.

I do not mean to embarrass Mr. Hutchins by suggesting that he has not made up his mind about his attachments to the philosophical ideals of Plato, Aristotle and St. Thomas Aquinas. On the contrary, it is Mr. Hutchins' critics who, seeing that they cannot be free in their irrationalism unless Plato, Aristotle and St. Thomas stand completely discredited, consider it to be part of their aim to eliminate these thinkers in order to survive. In a word, the situation which is being forced on Mr. Hutchins concerns not only his allegiance to metaphysics, but also (and even more) his allegiance to metaphysics such as it is understood in the tradition of these Greek and mediaeval philosophers. Metaphysics has been degraded to mean all sorts of things in the modern world, and had Mr. Hutchins remained pleasantly vague in what he meant by metaphysics, his critics would have experienced nothing more than the nebulous spanking of delicious innuendo. In short, there would not have been a problem at all.

But when Mr. Hutchins speaks of metaphysics, he thinks of Plato, of Aristotle and of St. Thomas Aquinas. So, after all, there is a problem. It may be true, indeed, it *is* true that metaphysics as Mr. Hutchins understands it is part of a universal and perennial philosophy which no historical vicissitudes can change. It is also true, as Gilson has insisted, that the history of human error is itself a vindication of a perennial philosophy. In the name of such a universalism, Mr. Hutchins is quite right to speak of metaphysics without being concerned with time or place or circumstance; for, so understood, metaphysical wisdom is as permanently located in history as is human nature itself. And yet, it is this very vision that Mr. Hutchins' critics contest to him. What for centuries has been conceived to be a part of the *natural* equipment of the human intellect is now being called a pretension to dictatorship, a provincial authoritarianism and even worse. We have reached a situation, in fact, in which Mr. Dewey sees nothing amazing in asserting that any educational scheme which is "based on the existence of ultimate first principles, with their dependent hierarchy of subsidiary principles, does not escape authoritarianism by calling the principles 'truths.'" [29] Nor does he see any incongruousness in saying that Mr. Hutchins appeals to these truths because he distrusts *freedom*.[30] Remarkable freedom, surely, which cannot withstand the touch of truth.

[29] Cf. *The Social Frontier*, Jan., 1937, p. 104.—Cp. R. M. Hutchins, *op. cit.*, p. 95.
[30] *The Social Frontier, ibid.*

Let us not miss the point. The point is not simply whether Mr.
Hutchins is right or wrong. For my part I think he is right, in spite
of his unfinished discussion in *The Social Frontier*.[31] The point is
rather that the universalism of truth, which Étienne Gilson's *Unity
of Philosophical Experience* should have made a tangible issue for
American philosophers and educators, is so completely absent from
view that anyone who appeals to fixed truths is being accused of
authoritarianism. What is more curious still, the defender of metaphysics and of first principles is so far removed from the understanding of some of our contemporaries that he is being accused of
foisting *sectarian* doctrine upon the American public.[32] Now *that*
is the point. I am not, therefore urging that Mr. Hutchins himself
adopt a "sectarian" attitude toward Plato, Aristotle and St.
Thomas in his defense of metaphysics. I am rather saying that Mr.
Hutchins' critics and their associates, having made truth a com-

---

[31] *The Social Frontier*, Feb., 1937, pp. 137-139.—It is not difficult, however, to
"complete" this article from *The Higher Learning in America*. No doubt, Mr.
Hutchins would have been forced to repeat in his discussion with Mr. Dewey what
he had already said elsewhere. The only excuse for wishing that Mr. Hutchins had
repeated himself on this occasion is that the cause of intellectualism cannot be defended too often in the face of the imperialistic claims of the disciples of scientism.

[32] Mr. Arthur E. Murphy, for example, in reviewing the first volume of the Pro-
ceedings of the Conference on Science, Philosophy and Religion (cf. "Sectarian
Absolutes and Faith in Democracy," *The Humanist*, I, 3, Autumn, 1941, pp. 106-
112), has expressed the opinion that some members of the Conference, including
Professors J. Maritain, P. Sorokin, F. E. Johnston, M. J. Adler and the present
writer, are intent upon using "the present crisis to push the claims of sectarian
doctrines" *(art. cit.,* p. 107). The only reason for calling attention to Mr. Murphy's
emotional reactions to the errors of our ways is the radical scientific sectarianism
that he thinks he must defend. The only position from which metaphysics—and
metaphysics is all that is in question here—can be considered to be a sectarian
doctrine is that of the sheerest positivism. Having based democracy on positivism,
Mr. Murphy is naturally opposed to those who refuse to accept skepticism as the
condition of liberty. In any case, the issue between an imperialistic skepticism,
which must legislate all truth out of existence in order to be free of it, and
metaphysics has been stated more recently by a more temperate positivist: cf.
Charles W. Morris, "Empiricism, Religion and Democracy" *(Science, Philosophy and
Religion,* Second Symposium, New York: Conference on Science, Philosophy and
Religion, 1942, pp. 213-241). But in any case the imperialism is on the side
of the positivists, for it is they who find it absolutely necessary to reduce knowledge
to science and the methods of knowledge to experimentalism. In the name of what
scientific principle does Professor Morris know that there are not other ways of
knowing besides that of the experimental sciences? Even those who have no intention of returning to the metaphysics of St. Thomas Aquinas are admitting that
science cannot possibly legislate beyond its own limits and should not pretend to
do so: cf. Charles Hartshorne, "A Philosophy of Democratic Defense" *(op. cit.,* pp.
130-172). What is of immediate importance, however, remains clear: only the sectarian devotee of scientific positivism can consider philosophical truths, such as
those that can be found in Plato or Aristotle, to be sectarian absolutes.

plete stranger to man, compel any defender of metaphysics to make an historical choice in order to preserve his allegiance to the universalism of truth in the history of human thought. There *is* truth, men *have* known it, and we can know *that*. Nothing less will do. The history itself of human thought must be contested to those who worship anarchy. It is they who are the utopians, they whose only future is to run away from the image of the human intellect itself. *That* image is written in the pages of history. Hence, though it be true that the proper name of no man (as Mr. Adler has wisely said) circumscribes the truth, yet there are many in our day who think that the proper name of every man circumscribes only chaos; and for this reason, it is our special task to argue both that truth exists and that some men at least have discovered it.

As it is clear, therefore, my aim is not at all to urge upon Mr. Hutchins any sectarianism. I am suggesting only that the wilderness in which he has been defending the universalism of truth is a very sophisticated wilderness and has a long history behind it. His critics are stuck fast in that history, and they understand his message only as an effort to undo the living present, a present which is to them the historical paradise of the liberated, but which is to him the wilderness of the blind. Mr. Hutchins' criticisms stick deep —as they should. He is not merely accusing the encyclopedism of American education; he is accusing the bankruptcy of the present moment in history. He is proclaiming, in terms of education, the failure of the modern world to achieve order and liberty in man and in society; he is writing the chapter on education in the anthropocentrist bill of errors already drawn up by Maritain.

VI

Gilson knew whereof he spoke when he observed that "too many among us are still looking at irrationality as the last bulwark of liberty." [33] This is no merely academic issue for the Catholic educator or for anyone else; nor is the war an issue from which we can isolate ourselves by retreating into our libraries for the duration. For once, we look forward to the future with uncertainty not only as to the outcome of the struggle against Hitlerism, but also as to the chances of civilization itself for survival even after the night of barbarism is over. I am suggesting that the Catholic educator has

[33] E. Gilson, *The Unity of Philosophical Experience* (New York: Ch. Scribner's Sons, 1937), p. 293.

a grave responsibility, and a remarkable opportunity, to contribute to the making of a new world, and that in order to meet this responsibility he must take stock of himself in his full significance as a Catholic man. More than at any other time in history the Catholic educator is now called upon to unlearn his own errors in order to participate in the future with the justice which the Catholic love of man requires. For there is a certain historical nakedness that has struck our age. Many of the habits of the world in which we have lived are disappearing, and the *stability* with which well established ages enter their future through the very strength of tradition is not here to help us now. We have not yet realized how much traditions are necessary to society, or how great an offense against the human need of habits is the attack upon the institutions of the past. Traditions are to a society what habits are to the individual. They can be virtues and they can be vices, and therein lies the grave problem for the educator; but, in any case, traditions are as necessary to a mature human society as intellectual and moral virtues are necessary to the true autonomy of man. It is part of the complex calamity of our age that we should have to fight not only against the slavery of Nazism, but also against the disintegration of the West. Without a victory against such a slavery, the future will sink into barbarities that only those who hate God can devise. With a victory, the West must still be saved from the dispersion that centuries of revolt against God and against man have produced.

But the West which must be saved is not merely a continent called Europe; it is an ideal called man, an ideal once formed by the Jewish and Christian ideals of personality, the Greek ideal of nature and intelligence, the Roman ideal of law. It is the ideal of a God whose creatures we are by nature, and whose sons we are by adoption. It is distinctively a Christian ideal of the liberty and the sanctity of human personality, as well as an ideal of the spiritual significance of the temporal order. What the Catholic educator must strive to accomplish by all the arguments at his command is to convince his contemporaries of, and to teach himself anew, the true nature of this Western man. As Maritain has demonstrated in his *Humanisme intégral,* we do not have to return to the *historical* ideal of the middle ages in order to achieve this purpose.[34] Nor did Gilson preach any *stratified* mediaevalism in addressing a Harvard audience on *Mediaeval Universalism and its Present Value.*[35] It

[34] J. Maritain, *Humanisme intégral* (Paris: F. Aubier, 1936), ch. IV.
[35] E. Gilson, *Mediaeval Universalism and its Present Value* (New York: Sheed and Ward, 1937).

remains true that the mediaeval man had a deep appreciation of reason, of liberty, of personality; he lived and thought as though all men were united by universal bonds, religious, philosophical, moral and political, which were, and are, the deep roots of the true Europe. Such a mediaevalism is not wedded to any moment in history; it is not an epoch but a universal human ideal. It is as perennial as man himself, and it is to such an ideal that the Catholic educator must return. The middle ages have gone, never to return; the mediaeval ideal of the temporal order is likewise part of past history; but the mediaeval ideal of man, so deeply felt, so imperfectly realized, so shortlived, remains as a genuinely universal frontier for all future history.

On the return to such an ideal hangs the future of civilization. This is not, in any obscurantist or sentimental sense, a *mediaevalism*. Only those for whom to be modern consists in being anti-mediaeval have special chains that bind them to the *historical* middle ages. For it is they who are the disciples of mediaeval errors that have become modern tragedies. The tragedy of the modern world is that it has never repaired the spiritual illness which overtook the Christian man at the peak of the middle ages and made it impossible for him from that moment onward to be an integrally human person who could seek and find in the condition of his creaturehood the sources of his spiritual autonomy. No one who has any love for what the mediaeval world accomplished, for the ideal of man to which it clung by faith alone long after it had failed to cling to it by reason—I say that no one could wish to return to the historical calamities that befell such a noble ideal of man and of society.

And in truth, the trouble does not lie with those who have seen their ideal of man realized, however fleetingly, in mediaeval thought. Everyone knows the great love which Maritain has for St. Thomas Aquinas; and yet, it remains an indisputable fact that no philosopher has done more to disengage the thought of St. Thomas Aquinas from the historical thirteenth century than has Maritain himself. If, for example, he considers that the existentialism of St. Thomas Aquinas is the philosophy of the future, if he considers that the integral humanism of St. Thomas Aquinas will be the soul of the new Christian society to come, even as St. Augustine has been the great master of Christian thought for the last fifteen centuries, the reason for this fact is not any nostalgic mediaevalism; it is the philosophical conviction that, on the occa-

sion of meeting the issues of his age, St. Thomas reached a true and
permanent conception of the human intellect, a conception, therefore, which Maritain presents as a true theory of man rather than
as an historical relic from the thirteenth century.[36]

It is not Mr. Maritain, it is Mr. Dewey, who is tied to the past; it
is Mr. Dewey whose only future is merely to run away from the
past. He is bound to the past, to its history, to its errors, to its
dilemmas. In revolt against all ages and all history, living *only* in
the future, Mr. Dewey is yet the disciple of the sheerest historicism.
His future is not an open one; it is simply an empty one: it is, at
least in the order of the intellect, the end of the West. This is not
a future but the summing up of the decline of reason in the Western world during the last five hundred years.

I do not say this in criticism of Mr. Dewey. I say it only as a lesson for the Catholic educator. Entirely apart from the Nazi threat
to the very life of Western civilization, we have reached a moment
of decision. Even the old errors seem to have run their course, and
it has required only the passage of time to expose the inadequacies
of half-truths. Now, more than at another time, the Catholic
thinker must realize the preciousness of his heritage and he must
profit by the lessons of history. What the middle ages failed to accomplish, what mediaeval thinkers strove so much to accomplish,
what has become an ever thinner light in the modern world—
this it is the mission of the Catholic man to save, to perfect and to
fulfill.

And he must undertake this work *now;* for this is the moment
in history when the drama of anarchy that has been going on in
Mr. Dewey's intellect for half a century is also rending the actual
world of history. So long as some notion of reason, of personality,
of liberty and of law was in existence, the European man could be
said to have retained an obscure perception of his meaning as a
creature of God and of the demands of his creaturehood. Now,
however, the last descendants of the nominalist dispersion are
caught between two infinities—the infinity of a God whom they
cannot ignore and the infinity of a world of matter in which, alas!
there is no river of Lethe. Mr. Dewey has been reading the history
of those who are the children of God but who, in despair and then
in revolt, have made themselves the masters of nature. But what
mastery is it to sink in the infinity of matter in order to forget the

[36] J. Maritain, "L'Humanisme de saint Thomas d'Aquin" *(Mediaeval Studies, III,
1942, pp. 174-184).*

infinity of God? Mr. Dewey has mistaken as a desire for power the terrible impotence of those who run away from their own creature-hood; as though man could remove from his nature the desire for God by making history to his own image. This is the last boundary of Mr. Dewey's secularist paradise—a present of perpetual revolt from God and *against* an intellect that remembers Him, a future of perpetual servitude to matter. It is the tragedy of Mr. Dewey, how-ever, that he is powerless to keep an anarchical skepticism in an abstract void: in the actual world of men, those who worship chaos also worship violence, those who despise reason also despise the universal bonds that join men together, and those who hate the image of God in man destroy man in order to feed their hatred.

How much the theologians must preach the first two command-ments to the world of the future!

And how much the Catholic philosopher is called to practise and to preach an orderly intellectualism! He must take to heart the les-sons of the concluding chapter of Gilson's *Unity of Philosophical Experience,* for those lessons are the pillars of the true metaphysi-cal transcendentalism. It is his task to rebuild the whole edifice of knowledge, and he must begin in the beginning. Against Mr. Dewey's *methodism* he must return to *metaphysics.* He must re-capture the traditional ideal of knowledge as an analogical and hierarchically ordered whole. But he must recapture it in its en-tirety. He must fight the notion that in the beginning there is method; for from such a notion, in the end, there results only the void. He must discuss anew the meaning of teaching and learning from the point of view of metaphysics as the true natural wisdom of the intellect; for only then will he be able to subordinate *method* in teaching to the analogical nature of *knowing.* Method in teaching is as diversified as are the sciences themselves. The only true transcendental principles of knowledge are found in metaphysics. When Mr. Dewey established a theory of education which pretended to legislate *to* the various disciplines a universal method of teaching, he was extending to the college and the uni-versity his methodic faith in chaos. It is simple, and also true, to say that *here,* here in the presence of Mr. Dewey's impassioned methodism, the Catholic educator must work for the re-establish-ment of wisdom. But what Catholic thinker does not see how im-mense such a task is, or how much the future of man depends upon it?

IV

THE SYNTHESIS OF UNIVERSALISM AND NATIONALISM ACCORDING TO THE CHRISTIAN PHILOSOPHY OF LAW

By Yves de la Brière, S.J.

*Professeur à l'Université Catholique de Paris
et
Rédacteur aux Études*

THE SYNTHESIS OF UNIVERSALISM AND NATIONALISM ACCORDING TO THE CHRISTIAN PHILOSOPHY OF LAW

I

THE UNITY AND DIVERSITY OF MAN

The basis of the entire construction is the fundamental unity of mankind. Participation in one and the same nature, corporeal and spiritual, physical and moral; with the same origin, same destiny, same essential rights and duties—these are the things that create among all men, among all peoples, a first natural community whose value all subsequently conceivable communities must consecrate; and whose requirements, postulates and just aspirations they must all fulfill.

Another fundamental element is the subdivision of the great human family into numerous social and political groupings, independent of one another, differentiated by ethnography and geography; by soil or climate; by social economy, conditions of life and labor; by moral or psychological differences, and above all by historical destinies. Among these groups, the combinations and the proportionings vary infinitely through time and space according to the diversity of successive migrations, of mutual action and reaction and of other vicissitudes that mark the life history of mankind. Such a variety of political and social groupings, of nations and of States manifestly presents itself as a spontaneous, permanent fact, with the universality of a general law of the life of societies here below; as a condition that favors the harmonious development of numerous human potentialities for the good of each group and the good of the whole; briefly, as a practical, normal, and rational exigency of the nature of man and of the nature of things.

Side by side, then, with the natural phenomenon of man's unity there exists the no less natural phenomenon of man's diversity, manifested by the variety of nations and the respective independence of political communities.

The imperative demand of morality and of law, according to the natural and providential order, has for object not the impossible

97

and unreasonable uniting of all the peoples of the earth into one
and the same community, into one and the same State or Universal
Republic, but the establishment, rather, of a system of normal relations among nations and States in order to guarantee to all men the
reciprocal exercise of the rights and duties consequent upon human sociability and solidarity—rights and duties of mutual justice and mutual benevolence which result from the rationality
of man and the very nature of things. Such is the fundamental code
which, in a very different sense from that given by Rousseau and
the 18th century ideologists, we term the Natural Law.

This code, imposed by the evident requirements of rational nature, may be reduced to a very small number of essential precepts
of which each subsequent common or written law thereafter promulgated must be the application or just interpretation, in harmony with the concrete conditions of national and international
society according to time and place:

Precepts of mutual justice: respect for the property and rights of
others; observance of contracts; fidelity to promises.

Precepts of mutual benevolence: mutual aid and assistance in
the perils or needs which are the common lot of mankind, at least
when it is within one's power, and when circumstances make it
urgent and opportune to give that help.

Such precepts are imposed universally upon the human conscience by the Natural Law which requires, moreover, that among
different peoples, among different political communities, a body
of positive laws, duly sanctioned by public institutions, ratify the
general and reciprocal obligations of such fundamental rights and
duties.

Then comes the positive construction with the Natural Law as
its foundation: a construction which at first, and for a long time, is
limited to a group of nations belonging to the same geographic
region, and having more or less habitual relations with one another, while ignoring almost completely the rest of the world: a
construction which gradually covers a greater part of the earth as
international relations develop: a construction which, finally, extends over the whole world, after geographic discoveries and means
of communication have brought together in regular intercourse
every continent and all peoples of the earth.

At the outset, the positive laws of this *jus inter gentes* are constituted by international custom, which has slowly permeated the

ideas and manners of a certain number of nations geographically
and socially bound together. This custom introduces a certain
number of practical rules considered obligatory, and whose voluntary transgression constitutes, in the eyes of every nation, an offense liable to punishment. Such is the Law of Nations in its primitive form and in its first becoming.

Founded on the Natural Law, postulated by the objective requirements of the common temporal good, the obligation of this
international custom, in the various nations it affects, has for its immediate determination, at least tacitly, the consent and agreement
of the governing authorities or political rulers of these nations.
International custom, is, however, influenced by the ethical errors
which prevail in the historical milieu where it is formed. It is
clear, then, that it becomes morally and lawfully obligatory only
within the same limits and under the same reservations as the internal law of these nations, in whatever concerns the objective
character of a just or an unjust law.

The time comes when international custom no longer suffices
for the Law of Nations. The community of peoples and of States
having expanded and civilization having become more complex
and refined, the common temporal good demands that the architecture of the Law of Nations be further elaborated. To international usage are added written conventions which regulate affairs
of common interest in greater detail by way of contractual and
positive stipulations.

With time these written conventions in their turn prove insufficient. They require to be supplemented by the creation of permanent organisms such as institutes, offices, etc., whose function
is the regular administration of the collective interests of an ensemble of Powers.

The development of international life may require, finally, the
establishment of a single center of administration and co-ordination for those affairs which concern the pacification and co-operation of all or nearly all the Powers of the civilized world. Then
only would the international community assume fully the organic
character demanded by the common temporal good.

Yet, however elaborate such a construction might become, it
would have always to obey the essential laws of its origin. It must
translate into institutions of public equity the exigencies or objective indications of the common good in the collectivity of nations

and States. To be legitimate, each of its positive laws must constitute an application or a rational interpretation of the authentic postulates of the nature of man and of the nature of things.

Briefly, the international organization will endure in proportion as it is more or less firmly rooted in the Natural Law.

In any spiritualistic philosophy—*a fortiori* in a Christian philosophy—the authority of the Natural Law rests on the fact that it views the nature of man and the constitution of things in the light of that eternal, divine and superior law from which each and every just law here below derives its binding force and its highest ratification.

II

The Lesson of the Natural Law Confirmed by Revelation

With respect to the Law of Nations as with respect to the internal law—private or public—of a single State, with respect also to domestic society and the civic community, several philosopher jurists, who do not by any means profess juridical positivism, nevertheless call into question the very existence of a natural law having the structure we have just outlined.

The confusion and distressing contradictions prevailing in this field, of which the history of thought and of human institutions all too often gives evidence, lead these jurists to consider as illusory the conception of an objective rule discernible by right reason as the proper foundation of all positive law.

These same philosopher jurists believe that the chief solid notions, in the domain of law, that obtain the salutary acquiescence of the civilized world are, in fact, derived from Christian doctrine and Catholic tradition. Not only do believers maintain this, but even non-believers pay tribute to Christian and Catholic influence, showing itself in the mental habits that have become current in the social and intellectual milieu to which they belong. Such a position might be called *juridical fideism*.

The element of truth which must be acknowledged here is the important service rendered to the cause of Natural Law and the Law of Nations by Christian doctrine and by Catholic tradition. This fact is commented upon, in relation to an analogous question, by the Vatican Council in the constitution *Dei Filius*. In fact, this Council defines that the knowledge of the true God and of other truths required to discern the true religion may be attained with certitude by unaided human reason in the exercise of its natural activity. Alluding, however, to the dogma of the fall of man and to the consequences of the fall, even after Redemption, the Council adds that, in mankind's present state, the causes of ignorance and of error are many and difficult, moreover, to correct. For this reason the Council affirms the beneficialness of positive revelation, as taught by the Church, in the sense that wherever it penetrates even such truths as are naturally knowable can be discerned more "readily, by everybody and without admixture of error" (*expedite, ab omnibus, nullo admixto errore*). The same may be said concerning the truths of social ethics which are also the object of natural law, particularly those that constitute the basis of *the law of nations*.

But this efficacious rôle of Christian doctrine and of Catholic tradition in making known to many and preserving for many the concepts of natural law does not preclude the natural law from remaining the natural law.

In speaking of the natural law, the aim is not to include or exclude this or that influence which may contribute effectively to its diffusion. The point is to recognize that the concepts under consideration belong to the natural and human order and are normally discernible by right reason. Such, beyond all doubt, is the case with reference to the rational exigencies of the social nature of man in view of the common good of human societies. No juridical fideism can suppress this truth which concerns the very essence of the objective requirements of the natural law.

Moreover, though it is true that wherever the light of Revelation exerts its influence human nature is thereby helped to grasp and to retain moral and philosophical truths of a high order *expedite, ab omnibus, nullo admixto errore,* it would be altogether fallacious to claim that, without the light of Revelation, human reason using only its natural powers has never succeeded—notwithstanding many fluctuations and deviations—in discerning and retaining with certitude a goodly number of moral and juridical truths in the code of rights and duties of the individual human conscience, in the codes of domestic and civil society, and, finally, in the code of rights and duties among nations. In every domain fideism must be held responsible for the dark pessimism with which, to its great disadvantage, human nature has come to be viewed.

The Natural Law exists not in philosophical abstraction alone, but in controllable reality. The Christian religion does credit to itself when it thus bears explicit testimony to the objective value of our rational and natural knowledge. Therein, too, lies the solid ground for a philosophy of law.

To sum up: the exigencies of rational nature with regard to man's sociability indicate an objective order and a divine intention governing all the societies, institutions and legislation of mankind.

Two societies present themselves as universally necessary, however varied may be the conditions of their concrete realization: domestic society (the family) and the civil community.

Beyond the limits of each civil community appears the universal community of nations, characterized by the twofold phenomenon of human unity and diversity. It, too, is governed by a system of rights and duties among nations which bears the name, *Law of Nations.*

This law of nations is based primarily on the common duties of justice and charity universally demanded by human rationality and sociability.

It has for secondary norm the requirements of the international common good as manifested by the historical and social development of the community of nations.

The circumstances of contemporary life have brought about a considerable evolution of international relations, which, in turn, requires that the organic institutions of international life be perfected to a degree heretofore unsurmised; for example, institutions of collaboration and pacification answering new demands of the common good.

Ultimately, it is the positive and contractual law that decides the various and contingent modalities of determination. But always the latter, if its effects are to be legitimate and useful, must be rooted in the natural law, in the fundamental demands thereof and in whatever it justly implies as befitting.

The rational and salutary primacy thus affirmed is the primacy of social morality.

But the rules of social morality referred to are those which by reason of their character and exterior object are amenable to positive prescriptions and sanctions in the form of man-made institutions and legislation.

By the very fact that they are moral rules they become juridical rules. This is the natural law.

It is the natural law applied to international duties and international organisms.

It is the radiance of the one superior order of morality and law, of justice and charity, in the juridical relations of State with State, nation with nation.

To believers, the social teachings of the Church might be said to bring a solid, well-balanced and luminous answer which dispenses with any other.

Yet, the authority of the Church, which, in this sphere, teaches and confirms so many liberating truths, does not by any means claim that all legitimate certitude on this point is derived from the one positive, transcendental and divine revelation. On the contrary, it affirms that in this realm of the legitimate order of the temporal City, it is the right reason of man that is immediately and normally competent to discern the objective rule from which may be deduced the structure of a well-ordered State, as well as the just determinations of law.

Far from advocating inordinately a sort of supernaturalistic monopoly or juridical fideism, far from underrating the rôle of human reason, the Church proclaims and recognizes, particularly in the Vatican Council, the legitimate competence of reason in such matters as are commensurate with its capacity, here below. In point of fact, after the memorable indictment in the Encyclical *Mit brennender Sorge* of March 14, 1937, what was the remedy against the aberrations of racial totalitarianism proposed in the matter of the principles governing the State and the law? Read the text itself. No answer could be plainer: *Acknowledgment of the natural law*. The homage there paid to that law is noteworthy:

". . . We refer especially to what is called the natural law, written by the Creator's hand on the tablet of the heart (Rom. II, 14), and which reason, unless blinded by sin or passion, can easily read. It is in the light of the commands of this natural law, that all positive law, whoever be the lawgiver, can be gauged as to its moral content, and hence, as to the authority it exercises over conscience. Human laws in flagrant contradiction with the natural law are vitiated by a flaw that no force, no power can mend. . . . The real common good ultimately takes its measure from man's nature which strikes a balance between personal rights and social obligations, and from the purpose of society established for the benefit of human nature. . . ."

This doctrine has been constantly and forcefully inculcated by all contemporary Popes in their teachings on the spiritual problems of the Temporal City; notably by Leo XIII in the Encyclical

Libertas praestantissimum of June 20, 1888, wherein he praises liberty but condemns Liberalism. In this same encyclical, the Pope hails as the necessary and dominating inspiration of all positive legislation those first truths, those great natural principles that must be considered a noble heritage, common to all humanity.

This doctrine of the objective value of the natural law is none other than the one taught with such forthrightness by the professors of our Catholic Universities: Vareilles-Sommières, Lucien Brun, Hervé Bazin, Claudio Jannet, Gustave de Lamarzelle, du Plessis-Grénedan. Worthy of special mention in this connection is the illustrious founder of the "Institut Catholique" of Paris, Mgr. d'Hulst, who treated with such elegant distinction and convincing competence the *Morality of the Citizen* in his Lenten conferences of 1895 at Notre Dame of Paris.

Let us define now, with greater precision, the term *natural law*. By it we mean the rules that are deducible from the exigencies of man's rational nature in whatever concerns the common good of human society; that clearly translate the intentions of the Creator, and are susceptible of positive codification, application and sanction by temporal authority.

III

CHRISTIAN LOVE OF COUNTRY

Patriotism is a moral virtue which disposes man to fulfill the duties he owes to his country and to love it as it deserves.

Normally, our country is identical with the political community of which we are members. But the notion of fatherland adds to the idea of political community and of civic loyalty a nuance of moral sentiment analogous to family feeling. One's country must not merely be served and obeyed, it must be loved. This shade of difference is marked by the very term *terra patria,* the fatherland, which evokes the idea of a tradition, of a heritage, of a patrimony transmitted from generation to generation. The idea of country is one of the sweetest and most beautiful in the domain of social psychology. It stirs in the human soul profound emotion and passionate devotion.

That we must serve and obey our country and perform every service it legitimately requires of us is a fact sufficiently established by ethics and the natural law. It is a matter of complying with a divine command, with a clear and supreme intention of the Creator inscribed in the nature of man and the nature of things.

The individual and the family cannot subsist, much less can they satisfy and guarantee fulfilment of the legitimate physical, intellectual, and moral exigencies of their rational and social natures, unless they find support in a permanent community of greater magnitude and power which provides the necessary safeguards; this precisely is one's country. The fatherland, in turn, can and must exact from its children all the services that are indispensable to the realization of social aims, to the conservation and defense of the general interests over which it exercises guardianship. Service or obedience to country is obedience to rational nature, and, consequently, to God Himself, since it is compliance with an ordination of the Creator.

This sort of duty to country bears not simply the stamp of an administrative ordinance, however just and necessary the latter be. It has the added significance of an affection of the heart— an inclination of love. The fatherland is, in fact, not only the tutelary guardian of the family, but an extension and prolongation of it. The moral sentiment which it arouses and to which it lays claim is closely related to that which every well-bred child feels for his family.

The fatherland appears as the collective heritage of one's ancestors: the land they inhabited, the works, the improvements, the constructions they wrought; the useful and glorious deeds they performed from generation to generation; the literary and artistic productions with which they enriched the common heritage; the joys and enthusiasms as well as the losses and sorrows they experienced in their collective consciousness—in a word, the inheritance, both spiritual and temporal, that fathers have transmitted to their sons from one generation to another. The homeland is that noble, precious and beautiful community that our fathers built from age to age by their labor, their love, nay, at the price of their very lifeblood. The present generation is only its trustee. It must realize its duty to guard and fructify this magnificent patrimony in order that it may be transmitted intact and enriched to future generations. Under the magic symbol of the same flag, it shelters, along with the treasures of common glory, both the graves of our ancestors and the cradles of our children.

We all carry in our hearts the well-loved image of the homeland. It is one of those sacred and invisible treasures that elude all spoliation and go with us wherever we roam. With the great Brazilian, Rio Branco, we gladly repeat, *"Ubique patriae memor."* The homeland!—its territory, its natural and artistic riches, its past and its present, its monuments, its splendors and its ruins, its great men and its great books—all these form the patrimony that belongs to each and every one. Its joys are our joys, its sorrows our sorrows. Whatever magnifies and honors it stirs our enthusiasm deeply, just as whatever threatens, mutilates, or outrages it wounds us to the quick and offends our inmost sensibilities. No earthly sacrifice is deemed excessive when the rights and love of country are at stake. We touch here upon one of the noblest and most generous of human emotions.

Bossuet, in his own magnificent language, has pointed out the origin and deep meaning of patriotic sentiment, of thoughtful love of one's ancestral land and tradition:

Human society requires that we love the land wherein we dwell together. We look upon it as a common mother. We become attached to it and this attachment creates a bond. This is what the Latins call *caritas patrii soli,* love of the paternal soil, and they look upon this love as a binding tie among men. As a matter of fact, men do feel closely united when they reflect that the same land which was the scene of their birth and life activities will cradle them together in death.

Christianity consecrates this noble love of country, already demanded and legitimized by the very nature of man and the rational order of things. The example of Our Lord Jesus Christ Himself is the best evidence. He who had so exalted the universal precept of divine charity towards all men and all peoples, manifested a deep and special love for the fatherland whose Son He was by His temporal birth. With what hallowed pride did He not evoke the religious and national glories of Israel: Moses and the prophets, the great kings, David and Solomon. In His eyes Jerusalem was the illustrious city of David, the "City of the Great King." To Him the temple of Jerusalem appeared as the magnificent symbol of the spiritual and temporal glories of the people of Israel. He shed tears of filial sorrow when a prophetic light revealed the future disasters that were to befall His beloved country—albeit as the just punishment of its crimes and ingratitude. Jesus wept as He viewed Jerusalem hemmed in by the trenches of the Roman legions, as

He beheld the walls of the City of David stormed by the victorious aggressor, the gigantic constructions of the Temple devoured by the flames, and the children of Israel who had not perished by sword or famine dispersed in cruel slavery throughout the Greco-Roman world—supreme catastrophe of the fatherland submerged in mourning and in ruins!

That Jesus loved His native land, gloried in its glories, wept over its disasters, is proof sufficient that love of country holds within the human heart a legitimate place in the hierarchy of virtues midway between man's more restricted love of his own family and the more comprehensive love he owes to all humanity in the essential and harmonious order of divine charity.

IV

THE CONTROVERSY OVER NATIONALISM

The moral problem of patriotism involves, as we have seen, the more modern question of nationalism.

This term is used today to designate two things, perfectly distinct, though capable of being conjoined.

On one hand, the word 'nationalism' may be used to designate the theory that sets up as an axiom the absolute right of peoples to dispose of themselves, the supreme right of each sufficiently differentiated people to form, if it so wishes, a distinct and independent State. This is the famous *Principle of Nationalities*.

On the other hand, the word 'nationalism' may be taken to designate a conception of State government which, among preoccupations of the same order, gives preponderance to the national interest, considered as consisting in the might and power of the State. Nationalism so understood is not patriotism as such, but a safeguard of patriotism and particular vigilance in its regard.

We cannot discuss here the first meaning of the world *nationalism,* namely the theory of public law, or rather, of the philosophy of public law, which bears the name of *Principle of Nationalities,* because it raises too many complex problems of law, history and philosophy. Moreover, whatever be the solution offered of the controverted points, the conception of patriotic duty remains unaffected. In any case, the only question thereby settled would be which political community possesses, in point of fact, over a given population, whose case happens to be under litigation, the superior rights and titles pertaining exclusively to the ancestral land —to the mother-country.

When the *Principle of Nationalities* is studied directly and in detail, as a problem of the philosophy of public law, the conclusion reached is that the wish of a particular people bent on forming a distinct and independent State constitutes a claim worthy of serious and fair consideration, but does not in itself constitute a supreme and absolute right. It may, according to the case, create or not create the legitimate right to separation and independence; for it may or may not accord with other legitimate considerations of law and of fact that are vital to the common temporal good, to the acquisition of those social advantages which constitute the universal and fundamental reason for existence of every political community. We cannot accept, then, as a decisive and sufficient rule—in the delicate and complex problem of the dismemberment and reconstitution of States—a formula so simple and summary as the *Principle of Nationalities,* as the nationalistic theory of the absolute right of peoples to self-disposal. This, however, is not the subject under discussion when we speak of country and of national duty.

The second meaning of the word *nationalism,* on the contrary, is of direct concern here, since it brings up the ethical question of the extent of the fatherland's rights over its sons and of their duties towards it. Indeed, it coincides in extent and amplitude with national duty itself, as viewed by the philosophy of public law.

The principle of patriotism and of national duty, however, is no longer in question. We enter now upon the study of the subsequent and complementary question: Which among the considerations that really matter in right administration of the country's interests ought to weigh most in the minds and conduct of such as have an efficacious and clear-sighted love of their country?

The answer may vary according to the rightful concerns of each patriot. Many, for example, might judge that the best temporal service they could render to their country would be to secure the enactment of good social legislation, or perhaps, of a good relief policy, or again, of a good financial policy; in a word, the felicitous and intelligent handling of one or the other problem of close interest to the proper administration of public affairs and promotion of national prosperity.

Now, the specifically nationalistic point of view is *the preponderance of the national interest itself,* envisaged as the strength,
the greatness and the power of the State, at home and abroad
—this being the general measure of the value and success of all
national activities. With regard to internal policy, the main concern of nationalistic milieus is the problem of organizing public
powers, so that the State may be firmly and authoritatively directed; with regard to external policy, the distinctive preoccupations are the problems of diplomacy, of armed forces, of expansion, to the end that the prestige of the State may be everywhere
upheld with influence and honor. The power of the State being
thus ensured, Nationalists believe that the other aims of social and
political life will be the more easily attained, each in its proper
rank and order. National interest being the dominant and characteristic preoccupation of Nationalism, it follows that the patriotism of Nationalists is more vigilant, more restless, more sensitive
and more exacting than that found in environments where the
prevalent tendencies are other than nationalistic.

We repeat, then, that, in this sense of the term, *nationalism*
wears the aspect of a vigilant patriotism. Its characteristic concern
will be the national interest under the form of the power of the
State, fortified within and without. In a great many countries of
our contemporary world, this conception of nationalism is represented by a compact and active fraction of public opinion. It corresponds to a policy, a sensibility, a mysticism. From the standpoint of country and national duty, it behooves us to inquire what
verdict must be rendered on current nationalistic ideas and influences, in the light of Catholic Christian morals.

The general solution of this doctrinal and spiritual problem depends entirely on the meaning attached to said supremacy of the
national interest through the power of the State.

Is this supremacy absolute, or is it merely relative and condi-
tional?

Absolute supremacy of the national interest is the doctrine of
extreme or exaggerated nationalism—ultra-nationalism, which
sets up as a final and universal end the predominance of the State,
to which everything else, without exception, must indiscriminately
be sacrificed.

It is the absolutist conception of the *"raison d'État"* and of the
universal right of the City. It is national interest become the supreme object of worship, replacing all else and preferred to all

else. It is the deification of a human interest, legitimate in itself, but regarded here as neither limited nor conditioned by any other right, as constituting alone, in itself, the sovereign good. It is, in a word, the revival, pure and simple, of the pagan worship of the deified City—of the State identified with God.

In every country this absolute and excessive cult of the national interest has avowed followers, often arrogant in their fanatical manifestations and claims. In a certain number of consciences the nationalistic religion replaces every other belief, every other religion.

Such is the nationalism which is contrary to natural law and social morality—condemned by Christian and Catholic doctrine. In many famous encyclicals, and especially in the *Ubi arcano Dei,* Pius XI reprobated this "immoderate love of nation" which refuses to recognize any higher norm. Prior to this, Pius IX, in the *Syllabus* of 1864, had condemned the proposition alleging that love of country justifies, of itself, every perjury and every criminal deed that would otherwise conflict with the moral order and the Divine law.

Every country has its share in these errors and excesses. But in Germany—more than anywhere else—this deification of the soil, of the race, this investiture of the State with supreme and unlimited rights is rampant. Having served as pretext and warrant for the most appalling abuses of power, it is affirmed with defiant brutality, in word and deed, by those extreme partisans of nationalism and pan-Germanism known today as Hitlerians or Nazis. No, the doctrinal errors of the absolute nationalist are, unhappily, not something to be laughed off as the pure figment of a fevered brain in quest of some heresy to tear apart!

That in absolute nationalism which is most contrary to social morality and a sound philosophy of public law, is the unlimited, unconditional value this doctrine attributes to the law of the City—to the national interest.

The law of the City and the national interest, like all other legitimate and justifiable institutions, deserve respect, consideration, devotion, loyalty. But, like other human values, they must harmonize, reach a compromise, come to terms with other rights, with other values, whose claims are either equal or superior to their own.

The rights of God necessarily prevail over human rights, over all earthly values. Social morality rules governments as strictly as individual morality rules the conduct of individual men. Even service to country is subject to imperative rules of right and duty. The City does not possess unlimited and unconditional rights over its members; it is in duty bound not to absorb or confiscate the legitimate and primordial rights of individuals and families, but to respect and hold them sacred. In other words, there are moral and objective limits to the authority that the City may legitimately exercise, even in the name of national interest, over its citizens—sons of the same fatherland.

Briefly, every country must recognize that, lying beyond its boundaries and holding relations with its own government and people, there are many other nations, many other countries, *whose rights and claims are on a par with its own* and quite as sacred. The power presiding over the destiny of each nation is bound to observe towards all other nations the rules of social justice and charity; above all, scrupulously to respect the property and rights of the rest.

Consequently, in the name of morality, in the name of law, in the name of universal good, the supremacy of the national interest is limited and conditioned by a great number of definite and imperious obligations. Not every political measure is licit simply because it is undertaken for the country's advantage. Not every means becomes acceptable on the sole ground that it promotes the national interest.

In a word, the supremacy of national interest—of the external and internal power of the State—is, in comparison with other reasonable objectives in the government of public affairs, to be regarded as relative, not absolute.

If, however, it is considered as relative; as respecting the rights of God, of morality, of individuals, of families and of other nations, then the conception of nationalism becomes just and admissible.

Against a nationalism thus limited and conditioned social morality can urge no objection on principle.

V

THE PERILS AND THE SAFEGUARDS OF NATIONALISM

Having recognized that nationalism must, in principle, accept the conditions and limitations which make it compatible with morality and law, it may be useful to reflect on the advantages and disadvantages of the nationalistic standpoint in so far as it is added to the patriotic standpoint which coincides with a strict duty of conscience.

Even when legitimate, nationalism appears as an accidental phenomenon arising from abnormal circumstances. The terms: vigilant patriotism, anxious patriotism, used to describe it, suggest that the national interests are threatened or exposed to harm, and that it is of great moment to remedy this situation by strengthening in an exceptional way the armament of the nation.

At its origin, nationalism is, in fact, a reaction of the national sensibilities against dangerous influences tending to disrupt the nation. Dangerous influences created, for example, by the menace of an alien power or the penetration of foreign capital attempting in a sly or brutal way to subjugate the fatherland. Dangerous influences created by the diffusion and internal contagion of doctrines and methods that enervate and disorganize the nation and engender a disregard of all just political necessities concerning the national interest. Nationalistic movements often arise to counteract such tendencies, to safeguard the rights of the State, and to proclaim the supremacy of the national interest.

Under such circumstances, nationalism may be legitimate in its origin and may answer, to advantage, a requirement of the public good.

It presents, moreover, the real advantage of directing the activities of its devotees towards the ideal of working for the national interest, whose moral and spiritual value is far superior to the narrow-minded quarreling, the sordid rivalries, the backstairs electoral and parliamentary operations that too often disgrace the domestic political organisms of many countries in both the Old World and the New. Certainly, the nationalistic idea takes a loftier and more generous flight.

After the advantages, we must consider the pitfalls and perils against which nationalism must guard itself in order to remain conformable to the superior rules of morality and law.

The threefold danger to be examined concerns the foreign, the domestic and the religious policies.

With regard to foreign policy, nationalism tends to be so exclusively concerned with national interests that little or no attention is paid to the rights and welfare of others, to the rules of justice and international benevolence, to the duties of co-operation— of mutual and collective collaboration, binding upon the universal community of States and peoples. Nationalism must never forget to combine equitably international with national duty.

As regards domestic policy, nationalism, rightly concerned about the organic power of the State as the normal condition for the realization of many social advantages, may be inclined to underestimate the various other political objectives not directly related to the organic power of the State. It may forget that social legislation, relief and security legislation, financial legislation, not to mention those laws touching the spiritual life of a country, correspond to essential needs of the nation's general activity; more briefly, to real national interests. What nationalism must particularly guard against is the narrowness of exclusivism, of a one-sided point of view.

With respect to the religious policy, finally, the nationalism of all peoples and of all parties without exception must guard against the perpetual tendency to consider Catholic questions, which, by definition, are of the universal order, from the exclusive standpoint of the national interest which is essentially particular to each nation. It is, in fact, confusing the point of view seriously to consider such questions as a papal election, the choice of a Church dignitary, the organization of religious missions in foreign lands, the distribution of apostolic tasks among missionaries of this or that nationality, according to the greater or lesser advantage which might result for the language, the influence, or the politics of this or that people, of this or that government. A too facile and ill-regulated excess of nationalism may even lead certain well-meaning persons into a complete misunderstanding of religious questions concerning the universal and eternal fatherland of souls.

In short, let the just care of the national interest be maintained within the limits assigned by morality and law. Let it respect the boundaries of other regions, of other sanctuaries. Its own lawful domain is already vast enough. Love of country touches the noblest, deepest, most generous passions of the human soul. Let the sacred sense of justice regulate the activities of this unselfish love.

The term *nationalism* gives rise to many subtle controversies. It requires to be distinguished and even subdistinguished owing to its essentially diverse acceptations and its unequally justifiable applications before the bar of reason, morality and law. When it comes to this concept, we must be particularly on our guard against summary generalizations and emotional simplifications.

Patriotism, however, of which nationalism functions as the armor, is a concept which, in its clear and well-defined meaning, corresponds to an indubitable truth, a noble duty, a high moral virtue. As an object of devotion and of love, the homeland constitutes a spiritual treasure, a magnificent heritage handed down by the generations of the past to the generations of the future.

As I write these pages for *The Catholic University of America,* on the occasion of the fiftieth anniversary of its foundation, I cannot refrain from saluting with fraternal sympathy the labors wherewith it has valorously performed, in the New World, the twofold task—which is that of the Christian philosophy of law— of reconciling Universalism with Nationalism in the intellectual and moral formation of an élite.

False and pernicious ideas, on one hand, improperly exalt Nationalism to the exclusion of Universalism; or, contrariwise, exalt Universalism to the detriment of Nationalism.

But what human wisdom reinforced by Christian Revelation teaches is the harmonious synthesis of a just Universalism with a just Nationalism. When each of the twain is kept in its proper place, we have order, we have peace, we have the true formula of law, we have—we may even say—the "catholicity" of law.

This harmonious synthesis of all that is sanely human and legitimately national is what must be sown in the minds of men by the noblest home of study and learning which we call the *University; most especially by the Catholic University;* in the Old World and the New; in the fraternal service of the one law and the one kingdom of God.

V

THE CHURCH AND NATIONAL CULTURES

By Andrew J. Krzesinski, Ph.D., S.T.D.

Professor Agregé of Philosophy
in
The University of Cracow
(now in The University of Montreal)

THE CHURCH AND NATIONAL CULTURES

Introduction

A close examination of the history of nations confirms the fact that Man everlastingly strives to achieve a higher level of existence, and that his spiritual being urges him continually to create a new world about him, upon which he exerts his personal influence. This may be called the world of culture.

Among different nations culture assumes many forms, taking on national characteristics, although it also exhibits elements of a universal character.

Of the many cultures which have appeared upon the arena of world history, some, like the Egyptian, the Sumerian, the Babylonian and the Dravidian, belong to the past. Others, such as the Chinese and the Hindu, live on, but having surrendered to the influences of their past, betray signs of lassitude and tend to feed upon the accomplishments of bygone ages. The Greek and Roman cultures, somewhat younger than these, lost their vitality with the destruction of the Oriental and Roman Empires. They did not, however, by any means become extinct.

Many of their most valuable contributions have survived in modern nations which began by organizing their own several national States upon the ruins of the old order. Such contributions formed as it were the seed of these new cultures, which were quick, however, to assume an original form of their own.

These newer cultures that developed among the Romance as well as German and Slavonic peoples are of special interest as being closer to us; the more so that, having come under the benevolent influence of a new and exceedingly important factor—Christianity—they were enabled, in consequence, to reach the highest pinnacles of idealism.

On the other hand, these cultures show, in the case of certain nations which from time to time have sought to rid themselves of the Church's influence, the signs of rupture with Christian ideals. In modern times we have witnessed such unprecedented secessions from the teachings of Christ as those typified by Rus-

117

sian communism and by German racism and nationalism. The consequences of these secessions have been disastrous.

In the present article we shall consider, on the one hand, the beneficial influence which the Church has exerted throughout the ages upon the development of national cultures; on the other, the deplorable consequences for national culture of the acceptance of radical nationalist theories like the racist doctrine of National Socialism.

Communism, with its appalling consequences for Russian national culture, will not be the subject of our present discourse.

I

CULTURE AND NATIONALISM

Culture is the product of man's creative effort. Man is not satisfied with any given reality, but constantly strives to enrich the external world and his own personality with new acquisitions, material and spiritual. Whatever lies in the sphere of culture is to that extent purely the creation of man. Indeed, were the results of man's creative work to be annihilated by some means and the acts of his genius suspended for a certain time, the very ground we tread would revert to a jungle, a steppe, or a desert, while man himself, as well as subhuman nature surrounding him, would dissolve into a maze of mysteries—riddles unintelligible to us.

The faculty of thinking enables man to comprehend the earth, to soar above the stars, to reach the furthermost recesses of the universe, to search the innermost depths of his own soul and to reflect upon his existence and origin. Man tries to comprehend, control, resolve and explain everything in the terms of causal relationships.

Such a world, becoming progressively more intelligible to him, no longer shackles him, nor do the phenomena appearing therein frighten him.

The tempo of progress toward intellectual culture determines the measure of growth of man's freedom. But this freedom which accompanies his thoughtful work of re-creating the external world, by no means suffices him. Thus, even though he enriches this world with the most magnificent acquisitions of art and science, a feeling of inherent weakness never leaves him. For nature's laws operate inexorably upon the external universe, regardless of man. True, he may convert matter and, to a limited degree, shape it into new forms, but he cannot destroy matter nor create even an atom. Man strives to achieve freedom similar to that possessed by the Creator, i.e., he wants to be master of his own world. He achieves this freedom in the realm of religion and ethics.

The laws of morality which he discovers in his practical mind, or conscience, by way of profound search and reflection, the laws enjoined by God Himself and moral truths learned from revelation, constitute the principles underlying man's highest creative activity. The world which he creates, augmented by the invisible gifts of God, is his own world—the culmination of his free, creative effort in the realm of culture.

Every true culture is saturated with a dynamism which manifests itself in the process of mutual integration and harmonization of all elements belonging to its proper sphere. Owing to this dynamic character culture becomes universal and possesses attributes whose acquisition deserves the effort of all cultured peoples.

If we define culture as the sum total of man's experience, gained in seeking ultimate spiritual perfection—control over himself, control over the surrounding universe and adequate adjustment of his relation to God and all peoples[1]—then, considering its universal quality, we must recognize the fact that the cultures of all peoples alike are necessarily the outcome of this selfsame creative process.

Does this mean that cultures do not differ from one another? Quite the contrary. Aside from their fundamental universal character, cultures differ in quality, kind, extent and style. Each of them exhibits national influences. This is a natural phenomenon, since culture is created by man, who belongs to some definite national group. Being a member of it, he perforce succumbs to national influence, adjusts himself to the general intellectual level, absorbs national likes and dislikes, is influenced by national problems and tendencies, disposes of special talents which enable him to achieve his goals and invest current events with special interest for himself. For this reason, the culture which man creates takes on a national color.

However, one may not deduce from this that man—the creator of culture—is merely its fortuitous component. Were that so, it

[1] Andrew J. Krzesinski, "Is Modern Culture Doomed?" Devin-Adair, New York, 1942; cf. pp. 1-3.

would preclude all progress in culture. Frequently, human thinking surges unexpectedly upwards to achieve lofty goals—sharply
transcending mediocre levels; in moments of highest inspiration
the thoughts of men elevate themselves like pillars of flame, illuminating new perspectives, blazing new trails.

It would be difficult to ascertain in such cases, whether and to
what extent human inspiration has been influenced directly by
national considerations.

Notwithstanding, it is unquestionable that the co-operation of
the national elements in culture tends to its advantage. People
work harder and achieve greater results when the goal of their
creative efforts involves their interests, preferences, strongly-felt
needs and tendencies. It is evident that elimination of the national
element from culture would deprive it of its originality and, what
is worse, would cause it to decay.

Parallel with nationality as an influence whereby culture's mold
is determined, is the racial factor, though, in point of fact, this
racial factor is not potent enough actually to give specificity to
culture. Rather, it expresses itself only in the distinctive overtones
it imparts. Hence, although it is correct to speak of Chinese, Indian, French, Italian, English, Polish or German cultures, it would
be improper to speak of Yellow or White culture. Taking Germany as an example, one may speak of the culture of a certain race
only on condition of identifying race with nation.

II

THE CHURCH IN RELATION TO NATIONAL CULTURES

We may now inquire: What is the relation of the Church to
national culture and race? Does it exert a benevolent influence
upon them? Did nations in times past really exhaust the possibility of benefiting by the Church's charitable activity? Do they, or
can they, benefit by it now?

In answering, we must consider, on the one hand, the organization and doctrine of the Church; on the other, the facts of history
concerning the relations between the Church and different States.

The Church is a community which integrates all peoples who
share a common faith, sacraments and moral principles, and recognize Christ as their ruler and the Pope as His representative

on earth. Its organization is strictly universal, which means that it does not countenance national or racial discriminations. Regardless of race or nationality, every man is entitled to be a member of the Church.

In this vast commonwealth known as the Kingdom of Christ, there are no boundaries. All of its members constitute one great family. They live a higher supernatural and blessed life. Through Christ's agency, they share in God's life even on earth. That is why they are termed "Children of God." Christ to them is the highest personification of good and each of them is to pattern his own life after Christ's.

All believers in Christ journey through life with their eyes fixed on God. Their faith reveals to them the kingdom of future glory, giving them glimpses of the life to come. This strengthens and confirms them, encouraging them to persevere and make progress. It gives inspiration that lightens their burdens and duties, enables them to surmount the greatest obstacles, steadies their character and rallies them to a more co-ordinated spiritual effort. The hard things of life become sweet; the tears and agony of those who suffer find consolation in faith. It is evident that God, whose guiding hand appears everywhere, is worthy of man's greatest sacrifice.

Only men of faith are able to retain peace, an unbroken spirit and joy in the presence of overpowering calamity. That serene, joyous disposition and optimism are of the utmost importance to every national culture. Men who are engaged in creating and promoting its growth are revitalized and reassured. Their creative powers are made more productive. Physically and spiritually they are stronger than their fellow citizens without faith. Inertness and lassitude are replaced by energy and vitality. The basis is both physiological and psychological.

From the physiological standpoint, it is certain that quickened circulation of the blood reacts favorably upon the entire physique. Optimism and emotional activity, generated while an individual is under the influence of some powerful ideology, tend to increase circulation. Growth of physical powers is a natural consequence. In such moments man is able to accomplish difficult tasks which in the throes of spiritual depression he would not even attempt. These facts may be easily verified and checked with the aid of scientific measuring instruments.

The psychological factor is far more potent. That optimistic ideas have a dynamic tendency cannot be gainsaid. Such tend to assume the character of norms; they integrate thought, will and emotion. Ideas whose absolute value the mind has recognized rise like mysterious lights in human consciousness, illuminating paths of progress, defining and centralizing concepts and judgments, eliminating at the same time contradictions and incongruities.

This process extends even to the innermost secrets of the mind, which it stimulates to harmonious unity of thought. Ideas grow and achieve structures of thought that are above the average human concept. As a result, thought is quickened and revitalized.

But the activity of ideas is not confined to the sphere of thought alone; they react upon the emotions, which in turn have the power to impart a pleasurable coloring, as it were, to our ideas. The effect, therefore, of the emotions thus aroused is to quicken and enliven thought, to heighten its freshness and interest and thus incite it to creative activity in accordance with the patterns of the ideas in question.

Neither can the will remain long inactive. It soon gives way to the influence of the ideas colored with emotion and begins to act upon them and to be guided thereby. Its activity manifests itself in the form of tendencies and various acts which reflect a harmonious and integrated psychical whole.

Thus, superimposed upon human consciousness, the faculty of concentration comes into play, spurred on by the dynamic nature of ideas which take on the character of higher values.

This is of the greatest importance to human creative energy and activity. First—the memory serves better in moments of spiritual elevation, revealing long forgotten facts and thought processes, thereby forming without hindrance new chains of thought and adequate conclusions. Second—emotion, feeding constantly on harmonized thoughts which are based on concrete ideas, finds itself in the state of readiness for action. It accompanies the conscious thought, animates it and further encourages its activity.

When motives for an idea appear well founded, the will decides upon action, deepens the trend of thought and elevates the worth of the idea.

The importance of the interaction of ideology and its accompanying emotional states for human creative power may be easily demonstrated. For example, one may examine mind and memory in the various ideological and emotional states which accompany them.

Whenever the ideological scales are tipped—particularly when optimism gives way to depression—the human mind surrenders itself to preconceptions and prejudices, becomes saturated, as it were, with inferences which prevent objective judgment and paralyze constructive activity. But once the ideological balance has been restored, objective thought and judgment reassert themselves and creative activity is again in evidence. In the former case, memory often misleads in the very matters in which it was wont to function normally; in the latter, it speedily returns to its normal condition.

Differences in the efficiency of memory are easier to observe at times of rise and fall of the emotional barometer. In pleasant emotional states—when human hearts reach their zenith of contentment and calmness—thinking is quickened and the memory works efficiently. Under irksome and unpleasant circumstances memory loses its efficiency and often fails completely.

To be objective, any study of these two contrasting states requires that subject-matter or content be identical in either case. Moreover, it is necessary that the changes of state under investigation—both ideological and emotional—be sincere and free from every trace of artificiality.

Such studies of the influence ideology exerts upon human activity disclose that the more profound the ideology and the more perfectly it strives to comprehend man's destiny and that of the universe, the more intense and efficacious is the creativeness it inspires. It is not to be wondered at, therefore, that Christianity, whose doctrine is more profound and sublime than any other, is the ideology that reacts most favorably upon the development of human genius.

The Christian ideology not only enhances the development and concentration of man's creative forces, it also enriches national cultures with moral standards and religious truths. This contribution of Christianity is of such inestimable worth that nothing else could conceivably replace it, even were it the product of the most intensive work of the greatest minds the world has ever known.

Teaching justice and the brotherhood of man, the Church strives to remove wrongs, to fight poverty, to eliminate class prejudices, inequalities and hatreds. She exacts mutual respect and fosters harmonious living among men. In season and out of season, the Church reminds the world that human equality and love for all men are the fundamentals of Christian morality.

In the light of what the Gospel teaches, the laws of civil society are to be obeyed and discipline is to be maintained within the State.

All these doctrines are of the utmost importance for national cultures. Under their guiding influence, national cultures are protected from inertness; from chauvinistic no less than anarchistic trends. Above all, they are made to assume a more and more humane character and constantly to advance in perfection.

III

CHRISTIANITY AS GUARDIAN OF NATIONAL CULTURES

Coming now to the relation existing between the Church and national cultures, let us note that the Church, almost from the Pentecostal day of her birth, through the long centuries, down to the present time, has never ceased to safeguard and protect the cultures of nations.

Everything in them that exemplified truth, goodness and beauty was accepted and confirmed by the Church, which regarded all such values as the common property of all mankind. This is especially true of the two cultures with which the Church first came into direct contact: the Greek and the Roman.

Greek philosophers, particularly Plato and later Aristotle, were highly respected within the Christian fold, and it is after the systems of these great thinkers that Christian philosophy was deliberately patterned. St. Augustine tried to accommodate Plato's philosophy to revealed religion, while St. Thomas, the great systematizer, did the same with even greater success, in reference to the philosophy of Aristotle.

In like manner, the Church adopted the findings of science, literature, the fine arts and by their use created new works inspired with the soul of Christian idealism. This inexhaustible capacity for utilizing spiritual treasures and for creating by means of them new works of beauty and grandeur is exemplified, perhaps most strikingly, in the sphere of architecture.

Whatever possessed to any notable degree a cultural character has always been the object of special solicitude on the part of the Church. In fact, the treasures of many known cultures, such as the Greek, the Roman, the Egyptian and others, would not have survived in anything approximating their present volume, were it not for the painstaking efforts of the Church.

Whatever collections exist today, preserved from destruction and kept intact for future generations, are monuments standing to the lasting credit of the Catholic Church. Here, thanks to her, are perpetuated many works of art and literature: treatises of philosophers and scientists, works of poets and writers, sculpture and paintings, even statues of pagan gods.

Parallel with her effort to extract and conserve whatever was worth while in cultures has been the Church's policy of preserving each of them in its own distinctive character. That is why she fosters diligently national customs and traditions which are not at variance with the teachings of Christianity. By encouraging the characteristic qualities and attributes of the culture in which a given nation has excelled, the Church has been instrumental in promoting its national aspirations as well as the national character of its culture. So profound is the Church's respect for national cultures, that she countenances among her members freedom even in the determination of ritual. Hence, notwithstanding her universal character and tendencies, the Church preserves various national rites, such as the Greek, the Latin, the Armenian, the Old Slavonic and others.

Always the teacher and educator, possessing complete knowledge of human nature, the Church knows that, by ministering to national spiritual needs, by making room for special talents, a healthy growth of moral and spiritual values within a culture will be achieved.

All European nations, appearing upon the stage of history since the fall of the Roman Empire, have profited by the teachings of the Church. Under her direction they have progressed by degrees from a primitive state of civilization to higher levels. It will be found that the earliest beginnings of Christianity in any of these nations coincide with the inception of a distinct national culture. Translations of the Scriptures, sermons and religious poems survive as cultural monuments of the nations whom the Church nurtured as a mother would her children, instructing them in the sublime and saving truths of her doctrine. Unfortunately, however, only too many nations, unfitted as yet for spiritual life, have in the past resisted the charitable leadership of the Church and, though accepting her teachings, have often reverted to their instinctive barbarism, living in hatred of other nations, seeking cruelly to exterminate their brothers in Christ.

Equally magnificent have been the contributions of Christianity in the social sphere. Many misconceptions concerning the nature of the social organism were demolished thereby, the result being a far-reaching revolution. As if by magic, class differentiations and social distinctions began to disappear. The master recognized his former slave as his brother, the mistress, her handmaid as her sister. The shackles of slavery gave way to the concept of equality. The revolution in social institutions went so far that the rich gave away their fortunes to the poor, seeking to eliminate all distinctions based upon wealth.

Nations and their cultures benefited immensely from this altered point of view; free citizenship was no longer limited to the patricians and the rich. Elevation of the masses to citizenship brought great numbers of new workers into the workshops of culture. Mental growth was accelerated by the spread of education, swelling the forces working for the advance of culture.

By upholding the view that the lawful authority of rulers of States comes from God, the Church contributed to their power for good, since the Christian faithful subject to their authority considered it a conscientious duty to co-operate for the common good of all citizens.

Equally positive and effective were the regulations established for foreign missions in countries abroad. In places where Christianity had not yet mustered a considerable number of followers, the native cultures even there found in the Church an ardent advocate of their cause, eager to protect their valuable elements.

In a statement issued in 1659 by the Sacred Congregation for the Propagation of the Faith to bishops and missionaries in China, the following instructions were given: "Do not try to induce people to give up their native customs, insofar as these do not conflict with faith and morality. It would be as ridiculous for you to do so as to try to move the French, Italian or Spanish cultures to the Far East. Instead, you should introduce there the faith alone, which recognizes the legitimacy of every custom and of national cultural habits, and enjoins that such be respected."

Closer to our own day (Easter of 1922), the same Sacred Congregation, in a letter addressed to the heads of foreign missions, inquired "whether in the decoration of sacred edifices and missionaries' residences the forms of foreign art are the only ones being used, or whether, in so far as possible, the characteristics of native art are being befittingly retained."

A letter in a similar vein by Archbishop Celso Costantini, then

Apostolic Delegate to China, urged the necessity of employing the native art in the construction of Christian churches in China.[2]

In modern times, the Church has repeatedly insisted on the application of this criterion in matters of ecclesiastical architecture and has even extended the principle to include all other phases of national culture in missionary countries.

The fruits of the care taken by the Church to foster national cultures have already become apparent. In the Far East we find Christian natives who, though above the average, are nevertheless part and parcel of their environment. The only external evidence of their Christian upbringing is that generally they are better clothed, more resourceful, more prosperous and on a higher intellectual plane than their fellow citizens belonging to the Hindu or Buddhist cults.

The *internal differences,* however, are far more profound. Members of the Christian faith in the Far East often are physically and spiritually more efficient, more adaptable and better trained for enlightened citizenship than adherents of other beliefs. These differences are most instructive and interesting when viewed at close range.

The author of this study had the opportunity of visiting the Far East in 1936 and 1937. As a result of research, he reached the conclusion that peoples of the Far East possess many virtues and natural attributes that would tell heavily in favor of their national cultures if these were integrated with Christianity and if the Christian faith were commonly accepted by a majority of the natives.

Instance after instance, country after country in the Far East, could be cited as illustrations to support this thesis.

Let us consider, for example, such countries as Japan, China and India. In Japan there are but few Catholics and yet, because of their changed outlook, many of them have been able to gain the confidence of the government and society. While the majority of Japanese are only distinguished by intense patriotism and sacrifice for the Emperor, the Catholics are characterized by honesty and ethical standards.

In China, where ancient forms of rugged individualism have, until recently, precluded a full growth of patriotism and made for much internal dissension—now forgotten in the war of resistance

[2] Archbishop Celso Costantini, "The Need of a Sino-Christian Architecture for Our Catholic Missions." (Bulletin No. 3 of the Catholic University of Peking, September 1927, pp. 7-15.)

to Japanese aggression—the native Catholics reveal themselves as devoted patriots, a strong force for national reconstruction, showing every disposition to work for national solidarity and the creative upbuilding of Chinese culture.

Typical of this spirit is a letter of Bishop Paul Yu-Pin, Vicar Apostolic of Nanking, dated July 22, 1937, which adequately sums up the reactions and feelings of the Catholics in that great country.[3] He wrote:

"We must give an example of obedience to the Government; we must rise like one man and perform our duty—a duty which the war places on us. We must bear arms in defense of our country and die heroically, if we must. All of us who cannot go to the front must work behind the lines, since that is almost as important as work at the front, in modern war. In time of war no Christian may stand on the sidelines. Those who possess property ought to surrender it to the government. Those who are strong should fight. We direct that all schools within our diocese shall make ready to receive the wounded, if need arises. Women and children must train themselves in the art of nursing. From today on, no effort should be spared in gathering wool, cheesecloth, cotton and whatever may be useful."

In India, the Catholics are exerting great efforts to liquidate the caste system which divides the entire nation into many separatist groups, each avoiding the society of the other. They have become the progenitors of a wholesome democracy, whereby equality of citizenship may be realized and the cause of national unity advanced. Thus they are contributing the wherewithal to construct a powerful Indian State and to enrich the composition of the native culture with the most ideal elements. Under the guidance of their bishops, they strive also to bring about indispensable social and economic reforms, in conformity with the principles of Christian social justice. In a country where so many millions live in dire poverty these reforms are imperative.

In all countries where Christianity has gained a majority in the population, as well as in the missionary countries, the activity of the Church in behalf of the national culture has been invariably beneficial.

[3] Bishop Paul Yu-Pin, Pastoral Letter, July 22, 1937. (Cf. "The Voice of the Church in China." London, Longmans, Green and Co., 1938, p. 43.)

IV

BREACHES OF FAITH WITH THE CHURCH ON THE PART OF CERTAIN EUROPEAN POWERS IN THE COURSE OF AGES

Not all nations that accepted the tenets of Christianity have remained true to the Church. Many of them, despite their early religious zeal upon conversion, came later to show infidelity to its principles. At different periods of their history they began to engraft upon the Christian religion a schematic and conventional formalism, instead of maintaining its essential structure intact.

The principles of justice and brotherhood among men, upon which all the teachings of Christianity pivot, became a dead letter. Within such nations the poor were left at the mercy of the rich who preyed upon the misery of the former, misusing their wealth for their own selfish satisfaction. The treatment they accorded to neighbor nations was invariably cruel. For this reason we find on the one hand a tendency to exterminate neighbor nations; on the other an increasingly distressed condition of the poor dwelling "within their gates."

The most prone to strike at the very foundations of Christian ethics were the Germans, who ruthlessly destroyed the monuments of Greco-Roman culture and exterminated the Slavonic nations adjacent to the present Northern and Central-Eastern parts of Germany.

Despite the undoubted progress in many fields that came with their acceptance of the Church's teachings, many of them later forsook some of the most essential ethical principles of Christianity.

Why has this happened? How is one to explain this breach of faith with the Church's ideology by so large a part of a nation that had the opportunity of becoming intimately acquainted with it?

The answer is not difficult to find. Like many other European nations, they were not adequately prepared to receive the religion of Christ. To conquer their faults and sensuality would have required a prolonged period of sustained effort. One might note, also, that the process of conversion was carried to completion too quickly. This explains why, instead of triumphing over the weaknesses of the national character, Christianity became but a thin veneer, with the result that in every crisis the more deeply rooted primitive instincts cropped up and led to the perversion of the Church's ideology—to a moral downfall of the nation.

If we compare European nations in general with those of the Far East, we must perforce admit that the latter, particularly Hindus and Chinese, possess many natural moral attributes and that they are, in consequence, if not better, at least, as well prepared to receive Christian ideals as were the European nations before their conversion.

It is unfortunate that Christianity did not simultaneously find its way to the Far East. This would have been of momentous importance for the Church. For the nations of the Orient might have better appreciated the value of Christian moral principles and yielded more readily to their influence. Deeply religious in temperament, they might have profited more by Christianity than did the European nations and could then have helped Europe to maintain its moral balance and avoid spiritual collapse.

It now remains to discuss Nazi nationalism and its relation to Christianity.

V

Nazi Nationalism and the Church

German National Socialism, otherwise known as Nazism, or racism, represents an unusually ambitious attempt at basing culture and all aspects of individual and collective life upon a purely terrestrial foundation, without reference to the Christian order. In this respect it resembles Russian communism, differing only in this—that it glorifies the nation rather than the working class. Its chief ideological expedient is the concept of racial superiority.

That so-called races differ notably from one another as regards psychic and physical qualities cannot be denied. Some are well developed both physically and spiritually, while others are far from this goal. Unquestionably there are heritable physical differences that mark off one *biological* race from another, and, as for race in the *sociological* sense, the higher its cultural level, the more pronounced are the physical and psychic attributes that distinguish it.

The racist theory is not a German invention. Among the earliest exponents of the doctrine was a French writer, M. Arthur J. de Gobineau, whose work, entitled *Essai sur l'inégalité des races humaines* ("An Essay on the Inequality among Races of Men"), was published at Paris in 1853 and 1856. He attempted to prove that the Nordic race is superior, and among the latter included Germans as well as Frenchmen residing in the northern and central provinces of France. He stayed within the bounds of his special interest and did not engage in criticism of Christianity. His most characteristic statement was to the effect that: "Christianity neither creates nor changes the aptitude for civilization."[4]

Much interest was shown in his work, particularly in Germany. Many public discussions were held concerning its central theme, and here and there Gobineau societies sprang up. It cannot be said, however, that the discussions proved popular.

Interest therein was reawakened in 1898, after the appearance of a new book on racism by Houston Stewart Chamberlain, entitled *Die Grundlagen des neunzehnten Jahrhunderts* ("Foundations of the 19th Century," München, 1898). The author, a native born Englishman, had become so infatuated with the German race that he domiciled himself in Germany, accepted German citizenship and undertook zealously to extol the German-Nordic race. In his book, he placed that race above all others and made no effort to conceal his antipathy for the Jews.

Portraying the Nordic-German race in the best light possible, both these writers credited it with unique cultural abilities.

But if racism was not a conception of German origin, it soon won adherents in Germany, because it flattered German national pride. Indeed, after World War I, racism became the favorite topic of discussion. Disillusioned and humiliated in 1919 by the treaty of Versailles, spiritually depressed Germany had reached its lowest ebb. At this point, Hans Günther, Adolf Hitler and Alfred Rosenberg entered the arena of German life. They seized upon the concept of racism as an expedient for reviving a waning national spirit. Günther[5] prepared a complete program of action and organization for the German people, basing it upon the principles of racism. Hitler devoted himself mostly to the ex-

---

[4] "Le Christianisme ne créé pas et ne transforme pas l'aptitude civilisatrice." (M. A. Gobineau, *Essai sur l'inégalité des races humaines*. Paris, 1853, p. 102.)

[5] Hans K. Günther, *Rassenkunde des Deutschen Volkes*, 3 ed., 1930.

position of political racism, while Rosenberg revaluated the Christian ideology in terms of the new doctrine.

In this new form, racism achieved an ultra-nationalist character, breathing hatred of everything non-German, expressing the urge to dominate not only Europe but the entire world. Taking a quick hold in cities and villages, the idea soon swept the entire nation and became a popular movement. Its growth was further accelerated by its anti-Communist orientation.

Broken spiritually, threatened by a powerful Communistic movement, the Germans looked upon racism as their only means of salvation. Racism was represented as the panacea for all national failings and sicknesses, as an instrument with which to achieve every national ambition.

Adopting the reversed broken cross or swastika as emblem of its ideology, the National Socialist Party grew by leaps and bounds— its black symbol being more and more flaunted from balconies, in shop windows and in homes. Hitler, its founder and director, waxed in power and influence, until in 1933 a majority of votes carried him into the office of chancellor or prime minister and soon thereafter made him president of the Third Reich. His subjects called him Führer, or leader. In his new rôle he became master of all the Reich, wielding the power of life and death over its citizens, such as no one before him had ever possessed in Germany.

From then on racism became the absolute social and political creed, while Hitler's *Mein Kampf* ("My Struggle"), first printed in 1925-27, became the Bible of the German people. All public and private life was organized strictly on the principle of racism, with the government extending its jealous hand over the care of youth. Alfred Rosenberg, author of *Der Mythus des 20. Jahrhunderts* ("Myth of the 20th Century"—first printed in 1930), became the leader of German youth and his book was placed in every school library throughout the country.

It may be said that just as the reversed, black swastika represents a crooked or broken cross, so also the entire ideology of Hitlerian racism represents a complete perversion of the Christian ideology and all other systems based upon the existence of God and man's future life. However, neither the psychosis of defeatism which overtook Germany upon the conclusion of World War I in 1918 nor the fear of Communism fully explains the extraordinary success of racism. We must seek further and deeper reasons for this history-making capitulation of a great portion of the nation to a new, atheistic doctrine. Where are we to find them? No-where else than in the structural and cultural weaknesses of the German character.

A perusal of German literature of the latter half of the 19th and the 20th centuries, in the fields of belles-lettres, science and phi-losophy, leaves an unfavorable impression because of the surpris-ingly large number of warped mentalities one encounters therein. The works of German writers, scholars, poets, philosophers, an-thropologists, psychologists, sociologists and all types of learned men suggest that one has to do with minds that are tendentially destructive.

Historically, it must be noted, that all movements which have aimed at the destruction of the Christian ideology have had their origin in Germany. It was there that Marxism found its birth-place, Communism being an outstanding example and the root whence most other materialistic philosophies have sprung.

In the company of Marx and Engels, the pair who fathered Communism, we see Strauss, Feuerbach, Vogt, Moleschott, Büchner and a whole group of similar mentalities. By the side of Paul Alsberg[6] and Ludwig Klages,[7] anthropologists and psychol-ogists who propounded the so-called "life pan-romanticism" doc-trine and proclaimed it the worthy goal of every Dyonysian,[8] were: D. H. Kerler[9] and Nicolai Hartmann,[10] postulatory atheists who recognized the right of every man to live as he pleases, regardless of rules, conventions, or consequences.

Among the latter group we find Friedrich Nietzsche[11] and Leopold Ziegler.[12] Nietzsche was a cunning egoist who visualized his "I" in everything: in his ideas, his likes, in gratification of the senses and in his contempt for all the priceless acquisitions of civilization. He represents a type absolutely devoid of self-control, desirous of destroying every cultural work, while seeking to impose his own rule upon the ruins.

Nietzsche does not recognize God. "If there were Gods"—he

[6] Paul Alsberg, *Das Menschheitsrätsel*, Dresden, 1922.

[7] Ludwig Klages, *Mensch und Erde,* Leipzig, 1920; Vom Wesen des Bewusstseine, Leipzig, 1921; *Vom Kosmologischen Eros*, München, 1922.

[8] *Dyonysius, sensuous Tyrant of Syracuse,* 430-367 B.C.

[9] D. H. Kerler, *Weltwille und Wertwille,* Leipzig, 1926.

[10] Nicolai Hartmann, *Ethik*, Berlin-Leipzig, 1926.

[11] Friedrich Nietzsche, *Also Sprach Zarathustra,* 2 ed., Leipzig, 1893; Jenseits von Gut and Böse, 3 ed., Leipzig, 1891.

[12] Leopold Ziegler, *Der Gestalltwandel der Götter,* 3 ed., Leipzig, 1922.

shrieks in a moment of exaltation—"could I endure not to be a God? Hence there are not any."

Voicing his hatred and contempt for Christianity and its moral teachings, which he terms a refuge for the weak and for the rabble, he would set up in its place a morality of brute force which would be used to crush all opponents and to subject them to his iron will To break every law of society, to obliterate all concepts of moral decency, to extinguish the lights of civilization—anything, in fact, standing in the way of his will to conquer—would justify for him the use of any means.

In his own estimation, Nietzsche is a "superman," the supreme aristocrat of the brain. Only that is good which will enable him to reach his goal.

The other, Leopold Ziegler,[12] in a moment of atheistic reflection tinged with anthropological mysticism, avers that man, after dispensing with God, should take His place and endow himself with all God's attributes. Ziegler insists that for this reason he is really a "religious man"—a "devout believer."

Both thinkers, Nietzsche and Ziegler, beyond all others, charted the course of Nazi ideology. Their influence, in conjunction with other contributing factors, gave rise to radical nationalism. Nor may one object that none of the above listed writers was popular enough or sufficiently known to have had considerable influence upon current German thought. Everyone of them in fact had numerous disciples and readers and some of them were exceptionally popular with the public.

Among the latter were especially Büchner and Nietzsche. Büchner's book, entitled *Kraft und Stoff* ("Force and Matter"), first published in 1855, saw a whole succession of editions and reached an incredibly wide circle of laboring class readers. Nietzsche was a favorite with the German intelligentsia and was extensively read by the youth in schools. In fact, a large part of the country came under the unhealthy influence of these writers. Others, not directly influenced, succumbed to the general atmosphere of spiritual pessimism, or fell into a condition of ideological indifference.

Among foreign writers, the greatest influence was exerted by Charles Darwin, who propounded the theory of evolution of organic species through natural selection. His theory of a struggle for existence among all organic beings—the survival of the strongest in the battle for life—was acclaimed by Karl Marx as the greatest scientific discovery of all time; the key to all human progress and history.

So prepared, Germany proved a fertile and ready soil for the nationalistic ideology of Nazism. The seed thus sown was not slow to sprout and yield a plentiful harvest. What, then, are the guiding principles of this radical national movement which, starting in 1933, has succeeded in overpowering the will of an entire nation?

VI

THE IDEOLOGY OF NAZISM

If we carefully read Adolf Hitler's *Mein Kampf* ("My Struggle"), or closely acquaint ourselves with Alfred Rosenberg's *Der Mythus des 20. Jahrhunderts* ("Myth of the 20th Century") and his many other books; if we examine the whole range of an already vast Nazi literature, we shall find that the underlying principles of the movement are based on the following piece of reasoning:

The law of natural evolution, which governs the whole world, demands that a superior race be the master of inferior races. Racially the Germans are superior to all other races: Therefore, the German Race should govern the rest. The condition prerequisite to maintaining German rule is the continued preservation of the purity of the Aryan-German Race. Every German is obligated devotedly to guard this racial purity. It is his highest duty. Whatever he may do to accomplish this end, or to promote German power over all the other races, is good, licit and desirable.

Having before us the general scheme of reasoning of the Nazi writers, we may now go into the details. This will facilitate the understanding and co-ordination of the whole idea.

It will make clear why Hitler, when discussing reasons for the German World War defeat in 1918, says: "The deepest and final reason for the downfall of the Reich was the failure to give recognition to the racial problem and its importance in the historical progress of nations." [13] Owing to their failure to recognize their duty to the Race, Germans, he alleges, intermarried with inferior races and this weakened them both physically and spiritually.

[13] Adolf Hitler, *Mein Kampf*, 6 ed., München, 1930. p. 310.

In the animal world the interbreeding of individuals of different races results in inferior progeny, and the same holds true of the human world. A person who intermarries with a person of an inferior race becomes the parent of inferior progeny, thereby violating the natural law which stipulates that a superior person should dominate; for he cannot interbreed with an inferior person and maintain his superiority.

According to Hitler, only a "born idiot" or a "limited person" would consider this law brutal. Accepting the premises as self-evident and indubitably valid, for reasons that are obvious, he emphasizes that it is indispensable for human progress. The contrary view would impede any progress, and civilization would retrograde, its downfall resulting as a foregone conclusion.[14]

America presents an outstanding example: Wherever the purity of the Aryan race—largely a German race in North America—was guarded, there culture stands high; while wherever the Aryans interbred with persons of inferior races, as in Central and South America where the Aryans intermarried with colored races, there culture has sunk to a low level (p. 313).

All great civilizations of the past perished because the blood of races which created them underwent pollution owing to intermixture with inferior races (p. 316).

As regards culture, Hitler bids us remember that it is created by man; hence if one is desirous of insuring the survival of a certain culture, he must seek first of all to insure the preservation of the man who creates it. "Nevertheless, the survival (of culture) is connected with the iron right of necessity and the right to victory of the strongest and the best" (p. 316). In other words, such a man must be assured the means of livelihood, as well as the means of vanquishing the weak.

Victory comes only through battle. "He who wants to live, must fight; he who refuses to fight in a world of constant struggle, is not deserving of life" (p. 317).

As they stand, these principles are nothing more than an application of Darwin's doctrine of the struggle for existence among the lower forms of life—understood in the most brutal sense, in its most elemental form—to relations among men.

Everything we behold, be it in the sphere of culture in general or in art, science, technique and other fields, is in all cases the work of an Aryan. He is the true Prometheus of humanity. In his mind

[14] Adolf Hitler, *Mein Kampf*, page 312.

glows always a divine spark of genius, ever inflammable, acting as a beacon in a dark world of secrets and guiding the way to conquest over all other beings on earth. Were his genius to be annihilated, then within less than a few thousand years darkness would prevail over the whole face of the earth and all culture would eventually disappear (p. 317).

The antithesis of the Aryan is the Jew. He has changed little in the last two thousand years. Being dextrous, he is able to adapt himself to changing conditions of life, but his mind, bereft of any creative ability, assimilates only what others have created, and therefore he has not been able to create his own culture (pp. 329-330).

Hitler and his fellow Nazis perceive no positive virtue in the Jew and present him in the most unfavorable light. According to them, he lacks any idealism and his solidarity becomes evident only when he is in danger, or when it is a matter of sharing in loot. He is a disbeliever in a future life. His religion serves him primarily as an expedient for maintaining the purity of his blood as well as a norm for regulating his intercourse with his fellow Jews, but even more so, his intercourse with non-Jews (pp. 331-362).

Progress in the sphere of culture is not the work of the majority of a nation, but is due to the genial, creative powers of single individuals.

This explains why National Socialism opposes the parliamentary system within its confines. In view of its principles, he who seeks to be its *leader*—to wield the scepter of supreme and unlimited authority—must be prepared to accept the final risks and responsibility (p. 379).

The highest law and most sacred duty for a Nazi is this: Strive to safeguard the purity of the Race, since only through preservation of the best types can humanity be ennobled (pp. 444-449).

This law is also to form the foundation for the education of youth. Its first requirement is the building of a healthy body; it further requires mental inculcation of self-control and building of character, with special emphasis on exercising oneself in decision.

Finally, the child may be exposed to informative education in various fields. Learning, as such, should be regarded merely as a secondary or auxiliary agent. Boys and girls may not leave school until they comprehend the importance of racial purity in human relations.

Military service includes the formal education of boys, while

German girls become the property of the State and achieve citizenship only upon marriage.[15]

It is necessary, insists Hitler, to expand the power of Germany, to increase its holdings in Europe and to obtain colonies. To achieve this end, it is indispensable to make pacts with certain countries and form appropriate organizations within the State.

In no case, however, is a political tie-up with Soviet Russia to be considered. "From a purely military point of view," writes Hitler, "in event of a war waged by Germany and Russia against the Western Powers, even perhaps, against the entire world, such a pact would prove catastrophic. The war would be fought on German, not Russian territory. The very fact of the conclusion of such a pact with Russia would point to an early war, whose consequence would be the end of Germany" (pp. 748-749).

"Germany may achieve its goal through pacts. But it is impossible thereby to augment our military strength. Only by the sword can we conquer France and the other nations, secure land and insure the hegemony of the German race."

During this moment of reflection Hitler felt that "the merciless goddess of revenge" was his ally, and that he would fulfill his oath of November 9, 1918 (p. 406).

In another passage he reiterates this promise of revenge and cries out exultantly: "God, bless our military might; be just and decide whether we deserve freedom! God, bless our war!" (p. 715).

This mention of God is very characteristic of Hitler, especially if we recall that he placed in charge of all education of youth Alfred Rosenberg, a man who makes it a point to persecute religion at every opportunity.

We must, therefore, consider Hitler's use of the Divine name as no more than a figure of speech, since to invoke the aid of the living God, under such circumstances, would be blasphemy. He would, in effect, be asking God to aid him in a highly unethical enterprise: the usurpation of other people's lands, the shackling of their liberty—humanity's greatest gift from God—and the wanton infliction of suffering and death.

To be exact, Hitler does not limit himself to the use of the Divine name in isolated instances. The term "God" appears often in his speeches. Whether Hitler really thinks of God when he uses the term, or whether he employs it simply as a rhetorical ornament, is immaterial. The decisive test is the absolute denial

[15] Adolf Hitler, *Mein Kampf*, pp. 452-491.

of God implied in racism. The God that Hitler invokes cannot be the true God, but must be a new God created by the Nazis. This will become clearer as we proceed.

VII

RELIGION AND NAZISM

What is the relation of racism to religion? Let us give a concise answer to this question, basing it chiefly upon the views expressed by Rosenberg who promulgated them with the approbation of Hitler and the entire National Socialist party of Germany.

According to Rosenberg, religion has no justification for its existence unless it aims to express the inherent value of the Nordic race; unless it seeks to remove the boundary separating the human soul from God. The Christian religion is foreign to German racism. It is based on false premises which were contributed by Jewish, Syrian and Roman influences.[16]

This is not to say that it is lacking in value. It is only necessary to reform it, to purify it and properly explain it. Above all, it must be expurgated of the teachings of the Old Testament, in order to free its adherents from the deplorable influences of the Jewish mind.

Next, it would be necessary, according to the same writer, to purge legend from the New Testament, together with all those features which represent Christ as a meek lamb, Redeemer of sins and Son of God, offering His life in sacrifice for the redemption of mankind (pp. 615-616).

Finally, particular stress should be laid upon those events in Christ's life where He appears as God the Warrior; as an Orator, castigating the masses and throwing out the despoilers from the temple, as a Rebel and Inciter to riot, who brings forth an unsheathed sword and calls men to arms.

In this way, one would come to construct a positive, instead of a negative, Christianity upon the groundwork of the New Testament.

According to Rosenberg, Christ is not a God. He was only an outstanding personality and a hero, deriving His ancestry from the Nordic race of Ammonites. Being really an Aryan, He had no

---

[16] Alfred Rosenberg, *Der Mythus des 20. Jahrhunderts*, München, 1933, p. 76.

connection with the Semitic Jewish race. The most that one could say of Him is that he belonged to the Jews morally, since He was raised and educated among them (p. 76).

This new Christianity, surnamed positive Christianity, achieved through radical reform of the text of the New Testament, would, according to Rosenberg, lead to regeneration of the Nordic race, to revitalization of the Nordic blood, and would conform to the tenets of racism. Love of one's fellow man would find no place in this Christianity (p. 76).

"Undoubtedly," writes Rosenberg, "Christ's religion was the precept of love. However, the German religious movement which someday may develop into a national church, must declare that the ideal of love among men is to be absolutely subordinated to the national honor and that no deed can be named good by the German Church if it does not serve the interests of the nation." [17]

Thus, National Socialism is a veritable Moloch that devours the rising generation, alienating youth from authentic Christian ideals, repudiating love for one's fellow man and perverting the teachings of Christ to its own earthy needs and interests.

From the day of the advent of National Socialism in Germany —from the day when its members first adopted the brown shirt— all Christians, Catholics and Protestants alike (according to Rosenberg), have forfeited their right to existence. Henceforth, they too "must become Germans only, as well as fighters for national honor and existence. . . . They must become members of the new German Church which has become the hope of millions." [18]

The purposes and goals of this new German Church shall be twofold: (a) to remove from German life all factors which are racially foreign to it; (b) to promote the development of the forces inherent in the race.

These forces are to be stimulated continually, for only in this way is it possible to maintain intact the mythic unity and co-operation of the Nordic blood and the Nordic soul, as conditions prerequisite to any creative action.[19]

Further inspection of Rosenberg's views in connection with the theories of racism reveals the frequent use of such terms as

[17] Alfred Rosenberg, *Der Mythus des 20. Jahrhunderts,* 3 ed., München, 1932, p. 596.

[18] Alfred Rosenberg, *Zentrum und Christlicher Volksdienst* (National-Sozialistische Monatshefte, April, 1931).

[19] A. Rosenberg, *Der Mythus des 20. Jahrhunderts,* p. 665.

myth, race, the soul of the race. It may be well to define these terms for the sake of clarity. What, then, do they mean?

In scientific literature the concept of *race* is given two meanings: biological and sociological. In the former acceptation, it is confined to delineating the hereditary morphological and physiological characteristics of persons living in a group. In the latter, the concept of race expresses itself in terms of the common culture and history which bind together persons living in the same community.

In Nazi literature, the two senses of the term are often confused. The prevailing meaning ascribed appears to be that the German Nordic race and the German nation are one.

The *soul of a race* expresses all the qualities and strength of a race. "It signifies," says Rosenberg, "the race seen from the inside, as the race, conversely, is the outside of the soul." [20]

Finally, *myth* is given a meaning coextensive with the consciousness of personal strength, which a person recognizes as his due solely by virtue of his belonging to a certain race. "To awaken the soul of a race to life," writes Rosenberg, "means to know its highest worth and to acknowledge its predomination over other values, its proper organic place in the State, as well as in art and in religion. Our task during this century is to create from a new myth of life a new type of man." [21]

This element of "mythical" strength, which is open to the Nordic-German race, has ever been the instrument of progress and creative ability down through the ages. Most commonly it is found in men who have attempted to impose their own will with a lesser or greater degree of force upon persons opposing the existing order and striving to establish upon the ruins thereof something definitely new.

Among such, according to Rosenberg, was the Emperor Diocletian, notorious for his cruel treatment of the Christians. He is said to have possessed blue eyes and a fair complexion, which leads Rosenberg to conclude that he must have come from the German race.

Evidently Rosenberg considers the cruelties of which Diocletian was guilty as virtues, for he describes the Emperor as a "man without a personal fault" (p. 89).

[20] A. Rosenberg, *Zentrum und Christlicher Volksdienst* (National-Sozialistische Monatshefte, April, 1931).
[21] A. Rosenberg, *Der Mythus des 20. Jahrhunderts*, p. 22.

Measured by Rosenberg's standards, the highest-ranking figure of medieval times was the German mystic, Eckehart, reputed to have opposed the teachings of the Church and to have advocated unlimited personal liberty not only in reference to other men, but also in relation to God. Inasmuch as Eckehart is alleged to have energetically opposed any conception of God distinct from the human soul, Rosenberg does not hesitate to conclude that he was the creator of the renaissance of German culture (p. 228).

The best examples of the mythical strength of the German Race in modern times are said to have been Frederick the Great and Bismarck of Kulturkampf fame, both notorious persecutors of the Polish nation.

The longing for a life enriched with these qualities peculiar to their race has been universal with the German people throughout their whole history. It manifested itself strikingly in the cult of the Germanic God Odin or Wodan who symbolizes the aforesaid longing of Germans for their ideal life, he being the most esteemed of all their Gods—"He was for all Germans a faithful reflection of the primitive spiritual forces of the Nordic man" (p. 644).

The time is now at hand for the realization of this longing. Evidence must be given of the power of the German Race. The immemorial urge to base German life upon authentic German cultural foundations must needs be fulfilled, if the Germans are to ensure for their nation a leading rôle among all the nations of the world.

In accordance with its destiny, as typified by the Nordic-German virtues, the German people must become the leading nation among all the nations in Europe. All nations—according to Rosenberg's ideas—ought to recognize this by submitting to the German will. Such submission will be the best guarantee for the continued existence and future of Europe.[22] Those who oppose this will, do so at their own peril—willy-nilly, they shall be forced to give way thereto.

The Germans are sure of themselves, this assurance being an attribute of their race. They are gaining a growing consciousness of the strength which is patent to their blood. It is God-like; in fact, it is God Himself. Rosenberg expresses this thought in the following words: "The God whom we worship would not exist

---

[22] "Europe," says Rosenberg, "its existence and future, will today find their protection primarily in Berlin." (Cf. his *Der entscheidende Weltkampf, Rede auf dem Parteikongress in Nürnberg, 1936*, München, 1936.)

at all if our soul and our blood did not exist—that is how Master Eckehart would formulate it for our day." [23] German blood constitutes the Godly nature in Nordic man, and it is a source of grace and gifts which flow out from it more abundantly than from the sacraments of the Christian religion.

This is, then, naturalistic monism or practical atheism, dressed up and presented in the form of German Messianism, buttressed exclusively upon the conscious feeling of power, seeking forcibly to impose its will upon others. In some strange way this atheism is identified with the deification of the German nation in the place of God.

"The highest values brought by raciation to the German soul," says another Nazi writer, Walter Grundman, "are honor and freedom. These values are interrelated internally and they determine myth—the consciousness of power inherent in the German race." [24]

Concerning the other benefits which are to accrue to the German people through National Socialism based on racism, Rosenberg wrote on October 14, 1930 (the date of the first victory of the Nazi movement), as follows:

"The National Socialist movement is the only representative of free German thought and of thoughts on social justice; it is representative of the tendency to purify the entire national life from corruption and humiliation. Yesterday it was empowered to tell the whole world: Within our camp is the Germany of the future." [25]

Courage ought to be the chief virtue of Nazi Germany. Germans must eradicate cowardice from their midst. They must remember that "cowards have never built a world. Hence, whoever wants to progress must burn his bridges behind him." [26]

Unquestionably, those who have suffered themselves to be carried away by the Nazi torrent have burned their bridges behind them, forsaking the ideals of Christian culture and the priceless treasures contained in Christ's teachings. The first to be engulfed by the Nazi flood were the youth. With the co-operation of State officials, an Alliance of the German Faith, or German Church, was

[23] Alfred Rosenberg, *Der Mythus des 20. Jahrhunderts*, p. 685.
[24] Dr. Walter Grundman, *Gott und Nation*, 2 ed. Berlin, 1933, p. 82.
[25] A. Rosenberg, *Zum Sieg am 14 September* (Völkischer Beobachter, 16 September, 1930).
[26] A. Rosenberg, *Der Mythus des 20. Jahrhunderts*, p. 22.

formed, headed by Prof. J. W. Hauer. This Alliance has succeeded by means of the platform and printing press in setting up a powerful machinery of propaganda, reaching out into every city, town and hamlet in Germany, seeking to gather all citizens into the fold of the new church and to wage continuous warfare in its behalf.

In addition to the Alliance, or German Church, there exists in Germany the Neo-Pagan Alliance, devoted to the same ends as the former and differing only in this, that it plans to revive the cult of ancient German gods, especially of Wodan or Odin. Among its chief partisans was the late General Ludendorff, who lived in virulent hatred of the Christian religion.

Besides the two mentioned, we find also the Alliance of German Christians which occupies a position midway between them. Accepting in principle all the ideas of racism, it nevertheless tries to reconcile the Christian religion with racism by eliminating from the Christian doctrine everything not in accord therewith.

The last mentioned Alliance was founded for those who find it difficult to break off their ties with Christianity and prefer to adhere to its teachings in the small measure consistent with a preponderant devotion to race.

This *Alliance of German Christians,* which purveys racism to its members in painless fashion, resembles the *Living Russian Orthodox Church* in bolshevik Russia. The structure and scope of both are similar.

Adolf Hitler is looked upon by its members as a providential personality. Some consider him a redeemer of Germany, others an intermediary between Christ and all peoples.

Julius Leutheuser, counsellor of the Protestant church and member of the second group, writes thus:

"Adolf Hitler is our living witness of the present era, who confirms the good works of the eternal Divine Spirit in history; and who, through his activity, enables us to understand in a new way the teachings of Christ and His mission. Our watchword is not that Hitler is equal to Christ, but: Through Hitler to Jesus Christ." [27]

The comparison of Hitler to Christ shows to what an extent Christian doctrine has been perverted even within the membership of the German Christian Alliance.

Since German Christians in general had no wish to break with

[27] Julius Leutheuser, *Die Deutsche Christengemeinde und ihre Gegner,* Weimar, 1933, pp. 21-22.

the faith of their fathers, while the exponents of racism found in Christianity the chief obstacle to achieving the national goal they had set for themselves, this compromise movement was foredoomed to failure. Lacking in popularity, its influence upon the masses was insignificant.

On the other hand, the German Faith movement, represented by the new German Church, did take hold and became very popular with all classes of Germans. The plans for its construction were formulated by Rosenberg.

Amply subsidized by the Reich government, its activity encompassed every field of human endeavor. No amount of public money was spared to promote its growth; to hire speakers and propagandists who delivered countless talks and lectures. Special meetings and academies were constantly convoked, while the printing presses were kept busy turning out books and pamphlets.

In every case of protest on the part of aggrieved listeners, the police were invariably on hand to give support and protection to the speakers.

At the same time, increased pressure was exerted upon the Protestants and Catholics alike to make them more amenable to the influence of the new anti-religious movement. They defended themselves as long as they could, but their situation became daily more difficult. The chief means of defense was passive opposition.

The following incident serves as an illustration:

One day in 1935, Prof. Hauer, director of the German Church movement, appeared in Münster for the purpose of addressing a meeting. As usual, the daily press gave him much favorable publicity. Thousands of people appeared at the station. Catholic and Protestant students also appeared in great numbers. These came earlier than the others and surrounded the automobile in which Prof. Hauer was to ride. When he entered and the car moved on, they obstructed its progress and prevented it from moving rapidly.

At length, however, Prof. Hauer reached Münster-land-hall where he was to speak. To his great surprise he soon learned that the majority of his listeners were Catholic and Protestant students who, immediately upon his arrival, began to chant religious songs. The singing was continuous, the police were powerless to prevent it, and the Professor, unable to speak, finally departed.

There were many like cases in Germany, in which the police engaged in altercations with the crowds, administered many beatings and made many arrests.

On the occasion in question, however, there was no assault. Instead, on the following morning, police appeared at the residence of Bishop von Galen, announcing his arrest. The bishop asked a few minutes' delay to make a change in clothing. He shortly reappeared, dressed in the liturgical garb of his office. He was ordered to remove the clothing in favor of civilian garb, but refused. Baffled, the police left. In 1935 the Nazis did not feel themselves as strong as at present. They lacked the courage to arrest a bishop in a Catholic city, garbed in the regalia of his office.

With the passing of time, however, the Nazis became increasingly bold. Passive opposition became less frequent, since more and more it had to be atoned for in blood, in prison sentences, beatings and confinement in concentration camps.

The iron hand of Nazidom came down heavily upon both Catholics and Protestants. The former presented a more difficult problem, for they had the support of the German Center Party. Thanks to a measure of autonomy in its religious belief and to the teaching of religion in schools, the Center was strongly entrenched among German youth.

For this reason, the Center became the first target of the Nazis. In a speech delivered in the Reichstag on February 28, 1932, Rosenberg said: "Until the Center is conquered, there can be no renaissance of Germany." Promises, threats, treachery and other means were employed, ending finally in the dissolution of this party.

The next objects of attack were professional and trade organizations of youth. These organizations were destroyed at one fell swoop.

One would think that these acts would have satiated the Nazis, especially in view of the fact that the concordat they had entered into with Rome in 1933 stipulated freedom for Church activity. Notwithstanding this pledge, however, the Nazis, now literally drunk with power, seized all Catholic schools, withheld the right of teaching from religious orders, canceled the right to give religious instruction and did all within their power to undermine the influence of the Catholic clergy upon the faithful.

No means was neglected to achieve this end. One of the methods used was to ridicule and defame the clergy by summoning them into court to stand trial for trumped-up and imaginary misdeeds.

Finally, the publication of religious newspapers was suspended and State control was extended not only to the pulpit but to purely ecclesiastical matters as well. The minutest transgression of these police rules, the most trifling insubordination was punished by confinement in concentration camps and prisons, or by secret executions.

The Catholics continued to resist this effort to enslave them. Bishops met in assembly to study means of opposing the persecution and they frequently expressed their opinions in the public press, calling attention to Nazi errors. The Government, however, was quick to place a ban on such publication and to prohibit all such criticism, whether by letter or otherwise.

Some of the bishops showed unusual courage in defending the purity of the faith. Among these was Cardinal Faulhaber, Archbishop of Munich. In 1933, during five Sundays in Advent, he delivered a series of powerful sermons entitled: "Judaism, Christianity and Germany." In one sermon he turned to the Protestants and besought their support for the common cause. He found an immediate and enthusiastic response.

Equally courageous were the sermons in Dresden of Rev. Father George, S. J., Crown Prince of Saxony, who called attention to the danger to which Germany was exposed.

Yet, if we reflect on the enormity of the evil impending from the results of the Nazi movement, if we picture to ourselves the deplorable consequences that the Nazi propagation of racism portended for the German nation, then we are forced to confess that, considering the gravity of the danger, the Catholic reaction was comparatively feeble. Neither in its intensity nor its extensity was it at all adequate to forestall the catastrophe. Indeed, the issues at stake were of the utmost gravity, bound up with the highest ideals, with principles that should have been defended without compromise, with unflinching decisiveness, even to the point of death.

Still more feeble was the reaction among the Protestants, notwithstanding their numerical strength, although, in justice, it must be admitted that many of their leading pastors opposed the errors of racism and were subjected, along with the Catholics, to cruel persecution.

After they had been in the saddle for several years, wielding this almost unlimited power, the Nazis succeeded in bringing the entire German nation to heel and forcing it, in sheer terror, to conform to their designs. The secret police, known as the Gestapo, were able to extend their domination over the private lives of citizens through the medium of wire-tapping, violation of privacy of the mails and the use of every means and device.

They took over control of all public offices, the public press and book publishing plants; in fact, every field of German activity. At the present time there is not a single daily newspaper or other publication that does not conform abjectly to Nazi ideology, not one book that dares to deal with the Nazi order in critical or objective fashion.

From the very first, the Nazi government extended its paternalism to include the German youth—this in keeping with its cardinal tenet that all children are the property of the State.

Torn away from the influence of their parents and pastors, prevented from attending church services, the children soon became spies within their own homes, their very souls poisoned with hate toward everything non-German and inoculated with the virus of neo-paganism. They were urged to make no distinction between good or bad. Murder, treachery and robbery were held up as heroic deeds, provided such crimes were of use in subjugating other nations.

Moreover, the Nazi practice has been to instruct youths in sexual matters and to impress upon them their duty of maintaining the purity of their race; the need of sterilizing the sick and all hereditary defectives.

The consequences of such an upbringing have disclosed themselves in all their repulsive nakedness; they are moral deterioration, nationalistic chauvinism and the disappearance of all higher ideals.

Frequently parades are staged for the young, calculated to acquaint them with Odin and the other pagan gods of ancient German mythology. Great numbers of youths take part in these festivals, carrying sunshields and other symbols of the old pagan faith. They sing songs that breathe a hatred for God, the clergy, Christianity and all supernatural ideals. Here is one example:

> "Gone are the days; but the cleric remains
> Who robs our national soul:
> Be he of Roman or Lutheran rite,
> He teaches the Jewish faith.
>
> Gone are the days of the cross;
> A pillar of sun climbs the heaven:

> At last we shall be free from God—
> Free to sing the praises of the nation."

The war upon Christianity continues unabated. At every opportunity religion is ridiculed and abased, while its adherents, Catholic or Protestant, are treated almost like traitors.

The mouths of Germans citizens are gagged; they cease to speak or confide. They live in terror of all men and even their own children. Secrets are discussed only behind closed doors and in fear of betrayal by immediate relatives. Timid persons refrain from expressing their opinion on any matter, lest they betray their thoughts.

Persons not belonging to the ruling class live in constant dread of their lives. The slightest criticism meets with stern reprisal. Huge concentration camps have been established at Dachau, Oranienburg and other points and victims from all over the Reich are brought to them.

These unfortunates are tortured in a most inhuman fashion. Often they are transported in freight cars over a period of weeks, many of them dying on the way from cold, hunger, thirst and privation; others so weakened that they are unable to leave the trains.

Prisons are filled to overflowing. In an increasing number of instances, urns containing the ashes of loved ones are all that come back to the sorrowing relatives.

Here and there, before the war, persons in great anguish of soul were wont to whisper: "We look forward to war, but a war in which Germany will be defeated, since only then will personal freedom be restored to us."

Externally, Germany gives the appearance of a unified nation, harmonized ideologically, invincible politically. At every election the Nazis boast of a 100% majority. Usually on such occasions, nobody would stand on his rights or play the hero, seeing that a sanguinary penalty would be summarily exacted.

In 1935, Dr. J. Goebbels, Nazi minister of propaganda, made the unconsciously sardonic statement, "National Socialism has simplified thinking for the German nation and brought it back to its earlier and primitive form." [28]

What he said is indisputably true.

The Nazis have simplified not only thinking, but everything else

---

[28] Dr. Joseph Goebbels, *Wesen und Gestalt des Nazionalsozialismus*, Berlin, 1935, p. 6.

in their country. They have reverted atavistically to the earliest form of Teutonic barbarism and cruelty. It is to be regretted that Dr. Goebbels did not shed light on how this "simplification" was accomplished.

Such, in outline, is Nazi racism as incarnated in the private and public life of Germany. In what way does this racism affect German relations with other nations?

VIII

Racism as Applied to the Foreign Policy of the Reich

After vanquishing the German nation and usurping power in every sphere of that country's national life, the Nazis made ready to carry out their plans regarding other nations. The goal was well defined: To conquer them, to subject them to their will, to subjugate them in Europe and in the entire world, if possible.

Since no nation would submit to the dictates of Nazi Germany voluntarily, the use of force was indicated.

Before taking the final step, they proceeded to gather secretly—and with the connivance of international munition and oil mongers—huge stores of armament, ammunition, oil products, planes, tanks, the most modern guns and vast amounts of raw materials. After they felt sure that they were strong enough to meet any foe, they began to provoke their immediate neighbors. Under their brutally wanton attacks fell first Austria, then Czechoslovakia, Poland, Norway, Holland, Belgium, France, Yugoslavia and Greece.

Every treaty, every moral obligation, was violated—thrown to the four winds. The law of nations and all considerations of humanity were ruthlessly cast aside.

Against all precedent in the previous history of the world, the methods used in waging total war became so cruel as to shock the conscience of the whole civilized world. No one had ever dreamt that any nation could fall to so low a moral level—could stoop to such fiendish cruelty. Ravaged and outraged Poland stands as a monument of infamy testifying to the lengths to which Nazi savagery (with Russian aid) could go.[29]

---

[29] Russian Communism, which at the beginning of the Second World War aided Germany in the latter's destructive onslaught on European nations, represents the same danger to Western culture as Nazism, nay, in all probability, even a greater

One thing, however, must be admitted—the Nazis are capable of acting logically. Having announced their plans in advance and finding the principles of racism adequate, they carried them out unflinchingly.

IX

CRITICAL NOTES ON RACISM

We have seen that racism, coupled with unexampled nationalistic chauvinism, glorifies murder and brutality in vindication of the German people's claim as a superior race to rule the entire world.

(1) This theory of a superior race and its rights is based on Darwin's theory of the struggle for existence and the survival of the fittest, according to which the right to survive is reserved to the stronger animals able to vanquish the weaker. This theory assumes diabolical significance when applied to humans. In the subhuman world, the lower animals are guided by their instinct of self-preservation when confronted with starvation or enemies. Once their hunger is satiated, however, or the peril averted, they ordinarily desist from their instinctive cruelty, and thanks to this respite, the weaker animals are able to survive and thrive in the vicinity of the stronger.

Man, on the other hand, knows not the limits of the animal appetite and, if he be an adherent of German racism, he will never be satiated until the very last alien nation is subjugated. This is so because man is guided not by his savage instincts alone, but by universal reason, which never ceases to remind him that there are yet other nations still unconquered, which nevertheless ought to be conquered, in accordance with his absolutely general theory of life.

In proof, we may consider the long series of consecutive attacks upon neighbor nations undertaken by Nazi Germany.

(2) By basing the whole of German life upon German blood

danger. Poland, which has suffered so much at the hands of Bolshevist Russia, understands better than any other nation the nature of that danger, and the United Nations will do well to listen to Poland in this matter. The fact that they now fight shoulder to shoulder with Russia against a common foe must not blind them to the fact that Communist Russia itself constitutes a formidable menace to the civilized world. Hence, however necessary it be for us to give help to Russia now, it behooves us, at the same time, to take the steps needed to guard ourselves against this new danger, which is bound to loom large at the close of the present war.

exclusively, by divorcing it from the teachings of religion and
ethics, the foundation is laid for man's complete reversion to a
state of barbarism. Deprived of all moral inhibitions, man surrenders to his lowest instincts—to every animal impulse, the final
result being his complete moral downfall.

As was to be expected, Nazi Germany has, in an extremely short
space of time, sunk to this nadir of moral degradation, a condition
that is evidenced by its wholesale murder of civilians and the inhuman treatment it accords to subjugated peoples. All these facts
are symptomatic of utter obtuseness with regard to moral values.

(3) Nazi writers are ecstatic in their admiration of the alleged
virtues of the German Race. In singing its praises, they point to
the necessity of maintaining the purity of the German blood, in
order to promote the nation's further progress. However, once
German life has been based on strictly Nazi principles, this so-
called superior German race takes on the lineaments of an ogre
in its lust to subjugate and enslave other peoples, under penalty of
annihilation, should they resist its despotic will.

Thus, the entire civilized world is in immediate danger of
extinction at the hands of Nazi racism, and it is imperative that
adequate steps be taken to check its onward course.

(4) Racism, as developed by the Nazis, was represented as a
blessing for Germany and the entire world. In practice, it has been
a curse not only to Germany but to all European nations. It has
involved the European nations willy-nilly in the most brutal war
ever known in human history, and has brought Germany to complete spiritual collapse.

(5) According to the theorists of racism, the German Race was
to be kept in its purity in order that it might contribute to the
highest type of culture. Instead, Western culture is now tottering
on the brink of a precipice while the priceless treasures of culture
are a heap of smoking ruins. Hundreds of genial minds have been
exterminated, or their cultural efforts impeded for a long time to
come.

(6) German youths, having been reared in hatred of other
races as well as of the adult population, are bereft of every human
feeling and every ethical consideration, with the result that they
now lead lives at variance with fundamental moral rules.

The German nation now finds itself in a very difficult situation.
It will require enormous effort to bring it, and particularly German youth, back to normal ethical standards. Weakened spir-

itually, the Germans will be unable to cope with their ethical problem unless they are given disciplinary aid from without.

(7) German racism has impregnated the souls of all Nazis and undermined the moral sense of even those citizens who opposed it. How else may one explain the fact that in this most unjust of all wars the young and the old seem satisfied with their success in murder and plunder and give every evidence of solidarity in thought and action?

Where are the Protestants and the Catholics? Have they forgotten the teachings of the Master and the principles of Christian morality, that they show no reluctance to participate in this war? Have they nothing to say in reprobation of the mass murder perpetrated upon neighboring peaceful countries?

One need not be a Christian to comprehend the depravity of taking part in these unprovoked aggressive wars. Natural ethics alone ought to suffice to discourage such participation.

Is it their excuse that they fear for their lives, or dread confinement in concentration camps? This is no excuse, since moral principles are absolute. It would be better for one to choose death, rather than stain his hands with the blood of innocent victims.

By suffering death, they would have become national heroes and would have been instrumental in retrieving national morality. Instead, they have put the seal of their silent consent upon lawlessness and the progressive moral decay of the German nation.

It is sad to contemplate the fact that German citizens not only take part in this war which the entire world must condemn, but also revert to savagery which is revolting to the conscience of every normal human being.

(8) Racism has gone through every stage of conflict with reality. The consequences are tragic. It has emerged from these tests battle-scarred and burdened with heavy moral responsibility, a byword for catastrophe, the incarnation of every evil force that has ever aimed at the destruction of human ideals—of humanity itself.

(9) Nazi literature dilates upon the merits of the Nordic-German race. That self-praise is largely exaggeration. The German race has indeed contributed in some measure to science and art, but the same can be said with greater truth of many other nations. When it comes, however, to national morality, it is plain that on this score the so-called German race now rates lower than most others.

(10) Among the arguments for racism we find many assertions

which are arbitrary and destitute of any scientific value. For example, it is a groundless assertion to say that Christ was a descendant not of the Jews, but of the Nordic race of Ammonites, or that Diocletian sprang from the Nordic race solely because of his external appearance.

All assumptions to the effect that there is no God apart from the German race and blood are a logical consequence of German atheism, which is characteristic of the Nazis; this generally takes the form of neo-paganism or of some kind of pantheism.

(11) German racism amounts to a total rupture with Christ and Christian culture, and marks the spiritual downfall of official Germany.

No wonder, therefore, that the Church has opposed the Nazi racist movement with all its might. In an encyclical issued by Pope Pius XI, entitled *Mit brennender Sorge* ("With burning anxiety"), the errors of German racism were censured in no uncertain terms. The Sacred Congregation of Seminaries and Universities, by the order of the Pope, condemned on April 13, 1938, its errors and its destructive tendency to undermine the fundamentals of the Christian faith. Rosenberg's book entitled *Der Mythus des 20. Jahrhunderts* was placed upon the Index of Forbidden Books.

Herein, as on every occasion, the Church has shown herself the true friend of national cultures, doing everything in her power to preserve them and ensure their legitimate development; to enrich them and to purge them of evil and erroneous tendencies.

Conclusion

From our discussion thus far it appears that normal development of culture is dependent upon certain favorable conditions, one of the most important of which is freedom. Furthermore, culture must be based upon a sound ideology which is transcendent in character.

Favorable external conditions create a proper atmosphere which accelerates the progress of culture and imparts its national character. However, although these elements contribute to culture and promote its development, they are not absolutely indispensable. The Greeks, after losing their freedom to the conquering Roman legions, continued to work in the sphere of culture with a success unequalled by their conquerors. Likewise the Poles, despite their loss of freedom between 1795 and 1918, continued their cultural work, in the face of ever increasing obstacles. Their contributions, especially to art and literature, during this interval were magnificent.

It is quite otherwise, however, with the condition of a sound national ideology, which is indispensable for culture, since without it there is no hope of spiritual growth, or of peaceful relations with other nations. An ideology concerned exclusively with earthly things does not suffice. Its character must be transcendent; that is, it must be grounded upon religious truths and permanent ethical principles, emanating from a higher source—God Himself.

Without a transcendent ideology of this nature, a nation is bound to become a derelict—a positive menace to other nations. Its spiritual downfall is all the more dangerous in proportion to that nation's technical and scientific development. For the higher its technical progress, the better equipped will be the morally degenerate nation to vanquish other nations and carry out its egoistic designs.

The war that has been waged in Europe since September 1, 1939, gives eloquent testimony to the necessity of the above outlined solution. The elimination of religion and ethics from Nazi ideology has had a patently disastrous effect upon German culture. Whatever the human spirit was able to invent has been utilized to destroy other nations. Triumphantly the law of the jungle marches on, laying in dust and ashes the priceless acquisitions of culture accumulated in the course of many centuries. Fire-inflamed skies, charred ruins, starvation, disease and pestilence, millions of graves—these are the fruits of an ideology that has turned its back on ethics, on religion, on God.

We are living in the most calamitous of all periods for human culture. Never before has history witnessed such a spiritual retrogression. Never before have whole nations suffered so greatly under the iron heel of brute force as they do today.

It is evident, therefore, that, in the absence of religion and ethics, peace and cultural progress are impossible.

All mankind, regardless of race or creed, should oppose in the crusader spirit this destructive doctrine. They should help the victims of its adherents to throw off its despotic yoke and recover their freedom.

This is a moral duty incumbent upon all. No one is exempted.

After witnessing this tragic collapse of moral values and of spiritual culture, it is a genuine consolation to reflect upon the beneficent influence of Christianity, especially in its purest form as represented in the Catholic Church. The ideology and magnificent works of Catholic Christianity are balm to the troubled human heart; they chart the only path on which the millions of souls in flight from brutal forces may find salvation, and on which those who now excel in cruelty and moral degeneracy, may retrace their steps to repentance and spiritual regeneration.

Let us hope for a speedy and universal return to this saving ideology.

VI

NATIONALISM
By Luigi Sturzo, Ph.D., S.T.D.

NATIONALISM

I

The word 'nationalism' was born in the course of the past century, soon after the birth of three 'isms': 'liberalism,' 'socialism,' and 'communism.' All four words have highly respectable origins. Their ancestors were 'gentlemen,' in the philosophic, the religious, and the linguistic sense as well. Their names are *nation, liberty, society,* and *community.* The 'ism' was added to their adjectives, thereby retransforming these into substantives; in this way, just as liberal (which meant something different) [1] became liberalism, social socialism, common communism, so national became nationalism. Thus the 'ism' was accepted to mean either a theory founded upon those principles or qualities (according to particular viewpoints), or an organized activity which, adopting some special interpretation of the principle, built up a theoretico-practical system; or, finally, a collective sentiment favoring in any way the tendency represented by the 'ism' in question. Then, in answer to a linguistic and rational exigency, from these substantives (themselves derived from adjectives) sprang still other adjectives even more closely adherent to the new meanings of said substantives: thus from socialism came *socialistic,* and from nationalism came *nationalistic.*

The process whereby the meaning of words crystallizes may be more or less slow and confused, depending on whether or not they imply certain principles to be defended and certain values to be protected, precipitating in consequence a contrary reaction on the part of the upholders of opposite principles. Hence, in the course of the XIX century, the words socialism, communism, and liberalism came to have a new ideological content more precise and more characterized, as polemics and scientific studies, on the one hand, and practical experiences and realizations, on the other, led by degrees to a definition and delimitation of their contours. And

[1] The word 'liberal' took on a new significance in Spain during the revolt and the war of 1822, in contradistinction to the word 'servile' applied to the absolutists.

although dim no-man's lands—controversial points and contradictory elements—still survived, a common interpretation of those
words was eventually reached. They already possessed authoritative sources of interpretation and concrete criteria for their further
elaboration.

For Catholics, the Popes' condemnation of the theories of liberalism, socialism, and communism, as contained in the relevant
pontifical documents, constituted an important basis upon which
to appreciate and understand the significance of these words and
to ascertain the points of divergence and of convergence disclosed
in their process of adaptation, both spatially to different countries,
and chronologically to different times. But it remains incontrovertible regarding these three terms that, from the very beginning,
the 'ism' connoted an excess, a supervaluation of what the original
substantives (liberty, society, community) signified. Thus they
came to convey the notion of a fundamental *primum* (either an
ethical, or sociological, or political, or economic *primum*); that
is, a primacy or superiority over all other principles or ideas.
Therefore, the condemnatory verdicts pronounced by the philosophers, sociologists, political leaders and ecclesiastical authorities
were not, and are not, aimed at liberty, society, or community as
such, but at the exclusivism or the excess implicit in their respective 'ism' forms, which theorize them and raise them to the rank
of absolute and fundamental principles.

By the very fact that they are characterized as such, they cannot
but assume a finalistic nature of their own, in that the realization
of a principle so viewed is regarded as a prevalent good that must
in all cases be obtained—the more prevalent the good, the more
fundamental the principle—so that if a principle like nationality
comes to be regarded (as indeed it did in the course of its historical
development) as the unique principle, it becomes simultaneously
an all-absorbing goal, to which all else is subordinate. Hence, inasmuch as men of theory and of practice, in accepting the implication given the three words by the added 'ism,' had accepted a
graded order of ends more or less prevalent, of principles more or
less absolute (unique), there sprang up a profusion of theory and
of practice, with the result that there came into existence not only
one liberalism but a thousand, not only one socialism but at least
a hundred, not only one communism but at least ten. This multiplicity of meanings must be placed in relationship with the com-
plexity of the subject-matter and of the problems connected there-

with; hence liberalism as a philosophical, political and economic theory has had in the past and continues to have many and varied facets, while socialism and communism have had considerably fewer owing partly to their materialistic and practical character and partly to their philosophic poverty.

At all events there can be no doubt of the fact that between liberty and liberalism, between society and socialism, between community and communism, there exists not merely the difference between an abstract and its alleged concrete (or *vice versa,* as the case may be), but also the difference between a natural principle and its excess or deformation—deformation which might in fact be pushed to a point where it becomes a negation of the principle itself, as might not be difficult to prove in the case of community and communism.

*
* *

This introduction leads to a better understanding of the scope of the word nationalism because the addition of 'ism' to 'national' gives evidence of some excess or deformation with reference to the original conception. The nation appears with excessive traits which so alter its natural characteristics, that its theoretical basis comes to be a fixed principle believed fundamental and its realization is thought of as a supreme goal. In consequence the nation becomes not only a political *primum* but also a sociological and even an ethical *primum.*

Such, in brief, is the error or fallacy lurking in the term *nationalism* itself. Nationalism, too, must be classed along with the other already mentioned 'isms' which during the nineteenth century usurped the place rightfully belonging to the concepts from which they originated. Thanks to nationalism, the nation's character as the community of a people organized on the basis of its traditions, history, language and culture, has come to be perverted; for nationalism is interpreted as being the principal efficient and final cause of the community.

Nationalism, too, takes on a broad variety of colors ranging from the most extravagant to the quite moderate and all the way from the philosophic to the sentimental. For this reason it is difficult to classify it and give it boundaries that will be accepted by all; and if we venture to define its essence as we have sought to do, we shall find some who in good faith will accuse us of using too lurid colors in depicting it and of giving the word a significance beyond its common acceptance. Having made, however, an analysis at once philological and sociological, we have the right to advert to its results. On the other hand, we readily admit that—logic aside—there are strictly political and sentimental nationalisms which are benign in nature.

To confound patriotism with nationalism is to err not only linguistically but also politically. Nevertheless, we have to admit that for many the two substantives were and are quite equivalent. Similarly, for many, even today, the affirmation of freedom or the maintenance of a constitutional system where political freedoms are regulated, corresponds to liberalism. And how often have Catholic social doctrines been classified as socialism and communism! The fact of the matter is that the general public is seldom able to get at the intrinsic link between words and their significance, but subscribes by way of approximation to those meanings which prevail at any given time.

Why then, it may be asked, did the Popes condemn liberalism, socialism and communism without qualification, aiming their condemnations at the accepted meaning of those words at the moment the condemnation was pronounced, and disregarding the existence of attenuated forms (in some cases even attacking forms which were believed to be attenuated); whereas in the case of nationalism Pius XI (the only one of the past Popes who has expressly and on more than one occasion adverted to the problem) was at pains to make a distinction between 'moderate' and 'excessive' nationalism, directing his warnings only against the latter? [2]

For this there may have been several reasons, but the one which appears most convincing is that the Popes, in condemning an error whose index is the word which expresses it, are not themselves

---

[2] In his speech of December 3, 1930, to the Cardinals and Prelates met in consistory, Pius XI spoke against "harsh and egoistic nationalism." In the encyclical letter *Caritate Christi compulsi* of May 3, 1932, he draws a clear distinction between nationalism as love of fatherland and exaggerated nationalism: "Right order of Christian charity does not disapprove of lawful love of country and a sentiment of justifiable nationalism; on the contrary it controls, sanctifies and enlivens them. If, however, egoism abusing this love of country and exaggerating this sentiment of nationalism, insinuates itself into the relations between people and people, there is no excess that will not seem justified; and that which between individuals would be judged blameworthy by all, is now considered lawful and praiseworthy if it is done in the name of this exaggerated nationalism." In his allocution to the teachers of the Italian Catholic Action on September 6, 1938, he once more, after many similar speeches, denounced exaggerated nationalism "which does not unite peoples but throws them one against the other." *(Osservatore Romano,* no. 208 of 1938.)

creating either the word or the significance given it, but are
making clear its meaning with reference to the error it is considered to contain, according the general understanding in certain
places or times. It may well be that the word which epitomizes the
condemned error may have had from the very beginning other
meanings, or that it may have acquired such in the course of time
(who does not know how liable words are to be changed in their
meaning?) and hence it is quite conceivable that these other meanings may not come within the range of the condemnation.[3]

For example, in England Catholics may belong both to the Liberal and the Labor Parties (the latter calling itself Socialist). With
reference to the Labor Party, after the publication of the *Quadragesimo anno* where the famous words were written: "No one can
be at the same time a sincere Catholic and a true Socialist," there
arose a broad discussion to which Cardinal Bourne put an end by
saying that "in this country a man or woman is free to join the
political party which makes the greatest appeal to his sympathy and
understanding." Naturally enough he added that it was necessary
to be on one's guard "against erroneous principles," and especially never to commit oneself or one's conscience "into the keeping of any political party." [4] Obviously the liberalism or the socialism of those British Catholics (assuming them to remain true
Catholics) cannot be identical with the liberalism and socialism
condemned by the Popes. And who does not recall that for a long
time the phrase *Catholic Socialism* was used (even after the condemnation of Pius IX and Leo XIII) to indicate the *Social* school
of Catholics? In Italy between the 'Eighties and the turn of the
century, two notable books appeared: *Catholic Socialism* by
Francesco Nitti (who later became Prime Minister) and *Christian
Socialism* by Count Eduardo Soderini (a prominent Catholic).

With these reservations, it may be said that it is the common
understanding among Catholics that, in speaking of liberalism,

[3] Secretary of State Cordell Hull, in his address on World Conflict delivered July
23, 1942, used, in reference to *nationalism*, the very same qualification as Pius XI, as
witness the following passage: "One of the greatest of all obstacles which in the
past have impeded human progress and afforded breeding grounds for dictators,
has been extreme nationalism. All will agree that nationalism and its spirit are
essential to the healthy and normal political and economic life of a people, but
when policies of nationalism—political, economic, social and moral—are carried to
such extremes as to exclude and prevent necessary policies of international co-
operation, they become dangerous and deadly."

[4] See Luigi Sturzo, *Politics and Morality*, London, Burns, Oates and Washbourne,
1938, Chap. V.

socialism and communism, one means the *systems* condemned by
the Popes. The same is not true in the case of nationalism, for
while with regard to the three aforementioned concepts, the Popes
found that they rested upon erroneous theories which were matters of common public opinion, with regard to nationalism, they
recognized that the same public opinion was divided, often giving
to the word nationalism the meaning of a marked love of country,
in contrast to the internationalism of Socialists and Communists
(Second and Third Internationals), who, because of an ideal
either broadly humanitarian or narrowly class-conscious, dis-
counted or denied (at least as a polemical method) love of country. We say "as a polemical method" because both the German
Socialists of the Second International in 1914 and the Russian
Communists of the Third International in 1941 demonstrated by
their deeds that they knew how to fight even for their geographic
and political fatherlands.

Be that as it may: when the Pope disapproved of nationalism,
he was confronted by two concepts current in common opinion, the
first of which did not have as its basis anti-Christian theories, or at
least failed to show them, while hiding behind the cloak of a love
of fatherland (a bit more highly colored than other loves). Hence,
the Pope limited his condemnation to anti-Christian nationalism,
which he himself called "excessive."

In so doing the Pope was prompted by two practical considerations of some importance. The first was that of inducing nationalist associations and movements, often created for sentimental
motives or for the defense of the bourgeoisie and of the middle
classes against the excesses of workers' parties, to reconsider their
nationalism and so bring it within the limits of an equitable valuation of the interests of one's own country. The second was that of
avoiding the consequence that any just defense of one's own nation
or nationality or of a national minority should be classified as anti-
Catholic and anti-Christian and as condemned by the Pope. This
would have resulted: (a) in convalidating the accusation that Catholics as such are anti-national; (b) in lending weight to the un-
patriotic pretensions of internationalists during the most acute
phases of political struggle, such as was then going on in France.[5]

Although the same might be said of the many varieties of liberalism or socialism born in a century of fermentation of ideas and

[5] See Maurice Vaussard, *Enquête sur le nationalisme*, Paris, Editions 'Spes,' 1924.

political attitudes in all countries, yet one datum is easily ascertainable: that the abstract ideas of liberty, society, and community, have in themselves an ethical content whose negation or attenuation implies an error, while the word nation is not a logical abstraction, has not a meaning transcending the mere historical fact of a people possessed of such and such characteristics, and finally does not imply an error when one modifies its physiognomy. Those who know how accustomed the Latin mentality is to such formal schemes and how strictly scholasticism has fixed their type, will understand the jealous care that Rome brings to the fixation of the relationship between the word and its essential and permanent significance. The Anglo-Saxon is, in general, more pragmatically-minded; he does not link, but isolates; he is not set on synthesizing, but is satisfied with approximations. On that account, he can easily surmount the ideological and systematic implication of a word (or of a fact) by taking it for what it is worth at the moment—*hic et nunc.*

The result has been a series of misunderstandings between the Catholic and non-Catholic worlds that makes difficult any real appreciation of certain pontifical interventions and the problems connected therewith, whenever according to common opinion it becomes hard to understand the historical facts that have given origin to said pontifical interventions. The last of these, namely, Pius XI's strictures on excessive nationalism (which, as we shall see, has taken on the colorings of totalitarian and racial nationalism) deserves to be analyzed further than is the wont in current journalistic polemics, with a view to determining its sociological and spiritual implications.

II

Nothing important and characteristic affects society without an intrinsic reason and a historical occasion. Whatever novelty comes to be grafted upon human processes will be but the development, natural or violent, of motives which had not been hitherto noticed, but which in the linking-up of free initiatives with social conditioning were made efficient and vital.

Since in the dialectic of sociology (not that of Hegel or Marx, but real and human dialectic) today's affirmation originates from yesterday's negation while producing in its turn tomorrow's negation—and from different viewpoints the negation and the affirmation are convertible—it becomes necessary whenever something new is affirmed at a given historical moment, to seek out its characteristics, in order to define the negation it contains.

To carry out such an analysis in the case of nationalism as it appeared in the last century, it is necessary first of all to ascertain what were, at the moment of its appearance, the theoretical and practical positings of the idea of 'nation.'

There were, in fact, three great historical affirmations between 1789, the beginning of the French Revolution, and 1848, the historical date of national and social revolutions.

1. The first was the French affirmation: *nation* was then taken to mean the country, the State, and the people as a moral and political unit, facing the monarch, considered as the head of the State, but only insofar as he was the first citizen and the first public servant. The three meanings given to *nation* were equivalent, inasmuch as the people (the Latin *populus*) was the whole country and the latter was organized as the State according to popular will. Hence the opposition of *nation* to *roi* (king) , in order to deny the previous system of absolute monarchy and to affirm the collective will of the people.

Thus the word *nation* became the assertion of a moral and political personality acquired by the people. The paternalist and patrimonial State was a thing of the past. In the old regime the people had been considered as not of age; the territory as patrimony of the Crown; wars as of interest only to the king; State and crown finances as one. Only with Richelieu was a beginning made towards effectuating a political distinction between the ruling house and France, not enough, however, to preclude Louis XIV from saying: *"L'État c'est moi!"* The *nation* that rose up against such a monarchical system owing to the law of historical dialectics wore revolutionary and democratic colors and built up on the basis of popular sovereignty the new personality of the country: thus was born the France of *liberté, égalité, fraternité,* which was to last through so many vicissitudes down to the 1940 armistice.[6]

2. The second affirmation peculiar to the idea of nation came from Germany, and Fichte, with his famous *Letters to the German Nation,* was its prophet. The nation was taken to mean an idea

[6] The revival after the present war of the French Nation is the common aspiration of the United Nations; we hope that the new France will be less nationalistic and more Christian.

which realizes itself, a spirit which becomes fact; the individuals belonging to it are only phenomena of a reality which we think of as collective insofar as we live in it and for it. The nation as people and culture is a potential reality which creates and develops itself through interior forces.

This immanent conception of the nation found its literary and philosophic fulfilment in the romantic period, and its political expression in the federalism of a number of small entities striving towards unity. This lasted as long as Hegel's conception of the "Nation-State" as supreme and immanent realization of the "Idea" prevailed. It was then that the Prussian State (which Hegel had in mind when he was setting down its *divine* characteristics) absorbed traditional Germany, which was feudal and federalist. The Reich became the only expression of the Germanic nation in its interior reality conceived as "Power and Force."

The further evolution of the concept of immanent nation has come through the idea of race and through a merging of the philosophic ideologies of Fichte and Hegel, of Bismarck's Power and Force and of the materialistic myths of Blood and Soil. Its realization is to be found in the National-Socialist Third Reich.[7]

3. The third affirmation of nation to come to the surface in the nineteenth century was that of the political unity and independence of every nation, such as had been formed through tradition, history, language, culture and religion. It appealed to those countries subject to a foreign State or partitioned among several, often non-autonomous, States. Giuseppe Mazzini symbolized this idea. This ferment, which permeated Italy, divided into many kingdoms and partially subjected to Austria, was such as to excite the wars and revolts of Greece and other Balkan countries subject to the Crescent, prompt the nationality and independence movement within the Hapsburg Empire, and cause the fanning anew of Irish and Polish revolts.

What tended above all in the nineteenth century to bring about the formation of a new national consciousness was the romantic movement which affected the literature, legends, and sagas of every country; the revaluation of particular languages as against languages of general culture, used only by the higher classes and at Court. From this sprang a popular movement orientated toward the idea of freedom, first disseminated by the French Revolution

---

[7] See *Nationalism, A Report by a Study Group of Members of the Royal Institute of International Affairs,* Oxford, The University Press, 1939.

and the Napoleonic Wars and later by the social movements which reached down to the working classes, at that time kept in oppressive and miserable conditions.

In this historical phase, accordingly, we find the idea of nation taking on a threefold aspect: first, nation as popular will organized in the State (France) ; second, nation as soul of a people which realizes itself through innate virtue (Germany); third, nation as an autonomous and free political personality (Italy, Greece, Ireland, Poland, Belgium, Bohemia, Hungary and, later on, the Balkan countries) .

*

*   *

In order to grasp the inner significance of the three aspects which the idea of nation took in Europe between the end of the eighteenth and the first half of the nineteenth centuries, it is necessary to examine in some detail what *nation* has been in its reality.

Nation means individuality of a people; and this cannot come about without a stable geographical contiguity, a historical and cultural tradition, an economic interest. When to these preliminary conditions is added an awakened consciousness on the part of the people of one of those sociological syntheses which only great ideas, such as religion, liberty and independence, can bring about, then there develops the collective *personality* which we call nation. For us the *individuality* of a people means only the *de facto* differentiation between one ethnical group and another. On the other hand, the *personality* of a people indicates the active consciousness which springs out of the differentiated group, giving the latter its own cultural and political stamp.

Hence the starting-point in the formative process of a nation is one of *distinction* between contiguous and even related ethnical groups, which later tends to become one of *opposition* against those who in any way undermine its formation or block its developments and conquests. Indeed, historical experience and sociological reason make us aware that, ordinarily, the personality of ethnical groups in general and that of nation, in its political expression, are most frequently born in opposition and struggle, in defense of their own religion and language, traditional customs and family rights.

A special and interesting instance, which has not been brought to light by historians or sociologists, is to be found in the concept of nation such as it developed in the XIV and XV centuries during the ecclesiastical struggles which stirred the entire Catholic world. At that time national consciousness was beginning to assert its hold over several European countries in consequence of the transition of vernaculars from spoken to written languages, leading to the consolidation of kingdoms, such as those of France, Castile, Aragon, England, Scotland, Portugal, Bavaria, Austria, Bohemia, Poland, Hungary, while the Italian Renaissance, the flowering of universities and of many other lay and ecclesiastical cultural centers gave an exceptional rôle to the intellectual classes.

Nations were not then conceived as political States (a wholly modern development); then not the "State" but the "kingdom" (leaving the communes out of account) was the politico-feudal unit. Nations did not lay claim to independence from a ruling house foreign to their population and language. What St. Joan of Arc stood for in France was something unique, achieved not without struggle and, for its originality and extraordinary character, neither followed up nor imitated. "Nations" then upheld their rights against the Roman Church, that is, against the international or supranational power that had powerfully organized its external structure (from Avignon especially) throughout Christendom. There were two motives of opposition: the economic one of tithes, taxes and other levies which were to be paid to the Roman Curia and to its legates, and the ecclesiastical one of the appointments of beneficiaries and of bishops which the Popes had reserved to themselves or retained control of either from the canonical or from the economic point of view.

But beneath the juridical and economic motives there were stirring deeper questions. The chief one was that of the Council superior to the Pope,[8] which appeared like a democratization of the Church and represented a stand of the periphery against the center, of the intellectual bodies (universities) against the disciplinary organisms, of the lay against the ecclesiastical power, of the nations against the super-nation. Throughout the debates of the Councils and in utterances made outside the Councils there emerged the consciousness of the nation which, failing as yet to be a political fact and evading any ecclesiastical definition, relied for its strength on the various kingdoms that made up its structural whole.

Hence, in the Councils of Pisa, Constance and Basel (during the

[8] See Luigi Sturzo, *Church and State*, New York, Longmans, Green & Co., 1939.

first decades of the fifteenth century), we find that the commissions of the Councils are set up according to nationality and that even the concordats of Constance in 1418 were formulated for each nation or group of nations and with their representatives; not for each State between the Popes and the monarchs.

The sociological aspect of the then rising nation can be said to be more or less similar to that of the nation whose rebirth took place at the end of the eighteenth and the beginning of the nineteenth centuries. Different only were the terms of reference through which national individuality became conscious of its personality. While the nations of the fifteenth century developed at the expense of the medieval papacy (and with the Reformation at the expense of European Catholicity), nineteenth-century nationalities developed at the expense of absolute monarchies and of paternalistic regimes. But whatever the historical contours, national personality in its nature remains always the same and develops with its own inner rhythm.

*

*   *

In order to get a clear notion of this constant historical fact of the formation and development of national personality, one must go back to the primary concept of community. For the nation in its essence is not the simple political organization of society (State) nor the religious organization (Church) nor a voluntary society to be freely formed and dissolved at the option of its members. It is rather the moral binding sense of a people which, becoming aware of itself, seeks to distinguish itself from any other and to arrange its existence in the best possible manner according to historical circumstances. Thus the nation may tend to become a unitary democracy (France) or a federal democracy (United States of America) or a national church (England in the sixteenth century) or a national federation (Switzerland) or a national unitary State (Italy in the *Risorgimento*) or a bilingual liberal State (Belgium).

But once a country or a people has succeeded in developing a consciousness of its own national personality and in affirming it in the struggles with which history has confronted it, there is no stopping. Like all living moral personalities, the nation will have its increment and development, its involution and decrease, all necessary stages of life until the moment arrives when the national

personality itself will either fade away because its physical subject
has altogether or nearly perished (as in the case of the Armenians
and the Assyrians) , or will be transferred to a larger and different
personality, reviving in a broader circle of ethnical, cultural and
political unity, as Montenegro or Croatia in Yugoslavia, Sicily in
Italy, Provence in France, Bavaria in Germany, Vermont, Texas
or California in the United States.

Let us fix two historical phases: that of the formation of the
personality of a nation and that of its affirmation and increment,
and we shall see, and the whole world will bear witness, that every
nation tends to preserve its existence, personality and future with
all its energies and at whatever cost. There is something here that
transcends the fact of an ephemeral existence and a transitory feeling, which goes down to the very roots of human society and of its
formation in natural communities.

Since the prevalent sociological conceptions, from the positivist
and the Hegelian to the neo-racialist, might give rise to some misunderstandings with regard to our statements, it is well to warn the
reader that in speaking of personality of the nation we do not
ascribe to any social body whatsoever a "spirit" of its own or a
"soul" or an entity or reality beyond the single individuals who
compose it. For us a collective personality, whatever its nature, be
it family or nation, State or class, religious or philanthropic community, or even humanity's social whole, is only the simultaneous
reflection of the consciousness of the single members who understand the aim for whose attainment they have gotten together to
co-operate, or who understand that aim in a different way and dis-
sent therefrom, so that in the end there comes about that maximum and that minimum of consent and of reciprocal influence
which create action.

This is not the place to analyze the process whereby the collective consciousness of a people or of a nation is formed nor the factors into which it resolves itself. Let it suffice here to note that for
such consciousness to emerge the social group must have pre-
existent within itself those values that form the nexus of a natural
community, such as tradition, customs, language, territory, social
rights and economic interests. Men living together converge upon
these essential values of life, even though the community never
had an independent political configuration of its own. The totality
of these values, idealized as a reality either to be attained or to be
defended, forms the collective consciousness of the nation.

Moral and cultural personality, therefore, (in the broad meaning of the word, as a "particular stage of advancement in civilization"), is never an entity by itself, above individuals, or a reality that incarnates itself (as the French say, often abusively), as witness the talk about a permanent soul of France, or of Germany, which realizes itself from generation to generation.

Such pseudo-philosophic and pseudo-sociological conceptions of society have entered into common language through idealistic philosophy from Fichte and Hegel on and through positivist sociology, especially Durkheim's, and have recently been applied to the historical case of nation, raising the latter to the status of a primary social constituent and the ultimate goal of social man.

Our controversy on the philosophic plane is with Hegel's idealism and on the sociological plane with Durkheim's "sociologism," though it is our considerate opinion that the theorizers of "nation," who claim to be followers of Hegel and of Durkheim, are guilty of an extralogical omission in transferring to the nation the philosophic *primum* and the sociological *primum* of their respective authors. At this point old and new errors meet, though the alleged connections between the two planes are entirely groundless.

*

* *

If the nation, as a people's personality and consciousness of such personality, is a historical and natural fact, it must have its exigencies and its limits and, morally speaking, its rights and its duties, for the same reason that we attribute similar qualifications to every human community, be it the family or the State.

Manifold are the problems that issue from the fact of nation, according to the manner in which the consciousness of a nation originates and takes shape in the people and according to the historical form of its outward projection. We are confronted with problems relating to a given historical fact; relating to, yet distinguished from, the problems of human society as such; they assume, therefore, a particular and concrete aspect, never a general and abstract one. Leaving out of consideration the historical facts of nations as conceived or concretized in ancient times or in the Middle Ages or in the Renaissance and limiting ourselves to the last phase, from the end of the eighteenth century to the present day, we see first of all the nation arising out of a conflict between historical rights of the higher classes and political ideals of liberty and democracy of the middle classes. This conflict is resolved either through revolts or through wars.

North America was the first instance in point; no one then spoke of an American nation, but the various English colonies in America felt themselves ripe for their erection into independent States governed by the people. The awareness of such maturity and the related assertions of independence and of self-government which led to a confederation, were born of their struggle against England and therefore originated in revolt and war. Confederation and subsequent federal government were the political forms used to assert the independence of what was later to become the "American nation."

If we ask ourselves the nature of the principle upon which the American nation claimed its political personality, the answers will vary according to the criteria used. We think that in the process of civilization the colony, if it is ripe for independence, has the right to obtain it by demanding it or even by fighting for it. Such maturity is indicated not only by cultural and economic conditions but also by the existence of the consciousness of having reached it. The independence of national nuclei is a right which comes before the historical facts (owing to which it was either lost or never reached) and in given historical circumstances such a right may justly assert itself. At the same time it is true that the political independence of a community which we of today call a nation is also conditioned by the totality of historical international factors and that therefore it is unquestionably a relative and not an absolute right, provided of course that the community in question be in full enjoyment of all the natural rights belonging to individuals, families and the moral personality itself of a people.

The case of France, to which we have already referred in enucleating the meaning of the word *nation,* followed in close sequence that of the American colonies. And, in fact, it is proper to note that the democratization of France, or better, the loosening of the juridical and class ties of her *ancien régime,* was the historical occasion of the germination of the idea of *nation,* and that the word *république* was not taken to mean a popular government without king, but in the sense of a mixed government of people and king. And when, owing to a series of revolutionary events, the monarchy was abolished, it was only then that the expression *sovereign nation* was coined.

We will not hazard any ethical judgment upon the various

phases of the French Revolution (nor, for that matter, upon the American and Italian Revolutions) but content ourselves with certifying the fact, sociologically ascertainable, that the idea of nation is bound up with the larger participation in the common life of that class or social group which has consciousness of it and which makes of it a motive for its collective activity. The nation of the fourteenth and fifteenth centuries was the nation of the university men, the Humanists, the ecclesiastics and nobles, and the Courts acting against the papacy; the nation of the eighteenth and nineteenth centuries is the nation of the Encyclopedists, the Romanticists, the bourgeois and the mercantilists, both in Europe and in America, acting against the absolute and paternalistic monarchies.

The cases of Ireland and of Poland, from a certain point of view those also of Belgium and Italy, and even more so those of Greece and of the countries subject to the Crescent, had, as their justification, the existence not of a paternalistic government as in France, but of a foreign tyranny. Even in the eighteenth century the British were for Ireland strangers and tyrants. Against them, the right to revolt had to be invoked. We well know that, in the cases of both the Polish and the Irish revolts, the authority of Rome sometimes manifested its disapproval, and in the case of the revolts and wars of Italy against Austria we find even today Catholic writers, like Cathrein, who frowned upon them,[9] just as Taparelli refused to admit the legitimacy of the insurrectionary war of the Greeks against the Turks. The encyclical letter of Pius XI *Nos es muy* of March 28, 1937, made the resolution of such cases less difficult, because it fixed the criteria for the justification of revolts, although as is stated in the same encyclical, "the practical solution depends on concrete circumstances." It is from the point of view of these "concrete circumstances" that we must judge the civil struggles and wars of Switzerland in the nineteenth century, aimed as they were at eliminating the religious intolerance dividing that country and at forming a true "Swiss nation."

*

*   *

[9] Pius IX, of course, condemned the wars of the Italian Risorgimento, which ended with the occupation of Rome. The celebrated Abbé Antonio Rosmini, founder of the Rosminian Congregation, and Father Gioacchino Ventura, General of the Theatines (Regular Clerics), approved of the war against Austria for Italian independence, and Ventura himself strongly defended the right of the Sicilians to revolt and wage war against the Bourbon King of Naples in 1848.

What we would like to stress at this point is that we must not identify—as is often done—natural rights, belonging to human personality, with rights that are born historically with the formation of a nation. A nationality can undoubtedly claim a right to religious freedom, as the Oriental and Balkan peoples did under the Turks, or the Greek-Ruthenians of Poland under the Czars, and yet fail to claim at the same time the right to its own political personality. On the other hand, it could give strength to its political revindication by uniting the latter with that of despised or suppressed religious rights. Thus, in the Irish case, the fight for religious freedom, which was climaxed by the Catholic Emancipation Act of 1827, came under the natural law and did not depend on any national development, whereas the fight for political autonomy, which ended in the creation of the Irish Free State in 1921, was carried out on the basis of national and historical rights.

The difference is very great: we call the former absolute and natural rights, the latter relative and historical rights, in order to accentuate the fact that the latter come to fruition only as the historical process unfolds itself and are subordinated to the exigencies, the rights and the possibilities of common life among the several peoples.

We cannot determine here exactly where the rights of a nation become prevalent over those of its component families and over those of the State or of the States within the framework of which a people has its political organization. In any case, a gradation of hypotheses and of casuistic dosing would be of almost no value, since it would not, in the end, have any bearing upon concrete facts.

The nation must not be conceived as outside the framework of society or community or family groups, which have rights insofar as they represent the means of common life for individual men; because society is for the individual man and not the individual man for society; rights and duties belong to human persons through society and not to society as a real entity outside the individual men composing it. If this holds true for the family and for the State, which are natural societies with specific aims and well-defined juridical contours, the same must be true of a society with a historical character and with indefinite contours like the nation, because even when it coincides with the State (as in France or in Italy), it is always regarded as a morally and psychologically different entity.

To the exigencies and to the rights of the nation we can therefore set a theoretical limit: the nation is subordinated to human personality as a means to an end, and hence cannot be asserted against the natural rights of men (whether or not they belong to the same nation). On the other hand, in order to meet the individualistic danger, it is necessary to go back to the other principle that every community represents an inter-individual bond, brought about to prevent social dissolution caused by the egoism of individuals. The fundamental social principle (like the cosmic one) is the solidarity of the component elements. It is true that the social resultant can never invalidate the rights of personality, but it is also true that individuals in safeguarding their own personality must reconcile this, through observance of the duties of justice and love, with the solidary co-existence of their fellow men.

Among the communities based upon such solidarity, the nation holds a place midway between the family and the State, sharing with the family the feeling of natural affinity and tending along with the State to the goals of civil increment of order and of defense. And between the recognition of human personality on the part of social powers and the observance of human solidarity on the part of individuals there is also to be found a scale of relative rights and duties pertaining to the nation and its historical exigencies.

We will not be more definite at this stage, because it is always dangerous to attempt a too early solution of a concrete problem which, when all its terms have been set forth, will appear to us with unforseen peculiarities demanding solutions that lie beyond the range of our previous experience. But in order to fix the limits of the inquiry we may say that the rights and duties that spring from the maturation of a nation, considered in themselves and not confused with those natural rights and duties resulting from human personality, are only historical and relative rights— just as historical and relative as is the nature itself of nation.

III

At this point many will ask themselves in what sense nation differs from *national consciousness* or from *national sentiment* or, finally, from *national ideal*. Here are three commonly used expressions which stand in need of clear definitions.

"National consciousness" is the feeling that comes to the surface with the reawakening of the characteristics of a people in its historical phase and which gives effectiveness to the community. So long as a people remains unconscious of its personality, there is no nation in the sociological meaning of the word. Thus we may have periods during which national consciousness weakens and then reasserts itself. Finland provides us with a characteristic historical example. Her great nineteenth-century poet, Elias Lönnrot, woke her up from her long sleep. Austria in the period between Seipel and Schuschnigg began to feel herself different to the old Hapsburgian Austria, and sharply differentiated, too, from the *Grossdeutschland* of 1848 as well as from Hitler's Third Reich.

"National sentiment" is akin to patriotic exaltation and is likely to manifest itself at happy or unhappy moments in the life of the fatherland. It may also be interpreted as an expression of solidarity among the members of the national community.

"National ideal" is a longing to obtain what is lacking in order to bring about the realization or the completion of the nation. Thus Italy's national ideal at the end of the nineteenth century was to push her geographical boundaries up to Trento and Trieste; today Eire's ideal is to bring about its union with the six northern counties, while the undoubted national ideal of Holland, Belgium, Norway and of all the countries overrun by the Nazis is to regain their independence and freedom.

All this can be called nationalism by virtue of a journalistic or popular extension of the meaning of the word; but it is not nationalism in an etymological, historical, political or sociological sense. We must be careful not to mistake the former for the latter; for though it be true that *usus te plura docebit,* it is nevertheless necessary to react against such usages as lead to confusion. Today when we recognize more clearly the true traits of nationalism, even while accepting the factual and subjective attenuations of those who call or have called themselves nationalists, we cannot accept principles that involve errors and perverted doctrines.

Nationalism is a theoretical conception and a practical activity which tends to overvalue the nation and to make of it a dominant, nay, an absolute ethical-political principle. In order to give validity to the definition, we must find its verification in the characteristics of nationalisms as they have developed in their historical objectivity and as they have been theorized by their chief propounders.

The first nationalism we meet on our way is German nationalism before and after the formation of the Bismarckian empire. The anti-Catholic *Kulturkampf* of that time had its nationalistic motive. It is of no moment that the words 'nationalism' and 'nationalize' were then used in a sense other than today's meaning, for there existed the germs of what is known as nationalism;[10] when Bismarck wanted to Germanize Pomerania and Silesia through eviction of the Polish population of those provinces, he was influenced by a strictly nationalistic concept: that of the homogeneity of the Reich's population. Be it called Germanism or German Nationalism, it is the same thing. The Polish representatives in the Reichstag and the Catholic Center Party reacted against Bismarck's policies. The substance of Bismarckian policy was that German homogeneity could never be achieved except through the Lutheranization of the Catholic provinces. Hence the persecution known as the *Kulturkampf* was expressly aimed at the Poles and the Catholics. Bismarck failed in the undertaking and had to yield; even in certain Protestant circles his methods had excited some alarm; but the idea of national *Kulturkampf* persisted and spread, Heinrich von Treitschke being its chief theorizer. Treitschke's thesis was that the Poles, Jews, Socialists and Catholics had to be eliminated from the Reich by every available means and device, including deportation, expropriation, imprisonment and death, in order to arrive at a homogeneous nation. The idea of homogeneity was not an end in itself but was conceived as a means of strengthening the State's powers and of uniting the nation in order to achieve dominion beyond its own boundaries and to bring about the political and economic expansion of the population.

The Aryan theories of Gobineau and Houston Stewart Chamberlain lent themselves admirably to Treitschke's nationalism, and although the former was French and the latter English, their theories were well received by German minds, which always need a theoretical peg whereon to hang any and every practical initiative. The theory of a superior Nordic Aryan race was exactly

[10] *Nationalize* and *nationalization* are still used to mean national or State control or ownership of a territory, of an industry or a public utility, while *nationalism* stands for the political theory of the nation as a prevalent principle of collective life, and *nationalist* for a person belonging to the nationalist party.

cut out for them. Already in the XVI century Luther had maintained that the Germans were superior to the Latins, and this had become a sort of dogma with Lutherans. But the scientific apparatus of the XIX century was needed to give it substance. This was the era of the triumph of science over philosophy and theology—the time when positivist sociology was raised to the dignity of a science. Nationalist and "scientific" racism was born and grew up in this climate.

In France, after the establishment of the Third Republic, there appeared a nationalism which was the outcome of the loss of Alsace-Lorraine, but which soon showed its natural characteristics, becoming anti-democratic, anti-socialist, and anti-Semitic. But whereas in Germany nationalism was anti-Catholic, in France it was born pro-Catholic; the French clergy were against the Republic, either because they were for the most part favorable to the monarchy, or because they feared the anti-clericalism of the bourgeoisie and of the working masses. Leo XIII, by his letter of 1892, in which he advised French Catholics to adhere to the Republic and co-operate in the framing of wholesome laws for the good of the country, did away with the inner conflict caused by the tradition of loyalty to the monarchy (a conflict which for some Catholics was real) and eliminated the pretext for anti-Republican action in alliance with those who were planning a *coup d'état*. But unfortunately a large part of the clergy and the laity refused to follow the advice of a far-seeing Pope. The Dreyfus case which came up for trial soon afterwards brought about a deep cleavage in France, with the Catholic laity and clergy (except for a small but significant minority) on the side of the accusers and in league with the most rabid nationalists and anti-Semites. Regrettably enough, although Dreyfus's innocence was proved, the strife lasted up to the First World War and in certain quarters continues to the present hour. Even to this day there are some who think they do a service to the nation by branding Dreyfus as a traitor.[11]

At that time, however, there was in France no real theorist of nationalism like Treitschke or Gobineau—none whose fame could compare with the celebrity later attained by Charles Maurras. Drumont was only a demagogue. The truth of the matter is that

---

[11] On this point and concerning later nationalism, see Yves Simon, *The Road to Vichy, 1918-1938:* translated by James A. Corbett and George J. McMorrow, Sheed and Ward, New York, 1942.

several negative movements of diverse character such as anti-republicanism, anti-democraticism, anti-Semitism, were then flowing in a common channel, a fact that makes any theorizing difficult. What brought together industrial bourgeoisie, landed aristocracy, militarism and a large section of the clergy in France was their anti-social sentiment of fear and even hostility toward the working and peasant masses as well the petite bourgeoisie, all of whom were gaining in importance, strength and power, both in the economic and the political fields.

In fine, there was a class problem: because of the Socialist declaration of the First International and later of the Second International in favor of the dictatorship of the proletariat, the abolition of property and universal disarmament, the wealthier and more powerful classes were afraid not only of Socialist leagues but also of universal suffrage. The word *nationalism,* in its "bourgeois" and "anti-socialist" meaning, was used in antithesis to the word *International,* the mere mention of which sufficed to frighten the upper classes—a phenomenon that repeated itself after the First World War with regard to words like *bolshevism* or *Comintern.*

It was at first believed that anti-socialist laws would remedy the situation. Bismarck tried this method in Germany, but met with resistance on the part of the Center Catholics, whereas in France the Catholics, being politically unorganized and usually in favor of the Right, fell an easy prey to nationalism of the first and second types.

At that time Italian nationalism had yet to be born. One could hardly call *nationalism* what in Italy went by the name of *"irredentismo,"* that is, the tendency to look forward to the reunion with the mother country of Trento and Trieste, then under Austrian domination. Such literary irredentism did not prevent Italy from being a member of the Triple Alliance with Germany and the Dual Empire for nearly thirty years. "Nationalist" politics in the sense of colonial expansion can be ascribed to Francesco Crispi, who drew the ire of France and promoted the first war against Abyssinia. True nationalism was of a later date and came of aping Maurras; its poet was d'Annunzio.

*

* *

Can we speak of an English nationalism? Joseph Chamberlain, Cecil Rhodes and Rudyard Kipling are representatives of British "nationalistic imperialism."[12] The first asserted the superiority of the Anglo-Saxon race as "infallibly destined to be the predominant race in the history of civilization and of the world"; and in the name of such a race those British nationalists justified their dominion over the Celts, especially the Irish.[13]

Leaving aside the eccentricities of the Joseph Chamberlain group and also the traditional British attitude of sufficiency, according to which, before the two great wars, there were only colonials to be found beyond the Channel (with the exclusion of Paris), we find that theoretical and practical nationalism of the nineteenth-century variety never developed in England and this for two reasons: first, because the British are pragmatists and do not care for theories (witness the lack of Marxist influence on English laborism), and second, because the British already had an empire that was expanding almost automatically and without struggle in Africa and the Pacific, up to the outbreak of the Boer War which was due to the megalomania of Cecil Rhodes and to a failure to comprehend facts on the part of the government in London. The British people itself was divided on the issue of this war and showed its reprobation of the excesses perpetrated in the campaign. But in reality the Boer War was more a colonial than a nationalistic war, and ultimately brought about the formation of a dominion with equal rights for all the peoples within the Union.

Even the London Jubilee ceremonies of 1887 and of 1897 were tinged less with nationalism than with imperialism—nay more with "emotional imperialism," to use the words of Ramsay Muir. It was then, at a time when all "civilized" countries were bent on dividing among themselves the unoccupied portions of the world, that England, almost without wars, succeeded in carving out for herself the lion's share and so built up the modern British Empire, which later came to be viewed as made up of three parts: the British Commonwealth of Nations, the Indian Empire and the colonies. Very soon literary nationalism disappeared from the British stage; at the same time local nationalisms came to life: the Irish, the Welsh, and the Scotch, the first political, the second folkloristic, the third literary, headed by the novelist Compton Mackenzie.

Turning to this continent: in what sense is it possible to

[12] See Carlton Hayes, *Essays on Nationalism*, New York, 1928.
[13] *Cf.* J. M. Robertson, *Saxon and Celt*, London, 1897.

speak of American nationalism? Here the word nationalism did not take the same meaning that it had in Europe. Indeed, the word was only posthumously applied to movements which, historically speaking, had been identified with different terminology. And, inasmuch as one of the most serious and dominant problems in the internal politics of the United States was the equilibrium between a strong central government and the administrative (and, from certain points of view, the political) freedom of the several States, we find that the idea of American nationalism was linked with federalist policies, the increase in the number of federated States and their cultural and linguistic assimilation. The freeing of the slaves was then the most serious problem to be solved, being in the foreground of the reasons that led to the Civil War. The man who saved the nation and American civilization was Lincoln. Nevertheless, the problem of the colored man cannot be said to have been socially and morally solved except in part; from the national point of view the problem is a complex one and imparts to American nationalism a certain racial tinge.

Another important problem connected with nationalism gained significance after 1848, retaining it until the First World War. We refer to the great tide of European immigration. Here, too, we remark a racial discrimination between the immigrants of Northern and Western Europe, on the one hand, and those of Southern and Eastern Europe (the Mediterranean zone), on the other. The immigration problem was rendered more acute not only from the social point of view but also from the national point of view owing to assimilation difficulties: the persistence of traditional customs among the first and even the second generation of immigrants, the formation of compact ethnical groups within cities and States and the inferior recognition accorded newcomers in the labor market. But gradually the alternation of prosperity and crisis gave occasion to certain social readjustments, and the political events of the last fifty years gave birth to a more deeply felt national sentiment even among the immigrants. The latter little by little gave up the thought of coming to America in order to make money and then going back to their country of origin.

What, however, from our point of view, must be brought into relief—and it is something of fundamental importance—is that in Europe national assimilation was "fostered" through violent processes, as in Bismarckian Germany by the agency of anti-Polish, anti-Socialist and anti-Catholic laws and by dint of repression as in Alsace-Lorraine, or as in Ireland through the suppression of revolts and the denial of home rule, or as in the Balkans where the Turks as late as the nineteenth century had recourse to mass murders and populations were left no choice save that of revolt and war. In America, on the other hand, the system of liberty and culture was applied and national formation was given a chance to develop of its own accord. Consequently, with all due allowance for the rather frequent asperity of feelings and resentments arising between the old American stock and the immigrant groups, we have never witnessed their leading to persecutions (comparable to the anti-Semitic ones in Russia, Poland and Eastern Europe, and even in France during the Dreyfus case), or to organized attempts to prevent single individuals from following their careers and attaining to high positions in industry, politics and culture.

Thus American domestic nationalism, with all its natural deficiencies, never overstepped the boundaries of pragmatism and sentiment in order to become a sociological or political theory.

At the same time there was a development of American nationalism in the international field. This could be called isolationist or defensive nationalism. Its prototype and foundation are to be found in the Monroe Doctrine, whose juridical nature and political value are debatable, but which must be considered in the light of its origin at a time when the great European Powers might still dream of regaining their lost dominion over former Western colonies, thus making the American continent a fresh battleground for their rivalries.

Since weapons for defense are readily convertible into offensive armaments, the nation (be it federal or unitary) that has reached a certain degree of peaceful expansion, will naturally be tempted to embark on warlike adventures. Unquestionably the union of forty-eight States, the opening of the Panama Canal and expansion in the Pacific gave to the United States an "imperial character" which the founders of the Union never anticipated. The doctrine of the freedom of the seas and the creation of a powerful fleet, the policies with regard to Cuba, Puerto Rico, Nicaragua and the Philippines and the so-called "dollar-diplomacy" were its natural corollaries.

All this may be called nationalism in the sense of national policy, or even "imperialism," if you will, and as such is subject

to praise or criticism as indeed are all policies of all States in all
ages. But it cannot be called nationalism in the sense of nationalistic theory, such as was developing at that very time in Europe.

*

*   *

On the eve of the First World War, Charles Maurras, the theorist of nationalism who was to give this its greatest expansion, was
already active. Until that moment the prevalent theories had been
German, their propounders being philosophic, romantic, militarist
and political writers, or racial theorists like Gobineau. Those theories, however, had been confined within the Teutonic ideological framework; they had failed to impress world opinion. The
word nationalism itself, used here and there in an equivocal sense,
had not yet become the index either of a theory or of a party with
well-defined contours.

The doctrinal roots of Maurras' views are to be found in the
positivist school; like Auguste Comte he admired Catholicism as
a social hierarchic organization, headed by a monarchical sovereign, with an aristocracy of its own selected by the head, with a
firm juridical discipline and a dogmatic associative structure. All
these were elements that, even in the eyes of a convinced positivist
and atheist, as Maurras often declared himself to be, had great
value for the worldly social edifice because of the cohesion they
gave to the political formation of a nation. To win the Church
to nationalism—that would be a masterstroke, not only by reason
of the sympathies a party might enlist and the political service it
could render to the Church of its country, but also by reason of the
adaptation of the reciprocally influenced theories and practical
results to the construction of a nationalist State.

In the meantime, during the struggle with the anticlerical
French government, which had denounced the Concordat, closed
the churches, sequestered eclesiastical goods, thrown monks, friars
and nuns out of convents and priests out of presbyteries, the
Action Française was the most powerful organization to come to
the help of the Catholics and the *Camelots du Roi;* in resisting
the government officials, it went beyond anything desired by the
clergy themselves.

Furthermore, some bishops and priests, seeing this audacious
party assert itself in the street, began to entertain the belief that

the monarchy might really be restored. Hence their republicanism of convenience (even if we admit such after the Encyclical of Leo XIII) speedily waned amid the excesses of the anti-clericals and the audacities of the nationalists. Thus a good many Catholics joined the faction of Maurras, regarded for the moment as the defender of French Catholicism—a worthy successor to Jeanne d'Arc who just at that time was being reinstated as the protectress of the new Catholic France. Maurras favored the Thomistic revival in France against philosophers like Laberthonniere and Le Roy, who were later to be placed on the Index; against Blondel, who for a long time was held suspect. He advocated a corporative structure of class organization against the socialism of Jaurés and the syndicalism of Sorel. All these efforts were looked upon favorably by the French clergy, with the result that nationalism, which the Church until then had either opposed or slighted because of the immoral and anti-Catholic tendencies it displayed in the course of its formation in several European countries, succeeded for the nonce in winning the sympathies of a part of the French clergy— even in those circles which, thanks to an equivocal use of the word, go by the name of "Vatican circles." The hidden poison could not, however, remain long concealed, the more so that the movement's best known leaders in and outside France were obscene novelists like Maurras and Daudet, or, like Barres and others, pagan in their ideals and conception of life.

French literature was at the time nearly wholly in the hands of this nationalist tendency and it was literature apt to carry this French positivist and philo-Catholic nationalism to other countries. An Italian nationalism was born, represented by the poet d'Annunzio (amongst the most pagan and obscene writers of his day). Even in Belgium and Switzerland the movement spread and the Rightist Catholics of many countries became nationalists. This was precisely what happened in Italy where many prominent Catholics and their newspapers upheld the Libyan War which, together with the two Balkan wars, was the starting-point of the great upheavals in the European balance of power.

While nationalist sentiments were being thus excited in the West and France was resuming her "literary" campaign for Alsace-Lorraine, the countries of the Hapsburg Empire were striving to obtain a better settlement of the nationality problem, especially the Bohemians and Poles; at Trento and Trieste, Italian feelings too were burning with more ardent fire—the upshot being that the annexation of Bosnia-Herzegovina by Austria embittered both Slavs and Italians.

Thus nationalist and national movements, merging together, furnished motives and pretexts that led to war. Every nationalism creates its opposite, and the conflict of interests makes inevitably for war; war in such a climate is all but a foregone conclusion.

IV

Wars are always accompanied by an unleashing of violent passions, until victory or defeat, viewed in their sad reality, give the lie in fact to those satisfactions of human egoism that, at the price of so much blood, men have striven to achieve. And even when certain satisfactions and gains are won by one side, it may be said with truth that victory itself not seldom turns out to have been really defeat.

Thus all the nationalisms which had their field day as a result of the last World War became one of the most potent causes of strife and unrest, leading ultimately to a new and more tragic conflict.

It is not for us to inquire here into the exact measure of nationalism's accountability for the present war. Our task is to analyze its immoral and anti-Christian character and to follow to its logical and historical conclusions the movement whose growth we have been considering.

Of all nationalisms since 1918, French nationalism must bear the chief responsibility for the present European cataclysm. It was French nationalism that obstinately opposed any reconciliation with Germany—any *rapprochement* between the two peoples; it fought every attempt to make the League of Nations superior to the individual States and powerful in molding European public opinion; it exploited the French fear of insecurity to the point of sabotaging all efforts to achieve a reduction of armaments; it would not hear of making any concessions to Germany. When the policy of Briand approving the admission of Germany into the League of Nations and contemplating an end to the Rhineland occupation prevailed in the Locarno Treaty, French nationalism denounced this policy as treason.

But above all it was French nationalism that poisoned the Catholic world after the war, in France as well as in other countries, even in England, decrying every generous idea, every Christian sentiment, every peaceful initiative, inciting to hatred and resentment, spreading inhumane and anti-Catholic doctrines. At that time a cry of alarm was raised in Belgium after a poll among Catholic students revealed the fact that a majority of them were in favor of the *Action Française*. An inquiry conducted by the Catholic writer Maurice Vaussard was later published in the book entitled *"Enquête sur le nationalisme."* [14] This book makes interesting reading even today, for it shows how the word nationalism, which had received any number of different and even opposed meanings, caused many outstanding persons in France to evaluate wrongly the problem as events had determined it. At the same time, one senses on nearly every page of the book a preoccupation with something that weighed like a heavy burden upon French and Belgian Catholicism, urgently demanding clarification. There were some who held that "nationalism will be the next heresy to be condemned." [15] Other writers of the *Enquête,* interpreting nationalism as national consciousness or as the perfecting of such consciousness, broke lances in its defense. They maintained that the more alive nationalism is, the more effective will internationalism be.

But we find certain clear-headed prophets like Chaptal, the Auxiliary Bishop of Paris, who wrote:

". . . But if politics seizes this notion of nationality and makes of it an absolute principle, without limits or controls, then it becomes, like all other absolute political principles which have no counterweight or measure, a vehicle of oppression, of tyranny and of gangsterism. Under the pretext of giving to a nation the place in the world which will allow it to develop all its worth and its power and to go to the very end of the vital expansion which it claims for itself, the morality of nationalism justifies all atrocities and legitimizes the worst tyrannies. It is to be hoped that all nations will rise up against those nations that profess such principles. These are malignant nationalities. Nationalism is a heresy and a monstrosity." [16]

One of the clearest answers was that by Msgr. John A. Ryan of The Catholic University of America, who said: "Nationalism is obviously opposed to the teachings and the spirit of Christianity. . . . Nationalism manifests itself in various ways. At its worst, it considers as licit all acts and all means calculated to increase the

---

[14] Editions Spes, 17 Rue Soufflot, Paris, 1924.
[15] *La Revue Catholique des Idées et des Faits,* Brussels.
[16] *Enquête,* p. 25.

power, the prestige, or the wealth of the nation. It is hardly necessary to insist on the absolute immorality of this theory." [17]

One could expatiate at great length on some pages of the *Enquête,* showing, among other things, how blind illustrious men
and sincere Catholics were in 1923 and 1924 with regard to the condition of France and her future. As Émile Baumann wrote: "No
country is more divided than France by internationalism. She
feels within herself manifold symptoms of death. She has terrible
neighbors. She believes, on the other hand, that her mission is not
yet finished." [18]

The motives which prompted many Catholics to adhere to the
Action Française and to sustain its nationalistic program were expressed by Gaetan Bernouille, the director of the *"Lettres"*
(which published the answers to the inquiry). In his conclusion
he said: "We have no quarrel with nationalism itself but with
the deviations in its present development. Here again we recognize
the eminent rôle of Catholicism in the regeneration of France. It
is not a question of anathematizing nationalism but of rescuing it
from the worship of force and of interest and from the nefarious
influence of nationalist positivism, in short of christianizing it." [19]
To this rather superficial view Maurice Blondel was squarely
opposed; for he saw in nationalist theories "the formal antithesis
of Catholicism"; and Vaussard, in his interesting conclusion, spoke
of nationalism's "pitiless inhumanism." [20]

Soon after the publication of the sixty answers to the *Enquête,*
the Archbishop of Bordeaux, Cardinal Andrieu, wrote a letter of
indictment against the *Action Française* which, though receiving
the approval of Pius XI, roused the anger of a notable section of
French public opinion. But the definitive intervention of the Holy
See was not long delayed. By the end of 1926 it published the decree which the Holy Office had prepared back in 1914 but whose
issuance had been postponed by both Pius X and Benedict XV,
who did not think the troubled times between 1914 and 1922
propitious for such action. The decree put the writings of Charles
Maurras and the newspaper *"Action Française"* on the Index.
Pius XI further enjoined upon the faithful not to associate them-

---

[17] *Ibid.,* pp. 234, 235.
[18] *Ibid.,* p. 129.
[19] *Enquête,* p. 137.
[20] *Ibid.,* p. 378. In his speech of July 18, 1938, Pope Pius XI said: "The contrast
between exaggerated nationalism and Catholicism is evident. The spirit of nationalism is contrary to the spirit of the Creed and of Faith."

selves with the *Action Française,* and extremely severe canonical penalties were enacted against transgressors, including the denial of the sacraments.[21]

*

*   *

From French nationalism to Italian nationalism was a short step. The foundations had been laid and the teachings spread. They only awaited a man who could translate them into political practice. Mussolini's teachers had been Napoleon, Machiavelli and Caesar: great names, but belonging to the past. Undoubtedly the historical figures in question excited his imagination after he seized power. But before that, as a Socialist and a newspaperman, Mussolini's teachers had been Georges Sorel and Lenin with whom he had been in contact and from whom he had taken his ideas of revolution and dictatorship, and Charles Maurras (not d'Annunzio, whose "jealous friend" he was), from whom he borrowed his conception of nationalism. Fascism (for a short while called National-Fascism), having crushed in the four years between 1922 and 1926 all resistance and opposition, proclaimed the totalitarian State (the word 'totalitarian' was coined by Mussolini and did not exist before in the Italian dictionary) in the famous words "Nothing outside or above the State, nothing against the State, everything within the State, everything for the State." [22]

Mussolini's notion of the complete subordination of man to the State, which was at the bottom of Fascist theory, had for Italy the twofold sense of the transcendence of the nation (conceived, in Italy, as contained within the limits of the State and hence as being its equivalent) and of the resolution of every social activity into

[21] In June 1939 the leaders of the *Action Française,* after twelve years of open revolt, made a formal act of submission to Rome, stating that "in disavowing all their possibly erroneous writings, they completely repudiated all principles and all theories contrary to the teachings of the Catholic Church." Pius XII in the following month approved *"ad mentem"* the decree of the Holy Office which lifted the ban against the newspaper *"Action Française,"* the ban, however, against all its issues from 1926 to July 10, 1939, and against Maurras' books still remaining in force. The Pope's *mens* was that, *"firmis manentibus quae saepe a Sancta Sede proposita sunt, tum circa distinctionem religiosarum rerum a negotiis mere politicis, tum circa rei politicae subiectionem legi morali, tum circa principia et officia ad Actionem Catholicam promovendam tuendamque tradita,"* they were specially recommended to the French bishops.

[22] Mussolini, when writing the article on Fascism for the Italian Encyclopedia in 1932, stressed even more clearly this notion of the totalitarian State, saying: "For Fascism, everything is in the State and nothing human or spiritual exists, far less has value, outside the State."

political power, so that not only was the primacy of politics proclaimed on the basis of the State, but the latter absorbed into itself every reason of social living in that every right came from the State to the individuals and not from the individuals to the State.

To realize the totalitarian State, a complete administrative centralization is first of all required, with the transfer of the sum total of all powers to the government, the government itself becoming the blind executor of the will of a *leader* endowed (it does not matter how) on a *dictatorial* scale with all moral, juridical and political powers.[23]

For the dictatorial machine to gain momentum, it is necessary to suppress all political and civil freedom, all the fundamental rights of human personality and of the family, of communities and of cities, of universities and of churches. The chief instrument of such power is force. But the public force of the police is not enough; reliance must be placed on a secret police (which has assumed the well-known names of OGPU in Russia, OVRA in Italy and Gestapo in Germany). Recourse had also to be had to private armed bands: the armed gangs of the Blackshirts in Italy and of the Brownshirts in Germany.

Force alone is not enough; education is also necessary. Therefore, the totalitarian State has monopolized the schools, the sport activities of the youth, the cinema, the radio, the press; special schools have even been created in order to shape the "perfect citizens." Still another step: the effort is made to weaken or even to eliminate the influence of the family; hence, the special Fascist, Nazi and Communist institutions for youth. At the age of six, one became in Italy a member of the Sons of the She-Wolf, at the age of eight of the Balillas, then of the Young Italians, and so on for every age to the grave. In Germany children are conscripted into the Children's Group of the Hitler Youth at the age of six, facilities being accessible to children down to four years of age; from ten to fourteen years boys and girls belong to the Young Folk (*Jungvolk*) and Young Maidens, respectively; from fourteen to eighteen to the Hitler Youth (*Hitler-Jugend*) proper and the Bund of German Girls, respectively. Before being admitted to the Party itself or one

---

[23] *Dictatorship,* in its original Roman sense, indicated a power conferred during emergencies and for a limited period of time, of the use of which account had to be rendered to the Senate and to the people. Today dictatorship means the power of an irresponsible and absolute leader with unlimited power over everybody and everything.

of its organizations of adults, the adolescents have to go through
the rigorous training of the Labor Service (both sexes) and of the
Army. The Russians have the "voluntary" organization of the
Young Pioneers, embracing the ages from eight to sixteen; younger
children may be banded together in the Octobrist groups. From
the age of seventeen, a Russian boy or girl is eligible for the Communist Youth (*Comsomol*).

A State organized along such lines must have a goal: Fascist Italy
has dreamt of the Roman Empire, Nazi Germany has idealized the
Herrenvolk, Bolshevist Russia has aimed at world-wide Communist revolution. In order to assert itself, the State must rely
upon an ever larger and increasingly modern military organization. Mussolini once said: "What maternity is to woman, war is to
man," thus uniting two goals—natural and unnatural—one of
which destroys the other. The upshot was the complete mili-
tarization of the country.

There remained the Church. As long as the Church could be
useful toward bringing about or maintaining dictatorships, its
help was sought, and concordats were negotiated. But when the
Church became an obstacle to the spirit of the totalitarian States,
it was persecuted and even abolished. The Bolshevists tried to
form a church of their own, then they suppressed it, proscribing
its priests and closing its buildings, declaring freedom of worship,
but imposing so many restrictions that this freedom became illusory. Hitler promised that the State would respect both Catholics and Protestants, attempted to make out of the Protestant
church a Hitlerian church, stipulated a concordat with Rome. But
he soon failed in his promises to both Catholics and Protestants by
beginning a subtle persecution which aims at the complete de-
Christianization of Germany.

Mussolini settled the Roman question with the Vatican and accepted a concordat on Pius XI's terms. Generally speaking, he
attempted to avoid open conflict with the Church, by favoring it
up to the point where it did not threaten the development of
Fascism. Here the chief conflict arose out of the question of education of the youth and of their Catholic societies. In this connection, Pius XI published the Encyclical *Non abbiamo bisogno*,[24]
wherein he brought into relief the danger of a State monopoly in
the education of youth and the broader danger contained in view-

[24] Commonly known as "On Catholic Action," June 29, 1931.

ing the State as the end of man. Pius XI had already condemned in his allocution of December 1926 the Fascist "notion that the State is the last end, for which alone the citizen exists." In the aforesaid Encyclical there is a declaration which gives the crux of the issue existing between the Vatican and all totalitarian States: "We are, as we stated above, happy and proud to wage the good fight for the liberty of consciences." [25] And the same Pius XI adds: "Besides, there is involved another right of the Church, equally inviolable, to fulfill the imperative divine commission entrusted to her by her Divine Founder, to bring to souls—to bring to every soul—all the treasures of truth and good, doctrinal and practical, which He Himself brought to the world." [26]

Many are the documents and the speeches of Pius XI against the State called totalitarian. Being anxious that an exact understanding of current errors concerning race, nationalism and totalitarianism should be imparted in Catholic seminaries and universities, the same Pope Pius caused to be drafted the famous list of eight erroneous propositions, the last of which runs as follows: *"Singuli homines non sunt nisi per 'Statum' et propter 'Statum'; quidquid iuris ad eos pertinet, ex Status concessione unice derivatur."* [27]

This totalitarian Leviathan, even if it grants concessions to the Church and accepts concordats, can never admit that the spiritual formation of the people should escape its influence; that any autonomous force should resist it and that the Church should inculcate ideas, principles and theories that contradict the nature, and diminish the power, of the State. It is impossible for the Church to be free under a totalitarian State, which, as such, is intolerant of any liberty.

The fundamental reason is that the basis upon which State totalitarianism is built, is an absolute one. [28] Be this basis the nation, the empire, the race, or the class, we are in every case faced

[25] The Pope said "of consciences" and not "of conscience," for "liberty of conscience" is an equivocal expression too often distorted to mean the absolute independence of conscience, which is "absurd in a soul created and redeemed by God." *(Ibid.)*

[26] *Ibid.*

[27] "Each man exists only by the State and for the State. Any right he possesses is derived exclusively from a concession by the State." Letter of the Sacred Congregation of Seminaries and Universities, April 13, 1938.

[28] In his first Encyclical, *Summi Pontificatus* (October 20, 1939), Pius XII speaks against that civil authority which "puts itself in the place of the Almighty and elevates the State or group into the last end of life, the supreme criterion of the moral and juridical order, and, therefore, forbids every appeal to the principles of natural reason and of Christian conscience."

with a deification that brooks no limits set by another God—no moral limits and hence no juridical nor religious limits. The State so organized becomes the source of every right and of all social reality.

We are faced with a slow but logical realization of theories formulated in the course of nearly two centuries. From a limitless popular will without moral checks (Rousseau), through the idea of the State as supreme manifestation of the spirit (Hegel), one arrived at positivism which made of human society an absolute (Comte), an entity outside of the individuals (Durkheim), with everything reduced to mere struggle for material survival (Marx). But more vivid images and deeper sentiments were needed in order to impress the masses and arouse their fanaticism; nationality, race, empire, class were shibboleths suited to fill that need. The war of 1914-1918 with its destruction of the existing particular order of things led to an extraordinary flowering of one of the most terrible social evils with which humanity has ever had to contend.

Pius XI set forth the problem in these clear terms: "He who takes the race or the people, or the State, or the form of government, the bearers of the power of the State or other fundamental elements of human society—which in the temporal order of things have an essential and honorable place—out of the system of their earthly valuation, and makes them the ultimate norm of all, even of religious values and deifies them with an idolatrous worship, perverts and falsifies the order of things created and commanded by God; such a one is far from the true belief in God and a conception of life corresponding to the true belief." [29]

The world fell into the sin of idolatry when it raised the State, the nation, the race, the class, the dictator to the plane of principles of morality, of law, and of the existence of the human community. Thereupon, unruly and unbridled passions broke through the barriers restraining them, because the Heavens are closed to idolaters; to them man is no longer a brother or a fellow creature, but a thing crystallized in the name of a false deity; all those incapable of being assimilated to that deity (the nation, race, or class), become brute matter to be subjugated, eliminated, or destroyed.

*

*   *

[29] Encyclical Letter *Mit brennender Sorge* (The Church in Germany), March 14, 1937.

Up until the second half of the nineteenth century anti-Semitism was resorted to by the Russians or the Turks in the name of "reason of State." From time to time anti-Semitic pogroms were engineered by the police in order to appease the populace, which was given certain designated days for looting and revenge. But with the advent of nineteenth-century nationalism there arose a theoretical anti-Semitism (as we have already intimated), justification for which was sought by invoking the ideas of national homogeneity or, later, of racial purity, or of struggle against the internationalisms of the capitalists and of the proletarians, which allegedly were of Jewish inspiration.

After Hitler came into power, anti-Semitism assumed the twofold aspect of an outlawing of the Jews and their systematic extermination. The anti-Semitic regulations of the Reich were extended to Austria, Czechoslovakia and Italy before the war, and since the war they have been applied in all Nazi-occupied territories; but it should be added that anti-Semitic sentiments and prejudices are also rather widespread in the democratic countries of both Europe and America.

The Papacy has put up a strong fight against anti-Semitism, which exists even in Catholic circles. Pope Pius XI has taken an unforgettable stand in this connection. As early as 1928, by his express will, there was added to a Decree of the Holy Office dissolving a certain Roman association called "The Friends of Israel" (which for disciplinary and liturgical reasons clashed with Catholic tradition), this open declaration against anti-Semitism: *"Qua caritate promota Apostolica Sedes eumdem populum contra iniustas vexationes protexit, et quemadmodum omnes invidias ac simultates inter populos reprobat, ita vel maxime damnat odium adversus populum olim a Deo electum, odium nempe illud, quod vulgo 'antisemitismi' nomine significari solet."* [30]

The several speeches of Pius XI, upon the occasion of the introduction of anti-Semitic laws in Italy, are of great importance and some of them are declarations truly worthy of a lasting place in historical records. For instance, in September 1938, during the re-

---

[30] "Moved by the spirit of charity, the Apostolic See has protected the people (of Israel) against unjust persecutions, and since it condemns all jealousy and strife among peoples, it accordingly condemns with all its might the hatred directed against a people which was once chosen by God, that particular hatred indeed which today commonly goes by the name of anti-Semitism." Decree of the Holy Office of March 25, 1928.

ception of a group of Belgian pilgrims, the Pope, having asked for the missal, read with tears in his eyes that passage in the Canon where, after the Consecration, God is asked to accept the offering of the Mass as he accepted "the sacrifice of our Patriarch, Abraham." And the Pope added: "Abraham is called our patriarch and ancestor. Anti-Semitism is not compatible with the sublime reality of this text. It is a movement in which we Catholics cannot participate." "Nor," he declared, "is it possible for Christians to take part in anti-Semitism. We are Semites spiritually." [31]

Together with acute anti-Semitism, there has developed in Germany a totally immoral State-eugenics. Its aim is to regulate births —as if human beings were mere livestock—from an exclusively animal point of view, in total disregard of the regular formation of families. It also aims at the elimination of diseased subjects through sterilization. Both measures have for their alleged end the achieving of racial purity and of national homogeneity and strength. There was no need of any formal condemnation by the Church to apprise Catholics of the immorality of such practices. But since among the latter in Germany a dispute had arisen as to whether in certain cases the State had the right to order sterilization of its "subjects," the Church did not hesitate to speak out. Her constant answer is and has always been that it is not licit for anyone either to order sterilization where it is not necessary and

[31] Quotations taken from the article "The Church and Anti-Semitism" -in the *Catholic Record* of London, Ontario, Canada, January 7, 1939. The news was also published by the Catholic papers of Belgium and by *La Vie Intellectuelle*, Paris, February 10, 1939. In the *Osservatore Romano* of July 30, 1938, in an official account of the pontifical reception of July 28, 1938, Pope Pius XI, deprecating the racial anti-Semitic movement in Italy, is quoted as saying: "We may ask ourselves how, unhappily, Italy has felt the need of imitating Germany." At this point the Holy Father opened smilingly a parenthesis saying that "somebody—and this had already happened in other circumstances—might have accused him of prejudice because, as is well known, the Pope is a son of Milanese, the men of the *'Cinque Giornate'* who threw the Germans out of their town. No, this is not the reason; it is because the Latins never used *race* or similar words. Our ancestors had other, more beautiful, more agreeable words: *gens Italica, Italica stirps, Japeti gens.* To Pius XI these words looked more civilized and less barbaric." How humane were these words of the Holy Father, and how timely his recollection of the five days of struggle with the Germans at Milan in 1848! For the allusion is particularly significant in view of the fact that the Germans are now once more in Italy, although, to be sure, the "Germans" of 1848 were in reality "Austrians."

Here we take occasion to refer the reader to a recent commendable and well-documented work, *National Patriotism in Papal Teaching*, by John J. Wright (The Stratford Co., Boston, 1942).

against the will of the patient, nor to take part in such an operation even as medical assistant in public or private hospitals, or to lend one's services, in any manner whatsoever, to promote and spread the practice of sterilization.[32]

Bad as this practice is, what shall we say of the killings, ordered by public authority, of those who "because of psychical or physical defects are no longer useful to the nation, but rather a burden to it?" When this news first appeared in the papers, the temptation was strong to classify it as wartime propaganda meant to slander the German Reich. But presently we read in the *Osservatore Romano* of December 1940 the answer of the Holy Office to the question propounded by a bishop of an unnamed country. The question was: *"Num licitum sit ex mandato auctoritatis publicae, directe occidere eos qui, quamvis nullum crimen morte dignum commiserint, tamen ob defectus psychicos vel physicos nationi prodesse iam non valent, eamque potius gravare eiusque vigori ac robori obstare censentur."* [33] Naturally the Holy Office answered

---

[32] The decree of the Holy Office of February 21, 1940, states that "direct sterilization of a man or a woman, either perpetual or temporary, is forbidden by the law of nature," and that eugenic sterilization had already been condemned by the same Holy Office on March 18, 1931, in connection with the Encyclical *Casti connubii* of December 31, 1930. *The New York Times* of December 24, 1939, published an Associated Press dispatch, according to which Heinrich Himmler, Chief of all German police organizations and leader of the Elite Guard, was quoted as stressing the need for more and more children. Herr Himmler had this to say with regard to the plans of the Nazi regime: "Special sponsors will be appointed by me for all children of good blood born in or out of wedlock, whose fathers fall in the war. . . . Beyond the limits of bourgeois laws and customs which ordinarily are probably necessary, it can become an exalted task even outside of wedlock for German women and girls of good blood to become—not frivolously but imbued with deepest moral concern—mothers of children begotten by soldiers moving to the front without knowing whether they will return or die for the Fatherland. Sponsors will look after the mothers and children during the war, and, if the fathers fall, after the war."

Moreover, Herr Hess, then Deputy Leader of the National Socialist Party, was quoted in the same dispatch as having announced the following regulations to be applied in all future cases of "war brides'" illegitimate offspring:

"1. At the birth registration of children of unmarried war brides the name of the father will be replaced by the designation 'war father' and where the name of the father is registered this designation will be applied to the name.

2. An unmarried war bride mother will keep her maiden name but with the title 'Frau'!

3. Where necessary the State will provide financial help, but the grandparents of war children will be expected to take care of them." These developments are perfectly in keeping with the anti-Christian and immoral principles of nationalism, denounced by Pius XI.

[33] "Whether it be legitimate, by order of public authority, to kill directly those who, though not guilty of a crime punishable by death, are because of psychic or

that such practice was "contrary both to natural law and to positive Divine Law."

Confronted with such facts, it seems in the nature of an anticlimax to protest against the suppression of minority schools, the forcing upon minorities of the language of the ruling national group, even in courts and in churches, the banning of private teaching, the obliteration of street names and epitaphs written in the language of the minority. These are all old methods of persecution, which nationalism has but enforced with greater asperity.

What has brought us back to the darkest ages of barbarism, with a speed and crescendo horrible to behold, is the mass deportation of minority groups in order to foster national homogeneity. In 1920, after the Greco-Turkish war, about one million Greeks were deported from Asia Minor. For more than a thousand years they had been living from generation to generation on the land, even under Turkish tyranny. And who does not recall the massacre of Greeks in Smyrna during that unhappy war? It is difficult to understand the complacency of the Western Powers towards this first large-scale deportation. It is true that the old Turkish regime had accustomed the world to the worst; but Ataturk had appeared upon the scene with the halo of the modern reformer. Only a few noticed the enormity of such a development, because nationalism veiled the crimes committed in its name.

Before the present war a deep impression was produced by the agreement between Mussolini and Hitler, whereby the South Tyroleans were offered the choice of returning to Germany or remaining in Italy. Out of a total of a little more than 200,000, approximately 75 per cent took the former alternative. As for those who chose to stay, the old policy was followed of using every pretext, good or bad, of administrative exigency, of military necessity, and so forth, to scatter them all over Italy, especially Southern Italy.

But the deportations of the present war are on an increasingly vast scale. The Poles, by the hundreds of thousands, have had to turn over their lands to the Germans. The German populations of the Baltic countries, numbering more than 80,000 were resettled, after the accord between Hitler and Stalin, in Pomerania and Poland. It was then rumored that the ancient German population of

physical defects no longer useful to the nation but rather a burden to it, and are thought to represent a handicap to the nation's vigor and strength."

the Volga region would be transported to Siberia or to other places. Such things are black crimes against the natural law.

It is difficult to ascertain what is happening today to war prisoners and to the subject populations of occupied or vanquished countries. We have had disquieting declarations such as the one stating the intention of destroying or scattering populations living in certain provinces because these are to be found within the alleged boundaries of Germany's *Lebensraum*. The system of the killing of hostages might easily come in the case of social structures based on the family, the clan or the feudal system, to be regarded as the only practicable way of enforcing on those communities the observance of the orders of the occupation authorities. In civilized and individualistic structures, that system lacks the same effectiveness and is both unjust toward the innocent and inefficacious owing to the lack of group solidarity. The reader will recall the cases of Lidice in Czechoslovakia and of other villages and towns in Yugoslavia. In the meantime, it is used with a view to destroying the social elites as appears, for instance, to be the case in Poland, Bohemia-Moravia, Belgium, Holland, Norway and France, as well as in the Balkan states.

The Vatican radio, as quoted by many Catholic newspapers in the United States, has often denounced the tortures and persecutions practised upon the Poles, from the religious as well as the moral and humanitarian points of view. The report which has aroused the deepest horror has been the news of prostitution being forced upon Polish girls, dragged into brothels organized for the use of the troops.

Similar policies, followed "because they are useful to the nation," together with those of compulsory sterilization and the killing off of the country's own nationals "because they are not useful to the nation," summarize all the inhumanity and immorality of a nationalism that has made of the nation a terrible deity and of the totalitarian State that deity's all-powerful minister.[34]

[34] The world has been horrified to learn from one news dispatch after another, arriving during the course of the past year, of the Nazi decision "to speed and intensify the extermination by massacre and starvation of the Jews remaining in occupied Europe." *(British Section of World Jewish Congress*—see general Press, Feb. 14, 1943.) It is believed that upwards of 5,000,000 Jews have already been "suppressed."

V

On the basis of our analysis so far, it is clear that the peaceful co-existence of nationalist, or—worse still—totalitarian, States is impossible. Wars of expansion and of conquest are a natural function of nationalist States; total war is the logical and historical outcome of the totalitarian State.

Let no one believe that we want to attribute the "invention" of war to nationalism and totalitarianism. War exists in the world in a more or less endemic condition. The rational tendency of man has always aimed at limiting war, at humanizing it, at realizing within positive law a natural law equal for all peoples, at forming an association of kindred nations. The *ius gentium* of ancient times, the patristic teaching which marked the first diffusion of Christianity, canon law and the formation of Christendom in the Middle Ages, the conception of natural law and its application to international law in modern times (witness Vitoria, Gentili, Grotius and Suarez), the beginnings of juridical associations among States, from the Congress of Vienna of 1814-1815, the Hague Conferences of 1897 and 1907, the Pan-American Union of 1890 down to the first realization by the League of Nations in 1919 of this tendency to associate—these are so many mile-stones marking the progress of mankind's never-to-be-halted march toward a practical and really peaceful brotherhood of peoples.

But if all States were based on the principle of nationalism, each one would be a law unto itself, both as regards internal existence and outward growth, and would not feel itself bound either by laws or by collective pacts or by bilateral treaties. It is true that a similar ruthlessness was advocated in the Renaissance and under the *ancien régime* by appeal to "reason of State." Yet, a moral and religious limit was acknowledged on all sides, and if that was violated, it was generally recognized that there had been a breach in the performance of duty both toward oneself and toward others. There were still such living organisms as the Church, the Estates, the parliaments, the municipalities, the universities, each of which had a personality of its own and strength enough to make it felt. Today, on the other hand, no social group has any strength left and the moral and religious limit is overridden by a pantheistic conception of nation. In the nation's name, everything is permitted, because it is no longer immoral. The tyrant of the Renaissance could say: "It is immoral, but it is useful to me." The nationalist tyrant, on the other hand, will say: "It is useful to me, therefore it is moral." The reversal is complete. War is no longer a baneful procedure used as a last resort in order to achieve justice (even where justice covers a *"latrocinium,"* to quote St. Augustine), but it is a normal means of domination in the name of one's own nation. Set two antagonistic nationalisms of equal strength one against the other (as, for instance, Germany and France until yesterday), and the consequence will be that the two countries in question will always be either under the incubus of impending war or suffering from the effects of past wars, won or lost. Such has been the situation for more than a century—from the revolutionary wars (1792) to the catastrophe of 1940.

When nationalism becomes totalitarian, war becomes total. It is no longer a question of limited wars, as under the paternalistic monarchies of the eighteenth century, with their armies based on the aristocratic classes, and it is no longer a question of popular wars and makeshift armies, created on the spur of the moment, as during the European and American revolutions from 1776 to 1848; it is rather a question of permanent armies of technicians made powerful by modern mechanized armament—the tank and the airplane; it is war that includes in its deadly embrace all the men and all the resources of a nation conscripted in a titanic effort at dominance by one power through annihilation of another.

The World War of 1914 offered a first specimen of total war; the present war is along more developed lines, with more efficient methods of destruction, aimed not so much at the territories as at the social structure of the countries involved. The old distinctions between *"nocentes"* (the harmful) and *"innocentes"* (the harmless) and the modern one between soldiers and civilians (combatants and non-combatants) have become meaningless and worthless. Indeed, the tendency to destroy to its roots an enemy population leads to the most atrocious and most unnatural deeds with systematic ruthlessness and ice-cold deliberation.

*

*   *

In order to quiet our growing apprehension in the face of this headlong race toward barbarism, it is alleged that these are not exceptional wars; that they are but imperialistic wars of which there has never been any dearth in the past. The descriptive term *imperialistic* is accentuated, as if it were something evil and immoral, which ought to disappear from political geography.

Just as we made a distinction between nation and nationalism, we will make here a distinction between empire and imperialism. The empire belongs to the historical nature of human societies; imperialism must often be taken as embodying a policy of dominion beyond the limits of right and of equity and hence to be condemned as something immoral. An empire may even be a desirable thing when it answers to the sociological characters of the populations forming it; in the historical international system, empires have served as bulwarks now against barbaric invasions (Tatars or Turks) as the Polish, Hungarian and Austrian Empires once did, now against the insecurity of the seas menaced by piracy (that of the true pirates and that of the States themselves) like the Spanish Empire in the fifteenth and sixteenth centuries and, since the eighteenth century, the British Empire and, more recently, the United States.

Obviously both in the formation and in the maintenance of empires there will often be deplorable facts and domineering tendencies. All this is in the nature of human society and is apparent in the small State of a million people as well as in the great empire of a hundred million people. But since good and evil must be related to the size of the entity producing them, if a wrong is perpetrated by a Swiss canton or by the Grand Duchy of Luxemburg, few will notice it; but if, on the other hand, it is committed by the United States, there would be no lack of accusers to write books on the Naboth's vineyard theme.

Just as we have in society big people and small people, wealthy and poor, the powerful and the humble, so we have among States analogous distinctions. The equalitarian idea conflicts with nature in the case of individuals and not less so in the case of peoples. The United States of America have grown in number from thirteen to forty-eight, and that was part of the natural development of things; if in the course of that development wrongs were committed, they may be imputed to the men directly responsible for them. No one will say that something wrong was right because the American people was involved. And the same may be said of the British Empire, or the German, or the Russian. The evil begins when, impatient at the slowness of its national growth and coalescence, a State or empire turns to conquest through unjust wars, or wars which, if justifiable in principle, are not so in their execution.

We have now reached a turning-point in civilization: all ethical conceptions, be they of natural law, or of *ius gentium,* or of Christianity, have been rejected in the name of a fundamental entity, the nation, and of its alleged rights as against those of other peoples.

Instead of striving for a peaceful living together of large, medium and small States, as nature and history have formed them, each in its own autonomy and all linked together by that international solidarity which is their fundamental law of existence and development, there has come to the surface a struggle of powerful nationalisms, drawing the medium and small States within their several orbits of domination and subjugating these by intimidation and force.

It was because of this that the League of Nations was opposed and reduced to impotence by the totalitarian States. We should mention, however, at this point the enormous responsibility of the so-called democratic States which because of their absenteeism or the uncertainty of their methods or their egoistic aims or their small faith in those very ethical and juridical principles that were at the basis of the League of Nations, allowed an institution to decay which could have rendered valuable services to international order. The Covenant of Geneva was far from perfect (though nothing after all is born perfect) and, furthermore, in that document all the mistakes of the peace treaties were reflected. The 1928 Kellogg-Briand pact on the renunciation of war as an instrument of national policy had a great moral basis but no juridical value. To say nothing of the unhappy reservations of Austen Chamberlain on behalf of the British Empire, no one had power to enforce observance of the plighted word in case of violation of the pact.

Just as Benedict XV traced the outlines of the international order to be established after the first Great War (his letter of August 1, 1917, will remain one of the most characteristic records of the intervention of the modern papacy in the life of nations), so Pius XII has fixed the ideal plan of international reconstruction with the five points of his Christmas allocution in 1939.[35]

---

[35] Pius XII's Christmas allocutions of 1941 and 1942 have been on the same subject, namely the International Christian Order. All three are in the same spirit and

The first point flatly contradicts totalitarian nationalism: the assurance to all nations of their right to life and independence. The same can be said of the remaining points, such as progressive disarmament; creation of juridical institutions; guarantees for the fulfilment of peace treaties and their revision as well; the acknowledgment of minority rights and the moral sense of responsibility for the observance of the precepts of justice and charity.[36] This is in substance Christian and natural morality applied to organized international society, in order to do away with the rule of the strongest, a rule which has become tyrannical owing to the lack of a moral conception limiting and checking it. How will it be possible to apply Pius XII's principles as long as peoples and their leaders continue to be infected with nationalism, and men do not reject the principles (if indeed such they may be called) of State totalitarianism? It is, therefore, absolutely necessary, in the face of the present world crisis, that excessive nationalism and State totalitarianism be rejected by Christian consciences, not only in the name of reason, but also in the name of religion. Unquestionably we are confronted with a collective apostasy that has overwhelmed European peoples and is already spreading to sections of the American peoples.

It may be debated whether and up to what point the right and wrong of the present war can be fairly apportioned among the belligerents. It seldom, if ever, happens that all the wrong is to be found on one side and all the right on the other. The very weakness and complacency of one side makes it responsible for the evil consequences, since it is owing precisely to such weakness and complacency that the emboldened enemy throws down the gauntlet of war.

What cannot be questioned and must be clearly borne in mind is that the nationalistic and totalitarian States of Europe looked only for the most propitious moment to impose by force a political

evince the same clear vision of the solution of post-war problems. His Christmas message of 1942, entitled "The Holy Season of Christmas and Sorrowing Humanity" (see the Catholic press for Dec. 31, 1942) is especially worthy of careful study.

[36] See *The Pope Speaks*, The Words of Pius XII, New York, Harcourt, Brace & Co., 1942. See also *America's Peace Aims*, The Catholic Association for International Peace, Washington, D. C., and especially *Principles for Peace: Selections from Papal Documents—Leo XIII to Pius XII*, edited for the Bishops' Committee by the Rev. Harry C. Koenig, S.T.D., National Catholic Welfare Conference, Washington, D. C., 1943.

and moral, a national and international, conception that is the negation of all the traditional values of Christian civilization insofar as these are realized for better or worse—more often for worse than better—by our infirm humanity.

We do not wish our readers to believe that nationalism alone, aggravated by totalitarianism, is the sole cause of this modern apostasy. Naturalism (taken in the sense of negation of every supernatural principle), sociological positivism, rationalistic philosophy have all permeated our society for more than a century. But while these errors, together with their derivatives, have been combated in the name of a sane philosophy and of the Christian religion, nationalism has been overlooked or, worse still, has been positively favored, even in the Church's so-called foreign missions, as Pope Pius XI strongly lamented.[37]

If it was opposed, it was opposed only on the political plane, which has led to greater confusion rather than to clarity among many Catholics. It would not be too much to say that the repeated warnings of Pius XI were the prophecy of one who was on the threshold of death. Pius XII accepted the inheritance when in his Encyclical he spoke of the error of totalitarianism as a divorce of "civil authority from every kind of dependence upon the Supreme Being—first Source and absolute Master of man and of society— and from restraint of a Higher Law derived from God as from its first source."[38]

Catholics should beyond the shadow of a doubt affirm and reaffirm that human and Christian universality which leads all to brotherhood in God, as against nationalisms which, raising themselves to the rank of deities, separate and hatefully divide mankind, each aspiring to dominate in the name of a self-attributed mission, and each substituting itself for God.

Pius XI, in the speech he addressed on July 28, 1938, to the alumni of the Pontifical Urban College de Propaganda Fide, re-

[37] In his speech to the alumni of the Pontifical Urban College de Propaganda Fide made on August 21, 1938, Pius XI told them among other things: "There is room for a just, moderate and temperate nationalism, associated with all virtues. But beware of exaggerated nationalism as of a malediction. It seems to us that unhappily everything bears us out when we call it a *true malediction*, because it is a malediction of divisions, of contrasts, leading to the danger of wars. For the missions, moreover, it is a real curse of sterility, because it is not along those lines that the fertility of grace can take root in souls and can cause the apostolate to flourish." (*Osservatore Romano*, 1938, no. 194.)

[38] See *America's Peace Aims, supra*, p. 21.

minded his hearers that "Catholic means universal, not racial, not nationalistic in the separatistic meaning of these two attributes." And he added: "Catholic Action must conform itself to these principles because Catholic Action means Catholic life. . . . It identifies itself with Catholic life, for what would life be without action? . . . Catholic life means activity based on charity, virtue, on the law of God which fills this life that therefore becomes God's life. There is no other way of Catholic thinking, and the latter is not racial, nationalistic, separatistic thinking in the sense which is clearly enough expressed by the last of these words. No separatism: we do not want to separate anything in the human family; for we understand—as is obvious—racism and exaggerated nationalism, *as they are commonly understood,*[39] to be barriers raised between men and men, natives and natives, peoples and peoples." [40] Pius XI had so well understood, as if by intuition, the evil impending for humanity, that in the last two years of his life, from the famous three Encyclicals of March 1937 to the eve of his death (when he wrote the document directed to the bishops of Italy, whose text has remained a secret), his constant thought was the one of guiding Catholics towards the repudiation of what he called racism and nationalism *as they are commonly understood*— the repudiation, namely, of the basis on which State totalitarianism was built. The Pope reiterated upon every possible occasion that "the contrast between exaggerated nationalism and Catholicism is evident" and that "the spirit of this nationalism is contrary to the spirit of the *Credo,* is contrary to the Faith." The Pope declared, in the audience granted to the nuns of the *Cenacolo* on July 15, 1938, Cardinal Pacelli (now Pope Pius XII) being present, that "he had never thought of these problems with such precision, with such, one might say, absoluteness, with such intransigence of formulas; and since God has given him the grace of this clarity, he wants to share it with his sons, because everybody needs it in times like the present when these ideas are attracting so much attention and inflicting so much damage. That very same day they had brought him very serious information and there could be no longer any doubt that it was a case of real apostasy." [41]

These words begin with the open confession that *"he had never*

---

[39] Italics ours.
[40] *Osservatore Romano,* 1938, no. 175.
[41] *Osservatore Romano,* 1938, no. 164.

thought of these problems with such precision" and continue as if the Pontiff were leaving a bequest: *"Since God has given him the grace of this clarity, he wants to share it with his sons."* These are moving words, uttered by a great man who, upon realizing the imminence of the catastrophe, opened his soul before the world. These words were caught only by a few; they were printed by the press of the world just like the texts of the many papal speeches to nuns and priests and pilgrims thronging the Vatican. Much later, a majority of Catholics and of non-Catholics, too, awoke from the stupor of nationalistic poisoning. But this happened only with the outbreak of the present war, nay only after the war had assumed the proportions of a world-wide struggle. Among the many causes of this, we must include the misconception of nationalism as fervent and active love of one's own nation, whereas in truth it was already possessed by an egoistic spirit, inoculated with an inhuman theory that has divided peoples and emboldened tyrants.

Words have their own life and evolution. When the word nationalism was coined, it meant the economic theory of "nationalization of certain industries of collective interest." Later the word was used to express the love of nation and the defense of its rights against the "Workers' International" and "class internationalism." Still later it was applied to the defense of "nationality" and of oppressed "minorities" (something which should have been called, as suggested by René Johannet, *"nationalitarism"*).[42] Finally it came to mean a given sociological-political theory and the nation was thought of in terms of a supreme entity, a law unto itself, without limits of human or divine bounds, while the national State was declared the totalitarian State. For us, today, in the light of recent experiences, *nationalism* should not hold any other meaning. It is not possible that there should be a common denominator of what is good (love of nation) and what is intrinsically bad (the deification of nation). Before the present war, in order to distinguish between nationalism and nationalism, the bad one was classified as *radical* nationalism (Vermersch, S. J.) or as *exaggerated,* in contrast to *moderate,* nationalism (Pius XI). But as Pius XI himself emphasized in the last year of his life, by nationalism *"as it is commonly understood"* today is meant the exaggerated kind, the kind in fact that separates peoples from peoples and is opposed to the Catholicity or universality of the religion of Christ, in view

---

[42] Maurice Vaussard, *Enquête sur le nationalisme,* Paris, p. 377, Editions Spes, 1924.

of which, notwithstanding all the differences of race, of nation, of social condition and of culture, all men are brothers. Over divisions must prevail solidarity, over differences fraternity, over hatreds love.

* * * * *
* * * *
* * *
* *
*

VII

PERSON AND SOCIETY

By ——————

PERSON AND SOCIETY

GOD THE CREATOR AND HIS WORK

Man, in comparing himself to his fellow men, is only too prone to judge himself superior to them; he congratulates himself on "not being like the rest of men"; his fatuousness even leads him at times to consider himself a "superman." Never, however, no matter how great his pride, does he set himself up, consciously[1] at least, as God, supreme Master and ultimate End of the universe. Upon even slight reflection, the limits of his being, the weakness of his powers, the ephemeral character of his earthly existence make abundantly clear his fundamental dependence. And should he wish to know upon whom he depends, let him rehearse the dialogue of Saint Augustine, let him question earth and seas, plants and animals, air and winds, sky and stars; all will answer: *Non sumus Deus tuus; quaere super nos*—"We are not thy God; seek Him high above us." And should he press them further: "You say that you are not my God; tell me at least something of Him," they will answer with a single voice: *Ipse fecit nos!*—"It is He who made us!" (*Confessions*, X, 6).

This Supreme Being, the Author of all things, must not be confused with the universe which He created from nothingness. All things receive their existence from Him; He receives His from no one, for He is self-subsistent. All things depend upon Him; He depends on none, for He possesses by essence the plenitude of being.

His infinitely wise thought conceived the plan of this marvelous universe; His all-powerful will gave it reality, effortlessly, by the sole virtue of His creative *Fiat;* His Providence governs it with admirable mastery.

All creatures, indeed, at the same time they received existence from God, were assigned by Him a reason for being, a finality which constitutes the law of their being. This law, expression of

[1] We say *consciously*. In reality, the sinner who rebels against God and opposes to the divine will the *"non serviam,"* sets himself up unwittingly as a rival of God—virtually proclaims himself God.

211

the will of the Creator, imposes itself upon matter by virtue of a physical necessity from which it cannot escape, upon the spirit as a moral obligation which it must meet by a spontaneous determination of its free will.

Man, situated on the confines of the two great domains of creation, participates both in matter and in spirit, and the duality of his nature distinguishes him from all the other creatures that people this visible universe. If he undergoes in his body all the necessities of the physical laws that regulate matter, his soul escapes from this constraint. By it and by the liberty which constitutes his exclusive prerogative, man finds himself placed "in the hands of his counsel" and established as the arbiter of his own destiny. It depends upon his free will to accomplish or not the end that God has assigned him; but he bears the full responsibility for his choice. If he conforms to the will of his Creator, he places himself in the order which his nature demands and finds there the peace and happiness for which he was created; if he refuses to submit, he deliberately places himself outside the divine plan, in a disorder which does violence to his nature and which of necessity plunges him into unhappiness.

It is then of supreme importance to man to know the thought of God as regards himself and the end which this thought has assigned to him, as well as the means given him to achieve that end.

THE END OF MAN

God does not revoke the gift of being that He made to humanity in creating it from nothingness. The existence of man has a beginning; it will never know an end. Death may indeed dissolve temporarily the human composite; this latter will be reconstituted on the day of the resurrection and will live forever *in perpetuas aeternitates.*

To this existence without end the Creator has assigned a finality which He could not fail to relate to Himself, since He is the Infinite Being, source of every created being. Created in the image of God, man possesses an intelligence made to know God, the supreme Truth, a will made to attach itself to Him, the Infinite Good, and to find in the possession thereof the satisfaction of all human desires—perfect happiness.

By his natural powers alone, however, man would never arrive at anything more than a purely abstract and rational knowledge of God; his condition as a created being confines him to the rank of servitor with no right whatsoever to the intimacy of his Master. But God has not limited to the unique gift of creation the magnificent munificence with which He has deigned to enrich man. Raising the latter above the strict exigencies of human nature, He has introduced him into the supernatural order, rendered him a participant in His own divine nature, caused him to pass from the condition of slave to that of child of God, and by this adoption has conferred upon man the privilege of knowing Himself one day "as He is," of loving Him and of being loved by Him with that intimate and profound love which reigns between a father and his children.

Such is the sublime destiny to which from the beginning God called humanity—the destiny, too, alas! which from the beginning the fatal gesture of the first-born of our race proudly repulsed. Nevertheless this foolish rebellion failed to rebuff the infinite Goodness that is God, for whom it became the happy occasion of a more magnificent reparation. Redeemed at the price of the blood of the Incarnate Word, men found again "the power of becoming sons of God" and it depends exclusively on them whether they shall one day possess the divine heritage promised them.

This coming into possession of the celestial heritage seals irrevocably the destiny of men. It takes place, however, only in eternity, upon the blessed invitation: "Enter into the joy of thy Master." But it is during his brief earthly existence that man prepares his eternity: *In momento aeternitas.* Hence the inestimable value of his mortal life and the unparalleled importance of the mission he must accomplish therein.

This temporal destiny of man does not differ essentially from his eternal destiny; but he fulfills it through means and in a manner commensurate with his mortal condition.

It is not given to him to know God here below "as He is," to contemplate him "face to face"; but his intelligence reveals to him, behind the screen of this created universe, the invisible presence and the all-powerful action of the Author of all things; faith introduces him to the secrets of the Divine Being inaccessible to unaided natural reason; and this knowledge, imperfect and veiled though it be, suffices to command admiration, submission and love.

The presence of man in the bosom of the visible world gives

the latter its reason for existence. Without him, this world would be no more than a useless mirror unconscious of the divine perfections it reflects; no voice would rise above the silent abysses to sing the greatness and to bless the munificence of the Creator. It is by man's tongue that the earth and the heaven proclaim the glory of God; it is he who commands all the works of the Lord to praise their Author. In his very person, matter, informed by spirit, participates in the life of the latter and rising above itself becomes capable of paying to God the tribute of praise, homage and submission that every creature owes to Him: *Benedic anima mea Domino et omnia quae intra me sunt nomini sancto ejus.*

It is also man's noble task to push to its complete achievement the work of the Creator by exploiting all the potentialities of nature and by making them serve toward his own material, intellectual and moral perfection. This world was entrusted to him that he might keep it and make the most of it by applying to it all the resources of his work and genius, and all effort expended to this end deserves from then on to be considered as a prolongation of the creative work of God.

Finally, by the part he plays in the transmission of the life that he has himself received, man assures to the visible universe interpreters by whose voice every creature will sing to the very end of time the glory of the Author of all good. In this way also he will help to people heaven by giving brothers to the angels and the elect to God.

The Social Nature of Man

Such is the magnificent task assigned to each man who comes into this world and the faithful accomplishment of which assures to him the fulfilment of his eternal destiny.

It remains to be seen what means are placed at his disposal to enable him to perform this capital task.

Assuredly human nature is rich in potentialities; but these would remain hopelessly sterile if the aid of exterior agents did not enable them to come into operation. Just as the germ, in order to push up its stalk, to cover itself with leaves, to burst into flower and to put forth fruit, requires the nourishing juices of the earth, the light and the heat of the sun, often the intervention of human effort; so the human being develops, becomes enriched and reaches the fulness of his personality thanks to what he borrows from the material world wherein he is immersed, from the fellow beings among whom he lives, and thanks above all to the constant and all-powerful aid of God.

Divine help will never fail men of good will and is sufficient in itself with their co-operation for the accomplishment of their eternal destiny.

Yet, in the normal plan ordained by Providence, each man needs, in order to realize his destiny here below, the aid of his fellow men.

Man, in fact, presents himself to us under a double aspect. If we consider him in himself, he reveals himself as a person, a being existing in himself, having his own destiny which he realizes on his own responsibility. But if we envisage him in the concrete reality of his existence and activity, both appear so intimately associated with the existence and activity of other human beings that it would be difficult to disassociate them therefrom. Man is a social being; he is made to live and develop in the society of his fellow men.

To this sociability of man, the very constitution of the human organism bears witness. Speech and hearing are given to man to enable him to carry on a constant commerce of thoughts and desires with other thinking beings. He comes into being only by the co-operation of two human beings who have become partners in order to communicate life to him and this life would be indeed precarious if those who were its authors did not consent to provide over a long period for its maintenance and development.

Moreover, man subsists only by dint of constant borrowings from the material world surrounding him. Left to his own unaided powers how could he triumph over grudging nature which surrenders its treasures only after a struggle? To overcome its resistance he will need a skilful technique, whose formula will have had to be elaborated by a long line of searchers and whose operation will demand the co-operation of a great many persons.

And if from the purely material plane we pass to the intellectual and moral plane, do we not reach an identical conclusion: the extreme dependence of man, in his thought and will, upon the social environment which shapes him and marks him with its deep imprint? Man finds his knowledge in the treasures of the science and experience accumulated by the generations that have preceded him upon this earth; his character is formed and tempered in the school of the family and of the various social environments in which he needs must live.

The *individual* about whom the majority of philosophical and sociological treatises speak is in reality no more than a pure abstraction; man is, for the most part, the product of the environment into which he is born, grows up and lives. Joseph de Maistre, could say with truth: "I have known Englishmen, Frenchmen, Germans and Russians, never have I met man," and Georges Valois observed very justly: "I have been the son, I am now the father; never have I been simply man."

Society is therefore the natural environment outside of which the human being could not reach his full development or fulfill his destiny. The plant dies when we pull it from the earth in which it has struck its roots, the flower fades when we pluck it from the stem that nourishes it. So man isolated from the society of his fellow men is hopelessly doomed to extreme material destitution and to the most complete spiritual poverty. This, in the last analysis, is the logical outcome of the individualism which, under pretext of assuring to man the full flowering of his personality, claims to break the bonds that bind him so tightly to his fellow men, to free him from all the constraints that social life imposes upon him and to constitute him the sole arbiter of his own destiny. Instead of the strong and vigorous personalities it congratulates itself on raising up, it has produced only a mutilated, impoverished and disabled type of humanity. From the dust of the individuals into which it has pulverized humanity no superman will ever arise; it can only give rise to "sub-men."

The Various Patterns of Social Collaboration

Human solidarity manifests itself under very different forms and modalities.

There is first of all the solidarity that manifests itself in completely spontaneous exchanges of services without any legal bond to associate permanently the persons who mutually aid one another. Such is the solidarity which is established between producer and consumer, between seller and buyer, between borrowers and lenders, between masters and disciples, between thinkers, scholars, artists and those who benefit by their wisdom, their knowledge or their art. Each of the parties engaged in the exchange of goods or the negotiation of a loan seeks therein a legitimate advantage while contributing to the advantage of the other party. But in the infinite web of relationships which are established thus in the bosom of the great human multitude there is no constraint, no pre-established agreement. The relationships are made or broken off according to the interest or good pleasure of the parties involved, who are in no way obligated to enter into the relationship.

There is nothing less stable than the balance of so many particular interests, concordant or divergent in turn. Production modifies its rhythm endlessly; customers develop other tastes or set up new demands; markets change and move; the exchange of goods and services takes a new direction.

Yet so strong is human solidarity that for every balance broken another is quickly reached, that the contacts broken at certain points are speedily re-established elsewhere and that, in spite of the thousand accidental shocks and troubles, nothing avails to obstruct in human communities the beneficial interchange of goods, services and thoughts. Similarly, in the healthy living organism, the circulatory system knows how to open for the blood new "anastomotic" channels whenever some accident happens to interrupt at a given point the natural course of the blood-stream.

The community which results from the interdependence and solidarity of particular interests powerfully aids the human beings it groups together to fulfill their destiny here below; it is nonetheless insufficient to secure for them all the benefits requisite to this end. The great error of liberalism was to have thought that the mutual exchange of goods and services would exhaust in itself all the possibilities of human sociability. This latter is further called on to procure for men benefits and advantages of a general nature, necessary to all, the enjoyment of which none of them, left to his own efforts, could secure for himself. The mere exchange of services does not suffice here; what is required is the collaboration of many individual activities, closely united in the pursuit of a common objective whose realization will benefit each of the associates. The community must give place to society.

Society is a stable grouping of persons collaborating for the realization of a common good under the direction of a single authority.

Unlike the spontaneous relationships which are established between the members of a simple community, according to their interests or their good pleasure, these associates are linked together by a formal legal bond that obliges them to co-operate in the common work and confers upon them the right to participate in the advantages which result therefrom. Society has this legal bond to thank for its stability; it is, however, to the co-ordinating action of authority and to the driving force this communicates to the activity of the members that it owes the effective attainment of its objectives.

Since it is the indigence and innate weakness of man which impels him to unite himself with his fellow men, it follows that man has from his very nature a right of association whose exercise no one may dispute. The use he makes of this right, however, gives rise to societies of very different nature and scope.

There are societies whose creation depends wholly on the free decision of the associates. The latter determine in all freedom the goal of their collaboration, fix as they wish the law that shall regulate their activity, designate at will the authority that is to take charge of the common interest. In this category belong those private associations that abound in all countries: industrial, commercial, professional, scientific, artistic, cultural, charitable, religious, etc. The same person will often, because of the various ends he pursues, hold membership in a large number of private societies.

These societies, however, are no more necessary than the limited benefit assigned them as their object; they answer a need of utility or convenience, not a necessity of human nature, and it is optional with any one to give or deny them his support.

There are other social ends indispensable to the perfection of human nature, which imperiously demands that they be attained, and such exigency calls for the constitution of societies rightly qualified to accomplish said purposes—societies of natural right. To this category belong conjugal unions, civil societies and international societies.

The first has as its object to ensure the propagation of the race and to provide for the education of the new generation.

The second is instituted to secure for its members those elements of perfection which their nature demands but which their individual efforts are powerless to realize.

The third, finally, is called upon to organize the activity of all States for the establishment of an international order by grace of

which each of them will be enabled to realize more efficaciously
the common good of its own subjects.

Societies of natural right, we say, and with reason. The nature
that demands them likewise dictates their essential laws, which it
is not within man's power to modify. To be sure, the conjugal
union is constituted by the free and mutual consent of the parties
concerned, but the latter, once the marriage vows are exchanged,
find themselves irrevocably bound by the inexorable law of marriage: unity, indissolubility, finality.

Men, incapable as a rule of prospering outside of civil society,
retain doubtless, in a certain measure, their free choice as to the
particular political community to which they prefer to give their
allegiance; they have the option of determining the form of government which is to govern them and of drawing up the charter
of their legitimate rights and immunities; but the laws which they
thereby constitute for themselves will be administered by whom-
ever they elect as heads in virtue of an authority that dominates
them sovereignly, because it comes from God.

In the same way, too, the international society, which already
exists in fact, tends to organize itself. It depends on the will of
men to create its institutions, to determine by what organ its authority shall be exercised, but it is not in their power to fix arbitrarily the objective which this society is to pursue, or the essential principles of international law.

This the Creator has done Himself and it is, once more, human
nature that by its exigencies reveals to us the Divine will.

The family, political society and international society—*domus,
urbs, orbis,* as Saint Augustine says—are the natural and consequently necessary legal groupings. It may be observed, however,
that these various societies correspond to needs which have different degrees of urgency.

The family, absolutely indispensable to the propagation of the
race, is the most necessary. Hence it appears from the very beginnings of humanity. Political society can exist only after the condition of density of population, rendering its constitution possible,
has been fulfilled and the collective needs necessitating it have
made their appearance. International society, finally, can be organized only after the different branches of the great human family have taken sufficient cognizance of their natural solidarity and
of the need of a common supranational good that can only be

realized through the united effort of their collective good will. With our colleagues of the *International Union of Social Studies* at Malines, we are convinced that this international society is actually in existence at the present time and that it is the duty of all the States to give to it at long last the juridical constitution it needs in order to accomplish its beneficent and pacific mission.[1] The grave menaces that weigh upon the world at the present day, strikingly confirm—so it appears to the writer—the truth of this contention.

Of the three societies of natural right, whose nature we have briefly outlined and whose economy we have examined, the second —civil or political society—will now claim our whole attention.

CIVIL SOCIETY AND THE COMMON GOOD

"Man," says Saint Thomas, "is naturally a part of some multitude, through which help is afforded him for living well"—*Homo naturaliter est pars alicujus multitudinis per quam praestetur sibi auxilium ad bene vivendum* (Eth. Lib. I, lectio Ia). And Leo XIII in his Encyclical, *Immortale Dei,* develops the same thought in the following words:

"Man is born to live in civil society; for being unable in isolation to procure for himself either what is necessary and useful to life or what makes for the perfection of spirit and heart, Divine Providence has put it in his nature to unite with his fellow men in society, domestic as well as civil, which alone is capable of furnishing what suffices for the perfection of life.

"Inasmuch, however, as no society can exist without a supreme head who efficaciously imparts to its single members a like impulse toward the common goal, it comes to pass, that for the civil community of men authority is needed to govern them—an authority which, like society itself, proceeds from nature and, therefore, from God Himself."

The essential function of authority, accordingly, is to co-ordinate harmoniously all the activities of the individual members and to apply them thus united to the realization of the social aim which it is its mission to promote.

This power, nonetheless, is conferred upon the civil authority exclusively in view of the social aim, the common good, for which it is responsible; it finds its limits in the very nature of this aim —this good. Hence, the fundamental problem of all social philosophy consists in determining what this common good—the end

[1] Cf. *A Code of International Ethics,* articles 9 and ff.

and term of all social activity—really is. Upon the solution given
to this question will depend the greater or lesser part that will be
accorded to the intervention and powers of authority on the one
hand and to the liberty and rights of individuals on the other.

The various solutions offered of this problem have issued from
totally opposite doctrines.

THE LIBERAL INTERPRETATION

Some wish to see in the common good of society no more than
the sum or, at most, the resultant of the particular goods of its
single members. The social body, if we are to believe them, is enriched or impoverished commensurately with the enrichment or
impoverishment of the individuals grouped within its bosom. Here
we have the theory espoused by individualistic liberalism. From its
point of view there is no need positively to direct individual effort
toward the social good; the latter results necessarily from the activity each individual exerts in his own personal interest. "Each
one," wrote Mirabeau, "is or believes himself free in his own
sphere, and each is led by the sight of his own good to work toward
the universal good" (*Social Philosophy*). Adam Smith, in turn,
observes that each individual being interested in increasing endlessly the value of his own product, works by that very fact to
augment the annual revenue of society, and he adds immediately:
"He generally, indeed, neither intends to promote the public interest, nor knows how much he is promoting it . . . he intends
only his own gain; and he is in this, as in many other cases, led by
an invisible hand to promote an end which was no part of his
intention. Nor is it always the worse for the society that it was
no part of it. By pursuing his own interest, he frequently promotes that of the society more effectually than when he really
intends to promote it. I have never known much good done by
those who affected to trade for the public good." (*An Inquiry into
the Nature and Causes of the Wealth of Nations*, Book IV, chap.
II.)

One may see without difficulty, however, that thus to identify
the notion of the common good with that of particular goods,
empties it of all proper content, that one takes away from social
activity its object, from society itself its reason for existence. The
State no longer has to regulate the activity of its citizens in view
of an end that surpasses the particular aims which they pursue.

"The world runs itself," Mercier de la Rivière gaily proclaimed, "the desire and the liberty to enjoy never ceasing to provoke the multiplication of products and the increase of industry, they impress upon all society a movement which becomes a perpetual tendency toward its best possible condition." (*The Natural and Essential Order of Political Societies*.) At the same time, the frontiers which separate the various political societies will tend to disappear and the exaggerated insularity that mercantilism attempted to impose upon nations will naturally be succeeded by a cosmopolitanism no less exaggerated, of which certain doctrinaires of liberalism will make themselves the champions. Not all the adherents of individualism are prepared to push the logic of the system so far. They prefer to retain for society and authority a reason for existence, but to reduce their scope to the mere defence of public order and liberty, both indispensable to the full flowering of those private initiatives on which, to their way of thinking, the prosperity of the body social depends.

This is, however, but a small concession and the concept of the *common good* still remains literally emptied of all positive content. The tutelary action that society is called upon to exercise adds, properly speaking, no new benefit to those which individuals have succeeded in procuring by their own initiative. Where is the *auxilium ad bene vivendum* of which Saint Thomas speaks, the positive aid given men in order to help them to live well?

Security is assured to those who have succeeded in building up for themselves a sufficient sum of particular goods. This is doubtless an appreciable thing, but what profit will accrue therefrom to those who lack the necessities? Liberty is guaranteed to all, but ordinarily it serves only the interests of the strongest and has for the weak only a very limited value. Social life is transformed into an arena open to the intense competition of unchecked appetites, to an exacerbated struggle for life which must inevitably end in the survival of the fittest and the elimination or enslavement of those less well endowed: *Paucis vivit humanum genus!*

Is there not, from that point on, supreme irony in speaking of collaboration for the common good, in connection with such a regime? In practice, moreover, the liberal system has broken all its promises. If it has been able, thanks to the stimulus it has given to the spirit of enterprise, to bring about a marvelous increase in the sum total of the wealth of nations, it has not been able to assure the equitable division of the goods so produced among all the members of the social body. The advantages resulting from the constant progress of science, the arts and technology, have become the perquisite of a very small portion of the community, while the majority of the population have found themselves pitilessly shut out from any legitimate benefit. "Wealth," observed Leo XIII, "has accumulated in the hands of a small number and the multitude has been left in poverty" (*Rerum novarum*).

The masses thus despoiled of the benefits that social life should, by virtue of its natural destination, procure for them, have ended by rebelling against this diversion of the common good to the profit of a minority. Their reaction has unfortunately led them towards an interpretation of human social life quite as erroneous as that which they very legitimately rejected.

THE SOCIALISTIC AND COMMUNISTIC INTERPRETATION

The powerful current which bears the masses toward Communism is a modern phenomenon, although communistic ideas date back to the first manifestations of human thought.

In all ages, indeed, the spectacle of the exploitation and enslavement of the weak by the strong, consequences only too usual of the unequal distribution of wealth, has impelled thinkers to seek in a profound reform of the social organization a remedy for these abuses. But it is the pseudo-scientific socialism of Karl Marx that has given to these aspirations a formula which claims to be definitive.

Socialists and communists agree in seeing in an entirely material felicity the supreme goal of human destiny. The social good, then, will consist, for them, in the greatest possible accumulation of material wealth and its equal distribution among the members of society. Now, the private ownership of capital makes of the proletarians passive instruments for the enrichment of those who dispose like masters of the means of production; the keen competition to which capitalists abandon themselves prevents them from deriving from these very means of production all the economic yield of which they are capable. It follows, therefore, that the quantity of material goods produced—the standard by which social prosperity is measured—is far from equaling the volume which the growth of capital and the progress of technology warrant, and that even this is most unequally divided among the totality of those who have contributed to its production.

It will be necessary, therefore, in order to step up to a maximum the quantity of consumable goods—which constitute the social good—and assure to all the benefit thereof, for the State to appropriate the whole of the nation's capital, with a view to assuring the rational exploitation thereof and to setting itself up as sovereign distributor of the wealth produced.

Private ownership of capital once abolished, all members of the social body find themselves on that footing of perfect equality demanded by their sameness of nature. No more masters, no more slaves; but all enrolled in the service of the common good under the orders of the social authority.

It goes without saying, nevertheless, that this authority will rule its subordinates with an iron hand. The gigantic enterprise of production it directs must be carried out according to a rigid plan, precise and minute, which leaves no place for caprice, improvisation, chance; all resources, all possibilities are inventoried, all needs measured; in the immense producing machine that society has become, each thing and each man is assigned his and its place, his and its task.

Such a regime tolerates neither whim nor spontaneity. An individual who departs from a given order is like a piece of machinery that slips a cog—a cog which jams.

Communism, then, is logically consistent with itself when it claims the right to regiment the entire man, body and soul, in the exclusive service of the collective enterprise of production.

Pope Pius XI analyzed very exactly, in his Encyclical *Quadragesimo anno,* this logical concatenation of socialistic thought:

"Socialism, completely ignoring the sublime destiny of man and of society, or not taking it into account at all, supposes the human community to be constituted only with a view to material well-being.

"Indeed, from the fact that an appropriate division of labor assures a more efficient production than does dispersed individual effort, the socialists conclude that economic production—whose material ends alone hold their attention—must of necessity be carried on collectively. And from this necessity it follows, according to them, that men are obliged, so far as production is concerned, to surrender and submit themselves wholly to society with a view to the production of wealth. What is more, such importance is attached to the possession of the greatest possible quantity of objects calculated to procure the advantages of this life, that the most exalted possessions of man, liberty not excepted, must be subordinated and even sacrificed, to the exigencies of the most efficient production."

Socialism, however, is fain to exonerate itself from the reproach of depriving man of his personal dignity and of obstructing him in the fulfilment of his proper destiny. True, it argues, in order to liberate the individual from the total enslavement in which capitalism holds him chained, there must be imposed upon him, in the order of production, the rigorous discipline of collective work. But this constraint is only partial and finds, in the order of the consumption and enjoyment of goods, a magnificent compensation in which the members of society will retain all their independence.

This attempt at justification did not escape His Holiness Pius XI. The Holy Father remarks:

"The loss of human dignity in the 'socialized' organization of production will be amply compensated, they assure us, by the abundance of goods which, socially produced, will be showered on individuals and which these last, as they see fit, will apply to the comforts and pleasures of the present life" (*ibid.*).

Vain attempt at escape! which does not succeed in diverting the Pontiff:

"Society, then, as Socialism dreams of it, cannot, on one hand, exist, or even come into being, without the use of manifestly excessive compulsion and, on the other hand, enjoys a license no less false, since in it no room is found for true social authority, which cannot be founded on temporal or material interests, but descends from God alone, Creator and Last End of all things" (*ibid.*).

Indeed, one cannot divide the life of man into two portions: one completely enslaved to the production of material goods, presented as the supreme end of his existence; the other consecrated to the search for a good infinitely superior to those for which he has been commanded to sacrifice the best part of his existence.

Personality, pitilessly immolated in the service of production, is not reborn during the rare moments of relaxation which the rigorous discipline of socialized work tolerates. Man, freed for a few hours from the collectivist "chain-gang," remains a degraded and mutilated creature, forever incapable of accomplishing his noble destiny. Facts, moreover, are stronger than theories. Socialistic thinkers may sincerely propose the eventual freeing of the human personality, but those who put their conceptions into practice cannot tolerate a personal autonomy that would escape their all-powerful control. The experience of Russian communism is proof of this. The Bolshevist dictators have understood that, as long as he keeps in the depths of his being the consciousness of a destiny superior to the material world surrounding him, man will never consent to play the rôle of a mere tool in the service of collectivist society's economic ends. Hence they have spared no effort to kill in him every vestige of truly spiritual life. They have waged relentless war on God, destroyed His temples, scrapped all cultural traditions, and at length barred all the gates by which the human spirit could envision vaster and more ennobling perspectives than those relating to Communistic society's materialistic ideal.

Communism, from then on, giving the lie to all its promises, sets itself up as a denier of human personality and identifies itself with the most radical totalitarianism.

THE TOTALITARIAN INTERPRETATION

Totalitarianism, as a political movement, is indeed a contemporary phenomenon; but the principles whence it springs are older and find their source in Hegelian pantheism, in the sociology of Comte and in Spencer's theory of social evolution, which gave birth to the "organic" school, the principal representatives of which were Fouillée, Espinas, Worms, Novicov, Izoulet, Durkheim, Giddings, Schaeffle, Lilienfeld, Gumplowicz.

For those who hold to this doctrine, society is the only truly living reality, existing in itself and for itself. It is "the most vital of known beings" (Comte), a great "physiological individual" (Fouillée), a monstruous "hyperzoaire" of which we are, as "metazoaires," only the modest components. Of this organism individuals are, in fact, the cells; the secondary aggregations spontaneously formed among them, the organs. Cells and organs receive from society soul and life, thought and will. For, just as society has its own life, so it has its own consciousness and its own will. Furthermore, by himself the human individual would not differ essentially from any other animal; it is his participation in the collective being that gives him a reason and a spirituality which raise him to the dignity of a human being: "Man is a man only because he lives in society. . . . It is society that forms the human type" (Durkheim).

Personality, if you will, but borrowed personality, and consequently illusory, which does not confer any autonomy. In the human body, too, the cells, the organs, the members live, but not

by virtue of a principle proper to themselves; their life comes
from the vital principle which moves the whole body, and that is
precisely the reason why, as simple components, they do not exist
for themselves, but only for the good of the aggregate in which
they are incorporated. Deriving, therefore—according to the *organic* doctrine—everything they are from the society which integrates them, they can have no personal end but exist solely for
the good of the superior organism which imparts to them being
and life.

Integral subordination of individuals to society, total abdication of their own personality: the sacrifice is not a small one. The
individual is assured, it is true, that he will automatically find his
compensation in the increase that will accrue to the single members from the greater vitality which their perfectly disciplined
activity gives to society.

That is quite possible; but we cannot forget that, as mere instruments of the common good, members have no right whatever
to said increase of life and prosperity; and that the increase in
question will, in any case, never constitute an adequate compensation for the sacrifice of human personality which the *organic*
interpretation implies.

It remains to be seen what, under this system, constitutes the
supreme end of society, to which every other value must be
subordinated.

Defined in general terms, it is the continuous enriching and
perfecting of the collective being. But the objective in question
differs according to the diverse aspects under which this collective
being can be viewed.

In the Soviet conception, the national community is considered
above all as a vast enterprise for material production, which must
be organized with a view to the greatest possible economic output.
That being so, everything therein will be ordained to this wholly
material end, and the individuals will have the right to citizenship
in Soviet society only insofar as they devote themselves to the
enrichment of the collectivity.

For National Socialism, society is essentially the incarnation of
a race, the purity of whose blood and the integrity of whose genius
must be safeguarded above all else; whose members, torn away in
the course of history, must be restored, and for which the *Lebensraum* (living space) its growth requires has to be assured.

Fascism is more closely bound up with the notion of the State, in which and through which the thought and the dynamic will of the collective being, namely, the nation, manifests itself. The sum total of the social effort will tend, therefore, to increase the power of the State, to reinforce its material organization, to intensify its potential moral energy. Life is the law of societies, and since all life consists in a constant struggle to exist and to exist in a better way, a people fulfills its destiny only insofar as it is ready to fight and strong enough to win the victory.

Economic prosperity, the integrity and grandeur of the race, political power, such—according to the different currents of thought and action of which the world is now a witness—are the supreme goals which the social authority assigns to itself in certain countries and which said authority claims to serve with an energy before which everything must needs give way. That, indeed, is the meaning of *totalitarianism:* the integral subordination of all values, material, spiritual, moral, to the service of the single end, the *unum necessarium*—supreme objective of the social will. Hence the inflexible conformism which is absolutely necessary in all totalitarian regimes and which they strive to realize by means suited to the genius of their several dictators. We know the frightful holocaust of human lives to which the Soviet dictatorship resorted in order to triumph over all resistance, local or individual. Elsewhere the inhuman horror of concentration camps is in force. And as the conformity of a purely external gesture furnishes but a precarious guarantee of submission and loyalty, it is upon conscience—the last refuge of personality—that the masters in power, with a tenacity and remarkable ingenuity of technique, direct their attack. Man, so it has been said, is a religious animal who seeks his stay and support in God. Totalitarian States owed it to themselves to commandeer for their own advantage this powerful and ineradicable human instinct.

The task to be accomplished was the banishment of God from the human conscience or at the very least the setting up of some rival deity. Bolshevism, materialistic as it was, undertook, like the other totalitarian regimes, to forge a mysticism of collective life. Everywhere this mysticism is inculcated, nurtured, propagated by every means and device. The totalitarian State, which claims for itself the right to fashion the whole man, takes charge of his mind from his earliest years and makes itself his educator; it imposes upon him its own conception of life and of the world (*Weltanschauung*) by means of the science which it controls, the press which it inspires, the rites and ceremonies which it institutes. Official propaganda, veritable "machine à cerveler et phosphoriser" (A. Roullet), goads on the citizen everywhere and always, literally hypnotizing him with its posters, its slogans, its appeals, its threats. With what extraordinary independence of mind must a man be gifted to resist this relentless hammering whereby totalitarian authority presumes to mold individual thought and conscience in its own image!

For such indeed is the supreme ambition of the totalitarian regime. Mussolini does not attempt to conceal it:

> "The Fascist State, which is the most exalted and powerful form of personality, is a force, but a spiritual force, a force which sums up all the forms of the moral and intellectual life of man. It is a form, an internal rule and discipline of the whole being; it penetrates the will as well as the intelligence. Its principle—central inspiration of the human personality living in a civil community—penetrates into the most intimate recesses of the individual and into the heart both of the man of action and of the thinker, of the artist and of the scholar; it is the soul of the soul. Considered as a whole, fascism is not only the legislator and founder of institutions, it is also the educator and promoter of spiritual life. It wants to refashion not the forms of human life, but its content: man, character, faith. And to this end, it wants a discipline and an authority which will penetrate into minds and rule there absolutely" (*The Doctrine of Fascism*).

". . . rule there absolutely!!"

There is but one being that has the right to formulate such a demand with reference to the human person: God alone!

COMPARISON AND EVALUATION

None of the three interpretations which we have just reviewed brings to the problem confronting us—the nature of the common good—a solution making equitable allowance for each of the poles of the person-society relation. On the one hand, the person sees himself unduly absorbed by society; on the other hand, it is society that resolves itself into an amorphous mob of independent and undisciplined individuals.

There are nevertheless degrees of error.

Certain *milieux* delight in contrasting the excessive indulgence of the Church for individualistic liberalism with the severity it employs as regards socialism and totalitarianism. Indulgence for individualistic liberalism? They forget assuredly Pius IX, his Encyclical *Mirari vos* and the *Syllabus;* they forget Leo XIII and his Encyclicals *Immortale Dei* and *Libertas praestantissimum*. Liberalism has been peremptorily condemned in its extreme formulas: when it exalts liberty to such a point that it scorns the rights of God, when it undermines the foundations of legitimate civil authority and lapses into anarchy. Apart from these extremes, the fact remains that liberalism upholds, although to excess, an essential truth of Christian dogma, that of the eminent dignity of the human person and of his inalienable rights. It is necessary—and the Church has not failed in this—to correct and redress its deviations; that, however, is no reason for incriminating in the same breath the attachment which it very legitimately has for liberty itself—"nature's highest benefit and the exclusive prerogative of beings endowed with intelligence or reason" (Leo XIII, *Libertas praestantissimum*). Furthermore, the rights of civil authority once recognized, it remains to determine the normal field of its activity and to fix the limits beyond which it must not go. Now, this work of delimitation cannot be done without taking into account the historical contingencies, the traditions and temperament of the nation, the present necessities of the body social, and one can easily understand that on this question there should exist among Catholics a very marked divergence of evaluations, in regard to which doctrinal authority abstains from intervening.

Quite different is the position of socialists and totalitarians. The former—in all sincerity or as a matter of policy—proclaim themselves respecters of the autonomy of the human person; as a matter of fact, their system leads infallibly to downright oppression thereof. Totalitarianism, with brutal frankness, depersonalizes the individual and delivers him up body and soul to the good pleasure of the State, restoring to honor the ancient formula of pagan philosophy: "Neither must we suppose that any one of the citizens belongs to himself, for they all belong to the State." (Aristotle, *Pol.* VIII, 1337a28, 29.)

Among some, therefore, at least in fact; among others, in principle, there is a pure and simple negation of human personality and liberty—a fundamental error with which the Church cannot agree.

This intransigent attitude does not prevent the Church from showing with regard to certain "socializing" tendencies or certain "authoritarian" preferences a consideration similar in every respect to that which she employs with regard to the "liberalizing" opinions already mentioned. On one condition, however, namely that the essential rights of human personality and liberty are respected.

Again for this same motive, the Church, without retracting in any way her doctrinal judgment, will tolerate and even sincerely accept a totalitarian regime which the orientation of the government and a residue of Christian tradition prevent from pushing to its ultimate consequences the erroneous doctrine on which it prides itself.

But between the just, yet opposing, claims of personal liberty and authority, Christian philosophy alone is capable of effecting that harmonious conciliation which is indispensable.

THE CHRISTIAN INTERPRETATION

Foremost among its considerations, Christian social philosophy places the person, that is to say, the human being subsisting in himself, having his own end which he must realize on his own responsibility, endowed as he is, for this purpose, with the faculty of freely determining his own acts. The existence of society answers a need of man's nature, seeing that he is unable "isolated, either to procure for himself what is necessary or useful for life; or to acquire perfection of mind and heart." (Leo XIII, *Immortale Dei*.) To determine what is the end of society, what the nature of the good it is destined to procure, inquiry must be made into what need it is that induces men to unite in society—what good they ask of social life.

This good will be primarily of the temporal order. It is here below, in this life, that men must accomplish this first stage of their destiny, upon which death places a final seal. In the present order of Providence, they doubtless need supernatural help and succor; but these are conferred upon them through the medium of a distinct society of positive divine right, instituted by Our Lord Jesus Christ—the Church. Apart from this, it devolves upon civil society alone to furnish its members with such means of the temporal order as they require to fulfil their destiny.

This good is collective or public. It is not incumbent upon society to procure immediately the particular and personal good of each one of its members. That is their individual task which they perform each one for himself and on his own responsibility, under the aegis of the general aid which society brings to all.

This good is common in this sense, that all members are invited to participate therein.

The equality of nature and of destiny among human beings does not permit that the social good, to whose realization they must all contribute, should become the perquisite of one or of a small number of them, to whose advantage all the others would find themselves subordinated and enslaved. This, however, does not prevent society, entrusted with the care of assisting the indigence and the weakness of its members, from distributing its aid and its services according to the needs peculiar to the different categories of citizens. "In the protection of private rights," wrote Leo XIII, "the State must occupy itself in a special manner with the weak and indigent. The wealthy class uses its riches, as it were, for a rampart and has less need of public guardianship. The poor, on the contrary, without riches to protect them from injustices, count especially on the protection of the State. The State must therefore surround with care and with a particular solicitude the workers who belong to the multitude of the disinherited" (*Rerum novarum*).

It is more difficult to determine with precision the constituent elements or the content of this common good. We shall attempt to do so later. Let us confine ourselves, for the moment, to distinguishing in the mission of the State a twofold function.

The first, quite negative, consists in protecting against every unjustifiable attack or limitation the rights and the liberty of the members of the social body. This care cannot, without serious ill consequences, be abandoned to the initiative of individuals; it follows that this tutelary function belongs of right to civil authority and constitutes its exclusive prerogative.

The second is of the positive order. It consists, on the one hand, in furnishing to private initiative the assistance required to enable the latter to realize more surely the objectives it has set itself; on the other hand, it consists in assuring, by means of its co-ordinating intervention, the harmonious union of all individual activities for the general prosperity.

However, here there is no longer question of a primordial task of the social organism, but of a supplementary intervention the scope of which will be determined, in each particular case and for each determinate group, according to the need for help and assistance which the true interests of the associates require. The State offers its co-operation, it does not impose it; it seconds private initiative but takes care not to stifle it.

Under this twofold form, negative and positive, the common

good which society places at the disposal of its members results, in the last analysis, from the collaboration of the members themselves, commanded and co-ordinated by authority. This collaboration implies therefore the subordination of the members to the common end, and this brings us face to face once more with the thorny fundamental problem of the relations between the individual and society.

Let us admit that, at first sight, Catholic thought seems to show in this matter a visible hesitation; some even think that they are able to make it contradict itself. Saint Thomas never tires of repeating that the common good takes precedence over the particular good as a whole does over its parts. He also affirms that a man, for just what he is and has, belongs to the community, even as a part, for just what it is, belongs to the whole: *"Quilibet homo hoc ipsum quod est et quod habet est multitudinis sicut et qualibet pars id quod est, est totius"* (*Summa Th.,* Ia IIae, q.96, a.4).

On the other hand, His Holiness Pius XI did not hesitate to say that "civil society is for man, not man for civil society."

Between these two doctrinal positions, the opposition is nevertheless only apparent. Saint Thomas himself has taken care to specify that man is not subject to civil society with regard to all that he is and all that is his: *"Homo non ordinatur ad communitatem politicam secundum se totum et secundum omnia sua"* (*op. cit.,* Ia IIae, q.21, a.4, ad 3). And the reason for this he gives elsewhere: The common good is more important than the particular good, provided they are of the same order. But it can happen that the particular good is superior by reason of the order to which it belongs: *"Bonum commune potius est bono privato si sit ejusdem generis. Sed potest esse quod bonum privatum sit melius secundum suum genus."* (*Sum. Th.,* IIa IIae, q. 152, a.4, ad 3.) The reservation here formulated removes the apparent contradiction which we pointed out above.

The common good, the proper aim of civil society, is, like this institution itself, of a purely temporal nature; the particular human good is, like man himself, of a complex nature.

Man is spirit and matter; he has a soul and a body.

It is by his soul that man rises to the dignity of a *person,* that is to say, of a being subsisting in himself, having his own end which relates him immediately to God, the supreme Good. It is through the material part of his being that he finds himself immersed in the temporal order, subject to the laws of nature and liable to all the necessities entailed by these laws; in this respect, he is—like a living being devoid of reason—only an *individual*. In him, from then on, matter is subordinate to spirit, individuality to personality which constitutes his pre-eminent and transcendent value.

A quite similar law governs the order of value of human goods. The good which for man exceeds all the other goods is the possession of God perceived here below by the veiled light of natural reason and faith, contemplated one day, face to face, in the brightness of the beatific vision. All the other goods of a purely temporal order are ranged, as means to an end, according to their comparative bearing on this unique and supreme good: those which man possesses as his own, his particular goods, as well as those which come to him from his participation in the common good of social life. Among all the goods placed on the same temporal plane, the order of values is established according to the principle of the primacy of the whole over the parts. The particular good of the individual will therefore, as Saint Thomas teaches, be subordinate to the good of the community and this latter can dispose of it absolutely according to the measure in which the collective interest of which it has charge requires. The renunciations, moreover, that the community imposes upon its members in this temporal order will be compensated by the greater advantage these members will find in participating in the common good augmented by their sacrifices. Under certain circumstances, it is true, the sacrifice commanded may be such as to despoil the individual of every particular good, including his physical life itself. Even so, these particular goods are not turned aside from their natural destination, which is to serve the supreme end of the human being. Quite the contrary: by giving, in order to obey the will of God, this supreme evidence of brotherly love, the individual brings about, as a result of sacrificing himself completely for the common good, the final liberation and the eternal salvation of his person.

Mgr. Bruno de Solages splendidly summed up this doctrine in his lecture at the *Semaine sociale* of Clermont-Ferrand (1937): "If one uses the term individual to designate man with regard to that part of himself which is submerged in the temporal stream and if one employs that of person to qualify him under the aspect by which he emerges therefrom to look toward the Infinite, one must admit that individuals are for society and that society is for persons.

"Individuals are therefore at the service of the common good of society, the essential aim of which is to favor the good of persons. It follows from this principle that, although society is made for man, the latter, nevertheless—because he can attain his ultimate end only through and, as it were, by means of the society that conditions his life—is in duty bound to serve it, and may find himself under the obligation to sacrifice for it his temporal goods and even life itself. This, however, is not tantamount to sacrificing himself as a person, but to realizing his personality in the supreme act of charity—*He that shall lose his life shall find it*. Likewise, for society to sacrifice what may seem its immediate temporal good out of regard for the moral law is not to sacrifice the common good of individuals who are persons and for whom, in consequence, regard for the moral law—condition of realizing their transcendent destiny—is the supreme common good."

From the pre-eminence, however, of the common good over the particular good of individuals, it does not follow that society has the right to dictate the law to its members arbitrarily and to dispose, according to its good pleasure, of their rights and their liberty. The just limits of the jurisdiction of authority are fixed by the exigencies of the common good. Now, inasmuch as the common good has no reason for existence other than to *aid* the members in the fulfilment of their personal destinies and to compensate for their natural deficiency, it follows that, in every case where their personal initiatives, isolated or spontaneously united, are sufficient for the realization of this task, collective help and the intervention of social authority become superfluous, nay harmful, as Pius XI teaches:

"The natural aim of all intervention in social matters is to aid the individual members of the social body, but never to destroy or absorb them.

"Let public authority therefore leave to groups of inferior rank the care of affairs of minor importance in which its effort would be dissipated excessively; from then on, it will be able to carry on more freely, more powerfully, more efficaciously its own functions, because it alone can effectively perform these, which are: to direct, oversee, stimulate, hold in check, as circumstances dictate or necessity demands. Let governments, therefore, be convinced that the more perfectly this principle is followed and a graded hierarchical order is realized between the various subsidiary organizations, the more excellent will be the authority and efficiency of the social organization as a whole and the happier and more prosperous the state of public affairs" (*Quadragesimo anno*).

Hence, as Pius XI remarks, it is the circumstances and the

necessities peculiar to each political group that determine the extent of governmental competence and the just measure of its interventions. A regime of wide individual liberty is suited to a highly cultured population of thoughtful and virile temperament, rich in initiatives, apt at controlling through strong personal discipline the exercise of their liberties. A closer supervision, on the contrary, is desirable in the case of societies less advanced in the ways of civilization or of communities in which an excess of individualism would threaten to upset the precise social equilibrium. Finally, in all cases, the civil authority will very legitimately reinforce its checks when it has to face some internal crisis or ward off some external danger; it will just as wisely relax its hold so soon as order and security shall have been re-established. There is no universal rule in this matter; each society must govern itself according to the formula which seems, in its eyes, best suited to the temperament and needs of its members, while striving, at the same time, always to leave its members the *greatest possible liberty compatible with the exigencies of the general interest.*

THE TRUE COMMON GOOD AND ITS CONTENT

"Individuals at the service of society, society at the service of persons." What does this mean but that society, thanks to the collaboration of the individuals (whose multiple activities it coordinates), realizes the common good, to wit: "the organized aggregate of social conditions thanks to which the human being can fulfil his natural and spiritual destiny." (J. T. Delos, O.P.)

Of the content of this common good we must now make an inventory.

1. We find it, first of all, to comprise peace which, according to the beautiful definition of Saint Augustine, is nothing else than "the tranquillity of order." Tranquillity of an order in which each citizen, protected in the full enjoyment of his rights against the usurpation of others, attends with perfect independence to the fulfilment of his destiny; in which society itself, efficaciously defended against all internal disturbance and all external aggression, performs with perfect independence its multiple functions. The establishment and maintenance of such a peace necessitates the existence of a juridical order founded on justice, a judicial organization offering guarantees of the strictest impartiality, an apparatus of constraint—police and army—capable of imposing upon all a rigorous respect for law.

2. Under the aegis of this peace and order, the widest possible field must be open to the fruitful unfolding of personal liberty. Here, however, we come upon an important distinction which the leaders of the *Semaine sociale* of Rouen (1938) drew between *liberty* and *liberties:*

The former, exclusive prerogative of rational nature, endows said nature with the faculty of tending to its end of itself, through the quite spontaneous movement of a will unconstrained by any physical determination. Respect for the inviolabity of this faculty, "excellent gift of nature" (Leo XIII), is a law that God Himself has established, and no created authority has the right to exert pressure upon it in ways calculated to turn it aside from the personal and supreme end assigned to it.

Liberties are the external manifestations through which the free determination of the human will expresses itself. As such they participate to a certain extent in the inviolable and sacred character of interior liberty. To a certain extent only, for being —relative to this liberty—only means, they have value only insofar as they aid it better to attain its end. On the other hand, because of their repercussions on the social milieu in which they are exercised, liberties may not escape the control of the civil authorities who have the right and duty to keep watch over them, to organize them, to limit them to the extent required by the common good.

Above all, however, "liberties at the service of liberty" (E. Duthoit, *Semaine sociale* of Rouen). Social authority is in duty bound to respect this first finality; it has no right to restrict the legitimate exercise of these liberties any more than the general interest demands, under penalty of unduly curbing and stifling interior liberty, which is not subject to its law. It will, on the contrary, make the laudable effort to set free said interior liberty by preventing or repressing the abuses to which the liberties lend themselves (alas! only too readily) when human weakness warps them from their natural function.

3. Of itself alone, however, liberty does not answer all the needs of human nature. Individual initiatives, isolated or spontaneously united, very often prove powerless to procure certain goods or to realize certain general conditions under which the individual may perform more perfectly the task assigned to him in this world. These goods and these conditions, indispensable to "the good life" and to "the better life" of all the members of

the community, are rightly demanded from the community itself and from the authority that rules it. Society finds itself henceforth invested with a positive mission of assistance whose measure and extent the circumstances and the necessities of social life determine differently for different social groups.

Let us define briefly the nature of this supplementary function in the various orders in which human activity may be called upon to exercise itself.

a) *In the religious order.* Elevated by a gratuitous favor to an order of relations with God that infinitely exceeds the capacities of his created nature, man cannot respond to this sublime vocation without supernatural help—grace which God alone can bestow, but which He confers only through the channel of the Church. In this domain, civil society plays henceforth only a quite secondary, though still important rôle. It has the obligation to bring to the Church the only aid it has in its power to give, namely, that of guaranteeing her legitimate liberty, of furnishing her with the material assistance without which her ministry, spiritual though it be, cannot function, of removing obstacles of a temporal nature that might hinder unduly her action on souls. Moreover, by rendering publicly to God the worship it owes Him as a collectivity of rational beings—just as physical persons do—the State cannot fail to create a social climate favorable to the blossoming of Christian life.

b) *In the domestic order.* The family, anterior to society, has received from God Himself its rights and laws, which civil authority is under obligation to respect and protect. God having willed (according to the words of Leo XIII) to place in marriage "the most fertile source of good and of public welfare" (*Arcanum divinae sapientiae*), it is of the highest importance that the legal order regulating its civil effects should harmonize entirely with the essential law of this institution entrusted to the Church's keeping. A civil legislation in conformity with the true exigencies of the common good will sanction the unity and indissolubility of the conjugal bond, the authority of the head of the family, the inalienable right of parents in regard to the education of their children; it will use every means at its disposal to assist families in the material difficulties—which, in our day more than ever before, make their noble task so heavy—by seeing to it that, in accordance with the entreaties of Leo XIII and of Pius XI, "every father of a family is able to earn that which, considering his condition and the locality in which he lives, is necessary for his upkeep and that of his wife and children" (*Casti connubii*). It will even strive, by more generous encouragements, to lighten the burdens and recognize the merits of those whose fidelity to the holy laws of marriage contributes to a greater extent toward populating the City.

c) *In the economic and cultural order.* It is in this domain principally that the intervention of society can exercise itself, for nowhere so much as in the acquisition of material goods and in the conquest of well-being, do the native weakness and indigence of the individual call more imperiously for the assistance of the body social as a whole. Let one but consider the enormous and persevering effort required for the arrangement of the terrestrial habitat, the establishment of regular and peaceful relations with similar human groups, the abundant and well-organized re-victualing of the community with resources of every kind not found in its own territory, the creation of legal and economic institutions of general interest capable of stimulating and promoting in every domain—economic, scientific, artistic, cultural—the fruitful unfolding of private initiative.

Left to their own powers, men would not succeed in realizing this minimum of well-being which Saint Thomas declares indispensable to the practice of virtue and the accomplishment of human destiny. They will succeed in doing so only by drawing on the beneficent helps which collective life places at their disposal: the treasure of science, of experience, of traditions which generations transmit to one another, enriching it unceasingly the while; the powerful and marvelous technology which the work of the centuries has elaborated; a juridical regime of work and of property which assures equitable distribution among the collaborators of the products of their common effort. In certain cases the collectivity will even supplement by its own initiatives the weakness or the insolvency of its members, arranging for the creation and management of enterprises or institutions of general interest.

In the accomplishment of its multiple tasks, however, social authority must never lose sight of the essentially supplementary character of its mission nor fail to recognize "this very serious principle of social philosophy" which Pius XI prized so much: "Just as individuals may be deprived, by transfer to the community, of tasks which they are capable of performing of their own initiative and with their own resources, so it would work injustice to the social order as well as harmfully disorganize it to take away from subordinate groups and entrust to a collectivity of wider scope and higher rank functions they are capable of performing themselves" (*Quadragesimo anno*).

CONCLUSION

Sieyès' celebrated "quip" about the Third Estate comes to mind, and, taking inspiration from his formula, we might not inaptly state the question thus: "What is the common good in the eyes of individualism? Nothing or practically nothing. What ought it to become according to the postulates of totalitarianism? Everything."

"Neither the one nor the other," say we in perfect accord with Christian thought. It is not at all necessary to abandon the common good in order to safeguard the dignity of the human person. Neither is it at all necessary to sacrifice the latter in order to do justice to the legitimate demands of social life.

Assuredly, the common good is made up of the contributions of individuals, and these contributions necessarily imply renunciation of particular goods, limitation of external liberties.

But these abnegations and limitations concern only the *means* destined to serve the person in the accomplishment of his end. The sacrifice is worth making, so long as participation in the common good replaces with interest the particular goods that have been sacrificed to it and so long as the retrenchment of external liberties strengthens and enriches that interior liberty whereby man of his own accord, with a wholly spontaneous movement, devotes himself to the service of God.

Nothing now stands in the way of our admitting with Saint Thomas man's subordination to society—*Homo ordinatur ad communitatem politicam*—since, with the Saintly Doctor, we refuse to interpret this as an absorption of his personality: *Non tamen secundum se totum et omnia sua.*

VIII

THE PANTHEISM LATENT IN TOTALITARIAN ABSOLUTISM

By GEORGE BARRY O'TOOLE, PH.D., S.T.D.

Professor of Philosophy
in
The Catholic University of America

THE PANTHEISM LATENT IN TOTALITARIAN
ABSOLUTISM

By *absolutism* is meant any theory of supreme, unlimited, irresponsible power vested in the government of a State, such that all individual liberties are extinguished by the constitution of an omnipotent civil authority to whose will and sovereignty there is no limit. It makes the private citizen the pawn of the State, which becomes the sole source and arbiter of all his rights.[1]

The mistake is commonly made of identifying *absolutism* with a particular form of government (for example, with one-man government—autocracy, in contrast to government by the people—democracy), or else with a particular way of ascending to governmental power (for example, by hereditary right instead of by election). All this, however, is beside the mark. What the term here signifies has nothing to do with the *organization* of government; on the contrary, it has significance only as applied to the *ideology* of government, that is, to the political theory those in control of civil society accept as warrant for their authority or right to govern. And thus it comes to pass that a monarch who, in practice, recognizes the fact that his power to govern is limited to the temporal domain and that he has no jurisdiction at all over what relates to the personal vocation and supernatural destiny of his subjects, is not absolutistic, whereas a democratic parliament or congress, refusing to confine itself within these limits, is.

However strange it may sound to unaccustomed ears, the assertion by King James I (Stuart) of *the divine right of kings* was not downright absolutism; for he acknowledged in theory, at least, a king's responsibility to God. On the other hand, Rousseau's declaration[2] of *the sovereignty of the people,* which is by many

---

[1] "Individual men do not exist except through the *State* and for the sake of the *State;* whatever rights they have originate solely by way of concession on the part of the State"—proposition (8), condemned April 13, 1938, by the S. Congr. of Seminaries and Universities.

[2] "If the State or City is neither more nor less than a moral person whose life consists in the union of its members, and if its foremost care is that of self-preservation, it must have a universal and compulsive force in order to move and dispose each part in a manner best suited to the whole. As nature gives the individual man

243

regarded as the very keystone of modern democracy, is absolutism pure and simple. This point is well brought out by Bishop Wilhelm Emmanuel von Ketteler who wrote in 1864:

"Everything depends, then, upon the way in which the constituted legislators look upon their legislative power in relation to justice and right reason. Their conception of this, in turn, depends essentially upon their religious convictions. Such formulas as: 'the law is the will of the king'; 'the law is the will of the king and the people'; 'the law is the will of the people,' have as yet no clear, unequivocal meaning. All these statements are susceptible of two possible meanings and which of the two is actually intended is of the utmost importance. Many believe that in saying: 'The law is the will of the king,' they have voiced the precise contradictory of the statement: 'The law is the will of the people.' This is entirely incorrect. Whether the law is the will of the people or the will of the king, is, in the final analysis, a matter of indifference. The question that decides everything is whether ultimately the law is the will of God or purely the will of man; or, to formulate this question more clearly, whether the men holding the office of legislators—the men who frame the laws in the form in which these are given to the people—act herein exclusively by their own will and by the will of those who appointed them, or whether they act under the conviction that it is their vocation and duty as law-givers to express an order grounded in the eternal will of God." [1]

Hence, by proclaiming the absolute sovereignty of the people, Liberalism states a principle that clashes with the sovereignty of God and, for all its affectation of democracy, stands committed to the absolutist conception of civil government.

Theoretically speaking, Liberalism vests this irresponsible and omnipotent sovereignty in the unanimous will of the people at large. But, inasmuch as perfect unanimity in the body politic is impossible of attainment, it substitutes as a practical equivalent the *majority vote of the people's representatives* in the national legislative assembly. Though in point of fact such a majority vote —thanks to political chicanery and popular indifference—seldom, if ever, represents the real will of even a majority of the people, it overrides every other consideration, including the commandments of God Himself. These fictitious majorities, for example, presume to vote away the very lives and liberties of the country's

absolute power over all his members, so the social contract gives to the body politic an absolute power over all its members; and it is this selfsame power which, directed by the general will, bears, as I have said, the name of sovereignty." *(Contrat Social,* bk. II, ch. 4.) And again: "Hence if the people so much as promise to obey, they dissolve themselves by the very act; the instant they have a master, they lose their sovereignty, and consequently the body politic is destroyed." *(Op. cit.,* bk. II, ch. 1.)

[1] *Die Arbeiterfrage und das Christenthum,* 3te Aufl., Mainz, 1864, VI, S. 73, 74.

youth through laws conscripting the latter for unjustifiable wars of aggression, as they likewise vote away the private property of citizens by imposing confiscatory taxes, in flagrant disregard of the obligation incumbent on the State no less than on the individual to obey the Divine precepts against homicide and theft.

To sum up, therefore, it does not depend upon the form or methodology of a government, whether or not it is to be regarded as absolutistic. This depends exclusively upon its ideology or theory of the origin and use of governmental power.

Ultimately, there are only two philosophies of government— *monism* and *dualism*. According to the monistic or naturalistic view, nature exhausts the whole of reality and humanity evolved and organized into civil society represents the highest expression of nature and the supreme or sovereign power in the universe. According to the dualistic view, nature—human and subhuman— does not exhaust the whole of reality; there exists, besides, a transcendent and supernatural Being, God, whose will is the supreme law of man and nature. By the principle of excluded middle, there is no third possibility; every government must find the warrant for its acts in one or the other of these alternatives.

It is recognized, of course, that monistic naturalism may be atheistic as well as pantheistic; for, in its materialistic form, monism denies the existence of all spirit and consequently of God, the Supreme Spirit. Its formula states that the real is coextensive with the sensible; that there is no transcendent God, but only nature. Pantheism's elimination of God is less blunt and brusque. It, too, affirms that nothing but nature exists, but, instead of denying Him outright, it prefers to identify God with nature. "Nature is God," it says. For this reason pantheism has been called "polite atheism."

Pantheism, accordingly, leaves room, as atheistic materialism does not, for a certain mysticism and pseudo-religious sentiment. At the same time, it furnishes equally good and far more respectable warrant for absolutism. Theism, on the contrary, by affirming the absolute supremacy of a God, transcendent to both man and nature, cuts the ground from under the theory of supreme and irresponsible power in the government of a State. If, therefore, absolutism seeks to assert itself on religious grounds, it has no choice but to fall back on pantheism.

1. *Theism at Variance with Political Absolutism*

In teaching that God, though really transcendent to His creation, is virtually *immanent* therein, theism does full justice to the element of truth latent in Pantheistic immanentism. The Catholic doctrine of God's immanence in finite things means that God, as Creator and Preserver, is present in all creatures by His action or causal influence, as the *First Cause* and *immediate Source* of their reality. But since in God, by reason of His pure actuality, the Divine action is identical with the Divine power and the Divine essence, it is true to say that God is present in creatures not only by His action, but also by His power and by *His essence* (which, however, is not to say, with the Pantheists, that God is present in finite things as *their essence*). In this sense, then, God's immanence in the world may be said to be not merely virtual, but supposital; for He is present everywhere and in everything not by influence alone but by His very supersubstantial reality—*per immediatonem suppositi,* imparting to each and every created being its very existence and power of action.

Since, however, creatures are to be referred to God rather than God to creatures, it would be more proper to express this intimate dependence of creatures on the Creator as the primordial source of their being by saying conversely: *All things are present in God,* instead of: *God is present in all things*—"For in him," as the Apostle says, "we live and move and are." [1]

This immanence, however, of creatures in God is not, as Spinoza misconstrued it, an immanence of accidental modes in the substance upon which they depend. [2] God's independence of creatures is other than the independence of *substance* in comparison to the *accidents* that require it for a subject of inhesion; it is rather the independence of an *efficient cause* or agent which remains *unmixed* with its dependent product or *effect.*

The term *from-otherness* (abalietas) used to express the dependence of an effect upon its efficient cause is by no means synonymous with *in-otherness* (inalietas), the term used to express

---

[1] *Acts* XVII, 28.

[2] "Per modum intelligo substantiae affectiones, sive id, quod in alio est, per quod etiam concipitur." (*Ethica,* 2nd ed., tom. I, pars I, p. 37—Nijhoff, The Hague, 1885.) Later, he adds: "Besides God no substance can exist or be conceived." (*Ethica,* pars I, prop. xiv, *op. cit.,* tom. I, p. 47.) Spinoza deduced this conclusion from Desartes' inexact definition: "Substantia est res quae nulla alia re indigeat ad existendum" (*Princip. phil.,* L. I.)

the dependence of accidental modes upon the substance in which they inhere. The dependence of an effect upon its efficient cause (agent) lies in this, that the *effect* cannot come into existence without the action of the efficient cause. (Thus *hearing* cannot come into existence without someone *speaking*.) On the other hand, the dependence of an accident upon its substance lies in this, that the *accident* stands in need of a subject in which to inhere. (Thus *knowledge* must exist *in* a *knower*—it requires a *knowing subject* in which to inhere.) To confuse, as Spinoza did, the cause-effect with the substance-accident relation is to give evidence of slovenly thinking.

Nevertheless, there was an excuse for this confusion; for the fact is that *in some cases* accidents are effects of the substance in which they inhere and certain effects are therefore accidents of their efficient cause. *Living substances,* for example, are capable of *modifying themselves,* that is, of producing *immanent effects* that *remain within their own substance.* Thus the student by reading a book produces knowledge within himself, which knowledge is at once an effect and an accidental modification of the student himself. This fact may have misled Spinoza, who was an anthropomorphic *panvitalist,*[1] into thinking that the term "accident" was coextensive with the term "effect." In reality, however, such identification of effect and accident is confined to the particular case of substances capable of *vital action.* An effect can be the accident of its efficient cause only on condition that the latter is a *living substance,* and even in the case of a living substance not all the accidents inherent therein are effects produced by said living substance. An effect, we repeat, can be an accident of its own efficient cause only if it remains within said efficient cause, and this holds true only in the realm of living substances and living agents. In the inorganic world no accident can be the effect of its own substance, and no effect can be an accident of its efficient cause. Hence, not all the effects of efficient causes are accidents of their efficient causes, and not all accidents (even of living substances) are effects of their substances.

To sum up, there are two distinct ways in which a *relative* can depend on its corresponding *absolute.* When the *relative* is an *effect,* its dependence consists in this, that it cannot be realized (either in itself or in something else) apart from the *action* of its

[1] See Spinoza, *Ethica,* P. II, schol. to prop. xiii, where he says: "All [individual things] . . . though in differing degrees, are *animated*" (italics mine).

efficient cause. When the *relative* is an *accident,* its dependence consists in this, that it cannot be realized *outside* a subject. An effect, therefore, can have its reality in itself outside its efficient cause, whereas an accident cannot, in the natural order of things, have its reality in itself, but only in a subject. To confuse these two distinct kinds of dependence by regarding *all* dependent things as *accidents* of the *absolute* whereon they depend leads to pantheistic monism, which interprets the multiplicity of individual things as so many accidental modes of one single substance—God.

To avoid pantheism, therefore, we must supplement the doctrine of God's virtual immanence in finite things with its correlative, the doctrine of His real *transcendence.* By this we mean that God is infinitely beyond the greatest of His creatures. For not only is the Creator infinitely greater than the sum of all He has created, but He exists after a manner wholly unique and wholly different to that in which any created reality exists. God differs *by all that He is* from finite beings and they *by all that they are* from God. None of the concepts we form from creatures is applicable to God and His activity *in the same sense* in which it is applicable to ourselves and our own actions.

Even when we say that God *exists,* we may not attribute existence to Him as if it were some quality that He possessed in common with creatures; for there is no generic concept whatever under which we can classify or bracket God along with finite beings. If God were *in the same case as* any of His *created derivatives,* far from being the supreme explanation which their contingency requires, He Himself would stand in the same need of explanation as they. Hence, God, as the Underived, the Unconditioned and the Undefinable, infinitely transcends all the categories of finite reality.

And, should it be objected that only the caused, the conditioned and the definable are comprehensible to us, and that unless we can compass God within our finite frames of thought, we leave Him wholly incomprehensible and entirely outside the sphere of human understanding, the answer is that God's incomprehensibility does not detract in the least from His value as explanation of the contingent world. For in postulating the Incomprehensible, it is not *God* that we are seeking to render intelligible, but *ourselves* and *nature.* It is to make ourselves and this visible universe of ours comprehensible that we postulate what transcends our comprehension, seeing that whatever is definable and comprehensible is destitute of self-sufficiency. The *de facto* existence of derivative and dependent realities is fairly thrust upon us in sense perception. Realities of this sort do not contain in themselves the explanation of their own existence and it is only by referring them to a Super-reality which, as *Ens a se,* has existence *from itself,* that we are able to account for them. Such an Underived Being is, by very reason of its self-grounded existence, altogether distinct from the totality of derivative things—"Now the *Ens a se* is *separate* by its very perfection, *immixtus ut imperet* (ὥστε κρατέειν), like the Intelligence (Νοῦς) of Anaxagoras and more so. There is, then, a real Transcendent. . . ." [1]

Immanence is one truth about God but not the whole truth. To divorce God's immanence from His transcendence is to have a one-sided view of Him. The balanced view is the one blocked out in those beautiful lines[2] of Hildebert of Lavardin (*circa* 1056-1134), Bishop of Le Mans, Archbishop of Tours:

"Above all, beneath all: without all, within all;
Inside all things yet not included: outside all things yet not excluded; . . ."

All creatures, including man, are dependent upon the Transcendent Being for that finite reality which distinguishes them from nothingness. In man, this dependence of universal nature on God becomes, because of his rational soul, a conscious dependence. Man feels himself under *obligation* to live up to an ideal of human perfection ordained for him by his Creator. By obligation is meant a restriction of *liberty.* Hence only a person, that is to say, a

---

[1] Sertillanges, *St. Thomas D'Aquin,* vol. I, p. 201 (Alcan, Paris, 1910). Anaxagoras says: νόος δέ ἐστι ἄπειρον καὶ αὐτοκρατές καὶ μέμικται οὐδενὶ χρήματι—"*But Intelligence is [something] infinite and self-ruled and is mixed with nothing,* "but," he adds, "it is alone, itself by itself. For if it were not by itself, but were mixed with anything else, it would partake in all things, supposing it were mixed with any . . . and the things mixed with it would hinder it, so that it would have power over nothing in the same way as it has now being alone by itself." (Fragment #6, Mullach's *Fragmenta Philosophorum Graecorum,* vol. I, p. 249a.)

[2] Super cuncta, subter cuncta; extra cuncta, intra cuncta.
Intra cuncta nec inclusus; extra cuncta nec exclusus;
Super cuncta nec elatus; subter cuncta nec subtratus.
Super totus praesidendo, subter totus sustinendo;
Extra totus complectendo, intra totus es implendo.
Intra nunquam coarctaris, extra nunquam dilataris,
Super nullo sustentaris, subter nullo fatigaris.
(*Orat. ad tres pers. SS. Trinitatis,* Migne, Patrol. S. L., 171, col. 1411.)

rational and free agent, is amenable to obligation. God steers irrational agents to their goals by *physical* necessity, but upon man
God imposes only *moral* necessitation, which is another name for
obligation. This necessity while prescribing the rule of action
does not abolish man's physical freedom to disobey.

However, for man to disobey this divine ordinance would be to
contradict his own rational nature and to repudiate his status as a
creature. Bakunin was quite right in inferring that if God exists,
man cannot be free. God, in endowing man with a free will, has not
endowed him with freedom to do as he pleases. If God had
exempted man from the obligation to live up to the ideal embodied
in his rational nature, He would be contradicting the work of His
own Wisdom.

From eternity God wills that all His creatures, actual or possible,
should observe the order constituted for them. This timeless
decree of the transcendent will of God is the *Eternal Law*, which
is "nothing else than the reason of divine wisdom insofar as it is
directive of all acts and all movements." [1] It is the Divine ordination of all things, created and creatable, as viewed in its absolute
and transcendent source, the Divine Nature itself.

In so far as this selfsame law is inscribed in the temporal terms
of created natures, it is spoken of as the *Natural Law*. This, so far
as it applies to *human* nature, is defined by St. Thomas as "the
participation of the eternal law in the rational creature." [2]

All creatures belong wholly to God and are essentially dependent on Him for all that they are. Hence they are essentially
subordinate to Him and absolutely subservient to His will.

In man this subjection to the Divine will is not, as has been said,
a matter of physical, but of moral, necessity; that is to say of duty
or obligation. "God, therefore," concludes Cardinal Cavagnis, "is
the author of moral obligation firstly on the score of His absolute
dominion over creatures; secondly because God's intelligence
imposes an order upon the human intelligence; thirdly because
the Divine perfection or goodness attracts to itself the will as the
adequate object of the latter's happiness; hence man, by a rational
necessity which is commonly termed moral, is held to observe the
moral law out of justice because of being God's creature, out of
reasonableness lest he go back on his own nature, and out of his

[1] St. Thomas, *Sum. Th.*, Ia IIae, q. 93, a 1.
[2] *Sum. Th.*, Ia IIae, q. 91, a. 2.

essential need for happiness lest he bring misery upon himself." [1]

This order of Divine Wisdom is not an impersonal one impotent to obligate the wills of the rational creatures to whom it is proposed. It is a transcendent *Someone,* not a *something* we are free to disregard. It is the subsistent *Intelligence* and *Will* of the Living God Himself, not an inanimate idol enthroned by ourselves and powerless to enjoin anything upon us. Therein it differs radically from a pantheist world-soul immanent in nature, from Plato's soulless model of the Good, from Kant's moral ideal which autonomous human reason makes imperative for itself—*They have mouths, but they speak not . . . feet have they, but they walk not.*[2] But when our Divine Ideal is a personal Being, really existent apart from ourselves and nature, it has the wherewithal to tie the bond of obligation.

Assuredly, moral obligation does not originate from the will of the individual; for it is absurd that anyone should obligate himself to himself. Nor is it possible to find in the corporate will of civil society the source of said obligation; the moral law does not emanate from the State, for the State no less than the individual must bow before its universally prevalent right.

The imperative "must-not" of this eternal law prevails over every other consideration however important, so much so that man feels bound rather to give up his life than prove false to the ideals of conduct which it prescribes. Should a soldier, captured by the enemy, be compelled to choose between betraying his country and facing a firing-squad, he has, morally speaking, no choice at all, but must go to his death rather than sully his conscience and his soul by doing what an eternal law inexorably forbids. No physical evil is comparable to the moral evil involved in the violation of a standard so divine.

The moral law, therefore, is not a self-assumed or socially-imposed code, but an immutable standard that has to be observed regardless of one's personal inclinations, social or individual interests. Nor can its binding force be accounted for by ascribing it to the corporate will of the State. Do we not honor as a moral hero the man who resists the effort of a tyrannical government attempting to seduce him into transgressing this sacred *unwritten law?* Not the State, therefore, nor public opinion, but the inalterable

[1] *Inst. Juris Publici,* vol. I, 457, p. 296 (Desclée, Lefebre, Rome, 1906).
[2] *Psalm* CXV, 5-7.

principles of morality divinely engraved in man's soul, are the supreme rule and standard of action both in social and in private life. Even the meekest of men, when the State attempts to browbeat him in moral matters, will reply with the Apostles Peter and John, that it is better "to obey God rather than men." [1] Montalembert called this utterance "the first *non possumus*," but unless he had in mind the qualification *papal,* he was wrong; for the sentiment is as ancient as mankind; it is the age-old answer of the human conscience to all absolutistic prepotence on the part of the State. More than four centuries before Christ, Sophocles embodied it in Antigone's reply[2] to King Creon:

CREON

"And didst thou really dare to transgress these laws?"

ANTIGONE

"Aye, for Zeus was not by any means the promulgator thereof to me, nor did Justice that dwelleth with the Gods below prescribe such laws among men; nor did I deem thine edicts to have power enough to enable a mere mortal to override the unwritten and unalterable laws of Gods (ἄγραπτα κἀσφαλῆ θεῶν νόμιμα). For they are not of today or yesterday, but from eternity they exist and no one knows the time of their appearing. Nor was I fain to suffer the penalty for them through fear of any man's viewpoint; right well I knew that I was doomed to die even though thou hadst not proclaimed it. Yet if I needs must die before my time, I account it mine own gain."

The source, then, of this all-outweighing obligation is evidently the original fountainhead of all rights and duties, namely, the eternal will of God. It is God who conceives from all eternity the ideals directive of all things to their respective ends. The ideals God sets as goals are simply the completed aspects of the natures He has given things as their Creator. Prior to all man-made laws, God, the founder of human reason, is the founder of the ideal which it befits a rational creature to achieve. God it is who from eternity conceives the natures of all things, assigns to them their goals and enjoins upon them their law of operation.

Hence man, too, socially no less than individually, is under obligation to be true in all his acts to his rational nature considered, not in itself alone, but in its relations as part of the universe which

[1] *Acts,* IV, 19-20.
[2] *Antigone,* vv. 450-462.

God has created. Man may not abuse his God-given prerogative of free will to debase his dignity as a rational creature, for he thereby resists the ordinance of an infinitely good God who bids him be reasonable, i.e., true to himself, true to what he really is, in order that he may be happy.

It follows that mankind must recognize in God the Supreme Law-giver not only for individuals, but also for the State; for the Creator made human nature social, thereby founding the State. It is by God's will that men unite in necessary civil society in order to supplement their natural deficiencies as families and individuals. In other words, the union of men to form the State is not a matter of option, but of obligation arising from the *prevailing right*,[1] which in this case is the Natural Law. But this, as we have seen, is nothing else than the Eternal Law of God insofar as it is promulgated in terms of human nature.

The wills, therefore, of human individuals are no more the source of the authority of the State than the State itself is the source of the rights of individuals. Rights are essentially correlated with duties or obligations. A right is a moral power and the State's power over individuals has its source in the obligation which *God's will* imposes on the human individual to live in civil society. Conversely, the rights that individuals enjoy as citizens do not have their source in any concession on the part of the State, but in the will of God enjoining upon the State the rigorous obligation to procure the common temporal good of its citizens without the least detriment to their personal vocation or eternal destiny. In short, all the rights of man, whether social or individual, have their common source in an obligation imposed by the transcendently sovereign will of God.

In the light of this truth, Jefferson's "principle that governments derive all their just powers from the consent of the governed" is an unfortunately ambiguous formula. If it is interpreted to mean that governmental power comes from the popular will independently of the Divine will, it is a patently false statement. On the other hand, if it is understood as meaning: "It depends on the consent of the people, to decide whether kings or consuls or other magistrates are to be established in authority over them" (Bellarmine)—as per the original from which Jefferson is said to

---

[1] A legal term meaning a higher right binding on all others not endowed with an equal right.

have borrowed it—then it states what is unquestionable. For at the inception of civil society, the people are empowered by God to choose their form of government, designate the subject of power, and fix the manner of accession to public office. Assuming the latter sense to be the one he had in mind, Jefferson cannot be said to have improved on Bellarmine, who makes this meaning much clearer.

The former sense, however, is the one in which Rousseau (of whom Jefferson was an ardent admirer) would have understood it; for the Father of Liberalism, as we have seen, made the popular will the supreme and unique source of governmental power, regardless of anything purporting to be an intimation of the Divine will—a position which was tantamount to denying the existence of a personal God. Quite consistently, therefore, Rousseau, in the concluding chapters (see book IV) of *du Contrat social,* subordinates religion to the State and sets up the purest kind of political absolutism.

Following in his footsteps, orthodox Liberals contend that the supreme social power or *sovereignty* belongs essentially and inalienably to the people, in such a way that the latter in electing their rulers and magistrates never alienate this supreme power, but merely delegate it (subject to revocation) for the sake of more convenient exercise. This, of course, makes government officials mere depositaries rather than possessors of authority. Civil authority is regarded simply as a sum of unit-wills integrated by adding together all the single wills of the citizen associates. The will of God has nothing to do with the constitution of a State, which is based exclusively on the several wills of the single citizens. These individual wills by common consent coalesce into a *general will,* which, having absorbed into itself all the liberties of said individual wills, emerges as the absolutely *sovereign* authority and sole arbiter of the rights of individuals, empowered to dispose of them according to its good pleasure.

This, as we have already remarked, is downright absolutism, and it is quite significant that Hegel, pantheist deifier of the State, who taught: "We must honor the State as the Divine on earth," [1] should have found in Rousseau's despotic *general will* something closely akin to his own conception of an immanent *universal spirit* and *divine will.* He says:

[1] *Philosophie des Rechts,* §272, S. 354, Georg Wilhelm Friedrich Hegel's *Werke,* volume 8 (Duncker & Humbolt, Berlin, 1837):

"To Rousseau must be given the credit of discovering and presenting a principle, which measures up to the standard of thought, and is indeed thinking itself, not in its form, such as would be a social impulse or divine authority, but in its very essence. This principle of Rousseau is will. However, he thinks of the will only in the restricted form of the individual will, as Fichte was likewise to do later, and considers the universal will not as the absolutely reasonable will, but as common will, emanating from the individual will as conscious." [1]

Indeed, one has only to substitute for Rousseau's manifold of coalescing single wills, omnipotent in the aggregate, the unitary will of a universal World-Spirit inherent in the body politic, and he arrives at Hegel's absolutist State which "has the supreme right over the individuals, whose supreme duty it is to be members of the State," [2] so that "the individual himself has his real existence, truth and moral status only in so far as he is a member of it." [3]

This perfect harmony between pantheistic immanentism and political absolutism will later engage our attention. Here, however, we pause to stress the fact that Christian theism is barren soil for absolutism; those who worship a transcendent God, distinct from nature on the one hand and from man on the other, can never recognize as absolutely sovereign the civil authority vested in the State. For in the God he adores the theist must recognize the Supreme Lord and Legislator of the universe, to whom all finite things—nature, man, society and those who govern society—are essentially subject. For the Christian, not the State nor popular caprice, but the unchangeable principles of morality imprinted in man's soul constitute the supreme standard of morality. The highest political potentate—whether he be styled emperor, king, president, dictator or anything else—is nothing more than the mere servant of God, applying a law he has received from God, and from which he dare not depart in the smallest detail under penalty of Divine castigation.

"For there is no power," says the Apostle, "but from God. . . . For princes are not a terror to the good work, but to the evil. Wilt thou then be afraid of the power? Do that which is good: and thou shalt have praise from the same. For he is God's minister to thee, for good. But if thou do that which is evil, fear: for he beareth not the sword in vain. For he is God's minister:

[1] *Op. cit.*, §258, S. 314.
[2] *Op. cit.*, §258, S. 313.
[3] *Op. cit.*, §258, S. 313.

an avenger to execute wrath upon him that doth evil. . . . For therefore also you pay tribute. For they are ministers of God, serving unto this purpose." [1]

This Christian conception of civil rulers as no more than ministers or servants, bound to serve God by executing His justice, is identical with the portrait given of them in the Old Testament:

"Hear, therefore, ye kings, and understand: learn, ye that are judges of the ends of the earth. Give ear, you that rule the people, and please yourselves in multitudes of nations: For power is given you by the Lord, and strength by the Most High, who will examine your works, and search out your thoughts: Because being ministers of his kingdom, you have not judged rightly, nor kept the law of justice nor walked according to the will of God. Horribly and speedily will he appear to you: for a most severe judgment shall be for them that bear rule. For to him that is little, mercy is granted: but the mighty shall be mightily tormented. For God will not stand in awe of any man's greatness: for he made the little and the great, and he hath equally care of all. But a greater punishment is ready for the more mighty. To you, therefore, O kings, are these my words, that you may learn wisdom, and not fall from it." [2]

All this, as Cardinal Billot observes, follows with inexorable logic for those who acknowledge the existence of an extramundane God. And hence he goes on to say: "That monstrous conception, then, of the State as the highest norm of public morality . . . coheres of necessity with the absolute denial of God, that is to say of the true living God, who is something more than a mere empty idea invented to overawe the common herd." [3]

Though they have immediate reference to absolutism in its Rousseauan or liberalistic form, the Cardinal's words apply with equal force to the latest styles as fancied by totalitarian theorists; for, on this point, the newer ideologies are far from original. Germany's National Socialists, for example, simply follow the beaten track of Liberalism when they ban religion from politics and make the temporal power of the State supreme arbiter in moral matters. How out of harmony such arrogation by the State of absolute supremacy is with the supremacy of an extramundane Creator of the universe, Pope Pius XI pointed out in the Encyclical *Mit brennender Sorge* which he addressed to the Catholic Bishops of Germany on March 14, 1937:[4]

---

[1] *Rom.* XIII, 1-6.
[2] *Wisdom* VI, 2-10.
[3] *Cf.* Appendix of his *Tract. de Ecclesia Christi,* Q. XVII.
[4] *Cf. Act. Apost. Sed.* An. et vol. XXIX (Ser. II, v. IV)—Num. 5, 10 Aprilis 1937.

"Our God is a personal, transcendent, omnipotent, infinitely perfect God, one in the trinity of persons and three in the unity of the Divine essence, Creator of the universe, Lord; King and Final Goal of the world's history, who neither admits nor can admit other gods beside Him.

"This God has given His commandments in a sovereign manner—commandments independent of time and space, of region and race. As God's sun shines indiscriminately upon all mankind, so His law recognizes no privileges and no exceptions. Rulers and ruled, crowned heads and subjects, little and great, rich and poor depend alike upon His word. His demand of absolute obedience on the part of all individuals composing any society whatever is grounded upon the utter completeness of His rights. And this demand of obedience extends to all the spheres of life, in which moral questions call for compliance with the Divine law and, by that very fact, for conformity between changeable human ordinances and the unchangeable Divine decrees.

"Only shallow minds will fall into the error of speaking of a national God, of a national religion, and make the fatuous attempt to imprison within the confines of a single people, within the ethnic narrowness of a single race, God, the Creator of the world, King and Lawgiver of peoples, in the face of whose greatness the nations are as tiny as drops in a bucket of water (Isaias XL, 15)."

In a word, political absolutism, claiming as it does unlimited and irresponsible power for the government of a State, amounts to an implicit denial of the transcendent God of Christian theism. In pantheism, on the contrary, absolutism finds an immanent deity after its own heart. This is the point we propose to establish in these pages.

2. *Pantheism a Form of Monism*

Pantheism is subsumed under a wider metaphysical doctrine known as *monism,* understanding by monism the theory that there is only *one* substance or ultimate reality.

The oneness affirmed of the ultimate reality may be either *logical* or *real.* In the former and looser sense, monism comprises atomistic materialism, which holds that there is only *one kind* of reality at the bottom of things, while admitting that this ultimate reality is *numerically manifold.* In other words, materialism's ultimate substrate of things is a plurality of material particles, which are specifically, or generically, but not really, one.

Monism, however, in the strictest sense of the word, is the doctrine that all things are reducible to a single primordial ground which is *really* and *numerically one*—to some unitary and universal principle, increate and eternal, which is commonly spoken of either as God or as the Absolute. But no matter how he names it, the absolute monist invariably identifies it with the material world and all things, including men. All cosmic realities—minds and bodies, organisms and minerals—however distinct or separate they may appear to common sense, are but different parts, modalities, phenomena, expressions, or manifestations of one and the same absolute reality.

This thorough-going monism is opposed, on the one hand, to *pluralism* (the doctrine that the world consists of many substances) and, on the other hand, to *dualism* (which posits an essential distinction between God and the world, spirit and matter, the conscious and unconscious, the living and the lifeless).

Such absolute monism may be either *idealistic* or *parallelistic*. Idealistic monism regards mind as the sole reality and matter as its product; hence it contrasts with *materialistic* monism, which regards matter as the sole reality and mind as its product. Parellelistic monism reduces everything to an ultimate reality that is neither mind nor matter, but the common ground of both.

Of these two main themes there are countless variations and combinations. Thus we have idealistic monism sung to us in a subjective key (Fichte) and in an objective key (Hegel). So, too, parallelistic monism is available in pantheistic and naturalistic keys; speaking of modern monism, Friedrich Paulsen tells us:

"We might perhaps designate this metaphysical conception, which has since prevailed in philosophy, as parallelistic monism in an idealistic key. In addition to it, we have also, it is true, especially in natural-scientific circles, monism in a materialistic key. The pure epistemologist prefers to remain on the standpoint beyond which Kant himself would not go: the corporeal world and the mental world are different manifestations of reality as such, which we cannot know, but may assume as a homogeneous unity. This would be the standpoint of agnostical monism, which Herbert Spencer occupies." [1]

In short, real or parallelistic pantheism admits the real (at least, phenomenal) existence of material things, which it looks upon as manifestations of a single ground called the Absolute. Idealistic pantheism, on the other hand, denying the real existence of extramental objects, declares that the things which appear to us as objects are really nothing but ideas or mental forms of a single thinking substance called the Universal Mind.

Among the various subspecies of pantheistic monism, two are

[1] *Introduction to Philosophy*, Thilly's transl., p. 60 (Henry Holt, New York, 1895).

sufficiently interesting to deserve special mention: I refer to the *emanationism* of Plotinus, and to *monopsychism,* William James' modern version of the Averroistic tenet of a universal *agent intellect.* Of these we shall have occasion to speak later.

Some authors distinguish between Pantheism (the doctrine that the universe is God) and Theopantism (the doctrine that God is the sole reality). Others insist on the need of a distinction between explicit pantheism and certain modern forms of absolute monism. Pantheism, they remark, starts with God and ends by identifying Him with the world, whereas modern monism often begins with the world, which it proceeds to deify into an absolutely independent and self-existent being; but since it speaks of this Absolute as Nature rather than God, such monism ought, in their opinion, to be called *naturalism* instead of pantheism.

However, so far as the purposes of the present discussion are concerned, these distinctions are of little importance. Nearly all monistic and pantheistic systems are in accord as to the following fundamentals: (a) the doctrine of *universal identity*—that there exists but one absolute reality which is all in all and in which all seemingly different things are identified; (b) the doctrine of *eternal becoming*—that the Absolute by virtue of a perennial evolution or unfolding develops progressively into all things in such a way as to achieve ever higher and higher degrees of perfection; (c) the doctrine of *humanitarianism*—that the Absolute manifests itself most perfectly in self-conscious human minds, in the individual and more especially in the social life of men, but that its manifestation of itself is less perfect in the lower forms of consciousness and life, reaching its nadir in the mineral world.

In other words, these systems are at one in seeking to imprison God, as *immanent mind,* in the world and especially in mankind organized as civil society. Herein, pending further progress, the evolving Absolute is reputed to have reached the high-water mark of its self-conscious existence.

3. *Monism's Mystical Synthesis of the Incoherent*

As an interpretation of reality, pantheistic monism flatly contradicts what is literally thrust upon us by *experience* and *reason.* Thus *external* experience, which comes to us through our senses, makes us clearly aware of the *multiplicity* and *variety* of visible things. As given to us in sense perception, material things frequently appear to us as not only differentiated but spatially separated. Natural beings, such as minerals, plants and animals, are presented to our senses as endowed with characters not simply different but opposite, e.g., consciousness and unconsciousness, life and lifelessness, spontaneity and inertia, immanence and transitivity.

The existence of plurality and difference is a fact also borne in upon us by *internal* experience, which makes us vividly aware of a distinction between ourselves and the outer world, between the ego and the non-ego, between the knowing subject and the known object. In certain cases, we are conscious of being ourselves the active and self-determining sources of what we do; in other cases, we feel ourselves to be the unwilling and passive recipients of effects impressed upon us by agents exterior to ourselves. Accordingly, the panetheistic doctrine of universal identity is in conflict with experience, which attests the real existence of plurality, otherness and differentiation.

It is likewise in conflict with the testimony of reason; for if the phenomenal differences of the universe are nothing but expressions, manifestations, or effluences of one and the same fundamental reality, then whence the distinction and opposition that mark them off from one another? In what sense can a unitary, independent, unconditioned, unlimited, uncaused and eternal Absolute be identified with the multiple, dependent, conditioned, limited, produced, impermanent, and corruptible realities that make up the visible human and subhuman world?

All the confusionism and incoherence characteristic of monistic thinkers is epitomized in their conception of the Absolute. Their deity is an impossible welter of contradictory attributes. More than two thousand years ago, the Academician philosopher Carneades (213-129 B.C.) excoriated Pantheism's pioneer theologians, the Stoics, for this radical flaw vitiating the very core of their ideology. In the Introduction to his translation of Sextus Empiricus,[1] R. G. Bury thus summarizes Carneades' criticism of Stoic "theology":

"The God of the Stoics is an incredible Being because he is composed of contradictory attributes. If He is to be infinite, omniscient, all-good, and imperishable, He cannot be either composite or corporeal or animate or rational or virtuous—all such qualities belonging to objects which lie in the sphere of becoming and perishing."

[1] *Sextus Empiricus,* vol. I, p. xxxv (Loeb Classical Library, Putnam's Sons, New York, 1933).

The State-God of the modern humanitarian pantheists is a tissue of still more flagrant contradictions. For the individuality characterizing all realities of nature is nowhere more apparent than in man. Peter and Paul, Fido and Rover have each their own individual natures, numerically distinct and even spatially separate from one another. But according to pantheists, Peter and Paul are numerically identical; Peter's singular nature is not simply *similar* to Paul's, it is *really* one and the same; all individual men (with Fido and Rover bringing up the rear), notwithstanding their distinctive individuation and genealogical differences, are merged into a single amalgamated Godhead called Humanity.

In it we do not have God become man—Christ, but man become God—Antichrist, *showing himself as if he were God*.[1] After Adam, in his preposterous ambition to *be as God*,[2] had set aside the commandment of his Creator, the comment that God pronounced upon his folly was truly ironic: "Behold the man is become as one of us."[3] The same remark applies with even greater force to pantheism's blasphemous deification of Humanity.

It is doubly ironic in that the monists, who find it so easy to swallow the contradictions entailed in fusing millions of human individuals into the absolute unity of the All-One, are the very ones who find it impossible to accept the doctrine of Three Persons in One God. Paulsen—monist and self-styled "thinking man"—declared: "If Christianity consisted . . . in the acceptance of the dogmas of the two natures or the three persons in one, . . . then of course it would be impossible for a liberal-minded and thinking man of today to accept it."[4]

Of the pantheistic humanitarians, who like Paulsen worship myriads of men merged into a single State-God, Gilbert Chesterton observed:

"It is evidently impossible to worship humanity, just as it is impossible to worship the Savile Club; both are excellent institutions to which we may

[1] II *Thess*. II, 4.
[2] *Gen*. III, 5.
[3] *Gen*. III, 22—this, the one and only *trinitarian* text in the Old Testament, plainly affirms a *plurality of persons* in God. "Behold the man has become as *one from among us*" (כְּאַחַד מִמֶּנּוּ). Accordingly, the orthodox Jew has to choose between admitting *polytheism* in the Scriptures and accepting the Christian or Trinitarian solution, which while affirming the *absolute* oneness of the Divine *essence*, affirms, on the other hand, a *relative* but real plurality of Divine *persons*—hence a *Triune* God.
[4] *Introduct. to Philos*. (tr. of Thilly), p. 250 (H. Holt., New York, 1895).

happen to belong. But we perceive clearly that the Savile Club did not make the stars and does not fill the universe. And it is surely unreasonable to attack the doctrine of the Trinity as a piece of bewildering mysticism and then ask men to worship a being who is ninety million persons in one God, neither confounding the persons nor dividing the substance." [1]

But the fact of the matter is, that pantheistic humanitarians actually do "confound the persons." For in consequence of their initial confusion of *real oneness* with *logical oneness,* they inevitably confound into one not only the individual *natures* of all beings, but even the very *persons* of men as well as the subhuman *selves* of irrational things. They make really *common* what are in fact the most *incommunicable* realties in nature, namely, human persons. For persons or rational selves are self-determining agents, fully aware of being in their own power, whereas irrational or subhuman selves are not in their own power, but mere puppets of either external or internal necessity. A person, as W. H. Mallock put it, "is in a true, even if qualified sense, the first cause of what he does, or feels, or is." And he adds: "If a man is not in any degree, be this never so limited, the first cause or originator of his own actions or impulses, he must be the mere transmitter or quotient of forces external to his conscious self, like a man pushed against another by the pressure of the crowd behind him. In other words, he would have no true self—no true personality." [2]

Nowhere in the universe do we find instances of more clean-cut distinction than between one person and another; yet it is precisely human persons that pantheists proceed to blend. "The heart and soul of all men being one this bitterness of *His* and *Mine* ceases. He is mine. I am my brother, and my brother is me." [3] Thus spake Ralph Waldo Emerson, whose solemn visage was chosen in recent years to decorate American postage stamps. In a like key, sang his equally vague poet friend, Walt Whitman, sharer with him in those selfsame postal honors: [4]

For me the keepers of convicts shoulder their carbines and keep watch,
It is I let out in the morning and barr'd at night. . . .

[1] *Heretics,* Ch. V, p. 96 (John Lane Co., New York and London, 1909).
[2] *The Reconstruction of Religious Belief,* pp. 75, 76 (Harper Bros., New York, London, 1905).
[3] *Essays—First Series,* Essay III, "Compensation," p. 136 (McKay, Philadelphia, 1888).
[4] *Song of Myself* (37), "Leaves of Grass," p. 61 (Doubleday, Page, Garden City, N. Y., 1926).

Not a youngster is taken for larceny but I go up too, and am tried and sentenced.

A few years ago an admirer of the foregoing lines remarked to me in a letter that true humility would, like Walt, outdo St. Philip Neri himself by discarding the last distinction between self and the criminal—"Not only does it say, 'There but for the grace of God go I' but it takes the next step, and with Walt Whitman says, 'There goes Walt Whitman.'" *Du sublime au ridicule il n'y a qu'un pas!* I do not recall exactly what I said in reply, but I remember it was something to the effect that by taking that one step further Walt Whitman had stepped over the confines of reason into the realm of unreason, where reason's indispensable principles of identity and contradiction are honored only in the breach. Catholic Christian thought, on the other hand, has never wavered in its allegiance to these paramount principles of reason— "God is my witness that our message to you is not both 'Yes' and 'No.' For the Son of God, Jesus Christ, who was preached by us— by me and Sylvanus and Timothy—was not now 'Yes' and now 'No,' but only 'Yes' was in him. For all the promises of God find their 'Yes' in him." [1]

Not so with the yes-and-no philosophers of monism—the prophets of the great All-One:

> Still though the one I sing
> (One, yet of contradictions made,) I dedicate to Nationality,
> I leave in him revolt (O latent right of insurrection! O quenchless, indispensable fire!)[2]

Paul and Timothy might prize their consistency, but Walt and Waldo boasted of their *contradictions:*

> Do I contradict myself?
> Very well then . . . I contradict myself;
> I am large. . . . I contain multitudes.[3]

The monist's mind, if not deep, is at least broad—able to swallow any absurdity without the least visible sign of discomfort. As for *consistency,* far from regarding it as a jewel, the pantheist

[1] II *Cor.* I, 18-20.
[2] Whitman, *op. cit.,* "Song of Myself," p. 10.
[3] Whitman, *op. cit.,* "Song of Myself," 51, p. 75.

is disposed to laugh it out of court. Emerson cannot hide his scorn for anyone so narrow as to take the need of it seriously:

"In your metaphysics you have denied personality to the Deity: yet when the devout motions of the soul come, yield to them heart and life, though they should clothe God with shape and color. Leave your theory as Joseph his coat in the hands of the harlot and flee.

"A foolish consistency is the hobgoblin of little minds, adored by little statesmen and philosophers and divines. With consistency a great soul has simply nothing to do. He may as well concern himself with his shadow on the wall." [3]

Naturally, belief in such a jumble of contradictions as the pantheist Absolute cannot be a matter of intellectual acceptance but, at most, of emotional adherence. Inasmuch as it involves assent to the absurd, there can be no question of rational conviction, but only of purely sentimental attachment. An intellectual belief on the order of what a Catholic understands by faith is excluded; what is required is an irrational allegiance, a voluntaristic faith, an emotional persuasion of the pietist or Kantian type.[1] Only blind emotionalism could possibly cling to that heterogeneous mass of jarring contradictions, that vast vague mixtum-gatherum which Pantheists call God. "Religion," as one monist confesses, "does not originate in dogma or in action, but in feeling; in feeling the finite becomes immediately aware of the infinite and the eternal. Every true feeling that springs from the fulness of the heart and turns toward the whole of things is religious." [2]

---

[3] *Emerson, op. cit.,* 1st. ser., Essay II: "Self-Reliance," pp. 64, 65.

[1] St. Thomas teaches that the act of faith has its immediate seat, not in the will, but in the intellect, which, however, elicits this act at the command of the will— "to believe is an act of the intellect, in so far as it is moved by the will." *(Sum. Th.,* IIa IIae, q. 4, a. 2.) Habitual faith is a supernatural intellectual virtue, rooted in the believer's understanding and enabling him to receive the Christian revelation upon the authority of an undeceiving and undeceivable God, who is supremely worthy to be believed. On Divine authority man can and ought to receive what is *above reason* (but never what is *against* reason, for our intellect is unable to assimilate contradictions, nor can it sincerely accept what is presented to it upon inadequate grounds). Hence Catholic faith is essentially a "reasonable belief"—ἡ λογικὴ λατρεία *(Rom.* XII, 1). For the evangelical, on the contrary, faith is not an intellectual conviction, but a mere blind enthusiasm or impulse of the heart, which clings to what appeals to the heart regardless of whether it conflicts with reason or not. Kantian faith is this same evangelical or pietistic faith reduced to naturalistic terms—it is an assertion by the will of religious ideals because of a practical subjective need. Pietistic faith amounts to a sentimental acceptance without any grounds or credentials whatever which the intellect can see and recognize as adequate.

[2] Paulsen (relaying Schleiermacher)—*cf. op. cit.,* p. 306.

Religion, therefore, as the pantheist understands it, is wholly a matter of emotion, a thing which waxes and wanes as feeling waxes and wanes. In other words, he is the naturalistic counterpart of the evangelical revivalist. In the best tradition of revivalism, he sets himself the task of stepping up the emotions of awe, admiration, and enthusiasm over Nature and Humanity. Whitman's *Song of the Open Road* [1] is a typical pantheist "pep-talk" having for its object the excitation of those feelings in which a pietistic sentimentalism, impatient of all rational definiteness, thinks religion to consist.

> Allons! with power, liberty, the earth, the elements,
> Health, defiance, gayety, self-esteem, curiosity;
> Allons! from all formules! . . . .
> Allons! to that which is endless as it was beginningless,
> . . . .
> Allons! the road is before us!
> . . . .
> Camerado, I give you my hand.

Small wonder, that Walt's far-fetched rapture over nothing in particular but everything in general should have evoked from D. B. Wyndham Lewis [2] this stinging, yet singularly appropriate, comment:

"Allons, then, cameradoes! (or cameradi), as the inexpressibly tedious Whitman (Walt) bellows. The future lies before us! Let us, taking up something or other, manifest our what d'you call it in the great free bounding universal thingumbob."

4. *Monism's Philosophic Roots*

The root-errors responsible for monistic thought are not confined to any one branch of philosophy, but are found in all. We shall touch briefly on the more important of them.

(a) First of all, monism is very often the outcome of certain confusions in the sphere of logic. Hegel, for example, confused *real* existence with *mental* (ideal) existence and further confounded mental existence (presence as a thought-object in the mind) with the subjective thought-process itself—"From what has been said we have seen that logic is the search for a system of the types or fundamental ideas of thought, in which the opposition between

---

[1] Whitman—*cf. op. cit.*, pp. 128-133.
[2] "On Straw," pp. 142, 143 (Coward-McCann, New York).

subjective and objective, in its usual sense, vanishes." [1] He has just explained that thought produces its own object, which is nothing else than the active thought's repetition of itself, and therefore "the product of its operation is equivalent to the fact, the essence, the intrinsic value, the truth. . . ." [2]

From here it is an easy step to the most prolific of all the logical sources of monism, namely, mistaking the unifying *mental mode* of *universality* for a *real mode* of things as they exist outside the mind.

This is the old Platonic error of *ultrarealism,* which affirmed the real existence of universalized thought-objects apart from sensible reality and independently of our mind's abstractive action.

However, as Aristotle points out, all the concrete realities of the sensible world are individualized, and the universal as such (i.e., the thought-object as isolated and generalized) exists only in the mind—"The reason is that actual sensation is always of singulars (τῶν καθ' ἕκαστον), while science is of the universals (τῶν καθόλου); and the latter are after a manner (πώς) in the soul itself." [3]

In the mental world we isolate in thought the essences of things from their unessential individuation, their likenesses from their unlikenesses, although in the real order of things these are never found apart. In other words, *isolates* or abstract thought-objects exist as separate and apart only *logically,* that is, in the mind, but their *unisolated* presence in our sense-data and in external things is as *real* as are those individualized things and sense-experiences themselves.

However, in consequence of the abstract or desingularized mode of their existence in the mind, these conceptual isolates become capable of *universalization* (generalization), that is, of being predicated of more than one individual thing. And thus it is that, although Peter, Paul and John have each their own separate individual human natures, the same isolate of human nature that I originally abstracted from Peter will serve over again to represent (make present to my mind) the human nature of Paul as well and also that of John. I do not need to form three separate representations, new abstractions being superfluous in the case of Paul and John. For the originally-isolated thought-object representing the

---

[1] *Logic of Hegel,* translation of Wm. Wallace, 1874, ch. II, p.39.
[2] *Op. cit.,* pp. 30-34.
[3] *De anima,* bk. II, 5.417b22.

human nature of Peter suffices to make present to my mind the human natures of Paul, John and countless other individuals. Reflection makes me aware of this and so I come to conceive said isolate as *universal,* that is, as *one* thought-object *mentally* referrable to *many* real individuals. I recognize that human nature, as it exists abstractly in my mind, is capable of receiving the predicate *universal* (meaning "representative of many"). But this *universality* is a *mental mode,* not a physical attribute predicable of singular realities like the individual human natures of Peter, Paul and John.

Ultrarealists who transfer from thought to reality this unifying mental mode of *universality* come inevitably to the monistic conclusion that all reality is *one.* In truth, however, the mode of universality (representability of many by one) —which in the widest concept of "being" transcends all distinctions and unifies the variety of all less general concepts—is a mode of thought, not of reality. The attribution of such a predicate to individuals leads to *idealistic* monism, which identifies the universe of things (nature) with *ens communissimum* (being in general), and the latter with *ens realissimum* (God).

(b) Monism may also be due to a perverted *metaphysics,* i.e., to misconceptions in the domain of *ontology.* In some instances, it arises from a confusion of the different ways in which a *relative* reality may be dependent upon its corresponding *absolute.* Such, as we have already seen, was the case with Spinoza whose error lay in conceiving the dependence of creatures upon the Creator as a dependence of accidents upon their substance, instead of as a dependence of effects upon their efficient cause.

Nor was Spinoza the only thinker that Cartesian metaphysics led astray. The *occasionalism* of Arnold Geulincx (1624-1669) and Nicolas Malebranche (1638-1715), by attributing causality (agency) exclusively to the Creator (First Cause) and denying all activity to created agents (second causes), virtually suppressed the real existence of creatures, making God the sole reality (theopantism).

(c) In the field of *cosmology,* monism results whenever nature's unity of order is misinterpreted as a substantial oneness of being or essence. The world is not a vast organism whose parts are substantially incomplete components unfitted to exist by themselves. On the contrary, the "parts" composing it are so many distinct and separate substances linked together to form, not one single *sub-stance,* but one orderly *system.* Cosmological monism is the outcome of mistaking this systematic oneness for substantial oneness.

(d) It is, however, in the domain of *psychology* that we find what is, perhaps, the most prolific of all sources of monistic aberration, namely, anthropomorphic *immanentism.*

Immanence is a term we have already used, in contrast to *transcendence,* for the purpose of designating God's intimate causal presence in the whole of His creation; this is its theological sense. In psychology and biology, the same term is used, in contrast to *transitivity,* to signify a characteristic of all *vital* action whether conscious or unconscious.

Etymologically, *im-manent* signifies *remaining-within,* and vital action is so characterized because the effects or completed changes in which vital processes terminate, *remain within* the agent initiating them and are not communicated to any external subject. All mechanical and physicochemical actions, on the contrary, are forms of *transitive* action, that is to say, of *interaction* between distinct substances. Mechanical action is intermolar, physical action intermolecular, chemical action interatomic, electrical action intercorpuscular. Always it is a case of one mass or particle acting upon another mass or particle distinct from and spatially external to itself. The living organism, however, is the ultimate recipient of the effect produced by its own action. The living reader, by his reading, modifies himself, not the book. The inert molecule of sodium nitrate, though it can nourish a blade of grass, is impotent to nourish itself. On the contrary, the blade of grass can nourish not only a cow, but also itself. Here the active source and receptive subject of the process terminating in the production of the effect are one and the same substance. Vital action, therefore, in contrast to the *transitive* or *communicable* action characteristic of inert substances, is of the *immanent* or *reflexive* type.

Man, being himself a living and conscious organism, is only too prone to transport his own immanent mental life into even unconscious things and to interpret the latter in that subjective light. It is this interpretation, *in terms of* our consciousness rather than *by means of* it, that constitutes what we may call *anthropomorphic immanentism.*

This error gives rise to *panvitalistic* (hylozoic) and *panpsychic* monisms which suppress all distinction between living and lifeless, conscious and unconscious, organism and environment, knower and known.

5. *Pantheism in Ancient Times*

Pantheism, in the sense of hylozoism (universal animation of matter) and panpsychism (which makes consciousness a universal attribute of nature), dates back to the earliest period of human speculation.

According to a theory widely held among anthropologists, one of the oldest superstitions of mankind was *animism,* i.e., the belief that ascribes conscious life to all natural objects. Sometimes, it is said, this belief took the form of *animatism,* according to which the things and phenomena of nature are endowed with life and consciousness, but not with individual souls. It is even thought that in certain cases early men entertained a philosophically monistic belief ascribing life to nature as a whole. On the other hand, animism normally took the pluralistic form which regarded all bodies as animated by separate souls, which might exist in a disembodied state. Souls of this sort were ascribed not only to men, but also to animals, plants, stones, tools and so forth. Such was the animism existing among the ancient Babylonians—"The earliest people in Babylon believed that everything possessed a spirit." [1] They ascribed a life or *Zi* to every natural object and phenomenon—"to trees, stones and plants, as well as such natural events as storm, rain, and wind," [2] and so forth.

Of this superstition Andrew Lang gives the following psychological explanation:

"Judging from . . . the myths of savages, early man may have half-consciously extended his own sense of personal and potent and animated existence to the whole of nature as known to him. Not only animals, but vegetables and inorganic objects, may have been looked on by him as persons like what he felt himself to be." [3]

That primitive man should have been anthropomorphic in his interpretation of external nature, is, after all, not a matter of great surprise. Modern men, too, even those who fancy themselves as "thinking men," display this selfsame tendency to humanize sub-

---

[1] E. A. Wallis Budge, *Babylonian Life and History,* 2nd ed., p. 100 (London, 1925).
[2] Morris Jastrow, *Religion of Babylonia and Assyria,* p. 48 (Ginn & Co., Boston, 1898).
[3] *The Making of Religion,* p. 54 (Longmans, London, New York, 1898).

human nature—to conceive everything in their own image and likeness. Charles Darwin is a case in point. On the analogy of the intelligent selection exercised by animal breeders and horticulturists, he assumed an unintelligent selection made by the blind factors of the environment, going so far as to ascribe to these irrational, nay unconscious, physicochemical factors of nature even nicer powers of discrimination than those possessed by human experts in artificial selection—"I have called this principle by which each slight variation, if useful, is preserved, by the term natural selection, in order to mark its relation to man's power of selection." [1] This is *anthropomorphism* with a vengeance! If he wished to put *human* and *natural* selection on a perfect par, Darwin, before likening the latter to the former, ought first to have expurgated *human selection* of the element of *intelligent control* lurking in it and vitiating its parallelism with the unintelligent havoc wrought by the blind factors at work in so-called *natural selection*. But what *intelligence* by its very etymology[2] signifies is precisely the *power of selection*—being derived from the Latin verb *legere* (to pick or choose) and the preposition *inter* (between). Hence, in eliminating *intelligence* one eliminates without residue all that there is to *selection*. Only at the price of *humanizing* it, can we endow inanimate nature with the power of selection.

Be that as it may, it is safe, so far as history goes, to assign India as the birthplace of anthropomorphic immanentism in its philosophic form. As such, it makes its first appearance in the post-Vedic period prior to 500 B.C. We find in the earliest *Upanishads* ("Sessions"), called the *Vedānta* (the suffixed *ānta* means *end*), *sc.,* the culmination of the Veda,[3] and, even before them, in the *Āraṇyakas* ("Reflections in the Woods"), traces of a pure-idealist monism or *acosmism,* with which Hindu speculation seems to have begun. *Ātman,* the Ego, is regarded as the sole reality. This true and ultimate Self of selves is said to be: "One only without a second"—*Ekadvitiyam.* The visible world of nature is but an illusion (*māyā*), a mirage which disappears on closer examination. Only one true existent remains unfalsified by this universal illusion and

---

[1] *The Origin of Species,* 6th ed., ch. III, p. 58; see O'Toole, *The Case Against Evolution,* New York, Macmillan, 1925, pp. 152, 153.

[2] *Cf.* Weekley's *Etymological Dictionary of Modern English,* 1921, col. 764.

[3] In later times, *Vedānta* was used to designate *Uttara-Mimāmsā,* one of the Six Systems of Hindu philosophy. (Max Müller, *The Six Systems,* 2nd ed., p. 113.)

that is a man's inmost self, which is one with the Supreme Self. In the oldest of the Upanishads,[1] it is said:

In the beginning this was Self alone, in the shape of a person (purusha). He looking round saw nothing but his Self. He first said, 'This is I'; therefore he became I by name. Therefore even now, if a man is asked, he first says, 'This is I,' and then pronounces the other name he may have.

Immanent in our bodies, internal even to our individual souls is this true unchanging, imperishable Self, which has swallowed up all the Vedic gods together with their gifts to man and which henceforth survives as the only reality.

However, the existence of the phenomenal world is too forcibly intruded on consciousness to be successfully ignored. A compromise was in order. So *Ātman* (the One) was blended with *Brahman* (the All), and *acosmism* gave place to a sort of *pantheism* identifying God with the world, the Ego with the non-ego —"He indeed is the same ·as that Self (Ātman), that immortal Brahman, that All." [2] This means that the reality of the impersonal world without is identical with the reality of the personal world within.

The pantheism which attains to definitive expression in the *Chhāndogya Upanishad* has two key-formulas. The first of these: "I am Brahman"—*aham bramā asmi,* occurs in the *Brihadāranyaka Upanishad* (I, 4.10), with the added explanation: "Now if a man worships another deity, thinking the deity is one and he another, he does not know." The second formula is the famous: "Thou art that"—*tat tvam asi,*[3] in which the neuter pronoun *tat* ("that" or "it") accentuates the impersonal character of *Brahman* (itself a neuter noun) denoting "objective essence" (known object). The words occur in the *Chhāndogya Upanishad,* where they are nine times repeated. Max Müller rightly styles this fusion of ego and non-ego, subject and object, knower and known as "the boldest" synthesis in the whole history of philosophy, but Hegel speaks in him when he adds, "and truest." (*The Six Systems,* ed. of 1903, p. 122.)

In substance, the two formulas mean this: I am Brahman, the One Reality; it alone *is,* all else is *māyā* (fiction, illusion); the

---

[1] *Bṛihad. Up.* I, 1. 1—*cf. Hindu Scriptures,* p. 49 Dutton & Co., New York, 1938).
[2] *Bṛihad. Up.* II, 5. 1 (*Hindu Script.,* p. 65).
[3] *Chhāndogya Up.* VI, 8. 7.

multiplicity and distinction of visible things are unreal, Brahman alone is real and worth knowing; when we know Brahman we become Brahman, the individual self being absorbed into the general Self.

Verily in the beginning this was Brahman, that Brahman knew (its) Self, saying, 'I am Brahman.' From it all this sprang.[1]

'As the spider comes out with its thread, or as small sparks come forth from fire, thus do all senses, all worlds, all Devas, all beings come forth from that Self. The Upanishad (the true name and doctrine) of that Self is 'the True of the True.' [2]

'As a lump of salt, when thrown into water, becomes dissolved into water, and could not be taken out again, but wherever we taste (the water) it is salt—thus verily, O Maitreyī, does this great Being, endless, unlimited, consisting of nothing but knowledge, rise from out these elements, and vanish again in them.' [3]

'As the bees, my son, make honey by collecting the juices of distant trees, and reduce the juice into one form.

'And as these juices have no discrimination, so that they might say, I am the juice of this tree or that, in the same manner, my son, all these creatures, when they have become merged in the True (either in deep sleep or in death), know not that they are merged in the True.

'Whatever these creatures are here, whether a lion, or a wolf, or a boar, or a worm, or a midge, or a gnat, or a mosquito, that they become again and again.

'Now that which is that subtile essence, in it all that exists has its self. It is the True. It is the Self, and thou, O Svetaketu, art it (that).' [4]

'These rivers, my son, run, the eastern (like the Gaṅgā) toward the east, the western (like the Sindhu) toward the west. They go from sea to sea (i.e. the clouds lift up the water from the sea to the sky, and send it back as rain to the sea). They become indeed sea. And as those rivers when they are in the sea, do not know, I am this or that river.

'In the same manner, my son, all these creatures, etc.
. . . .

That which is that subtile essence, in it all that exists has its self. It is the True. It is the Self, and thou, O Svetaketu, art it.' [5]

But the *identity* of self and not-self makes no sense; it is an unintelligible relation which the lips may speak but the mind refuses to assimilate. When Maitreyī said to her Brahman husband:

[1] *Brihad. Up.* I, 4. 10 (*Hindu Script.*, pp. 50, 51).
[2] *Brihad. Up.* II, 1. 20 (*Hindu Script.*, p. 60).
[3] *Brihad. Up.* II, 4. 12 (*Hindu Script.*, p. 64).
[4] *Chhāndogya Up.* VI, 9. 1-4. (*Hindu Script.*, p. 171).
[5] *Chhāndogya Up.* VI, 10. 1-3 (*Hindu Script.*, p. 171).

"Here, thou hast bewildered me, Sir," [1] she but voiced the inevitable protest of reason against this anti-intellectualist confusionism which leads straight to Buddhist nihilism.

In the sequel, as the later Upanishads (composed between 500 and 400 B.C.) show, the equation: "Ātman=Brahman," was abandoned as untenable and replaced by a *cause-effect* relation. Self, indeed, remains what it was before, namely the Self in us, but this Self has now become a Creator, who having made the world, enters into it to animate it after the fashion of a *world-soul*. Pantheism thus comes to be superseded by a kind of *cosmogonism*, which the *Taittirīya Upanishad* describes as follows: "He desired: 'I will be manifold, I will propagate myself.' He performed austerities. Having performed austerities, he created this whole world, whatever existed. Having created it, he entered into it." [2]

In spite of their shift from identification to causation, the Brahmanic philosophers did not escape monism. Their Creator does not transcend his creation, but incorporates himself in it and remains immanent in it as its soul. They forsook idealistic monism only to fall into monism of the parallelistic type. The reason is clear. Incorrigible immanentists that they were, the Hindu sages, if they thought of *efficient cause* at all, were bound to think of it anthropomorphically, after the analogy of a *living* cause like the human thinker. Now, *living* causes, as we have already noted, can produce effects not only in subjects *external to* themselves but also *within their own substance,* such that the subject these effects modify forms one substance with their immanently acting cause. To arrive at the notion of an *extramundane* Creator, however, one must renounce *anthropomorphism* and reason on the analogy of *transitive,* instead of *immanent,* causation.

Not long after its appearance in India, philosophic monism appears among the Greeks, but cast in a naturalistic rather than a pantheistic mold. Aristotle tells us[3] that the Physicists, as he calls the Early Ionian cosmologists, admitted only *one principle* and that a changeable one, "some declaring air to be the first principle, and others water." John Burnet answers those who suggest that Aristotle was guilty of an anachronism in classifying the Early Ionians as monists, by citing a pre-Aristotelian testimony from 500 B.C., namely, the Hippocratean treatise *On Human Nature.*

[1] *Bṛihad. Up.* II, 4. 13 (*Hindu Script.,* p. 64).
[2] *Taitt. Up.* II, 6.
[3] *Physics,* Bk. I, 2.184b 15-17.

In the passage he quotes,[1] the *all-one* (τὸ ἕν χαὶ πᾶν) doctrine is formulated in so many words.

Whatever may be thought of Thales and Anaximander, it is quite certain that Anaximenes (*circa* 588-525 B.C.) taught the panvitalistic doctrine that the world is an animal inhaling masses of air from the Boundless. Interpreting the macrocosm (nature) on the analogy of the microcosm (man), he argued that "just as our soul, which is air, holds us together, so also do breath and air encompass the whole world." [2] In this doctrine Anaximenes was followed by the early Pythagorean school.

The first Greek philosopher to espouse monism explicitly was Xenophanes (*circa* 570-470 B.C.) of Colophon. Says Aristotle: "But Xenophanes, the first exponent of the One (for Parmenides is said to have been his disciple), gave no definite teaching nor does he seem to have grasped either of these conceptions of nature; but referring to the whole universe (heaven) he states that God is the One." [3]

Foreshadowing the Eleatic monism of *pure being,* according to which the many which we see is *appearance,* whereas the one we do not see is *reality,* he affirmed the oneness of the Deity. However, he was not a monotheist, but a pantheist, confounding God with the universe. Among the surviving lines of his philosophical verses are these four outlining his conception of the All-One.[4]

1. There is one God, the greatest among men and gods, like unto mortals neither in form nor in thought;
2. He sees all over, understands all over, hears all over;
3. But without toil by the thought of his mind he disposes all;
4. For always he abides in the same place unmoved, nor does it become him to ramble from one place to another.

It remained, however, for Heraclitus (b. about 530 B.C.), one of the Later Ionian philosophers, to think out the *immanentist* premiss to its ultimate conclusion in an anti-intellectualist monism of *pure becoming.*

Impressed with the great fact of cosmic *change,* this oracular sage of "Fire and Flux" saw in the universe naught but an inces-

---

[1] *Early Greek Philosophy,* footnote 2, pp. 9, 10 (Black, London, 1930).

[2] Plutarch, *de Placitis phil.,* bk. I, 3 (Mullach's *Fragmentorum Philos. Graecorum,* vol. I, footnote 5, p. 241).

[3] *Metaphys.,* bk. I, 5.986b 22-24.

[4] *Cf.* Mullach's *Frag. Phil. Graec.,* vol. I, p. 101.

sant cosmic metabolism that spares nothing and renders all reality radically unstable, down to its very bottom. He denies all essential permanence in nature reducing it to a perpetual cascade of evanescent phenomena.

Claiming that wisdom does not consist in a knowledge of the impermanent manifold but in the appreciation of one highest truth or *Logos* ("Word") which underlies everything and is "true evermore," he ridicules Pythagoras for his curiosity about scientific matters. What, then, did he mean by that all-important *Word?*

Burnet notes that Heraclitus lived at a time when the Delphic precept: "Know Thyself," was a household word in Greece and when the Hellenes were beginning to take a lively interest in *the inner world of Self*. By that time, the human soul was no longer looked upon as the pale insubstantial wraith of Homeric days, but had become a warm and significant reality. Philosophic thought, hitherto engrossed in the study of the outer world (the macrocosm), was shifting its attention to the world of self (the microcosm). Plutarch[1] testifies: "Heraclitus, as if accounting it a great and signal feat, declared: 'I sought myself'; and that, among the inscriptions at Delphi, especially divine seemed the one: 'Know thyself.' " (Frag. #84.) And Plutarch explains that by the words *I sought myself,* Heraclitus meant that he *took pains to know himself.* And adverting to the unfathomable profundity of the soul as an object of study, Heraclitus himself exclaims: "You will not find the boundaries of the soul by travelling in any direction, so deep a measure it has." [2]

Whereas Anaximenes had hypothecated a *breath-soul* for both the human person and the world and envisaged the universe as an animated organism inhaling air from the boundless, Heraclitus postulated a *fire-soul* for man and for nature. Anaximenes' two world-forming processes of rarefaction and condensation he modified into a two-way metabolism, designating the former process as *combustion* (ἐκπύρωσις) or *evaporation* (ἀναθυμίασις). By this theory he professed to explain how the visible world comes to take form out of the *pure primordial fire.*

Reopening the question of reconciling the opposites (hot and cold, dry and wet), which the Early Ionians had sought to solve on *meteorological* lines, he searched for a new solution in the inner

[1] *Adv. Colot.* ch. 20 (Mullach, *op. cit.,* vol. I, p. 326).
[2] *Cf.* Diogenes Laertius, IX, 7.

world of *psychology*, assuming a psychophysical parallelism between the processes of human life on the one hand and those of nature on the other.

In the human being, he argued, *life* and *sleep* and *death* are the counterparts of *fire* and *water* and *earth* respectively, and so, thanks to that, we can make ourselves and the outer world intelligible in the light of this analogy. Proceeding, therefore, on the supposition that the phenomenal opposites (the hot and dry, the cold and wet) stand to one another in the same relation as the aforesaid phenomena of life, he compares *hot* and *cold, wet* and *dry* to *life* and *death, sleeping* and *waking*. For the soul is *fully alive* only when it is *awake,* and *sleep* is an *intermediate stage* between life and death. Sleep and death are due to an advance of moisture upon the dry. This is proved by drunkenness[1]—"A man when he gets drunk, is led by a beardless boy staggering, having his soul wet" (Frag. #70). "It is death to souls to become wet, and death to water to become earth." [2] (Frag. #59.) Waking and life, on the other hand, are due to the advance of warmth or fire upon moisture, which is thereby *dried up* or *evaporated*—"A dry soul is wisest and best." [3] (Frag. #72.)

Furthermore, there is a *regular alternation* in these parallel processes; for sleep alternates with waking and death with life. So, too, fire is fed by the exhalations of evaporating liquids (as is to be seen in the candle flame and the olive-oil lamp); likewise, fire turns liquids into exhalations (as is to be seen when water is evaporated into steam by heat). If there were no water (liquids), there could be no fire and, were there no fire, no exhalations would be given off.

Heraclitus, applying the same reasoning to nature (the macrocosm), sees in the interchange of day and night, of summer and winter an alternation parallel to that between life and death, sleeping and waking, and due to the very same cause, namely the advance of fire upon water and of water upon fire.

Consequently, he concludes that Anaximenes erred in making an *intermediate* state like "air" the *primary* stuff of the universe. For this primordial substance must needs be the *most living* of all, and hence *fire*, like unto the human *soul* which keeps our bodies *warm*. Since, then, the dry or fiery soul is wisest, the Wis-

---

[1] Mullach's *Frag. Phil. Graec.*, vol. I, p. 325.

[2] Mullach, *op. cit.*, vol. I, p. 323.

[3] Mullach, *op. cit.*, vol. I, p. 325.

dom that steers the universe—the supreme reality—must be *Living Fire*.

The process of eternal combustion is the key to both human life and the life of the world. It is a tireless rhythm—an incessant metabolism that makes and unmakes the universe. The equilibrium of this *two-way* process depends upon equal measures of fire being extinguished in smoke and vapor and being rekindled by exhalations from evaporating liquid. And so Heraclitus' great Word or message is the following:[1]

"This world, which is the same for all, no one of gods or men hath made, but it was ever, is now and always shall be an ever-living fire with measures of it kindling and measures of it going out." (Frag. #27.)

Because of this the world and ourselves are subject to a process of radical and interminable *flux*—"All things come into being by a conflict of opposites, and the sum of things flows like a river (ῥεῖν τὰ ὅλα ποταμοῦ δίκην)," says Diogenes Laertius (IX, 8), summing up Heraclitus' view. This holds true no less of nature than of man—"We step and do not step into the same rivers; we are and we are not." [2] (Frag. #83.) The truth which has hitherto escaped men is that all the *many* and *conflicting* things we know are really *one* and that, on the other hand, this *one* is also *many*[3] —"the one results from all things and all things result from the one." (Frag. #45.) "God is day, night, winter, summer; war, peace; satiety, hunger." [4] (Frag. #86.)

In fact, the oneness meant consists precisely in the balance of the conflicting opposites. He expresses this doctrine of the identity of opposites by saying:[5] "The *way up* (ὁδὸς ἄνω) and the *way down* (ὁδὸς κάτω) are the same" (Frag. #32), a principle which he applies both to man and to nature. By the "way up," he means the change of earth into water and of water into fire. By the "way down," he means the reverse change of fire into water and of water into earth. And these two ways are forever being simultaneously traversed in opposite directions, so that everything really consists of two factors, one travelling up and the other down. Hence Parmenides' criticism of the Heracliteans "in whose view *to be* and

[1] Mullach, *op. cit.*, vol. I, p. 318.
[2] Mullach, *op. cit.*, vol. I, p. 326.
[3] Mullach, *op. cit.*, vol. I, p. 320.
[4] Mullach, *op. cit.*, vol. I, p. 327.
[5] Mullach, *op. cit.*, vol. I, p. 318.

not to be are considered to be the same and not the same, and all things travel in opposite directions." [1]

Such was the Heraclitean monism of pure becoming, in which all things are said to evolve out of a war of opposites; for, according to Plutarch,[2] Heraclitus "called war the father of all things" (Frag. #37). In answer to this, Aristotle—as if refuting in advance the evolutionary *Dialektik* of Hegel and Marx—points out that the Heraclitean identification of opposites, far from starting the clock of evolution, would stop it—"It happens to those who claim that things can at once be and not be, to prove all things to be in a state of rest rather than in process of change, for on that supposition there is nothing for them to change into, seeing that everything is already existent in everything." (*Metaphysics*, IV, 5.1010a35-b1.) However, Aristotle refuses to take as anything more than verbal Heraclitus' alleged denial of the principle of contradiction,[3] remarking that seriously to deny it would lead to nihilism.[4] Granting[5] that what is *actually* one may be *potentially* many, he notes that it is only when actual oneness and actual multiplicity are predicated simultaneously of one and the same subject, that we have contradiction.

But Aristotle's definitive answer to Heraclitus lay in his discovery of *abstraction* (ἀφαίρεσις), the process whereby we isolate in conceptual thought the unchanging amid the phenomenal flux— that which does not vary from individual to individual, from time to time, from place to place—the intelligible essentials abiding in sensible things. Says Philip Wicksteed:[6]

". . . . Now Aristotle finds in the human 'mind,' which has faculties not granted to the highest brutes, a power to isolate in thought what is never isolated in fact. . . . This is the power of 'abstraction' by which we can think apart that which never exists apart. . . . In the mental world we must learn to isolate in thought likenesses. . . . which are never found in fact or experience isolated from unlikenesses and diversities.

"If we can do this, we shall have found the realm of abiding realities. . . . We shall then command a realm of abiding truth, but we shall find it not outside and above the change and flux of things and experiences but at their very heart, separable from them in thought but never in reality. Such 'ab-

---

[1] Mullach, *op cit.*, vol. I, p. 119.
[2] *De Isid. et Osir.*, ch. 48 (Mullach, I, p. 319).
[3] *Metaphys.* bk. IV, 3.1005b23.
[4] *Physics*, bk. I, 2.20-26; also 185a7.
[5] *Phys.* bk. I, 2.185b27-186a4.
[6] Aristotle's *Physics* (Loeb Classical Lib.), vol. I, p. xlviii.

stractions' exist *apart*. . . . from 'concrete' things and beings only conceptually; but their existence *in* existing things and experiences is as real as those things and experiences themselves and it is only by isolating or abstracting the conceptual that we can have any grasp of the permanent and unchanging amidst the flux and change of sense-experiences. . . .

"This is Aristotle's solution of the old problem as to where we are to find the permanent and changeless when we have no direct access to anything but the evanescent and varying. He places it in sharp contrast to the Platonic doctrine of Ideas; and in his first attempt to arrest and define it before he has gained the complete mastery of it to which he ultimately attained, we catch him in one of those rare moments in which pure intellect kindles on his lips into passion as he feels himself to be in the very act of bringing the unceasing flux under the control of an intelligible order—like one who has arrested the rout of a bewildered and panic-stricken army and is rallying it and inspiring it to victory." [1]

Eventually the Stoics were to develop Heraclitus' evolutionary monism into an elaborate system. Meanwhile, however, it found an opponent in another monist philosopher, Parmenides (b. 514/16 B.C.) , founder of the Eleatic School. To the wholly unactualized flux of Heraclitus he opposed the fully realized being of that which actually *is* (τὸ ἐόν) . He denied the fact of change as an illusion of the senses and affirmed a static monism of pure being.

Understanding the verb *to be* in its *existential* as opposed to its *copulative sense,* he posed (regarding reality) the disjunctive question: "Is it or is it not?" Because in order to think at all, we must think of something, he concluded that non-being is unthinkable and therefore incapable of realization in any degree. Hence if being is at all, it must be perfectly realized being, an absolute exempt from change or movement of any sort. Parmenides, therefore, rejected all becoming as an illusion and posited a unitary and static Absolute Being. "For thou canst not know," he says, "what is not—nor utter it; for it is the same that can be thought and that can be." [2]

"One path only is open to us to speak of, namely *It is*. In this path are numerous signs that what *is* is unproduced and imperishable, whole, homo-

---

[1] The passage to which Wicksteed here alludes is *Anal. Post.*, bk. II, 19.100a11-17, where Aristotle says, "when a rout occurs in battle, if one soldier makes a stand, another stands, and then another, until the flight is rallied. . . . When one thing without a difference has made a stand, then the earliest universal is present in the soul: for though the act of sense-perception is of the individual, the content thereof is universal—is man, for instance, not Callias."

[2] Mullach, *Frag. Phil. Graec.*, vol. I, pp. 117, 118.

geneous, immovable, perennial—(it cannot be said of it that) it once was not
nor (that) it will be, because it is now simultaneously all, one continuum." [1]

It must not be inferred, however, that Parmenides had arrived at
the most abstract of all concepts, namely, that of transcendental
being. He had not divested himself of the materialism of the Early
Ionians. For him *being* was a limited corporeal mass filling all
space—a continuum rounded into a spherical shape. Hence he
goes on to say:[2]

"For nothing else is or will be but *being*. . . . Yet since the extreme limit
of *being* is perfect, it is rounded off on all sides like a sphere, equidistant
at every point from the center; for it cannot *be* more in one direction than
another."

As a corollary to this comes his rejection of the Pythagorean
dualism of *limit* and *unlimited:*

"Mortals have made up their minds to name two forms, one of which
they ought not to name and that is where they go astray from the truth." [3]

We go between the horns of Parmenides' dilemma: "It is, or it
is not," by means of the Platonic distinction[4] between *relative*
non-being (*otherness*) and *absolute* non-being (*nothingness*), as
also by means of the Aristotelian distinction[5] between *actual*
being (what *is-actually*) and *potential* being (what *is-potentially*).
These show the Parmenidean disjunction between *absolute* being
and *absolute* nothing to be an incomplete enumeration of alternatives.

In general, Parmenides' error lay in his confusion of the *copulative* with the *existential* use of the verb *to be*. Sometimes (as in
the case of Descartes' famous: "I think, therefore I *am*") this verb
is used to attribute actual existence to its subject. As a rule, however, the function of the verb *to be* is to assert the *real identity* of
its subject and predicate. And similarly, the function of the
negating copula *is not* in a negative proposition is not to deny the
existence of the subject, but to assert the *real otherness* (or real
diversity) of the subject and the predicate. Thus in the negative

[1] Mullach, *op. cit.*, vol. I, p. 120.
[2] Mullach, *op. cit.*, vol. I, p. 124.
[3] Mullach, *op. cit.*, vol. I, pp. 125, 126.
[4] *Theaetetus*, 255 a-e—256e.
[5] *De gen. et cor.*, bk. I, 10.327b23 (Didot, I, 10.327b8).

statement: "A man *is not* a horse," the intention of the speaker is not to deny the existence of either a man or a horse, but simply to show that these two thought-objects always represent two distinct realities, never one and the same reality. It is only when the subject represents what is given not merely in thought, but in reality through sense-perception, that we are warranted in predicating "is" of a subject in the existential sense.

Parmenides, as has been stated, rejected change and movement as an illusion of the senses. To save the palpable reality of motion, the atomists, while not abandoning Parmenides' corporealism, were forced to give up his monism and to cut up his Unitary Real into an infinity of small, spatially-separated, but still unchangeable reals called *atoms*. In other words, they substituted for his static monism a pluralism of atoms moving about in empty space.

When the Stoics revived monism in later times, it was to the dynamic monism of Heraclitus rather than the static monism of Parmenides that they returned.

Zeno of Cittium (333-261 B.C.) adopted the Heraclitean *physics* of flux and fire as the basis of his materialistic pantheism. For the Stoics all that exists is one universal body which is identical with God. God is every bit as corporeal as the world. The primordial world stuff is an "artistically working fire" (πύρ τεχνικόν) which by its *upward* and *downward ways* makes and unmakes the world. Periodically (at the end of each cycle called a *great world-year*) the universe is consumed in a *world-conflagration* (ἐκπύρωσις), after which the cycle of cosmic evolution commences all over again.

The Stoic philosopher, Chrysippus (*circa* 282-206 B.C.), systematized Zeno's doctrines into a panvitalistic, panpsychic monism like that of Fechner and Paulsen. Following the path traced by Zeno, he taught the oneness of the world and its identity with God, who abides in it after the manner of a world-soul. Diogenes Laertius quotes him as saying in book I of his *On Providence:*

"Thus the whole world is a living being, endowed with a soul and having aether for its ruling principle" [1]—in a subsequent passage, Diogenes Laertius comments: "That the world is a living being (ζῷον), rational, animate and intelligent, is laid down by Chrysippus in the first book of his treatise *On Providence*." [2]

[1] Diogenes Laertius, *De vita philos.*, VII, 139.
[2] Diogenes Laertius, *op. cit.*, VII, 142.

Thus, under the inspiration of Heraclitean immanentism, the
Stoics constructed a thorough-going parallelistic pantheism. Like
the Hindu Cosmogonists of the later Upanishads, they make the
Creator immanent in His creation, so imprisoning God in matter
that there results from the union a single substantial principle
under the seeming dualism of parallelism. This unitary principle,
which is at once mover and moved, is the universal Being outside
of which there is nothing. In it all particular beings find their
origin and goal; in it they come to be and perish—flux and reflux,
as it were, of a perpetual evolution.

This fundamental principle or invisible force immanent in
visible nature is variously spoken of, on the one hand, as fiery
Spirit (Breath), God, Soul, Cause, Intelligence, Reason, Fate,
Destiny, Providence, on the other hand, as Fire, Heat, Air, Aether.
It is the spirit or breath which permeates the inert mass of the
world to move it even as the individual soul moves the individual
body, for which reason it is called the *soul of the world*.[1] Human
souls are but so many derivative sparks or manifestations of this
one universal fire-soul into which all things, including the souls
of men, are eventually reabsorbed and out of which they emerge
again in perpetually recurrent cycles of evolution.

The Stoics were pioneers in the application of pantheism to
political life. In view of their general ethical principle that every
man ought "to live conformably to nature"—meaning by nature
not only the nature of man but that of the universe—"the Stoics
say that the wise man will take part in politics, if nothing hinders
him." [2]

According to Zeno the individual man is subject to two com-
monwealths, a heavenly city and an earthly city: accordingly, he
ought to devote himself to the service of either or of both. The
wise man will realize to the full his citizenship in the spiritual
commonwealth of Universal Reason. It is nature and the constitution of the universe that impose on man the duty to live in
society.

This *collectivist* outlook of Stoicism, contrasting as it did with
the individualist attitude of the Cynic school, recommended it to
the civic-minded Romans. Seneca (A.D. 3-65), in words[3] which
may have suggested the theme of St. Augustine's great work (*De*

---

[1] Seneca, *Epist.*, 65, §24.
[2] Diogenes Laertius, *De vita philos.*, VII, 123.
[3] Seneca, *De Otio*, IV; *Epist.* 68, §2.

Civitate Dei), held that there are *two cities* in which a man may be enrolled: (a) the great cosmic community of gods and men, as far-flung as the courses of the sun; (b) the earthly Athens or Carthage of which man is citizen by accident of birth. This being the case, it is optional for a man either to serve both, or to renounce the one and serve the other.

In itself, such doctrine favors worship of the State and political absolutism, both of which were rife among the Romans of the imperial epoch. In fact the erection of temples to the divinity of Rome (*Roma dea*) and apotheosis of the emperors was "in the air" (Dill) from the time of Augustus to that of the great Stoic Emperor Marcus Aurelius (A.D. 161-180). The so-called cult of *Rome and Augustus* had temples and priests (*Augustales*) in all the provinces and municipalities of the Empire. Often this State idolatry took the form of an animistic pantheism adoring not so much the Roman State and its personal head as the *divine* in these, namely "the Genius of the Emperor" and "the Genius of the Roman people."

On the other hand, it cannot be said that Stoic philosophers intended to uphold despotism by their teaching. Many of them, on the contrary, were lovers of freedom and a few went so far as to defy the tyranny rampant in their day. Thus Lucius Annaeus Cornutus (A.D. 20-68) was exiled by Nero for criticizing too freely the Emperor's literary attempts; the *Pharsalia* of Lucan contains passages praising freedom and assailing despotism; the terms "free" and "freedom" occur no fewer than 130 times in the writings of Epictetus (*circa* A.D. 50-120). Of course, all this is inconsistent with the determinism or fatalism professed by orthodox Stoicism, but it acquits the Stoics of explicitly justifying absolutism as certain Hegelians of our time have done.

The last monistic system of pagan times was Neoplatonism. This *emanationist* monism, in that it derives the lower from the higher instead of *vice versa* may be described as the exact reverse of C. Lloyd Morgan's naturalistic monism of *emergent evolution*.

According to the founder of the School, Plotinus (A.D. 205-270), the primordial reality and source of all is the *One* (ἕν) or the *Good* (τἀγαθόν). This[1] is not "all things" (τὰ πάντα), as the pantheists contend, but "before all" (πρὸ πάντων)—pure Oneness "beyond existence" and "beyond knowledge." The One sheds

---

[1] *Ennead* III, viii, 8.

around itself, as it were, a lustre (περίλαμψις), after the manner of a sun[1] that loses nothing by shining. This effluence or lustre is *essence* (οὐσία) which is a transmission of light from the One and also its image (εἰκών). The image turning to the One sees itself to be an image thereof and *essence* thereby becomes *Intelligence* (νοῦς), which is the first emergent or emanation of the One—"The One turned toward himself and looked and this contemplation is Intelligence."[2] In this way, out of the superabundance of his perfection and with no loss to himself, the superior One gives forth what is inferior to himself. Intelligence then gives birth by emanation to "the *Soul* (ψυχή) of all," that is, the *World-Soul*, which completes the first fundamental *triad*. Next, the World-Soul evolves from itself *formative forces* (λόγοι), and the latter in their turn generate *matter*, with which they then combine to constitute material phenomena.

After this manner, in a series of deteriorating emanations, the universe of things comes into existence, not by a transference of any part of the nature of the One, but by an overflow of its inexhaustible perfection.

From the Supreme One at the top to the world of matter and sense at the bottom, we have a graduated scale in which each successively engendered unity emerges out of the inner essence of the higher and simpler form above it. Such is the Plotinian concatenation of emanations spanning the gulf between the Absolute and the world of matter.

After the One has pluralized itself into the primary triad (the One, the Supreme Intelligence and the Universal Soul), the World-Soul gives birth to the secondary triad, which is the tripartite division of human nature into: (a) the intellect; (b) the soul; (c) the body. Triadism, however, is a less emphasized feature in Plotinus' system than it is in the systems of Proclus and Hegel.

Proclus (A.D. 410-485), the only other notable thinker of the Neoplatonic school, teaches that every creative energy produces derivatives like itself, but less perfect; these derivatives strive to return to their source, the result being a circulation of things away from and back to their source. The process in question is triadic, comprising the following three steps: (a) the original

[1] *Enn.* V, i, 9.
[2] *Enn.* V, i, 7.

(μονή) ; (b) emergence from the original (πρόοδος) ; (c) the return (in a lower form) to the original (ἐπιστρωφή).

In such a return of the individual soul to God Plotinus believed the final happiness of man to consist. In this ecstatic reunion with the One whence all things have emanated, all sense of personality is lost and swallowed up in rapture.

Plotinus' metaphorical language leaves us in doubt as to the nature of the process by which creatures *emanate* from the One. It is clear, indeed, that he has in mind something more subtle than the crude effluxes of an *emanationist pantheism*. On the other hand, it is equally clear that the emergent process whereby the indivisible One is multiplied into the manifold of the sensible world is not *creation* (that is, *total* production) in the Christian sense of the term. Consequently, we are forced to conclude that the Neoplatonic series of *emanations* breaks the unity of the One *only in appearance* and not in reality, and that, like all such attempts, it fails to reconcile the monistic assumption with the real manifold existing in the visible world. In a word, it fails to solve the problem of 'the many and the one.' "Neoplatonism, the last effort of pagan philosophy to hold its own against the advancing tide of Christianity, hardly, perhaps, deserves the name of pantheism, since it gave to God an existence outside the world. But it held all things to proceed from God by emanation, and hence to be formed of the Divine substance."[1]

6. Pantheism in the Middle Ages.*

Pantheism arose in ancient times either as a philosophical ideology or as one of the many possible developments of pagan polytheism. It was easy for polytheism to become more or less pantheistic without losing, at least to the average mind, its fundamental characteristics. Its countless deities, dwelling not only on Olympus but everywhere, in trees and springs, in mountains and seas, could readily be conceived as so many manifestations of one supreme all-pervading deity. The old Roman religion especially had felt that a divine power is present everywhere: *numen adest;* the Romans had divinized almost everything, the little events of the household no less than the greater ones of public life.

---

[1] Joyce, *Natural Theology*, pp. 481, 482 (Longmans, London, New York, 1923).

* For this section (No. 6), on *Pantheism in the Middle Ages,* and part of the next, the writer is indebted to a European colleague who, however, prefers not to be named.

In such an ambient, pantheism aroused no distrust. It was not thought of as "introducing new gods into the State"; it could exist alongside the many religious cults that flourished among the Mediterranean peoples and their neighbors, cults which, with the extension of the Roman Empire, became known and followed even in Rome itself.

But after Christianity triumphed and became first the official religion of the Empire and later the common faith of the Western World, the whole status of pantheism was changed. It was no longer a mere philosophical ideology or a permissible belief; it became instead a heresy. Christian faith and, in consequence, Christian culture rest on certain fundamental articles which cannot be abandoned without destroying the whole edifice of the Christian religion. The existence of a personal, transmundane God, distinct from His creation, is one of these fundamental articles.

It is easy, therefore, to understand why there were so few pantheistic movements during the Middle Ages. True, they were not altogether absent, but they were not very influential and never attracted a large following. They deserve, however, to be studied for two reasons. First, because they present certain features which recur in more recent pantheistic philosophies and are sometimes more visible in the simpler forms of medieval pantheism. Secondly, because the pantheistic heresies of the centuries between 800 and 1500 were associated with other movements which were neither religious nor philosophical as such. Like various other heresies of those times, the pantheistic ideas formed but one element in a totality of heretical or "reformatory" ideas which were mainly concerned with social and political developments.

All heresies begin by singling out for attack one or more articles within a great and self-consistent system.[1] Either some statement which is incompatible with the rest is introduced, or some essential part of the system is denied. Heresies live from the truth they retain; they die from the falsehood they add. Sometimes it is an exaggeration and onesided development of a certain part of the doctrinal system that lies at the bottom of a heresy. It is but a short step to heresy if one part of the total system of Christian doctrine is overemphasized without taking into account its equilibrium with the other parts.

[1] Chr. Dawson, *The Great Heresies*, New York, 1938.

Something like this would seem to have been the case with some of the forms of medieval pantheism. Indeed, one element that lent itself to heretical distortion is to be found in Christian theology itself. If the idea of the *concursus Dei,* or the doctrine that all finite things are but ectypes of the Divine archetypal ideas, is over-emphasized and the notion of a personal and transmundane God is not brought in by way of counterpoise, a pantheistic conception may result.

Medieval pantheism has, however, more than one root. First of all, there is the influence of Platonic, and of Neo-Platonic philosophy. Platonism as such is not pantheistic. Neo-Platonism is not much more so. But both are liable to develop into a definite pantheism because of certain elements they contain. Plato's theory of ideas and the medieval "realism" which sprang from this theory can easily be given a pantheistic tinge, especially after they have undergone the modifications that their "Christianization" necessitates. Plato had conceived of the "ideas" as eternal, and as dwelling in some "supercelestial" place. Eternal things which are not God are inacceptable to Christian philosophy. The Platonic ideas were therefore considered as the Divine ideas of which particular existing things are but the imperfect images. But, in Plato's philosophy, the ideas in question are also the concepts that the human mind forms. Now, in God there is no difference between His essence and His existence; He *is* all His attributes. He is, therefore, also His ideas. But if so be these ideas are accessible to the human mind, then man has an immediate and adequate cognition of God's nature—the implicitly pantheistic error of *ontologism.* On the other hand, if everything "participates" in the ideas and the ideas are co-essential with God, then everything participates in God's very essence.

Neither was Neo-Platonism pantheistic in its basic conceptions, since Plotinus taught an "emanation" of the various forms of existence out of the "One and All." But here too, the development into pantheism was very easy. It was sufficient to eliminate the difference between the One and its emanations to make all reality co-essential with the One.

Among the "Platonists" of the Middle Ages there are two schools which, at one time or another, were considered to have taught a pantheistic philosophy. One of these is represented by Johannes Scotus Eriugena (*circa* 800-870), whose knowledge of Greek and whose work as a translator of the Pseudo-Dionysian writings had brought him into close touch with Neo-Platonic ideas, many of which had been incorporated in the writings of the Greek Fathers who occasionally took over whole passages from the pagan philosopher.[1] Scotus was not a pantheist, and his writings did not arouse any suspicion until a definitely pantheistic sect of the twelfth century referred to Scotus as an authority. Nor was the other school really pantheistic—the School of Chartres, headed by Bernard (*circa* 1065-1130) and Thierry (*circa* 1080-1155). Much has been said of a *panthéisme Chartrain,* and it is true that some passages, *e.g.,* in Bernardus Sylvestris (*fl.* 1145-1153), are rather suggestive of pantheistic ideas. But it seems that none of the masters of Chartres intended to profess a real pantheism. They did teach, however, an extreme "realism" and thus, in a sense, paved the way for pantheistic monism.

Platonism has also been the philosophical source of more than one monistic conception. It is true that materialism came on the scene before Plato. But that early materialism of Democritus at least made to dualism the concession of recognizing that the matter of which souls were supposed to consist was of a peculiarly subtle kind. At first sight, it might seem that there could be no greater opposition than that between the dualism of Plato and the materialism of Democritus. Nevertheless, Platonic dualism makes the gap between matter and mind so wide that the body may be regarded as existing independently of the spiritual element in human nature. The body, being only the tool used by the soul, or the ship steered by it, retains a considerable independency of existence. Psychophysical parallelism is definitely Platonic in its origins. And parallelism is closely allied to pantheism as we see from the philosophy of Spinoza.

It is noteworthy that it was precisely in the School of Chartres that Democritean materialism and atomism were revived; the philosophy of nature by William of Conches (*circa* 1080-1154) was the result of this rebirth of atomism. But William of Conches (who among other heterodoxies identified the Holy Spirit with the World-Soul) modified his ideas considerably when threatened with ecclesiastical censure. And here it may not be pointless to remark parenthetically, that modifications of this sort were generally not made out of mere fear of the condemnation and punish-

---

[1] P. Henri, S.J., *Les états du texte de Plotin,* Paris, 1938.

ment, but from a sincere desire on the part of the writers to stay within the boundaries of the approved faith. They were convinced believers, most of these philosophers and theologians who incurred centure. This is strikingly exemplified in the case of Abelard.

The twelfth century had not yet worked out the basic notions of philosophy to the degree of clarity we admire in later times, especially in the writings of Aquinas. Certain ideas and terms were used rather promiscuously. Among these were the terms *form, idea, concept, nature, essence.* Because of this confusion, it became possible for some philosophers to propose the theory that God was the form of everything—*Deus forma omnium.* The form is a non-corporeal factor in the nature of the existing composite. Such a theory, however, bordered dangerously on spiritualistic monism and pantheism, just as the notion of a "spiritual matter" or a common matter underlying every real being, whether corporeal or spiritual, bordered dangerously on materialistic monism and pantheism.

Both these forms of pantheism were propounded during the twelfth century. Amalric (Amaury) of Bène (d. 1207) taught a spiritualist monism and pantheism.[1] What his personal ideas were is practically unknown; no writings of his are extant. What is known of his ideas is contained in reports on the sect which bore his name, the *Almariciani* (or *Amauriani*), who were solemnly condemned in 1210. This sect, however, did not content itself with teaching pantheism—identifying all things with God, but succumbed to the Waldensian heresy on one hand and adopted Chiliastic ideas on the other. From the Waldensians the Almaricians got certain political and social ideas, and they professed a belief in the imminence or the presence of a "Third Reign," the reign of the Holy Spirit, of whom some of these heretics believed themselves to be incarnations.

Contemporaneously, there was a disciple of Amalric, Master David of Dinant, who taught that God was prime matter. For having done so he is severely criticized by St. Thomas.[2] His writings (condemned, too, in 1210) have disappeared, though Nicholas Cusanus seems still to have had one copy in his library. David

[1] On Amalric *cf.* De Wulf, *Histoire de philosophie médiévale,* tome I, pp. 240-242 (6ieme ed., Louvain, 1934).
[2] See St. Thomas, *Sum. Theol.* Ia p., q. III, a. 8.

had, so far as we know, no followers. His philosophy deserves mention not only because it is an instance of medieval pantheism but also because it shows the close relation between pantheism and materialistic monism.

The Almaricians cited the writings of Scotus Eriugena as one of their sources. In the sequel, these writings were condemned along with those of Amalric and David of Dinant. However, they did not altogether disappear, and they influenced in later times a man who has been likewise accused of pantheism, though he evidently remained, at least subjectively, a true son of the Church. This was Master Eckehart of Hochheim (1260-1327). The twenty-eight propositions of Eckehart, condemned in 1329 comprise some statements that unquestionably smack of pantheism.[1] However, this great Dominican preacher claimed in his written defense that these propositions were not taken from his original writings but mostly from notes people had made of his sermons. Eckehart died before he reached the council where he intended to plead his cause. Recent research and especially the publication of Eckehart's Latin works tend to disprove the charge against him. But the fact remains that certain statements of this German mystic were, as they stood, open to misunderstanding; and the fact that, even in modern times, Eckehart has been repeatedly hailed as a precursor of modern ideas, shows that the step might be extremely short from certain ideas of mystics to downright pantheism. Not only in those of Eckehart, but also in the writings of Tauler (1290-1361) and in the anonymous treatise called *Theologia Deutsch,* the reader comes across passages which, taken by themselves, suggest a definitely pantheistic view, and yet Tauler was very far from being a pantheist.

In reviewing the ideologies that have proved wellsprings of pantheism in medieval times and still more so in later centuries, we should not overlook one which became very influential in the latter part of the thirteenth century and which retained its importance up to the dawn of the modern age. We refer to the Arabian philosopher Averroës (1126-1198) who became famous throughout the Western world as the Commentator on Aristotle. Averroës himself, and perhaps even more so his Latin followers, taught the numerical identity of the intellect in all men. Averroës interpreted

---

[1] In the Constitution *In agro dominico,* March 27, 1329.

certain passages in Aristotle dealing with the νοῦς in terms of a theory incompatible with Christian doctrines, especially with the doctrine of personal immortality. The highest part of the human mind was conceived by him, not as a real part of human nature, but as something entering human nature from without—supposed to subsist as a thing apart—numerically one in all men, and therefore impersonal. Whether his interpretation was the right one, or whether St. Thomas Aquinas showed a better understanding of Aristotle, or whether Aristotle himself failed to arrive at a definite and unequivocal position, are still so many mooted questions.[1] In any case, the teachings of Averroës found many followers. In spite of the definitive condemnation of his philosophy in 1277, it continued to be taught in the Faculties of Art and became practically the official system of the philosophers as opposed to the theologians. From a theory which assumes a numerical identity of the intellect in mankind to a theory which identifies this intellect with God, there is again but a short step. Latin Averroism did much to prepare the soil for all sorts of philosophical offshoots that soon led far away from orthodoxy and from the philosophic synthesis which the genius of St. Thomas Aquinas had achieved.

7. Pantheism in Modern Times

During the first centuries of the modern era we find hardly any pantheistic philosophy of major importance, with the sole exception of the philosophy of Giordano Bruno (1548-1600). Bruno, however, made a profound impression on his contemporaries and on many historians of human thought, owing to the tempestuosity of his temperament and writings as well as to the nature of his philosophy, but most of all, perhaps, because his aggressive personality brought him into conflict with the Inquisition and led eventually to his being burnt at the stake. This tragic end has glorified Bruno in the eyes of certain historians, making him a true precursor of modern times—a hero of "free thought" and "progress." Bruno's philosophy, however, was far from being as original as some of his admirers would have it. His pantheism is a pan-vitalism or hylozoism stemming directly from Platonic conceptions, which, having played a prior rôle in the twelfth century, were once more revived by certain older contemporaries of

[1] Cf. F. J. C. J. Nuyens, S.J., *Ontwikkelingemomentne in de Zielkunde van Aristoteles* (Nijmegen, 1939).

Bruno. The Platonic or Neo-Platonic idea of a "world-soul," *anima mundi*, had a rather amazing success with a number of medieval philosophers; Abelard is one of them. The School of Chartres, too, fancied the idea. They identified this *anima mundi* with the Holy Spirit of Christian theology, truly a preposterous notion, and by vagaries of this kind aroused the wrath of the defenders of orthodoxy, *e.g.*, of St. Bernard of Clairvaux and of his friend William the Abbot of St. Thierry. The thirteenth century, however, seems to have paid little attention to this eccentricity, though it was still kept alive by the Averroists. As for Averroism itself, it continued to flourish in Italy, where it had become, so to speak, the official philosophy, especially at the University of Padua. The sixteenth century saw a revival of the idea in the philosophy of Cesalpinus (1519-1600) and of Patrizzi (1529-1597). The latter taught that the individual human soul was but a part of the *anima mundi*. There is a close resemblance between their ideas and the conception of Bruno, who believed that the soul is a mode of the Divine substance, which alone exists really as the *monas monadum;* the inferior monads were "contractions" of the Deity. In many of his notions and in his terminology, Bruno is the docile pupil of Scholasticism, whatever hostility he may have felt towards it. In point of historical position, his philosophy is related, retrospectively, to the materialistic pantheism of David of Dinant and, prospectively, to the parallelistic pantheism of Spinoza. Bruno's pantheism has been called a pantheism of "explication," because he thought of all things as evolving out of the one Divine substance. Similar ideas were proposed, in modern times, not only by Spinoza but also by Schelling.

As Bruno to Schelling, so Valentin Weigel (1533-1588) stands in relation to Hegel. But whereas Schelling knew Bruno's philosophy well and devoted to this man one of his dialogues, it is not clear that Hegel was acquainted with Weigel's philosophy. According to the latter, God knows himself only in and through human minds; the similarity between this notion and Hegel's thesis of the "spirit" or the "idea" developing in the three steps of the subjective, the objective and the absolute to its *an-und-für-sich-Sein* is remarkable. Weigel repeats, on the other hand, certain formulas that one meets with in the writings of the German mystics. God reaches knowledge of Himself in man and in him only in so far as man gives up his selfness (*seiner Selbstheit abstirbt*) in such a way that God Himself becomes man. The relation of this statement and of the ideas on θέωσις (*Vergottung*) in Eckehart is not to be overlooked. God is the totality of all things though not in an explicit manner. As the One is contained in all numbers, so God in all things.[1]

So far as the influence of their philosophy is concerned, neither Bruno nor Weigel made any impression on their times. Despite the decline of Scholastic philosophy and of religious mentality in general, there was still apparently enough left of sound religious thought to prevent a wider acceptance of pantheistic speculations. Men continued to feel more or less as the Fathers of the fourth Lateran Council had when they called pantheism a *doctrina non tam heretica quam insana censenda*.

Only in the mind of Spinoza (1632-1677) was a complete system of pantheistic metaphysics born. True, a certain pantheistic trend is also discernible in Leibniz' philosophy, but the latter was not avowedly pantheistic, neither was it based on pantheistic conceptions as was the philosophy of Spinoza. Leibniz (1646-1716) is more on the order of a Neoplatonic emanationist.

Spinoza makes his pantheistic notion of *Deus sive natura* the fundamental thesis of his entire system. His parallelistic monism is so well known that we may content ourselves here with simply summarizing (mostly in his own words) its salient features:

"Besides God no substance can exist or be conceived." [2]

"Particular things are nothing but modifications of God's attributes, or modes by which God's attributes are expressed in a fixed and determinate manner." [3]

"Hence it follows, that the human mind is a part of the infinite intellect of God." [4]

Spinoza rejects as an illusion of the senses all separateness and distinction of bodies saying: "And if we go on indefinitely in this way, we shall readily conceive, that the whole of Nature is one Individual, whose parts, that is all bodies, vary in infinite ways, without any change in the Individual as a whole." [5]

His panvitalism or hylozoism comes out in the following: "For what we have hitherto proved, has an altogether general bearing, applying not more to men than to other individual things, all of which, though in different degrees, are animated." [6]

---

[1] Ueberweg-Heinze, *Geschichte der Philosophie*, bk. III, 12th ed. 1924, S. 141.
[2] *Ethica*, p. I, prop. xiv (Nijhoff, The Hague, 1895, *Opera*, tom. I, p. 47).
[3] *Ethica*, p. I, cor. to prop. xxv (*Opera*, I, p. 58).
[4] *Ethica*, p. II, cor. to prop. xi (*Opera*, I, 81).
[5] *Ethica*, p. II, schol. following lem. vii (*Opera*, I, p. 87).
[6] *Ethica*, p. II, schol. to prop. xiii (*Opera*, I, p. 83).

His parallelistic view (parroted by Paulsen) is expressed in such passages as these: "The order and connexion of ideas is the same as the order and connexion of things," [6] and, again: "Body cannot determine mind to think, neither can mind determine body to motion and rest." [7]

Finally, one recalls his famous *logical* (not real) distinction between creating and created Nature, of which Spinoza wrote: "I wish here to explain what we are to understand by nature viewed as active (*natura naturans*) and nature viewed as passive (*natura naturata*) . . . by nature viewed as active we are to understand . . . God, in so far as he is considered as a free cause. By nature, however, viewed as passive I understand . . . all the modes of the attributes of God, in so far as they are regarded as things which are in God." [8]

A brief word may be in order as to the relation between Spinoza's pantheism and Cartesian dualism. Descartes, as is well known, influenced Spinoza in more than one way. Descartes had not only reinstated Platonic dualism, but had exaggerated this conception to an extreme never contemplated by either ancient or medieval dualists. Not only was the *res cogitans* wholly separated from the *res extensa,* but the latter was given a status that amounted to an absolute independence. The human body, according to Descartes, is of the same kind as the body of an animal, and the animal organism is nothing but a complicated machine. The human body indeed becomes the tool of the soul, as in Plato's philosophy, but it is a body that possesses a complete nature of its own. Such extreme dualism could not possibly be maintained. To overcome the difficulty, various solutions were proposed. Spinoza's monism was one of these. By regarding mind—*cogitatio*—and body—*extensio*—as two attributes of the one substance the intolerable gap created by Cartesian dualism seemed to be bridged. Spinoza was not, of course, a materialist; yet it needs but little shifting of emphasis to turn his philosophy into the grossest kind of materialism.

Two centuries later, Spinoza was to impress profoundly some of the most brilliant minds in Germany. Lessing, Goethe, Jacobi and others were unstinted in their admiration of his philosophy. Goethe was led to an acceptance of it less, perhaps, through conviction of its truth than as a result of his feeling for the sublimeness and aliveness of nature. To Goethe the world appeared to be, as he expressed it in a famous line of his *Faust,* the living vesture

[6] *Ethica,* p. II, prop. vii (*Opera,* I, p. 76).
[7] *Ethica,* p. III, prop. ii (*Opera,* I, p. 121).
[8] *Ethica,* p. I, schol. to prop. xxix (*Opera,* I, p. 60).

of the Godhead—*der Gottheit lebendiges Kleid.* Lessing professed at times a modified Spinozism to which he gave rather quaint expression in language borrowed from Christian theology; the world, he said, was *filius consubstantialis Dei.* We are reminded of certain ideas of Schelling, at least in one of the phases of that Proteus-like philosopher's development.

Before Spinoza's philosophy had aroused the enthusiasm of some of the intellectual elite in Germany—it never became popular—there had been in England one who deserves mention, if for no other reason than because he seems to have been the first to use the term "Pantheism." Toland (1670-1722) had published a work entitled *Pantheisticon,* in which he defended the thesis that God is not really distinct from the world. His pantheism, however, had as little influence as Spinoza's, if not less.

Pantheistic speculation in itself never seems to appeal to the average mind. This mind, if religiously inclined, finds far more satisfaction in the theistic doctrine than in the abstract, abstruse and conflicting ideas of pantheism. To make this ideology palatable to the average mind, it has to be associated with other sets of congenial ideas. Indeed, the historical importance of philosophical pantheism lies not so much in its immediate influence on larger masses, as in the fact that it *prepares the way for other ideas—*political, social, psychological—*which are incompatible with theistic conceptions.* Pantheism, by undermining the theistic outlook, opens the way for these other ideas.

This was especially true in the case of Hegel (1770-1831) whose philosophy was much too abstract, complicated and difficult ever to become really popular. To discuss Hegelian ideas, to quote expressions taken from his writings, to allude to his basic conceptions, was, for a time, quite a fad in certain circles. The same is true of Hegel's adversary Schopenhauer. But such fads are no proof of a real diffusion at large of Hegelian, or for that matter Schopenhauerian, ideas. However, the fact that affectations of this sort came into vogue is an unmistakable sign that men's minds had been previously prepared to receive a set of ideas definitely opposed to Christian tradition.

Not that Hegel himself was consciously anti-Christian. He professed, on the contrary, great admiration for the Christian religion and for Christian philosophy, and he knew more about the latter than did most of his contemporaries. Hegel had even studied Protestant theology, and his speculations on the mystery of the Trinity are to be reckoned among the factors that determined his philosophical development. He was also well acquainted with Greek philosophy and fully conversant with all philosophies proposed since Descartes. He regarded himself as representing the supreme achievement of all philosophical endeavors; his philosophy appeared to him as the synthesis and culmination of all philosophies preceding his own. No wonder that it comprises so many elements from older systems! Nevertheless, this philosophy is far from being eclectic or syncretistic; it is a very original and quite imposing edifice, being the greatest attempt at a complete synthesis, an all-comprehensive system, since the times of St. Thomas. It is quite significant that in our day there is a renaissance of Hegelianism as well as a renaissance of Thomism. The philosophical mind, longing for a comprehensive world-view, for some idea capable of providing a *punctum fixum* amid the turmoil of these times, turns either to Aquinas or to Hegel. This situation has been analyzed in a very penetrating way by one of the leading Catholic philosophers of Germany.[1] To become aware of the Hegelian influence in modern philosophy one has only to recall the names of Bradley, Bosanquet, Croce, Kroner.

Hegel's *panlogism* ("All that is, is reasonable") is as monistic as Spinoza's pantheism, a point which Hegel himself makes quite clear in his *Beweise für Daseyn Gottes:*

"Absolute Necessity (*Nothwendigkeit*) being posited as alone true and real, in what relation do mundane things stand to it? . . . This relation is disproportionate in every principle; they are contingent things. Moreover, they differ from Absolute Necessity; but relative to it they have no independent being, and even in conjunction with it they are nothing in themselves;— there is only One Existence (*nur Ein Seyn*), and it appertains to Necessity, the things (of the world) are it, as being accidents of it. What we call Absolute Necessity, is rather to be hypostasized as the Universal Being, as the Substance, as outcome through transcension of the mingling of self-mingled Unity."[2]

Reality and ideality are one—that is what Hegel's much misinterpreted *Alles was ist, ist vernünftig* really means. By so saying Hegel did not wish to imply that every blunder, every folly, every

---

[1] E. Przywara, S.J., *Wende zu Thomas oder zu Hegel?* (*Logos,* vol. XV).
[2] *Werke,* vol. XII, S. 437, 438 (Duncker & Humblot, Berlin, 1832).

mishap is *reasonable* as measured by the yardstick of human reason; he simply meant that he saw in each and every fact the concretization of the self-evolving idea.

This absolute Idea (*Idee*) proceeds in eternal self-movement from itself to become Nature and then, reverting to itself, becomes self-conscious Spirit (*Geist*) in Humanity. History is the product of this perpetual *Dialektik,* this reciprocal and progressive fecundation of the Idea and Nature. The higher the Idea progresses in the series of its manifestations, the farther do these manifestations move away from particular and concrete reality, becoming by degrees more and more embodiments of abstract ideas.

The individual mind, the "subjective spirit," is a lower manifestation of the Absolute than the forms of the "objective spirit" among which the State is the highest. Reason is essentially social, and so tends to culminate in organized society which is the State. The State is also the visible embodiment of law and morals. It is the State that makes possible the existence of society, the family and the human species itself.

This leads to what has been aptly styled the "divinization of the State"—"The State is the divine will as present spirit, which unfolds itself in the actual shape of an organized world." [1] The "absolute spirit" as it appears in the shapes of art, religion and philosophy, no longer has any body; it has become pure idea. The Hegelian State, by virtue of immanent divinity, is supreme, absolute, omnipotent—the highest being within the compass of the tangible world. Because of its supereminent dignity, the State takes indisputable precedence over the individual, whose sole function and final destiny is to be a member of it. Apart from this, the individual citizen has no significance nor reason for existence.

"The State is the realization of the moral idea—of the moral spirit, as the manifest, self-conscious, substantialized will which thinks and knows and executes what it knows, and in so far as it knows it. The State finds its immediate existence in morals, and its mediate existence in the self-consciousness of the individual and in his knowledge and activity. The individual, on the other hand, has his substantialized freedom in the State, as the essence, goal and product of his activity." [2]

"The State, which is the realization of substantialized will, having its reality in the particular self-consciousness elevated to the plane of the uni-

[1] *Philosophie des Rechts,* §270, Hegel's *Werke,* vol. 8, S. 334.
[2] *Op. cit.,* §257, *Werke,* vol. 8, S. 312.

versal, is the absolutely rational. This substantialized unity is its own immovable end; in this end freedom acquires its supreme right, even as this end has the supreme right over individuals whose supreme duty it is in turn to be members of the State." [1]

"But the State has an entirely different relation to the individual; inasmuch as it is objective spirit, the individual himself has objectivity, truth and moral existence only in so far as he is a member of the State." [2]

Monism of any sort ends inevitably in abolishing the dignity, the rights, nay, in a certain sense, the very existence of the human individual or person. When the human person is regarded as a mere "attribute" of the One Substance, or as an intermediate step in the evolutionary process of self-development by which the *Idea* reaches its final perfection, or as "part" of some all-pervading spiritual being, the upshot is that personality loses its characteristic properties. Hence, pantheism invariably destroys the dignity and rights of persons, raising the State—or, in certain modern instances, "society"—to the plane of a higher kind of reality. Since the all-embracing One is the only real existent, it follows that the more comprehensive such "suprapersonal" collectivities are, the closer do they approximate the reality and importance of the One.

The success enjoyed by Hegelianism was shortlived. It has since, however, been kept alive by a sporadic following, to achieve, as previously remarked, its second vogue in our day. The influence it exerted on subsequent thought has diverged in two directions. On the one hand, Hegelianism developed into the materialism of Ludwig Feuerbach and Karl Marx. This is not strange, for pantheism, as we have noted, may readily become materialism by a mere shifting of emphasis. Of this fact, the two XII-century pantheistic heresies of Amalric and David will forever remain classical examples. On the other hand, Hegel's doctrines gave birth to the humanitarian schools of the nineteenth century, in whose systems "society" or "humanity" replaced the Hegelian State. Thus *Humanity* is the Absolute in the philosophy of Auguste Comte, while *Society* became a word to conjure with in not a few schools, among which that of É. Durkheim is an outstanding example.

Partly dependent on Hegel, but also influenced by Spinoza, is the parallelistic monism of G. T. Fechner (1801-1887), the father of experimental psychology. As a philosopher, Fechner's influence

[1] *Op. cit.,* §258, *Werke,* vol. 8, S. 313.
[2] *Op. cit.,* §258, *Werke,* vol. 8, S. 313.

was not of great importance. As a psychologist, he became the foremost proponent of "psychophysical parallelism." This theory assumes a strict co-ordination of bodily and mental phenomena such that to each phenomenon of the first series there corresponds one of the second series. The correspondence, however, is not due to any causal connexion between the two series but to a sort of "pre-established harmony." The names of H. Lotze, C. F. Krause and F. Paulsen recall the more prominent exponents of this philosophy, though none of them attained to major importance.

In the field of philosophy this parallelism takes the form of a panpsychic monism, which ascribes consciousness not only to animals, but also to plants and minerals. As the idealistic pantheist Friedrich Paulsen (1846-1908) expresses it:

"There is, indeed, still another possibility. It is the hypothesis, of Spinoza and Fechner, of *universal parallelism*. No psychical process without concomitant movement, no process of movement without a concomitant psychical process."[1]

Paulsen goes to the obviously unscientific extreme of affirming that this parallelism "holds universally,"[2] that plants as well as animals, nay, even minerals possess conscious life in varying degrees, that the whole world is, in fact, one vast animal animated by a single *world-soul*,[3] which is strongly reminiscent of the hylozoism of the Early Ionians and the panpsychism of the Stoics.

Paulsen's parallelism, however, is an idealistic monism, because he regards the mental processes as being real and the physical processes as being merely phenomenal. Other parallelists, more faithful to Spinoza, profess a neutral monism which regards physical and psychical processes as two equally real aspects or manifestations of a single reality. H. Ebbinghaus is a typical exponent of this more materialistic view.

But these panpsychic monists, far from proving that psychophysical parallelism holds universally in nature, do not even make out a credible case for man, as McDougall has shown in his *Body and Mind*. The latter's criticism of psychophysical parallelism has "resulted in the demonstration of numerous incomplete correspondences between processes in the brain and nervous system, on

[1] *Introduction to Philosophy*, p. 91.
[2] *Op. cit.*, p. 99.
[3] *Cf.* Paulsen, *op. cit.*, pp. 232-242.

the one hand, and various types of mental processes, on the other hand." [1]

Among the *Interactionist* opponents of parallelism, Professor William James (1842-1910) may be instanced as a partisan of pantheistic thought. His *monopsychism,* as already noted, represents a sort of modern revival of Averroism. Admitting the possibility of causal interconnection between conscious and bodily processes, James held that thought is an impersonal activity originating not in ourselves but in a *Universal Mind.* Our individual brains, dipped, as it were, in this common sea of consciousness, undulate with its ceaseless rhythm. They are like so many *aerials* picking up the 'Hertzian waves' of thought. As "the thought-stream" courses through an individual brain it becomes momentarily tinged with the peculiar coloring we call personality. In reality, there is no person behind thought. What thinks in each of us is the cosmic mind or world-soul. Hence, we ought not to say: "I think," but: "It thinks." The primordial ground of thought is not a person or a substance at all, but a *process* without a subject. On this point, James is at one with Hegel.

We conclude this brief account of pantheistic or monistic thought in modern times by mentioning a recent form of naturalistic monism of which C. Lloyd Morgan's *emergent evolution* is typical. Besides Morgan and S. Alexander in England, two Americans, namely, R. W. Sellars and G. H. Parker, may be cited as prominent exponents of this view.

According to Morgan, nature, though a single whole endowed with unbroken *continuity,* consists of an ascending scale of more and more complexly organized units, starting with electrons at the bottom and culminating in the human organism at the top. At each higher level in this cosmic scale, higher units *emerge* out of the coalescence of the simpler units of lower levels. These higher units are *something more* than a mere summation of the lower units; for, over and above their *additive* properties (which Morgan calls *resultants* and which are predictable from a knowledge of the properties of the components), they show *new* and unprecedented properties (which Morgan calls *emergents*). These *emergents* are unpredictable on the basis of the properties of the components.

Unlike Plotinus, C. Lloyd Morgan prefers to stand the evolu-

---

[1] S. Eldridge, *The Organization of Life,* p. 431 (Crowell, New York, 1925).

tionary pyramid on its apex instead of on its base; to derive the perfect from the imperfect, the higher from the lower. We quote the concluding words of his book:

"In such credal terms I believe in a physical world at the base of the evolutionary pyramid and involved at all higher levels; I believe that throughout the pyramid there are correlated attributes and that there is one emergent process of psycho-physical evolution; and I believe that this process is a spatio-temporal manifestation of immanent Activity, the ultimate Source of those phenomena which are interpreted under evolutionary naturalism." [1]

8. Pantheism Logically Coherent with Absolutism

There is no doubt but that absolutism is the logical corollary of Hegel's pantheistic deification of the State. Heinrich Moritz Chalybäus (1796-1862), one of the best interpreters of XIX-century German thought, expressly tells us that any independence on the part of either families or individuals is "egotistic exaltation of the personal, and far inferior to the disinterested patriotism of classical times. Despicable indeed is this vain self-idolatry, which refuses to be absorbed in the absolute substance of the State." [2]

This close connexion between pantheism and absolutism was also pointed out by Pius IX in his *Allocution* "Maxima quidem" of June 9, 1862: [3]

"4. With a perversity equalled only by their folly they do not hesitate to assert that there is no Supreme, All-wise and All-provident Deity existing apart from this universe of things, and that God is identical with nature, and therefore subject to change, and that God is achieving realization in man and in the world, and that all things are God and share the very substance of God, and are one and the same reality as God, and that in consequence spirit is identified with matter, necessity with liberty, truth with falsehood, good with evil, right with wrong. . . .

"5. Furthermore, piling comments upon comments and ravings upon ravings, and trampling upon all legitimate authority, and legitimate rights, obligations, and duties they do not scruple in the least to substitute for true (and) legitimate right the false and lying right of force, and to subordinate the moral order to the order of material things. . . . They attack, too, and seek to destroy the right of all lawful ownership—conjuring up and imagining, with perverse mind and intent, a right circumscribed by no limits whatever, and this, they opine, belongs to the State which they rashly judge to be the primary source and fountainhead of rights."

[1] *Emergent Evolution*, p. 309 (Holt, New York, 1923).
[2] *System der Spekulativen Ethik* (1850), vol. I, S. 370.
[3] See § 4 and § 5 of "Maxima quidem" (Gasparri, *Cod. Jur. Can. Fontes*, Rome 1924, vol. II, N. 365-544, pp. 963, 964).

Over all created reality, over nature and mankind, the will of the Creator reigns supreme. To make God immanent in the nation as its national Soul or Spirit, is to rob Him of this supremacy and to transfer it to the body politic. Thus pantheism leads logically to absolutism; for, in its purview, all distinction between civil and Divine authority ceases, the social will of man being identified with the will of God Himself. Any dependence of the State upon a will or law higher than its own is then unthinkable. It becomes the absolute and universal master with no one above it to say it nay. The inevitable upshot is absolutism—irresponsible and unlimited authority vested in a divinely omnipotent State.

However, it is not implied that the average mind infers absolutism from pantheism in this strictly dialectical fashion. On the contrary, it would be unwarranted simplification of the problem to account for the totalitarian absolutism so rife in our day by deducing it from Fichte or Hegel in a purely logical way. In fact, for the great bulk of people to-day abstract systems of ideas hold no more interest than they did in earlier ages. An emotional factor must always enter if such speculative notions are to appeal to the man-in-the-street.

Formerly, when a more impassioned religiousness characterized the times, this emotional factor was supplied by popular piety. In those days heretical movements evoked not only the opposition of the ecclesiastical authorities and of the secular powers, then closely associated with the Church, but also the indignation of the popular masses themselves. In later times, when religion had ceased to be the dominant factor in men's lives, it was social, political, national and other humanistic considerations that stirred the passions of the multitude. But whether religious or profane, it is ever the emotional factor that lends dynamism to ideologies.

In times of economic security and international equilibrium, we are apt to give little heed to the rise of new ideas in academic spheres. But once these ideas get hooked up with others that appeal to the masses, or once popular movements come to feel the need of metaphysical or theological support, we are surprised to see heretofore dormant speculations, which had constituted no more than an undercurrent of the general mentality, push out into the open and begin to play a rôle which has to be reckoned with. That has been the case with Hegelianism. As a philosophical system, it still remains what it was in the latter part of the XIX century—the esoteric cult of a few eccentric minds. As a general attitude, however, it is very much alive and has given powerful expression to itself, first in Marxian socialism and then in nationalism and totalitarianism.

Passion and reason are hostile to each other. When the former triumphs, reason is ignored or else it is enslaved by passion. The *idées forces*, offspring of passion, either suppress reason outright or they exploit it for purposes of *rationalization* only, that is, simply to find plausible reasons for preconceptions which really have little to do with reason, which prove, on the contrary, to be utterly absurd when examined in the cold light of reason. As a matter of fact, the interplay of reasoning and "emotional thinking" is quite complicated and involved. That rational speculation does in a way prepare the ground for ideas dictated by passion alone and having an exclusively emotional appeal, is an undeniable fact. On the other hand, it is equally certain that purely sentimental notions, once they have captured the popular imagination, create an attitude of mind favorable to the reception of ideas previously shunned because of their purely rational nature and speculative origin.

That totalitarian propagandists in search of rational justification should claim to find it in the political philosophy of Hegel, is not a matter of surprise. Nevertheless, we would be deceiving ourselves were we to look on Hegelianism as the sole or even the main factor in bringing about the recent flowering of totalitarian ideologies.

Hegel himself, for all his deification of the State, would scarcely have approved of making even philosophy subservient to the interest of totalitarian politics. Philosophy was for Hegel the mind's supreme achievement, the ultimate step in the self-evolution of the Absolute; as such, it was judge of all else, in the capacity of last court of appeal. He would never have sanctioned its demotion to a subordinate place.

Much fun has been made of Hegel for his reported answer to the objection that, as a matter of fact, history had not developed according to the principles of his philosophy. *Umso schlimmer für die Geschichte*—"So much the worse for history," he is said to have replied. This saying is often quoted as evidence of the philosopher's colossal conceit. Conceited no doubt he was, but the words in question are susceptible of a deeper meaning than superficial criticism discovers in them. They are suggestive of a thought which, to tell the truth, is at variance with the fundamentals of

Hegel's system itself. However, inconsistency is something one must be resigned to finding in the verdicts of philosophers. What Hegel apparently wished to say was, that man is found guilty before the bar of history, in that it is through his fault that the Absolute has been prevented from developing according to its own immanent laws. The idea of metaphysical laws which are in some sense eternal, is one that seems to dominate the whole purview of Hegel. To him the idea that right is to be defined in terms of the good of a single nation, would not have been acceptable.

What would have influenced Hegel to reject such a notion were the elements of traditional philosophy surviving in his system. The very fact that he regarded his own philosophy as the consummation of all prior speculation is proof that he thought of himself as being in the line of intellectual descent from his predecessors and as indebted to them in consequence for the advances he congratulated himself on having made.

The whole progress of human thought and the march of all political, social, and cultural history was visualized by Hegel as an unfolding of successive phases of the grandiose pageant of continuous evolution—an evolution in which the histories of single nations were but so many partial and passing manifestations.

Nonetheless, it goes without saying that the Hegelian abolition of all distinction, first between the ideal and the real, next between the Creator and creation, and finally between one particular reality and another, destroyed the very possibility of upholding the dignity of individual human existence. At the same time, it cleared the way for the installation of some "whole" conceived as the only reality and only value.

We may characterize as truncated Hegelianism the scheme of ideas with which the totalitarian concept is associated—truncated because, in these latter-day ideologies, the Absolute of Hegel's system has been lopped off from the rest. In their purview, the Idea is no longer the starting-point and goal of all cultural and historical movements—a conception, incidentally, which is more akin to Scotus Eriugena's notion of *natura quae creat et non creatur* and of *natura quae nec creatur nec creat* than is commonly admitted. Instead, something, which in Hegel's system was merely an intermediate form, now absorbs the whole meaning of evolution, constituting its ultimate end, namely, the nation, or the State.

On the other hand, this amputation of an essential part of

Hegelianism, combined with retention of the remaining portion, was a procedure made possible in consequence of Hegel's own abolition of individuality and of the infinite distance separating God or the Absolute from finite beings. That, in the final analysis, coinvolved the elimination of the last consideration safeguarding individual rights and individual existence.

The rights, the dignity, the very existence of human personality find their only guarantee in the existence of a *persona archetypus* whose faint and deficient image the human person is—*Faciamus hominem in imaginem et similitudinem nostram.* Take away this idea of a *persona exemplar,* and only two courses lie open: either one must identify each and every man, or at least certain "elect" individuals, with God—such was the road taken by the followers of Amalric; or else we must strip man of his reality as an individual and view him as no more than a part of some greater whole which alone is credited with true reality and value. The latter course was the one that the totalitarians saw fit to follow.

9. *Totalitarian Pantheism*

Whether totalitarianism be national, as in Germany and Italy, or communistic as in Russia, makes in the long run very little difference. An attentive study of *Refléxions sur la violence,* the work that Sorel wrote in an essentially socialistic vein, will disclose to every intelligent reader the common origin of both these ideologies. Nor, indeed, can anyone fail to notice that in their practical achievements as in their political, social and economic ideals, the said two forms of totalitarianism hardly differ at all. Their temporary political alliance at the outbreak of the Second World War was but an outward manifestation of their inward affinity.

Marx's materialistic interpretation of history is quite as legitimate an offspring of Hegelianism as nationalistic totalitarianism. Marx himself and his interpreter, Lenin, were fully conscious of Marxism's indebtedness to Hegel. Marx, indeed, made no secret of the fact that his own revolutionary *dialectic* of the class-struggle was only a materialistic interpretation of the Hegelian *Dialektik*.[1]

It may be doubted, however, whether the spiritual fathers of Nationalistic Totalitarianism are equally well aware that their own intellectual parentage was the same. Certainly, Giovanni

[1] See Marx's "Preface to the Second German Edition," Eden & C. Paul's translation of *Das Kapital* (*Capital,* vol. II, pp. 873, 874, Dutton, New York, 1934).

Gentile, professed *idealist* and product of the Neapolitan school of Hegelianism,[1] ought not to have been ignorant of what he owed to Fichte and Hegel. Be that as it may, this reputedly official philosopher of Fascism, who was Mussolini's Minister of Public Instruction from 1922 to 1924, showed himself definitely dependent on Hegelian ideas even when criticizing other Neo-Hegelian philosophers like Benedetto Croce.

There is a Chinese proverb which says: *The darkest place is the foot of the lamp.* To all appearances, it is the German totalitarians who are least aware of their dependence on Hegel. In fact, the authors who attempt a philosophical rationalization of National Socialism are much more apt to refer to Nietzsche than to Hegel. As for Nietzsche himself, he was influenced by certain currents of French philosophy, also by Schopenhauer, but scarcely to any noticeable degree by Hegel.

Nietzsche, in that he invented the "superman," is regarded as a thinker who gave a strong impetus to individualism. While this is doubtless true, it is equally true that he sponsored ideas which could only result in the destruction of human individuality. Nietzsche's impassioned, uncompromising rejection of Christian morals as well as Christian philosophy and his implacable hostility to the idea of a personal God were bound to have that harmful effect. Moreover, his accentuation of the biological aspect of human nature furthered the development that later came to be known as the "philosophy of life."

This philosophy takes a variety of forms, but all of them more or less agree in singling out *life* as something absolute and ultimate. Henri Bergson, who set out from this point of view, came in his later works to modify his original conception, to such a degree, in fact, that he ended by teaching a theistic metaphysics, nor was he at pains to conceal his strong sympathy with Scholastic philosophy. Georg Simmel, too, has receded from his earlier position, mitigating his former tendency to look on "life" as an ultimate entity. Others, however, have persisted in the view that "life" is the sole reality and sole value, a conception not far removed from hylozoic pantheism.[2]

---

[1] See R. W. Holmes' *The Idealism of Giovanni Gentile,* pp. x-xiv (Macmillan, New York, 1937).

[2] Proposition No. 7 of those which the S. Congr. of Seminaries and Universities culled from Nazi literature and held up for reprobation on April 13, 1938, formulates their hylozoic pantheism (panvitalism) as follows: "Nothing but the KOSMOS

We should not allow ourselves to be deceived by the disclaimers these thinkers make of pantheism and of every sort of spiritualism, nor again by the fact that one of the most influential of their number speaks of "spirit" as distinct from "soul." Ludwig Klages, who has published a three-volume treatise entitled *The Spirit as Adversary of the Soul,* envisages the "spirit" as entering the human being from without in a way reminiscent of the Averroistic view. But, whereas that Arabian commentator, if not Aristotle himself, saw in the "spirit" the "active intellect" and highest part of human nature, Klages regards this intrusive spiritual element as destructive of man's original goodness, aliveness and nearness to reality. But no matter how we evaluate this "spirit," one thing is certain, namely, that Klages' philosophy is rightly classed as a pantheistic view. It is not surprising, therefore, that it met with such great success in totalitarian Germany. Any philosophy that tends to abase the dignity or to abolish, so to speak, the existential status of the individual, is invariably welcome to the totalitarian mind.

Another conception of human nature which found favor with German totalitarians was the one propounded by the Swiss alienist and psychologist C. C. Jung, originally a pupil of Freud. Having developed a philosophy of his own, Jung was put under the ban by psychoanalytic "orthodoxy." But after psychoanalysis itself had been condemned by the reigning party as being something "Jewish," Jung, who happens to be an "Aryan," was lionized by the German racists.

Among Jung's conceptions there is one at least that deserves mention here. He was considerably impressed with the similarities between some primitive, folkloristic ideas and certain "symbols" he believes to be active in the generality of human minds. To account for this fact he introduces the notion of the "collective unconscious." Whether he conceives this *collective unconscious* as a substantial unity or simply as a function common to all men, is not quite clear. It would seem, however, that he must believe in some sort of substantial oneness, for only on that supposition is the identity of a "collective unconscious" in all peoples and throughout all ages intelligible. Everything considered, the *collective unconscious* appears to hold in Jung's anthropology much the same position that the *agent intellect* in its numerical identity held in the system of Averroës. But whereas this intellect figures

or Universe exists; all things, including man himself, are but different forms of the *Living Universe,* developing through long ages."

as "above" the individual in Averroism, the unconscious in Jung's theory is "below" the individual.

There is, to be sure, no direct relation between the ideas of Jung and those of Klages. Both, however, are children of the same era—of an era that tends to do away with individuality and to set up some "collective" entity as the sole reality.[1]

Some authors endeavored to reconcile collectivism with the individualism, or rather, personalism demanded by Christian philosophy. Among these, were certain Catholic thinkers who, while unwilling to sacrifice the dignity of the single human person, sought, nevertheless, to accentuate the reality and preponderant rôle of the collectivity. Inasmuch, however, as the term "collectivist" had been pre-empted by the Bolshevists, these Catholics, who at that time firmly believed in the incompatibility of nationalism and communism, preferred to speak of their philosophy as "universalist." The most outstanding proponent of this *Universalismus* was Othmar Spann, whom Alfred Rosenberg denounced as "the modern spokesman of the Scholastic Middle Ages." [2] Spann, a former professor of economics in the University of Vienna, is author of a book entitled *Gesellschaftphilosophie* (1928). Yet, in spite of his wish to preserve the fundamentals of theism and even of Christianity, the *universalism* espoused by Spann robs the human individual of his independent existence by making this depend on membership in a larger group, *i.e.*, the State or nation. Spann goes so far as to deny all direct relation between individuals, whom he holds to be related to one another only through and in the greater "whole."

[1] This totalitarian dogma that the social group or "collective whole" alone is real and that the human individual has no real value apart from the group, represents the *exact reverse of the truth*. Absolutely speaking, the individual alone is real, whereas collections (classes, groups) are *mental constructs*, which, far from having any absolute extramental reality, do not even admit of realization outside the mind. Actually, a collection is not a single being, but a multitude of distinct individual realities whose sole unity is a logical or conceptual oneness ascribed to them by the mind. Collections are not *real wholes* but logical ones. This misplacement of emphasis that attaches importance to the *unreal* collection rather than to the *real* individuals mentally collected into a group, is an error unfortunately not confined to totalitarian ideologists. Certain symbolic logicians, too, interpret individuals in terms of classes. Thus Chapman and Henle treat the names of individuals "as designating a class having one member" (*Fundamentals of Logic,* 1933, p. 26), which reminds one of the hackneyed witticism about "constituting oneself a committee of one." When it comes to the absolute truth, a collection is not a real unit but a multitude of separate realities.

[2] *Mythus des 20. Jahrhunderts,* 61-62. Auflage, S. 696-698 (Hoheneichen-Verlag, München, 1935).

Any philosophy denying full reality to the individual invariably ends by becoming totalitarian. And once its development has taken this direction, it must—in so far as the philosopher proposing it is willing to consider some higher metaphysical principle—go one step farther and become pantheistic, whether the philosopher in question be aware of this logical necessity or not. On the other hand, every pantheistic conception must from its very nature, deny to the individual the full reality that is his by fact and by right; for evidently the distinction between individuals vanishes if, as manifestations of the One, they are all regarded as coessential and consubstantial with one another.

In his already quoted Encyclical Letter (*Mit brennender Sorge*) of March 14, 1937, addressed to the German Bishops, on the situation of the Catholic Church in the German Reich, Pope Pius XI exposes this pantheistic implication latent in National Socialism:

"Anyone who with pantheistic indefiniteness identifies God with the universe, materializing God as the world and deifying the world as God, does not belong to the fold of the true believers.

"Neither does that man who, following a so-called prechristian conception of ancient Germanism, substitutes in place of the personal God a gloomy and impersonal fate, denying God's wisdom and providence which "reacheth from end to end mightily and ordereth all things sweetly" (*Wisdom*, 8:1), and directs everything to a good end. Such a man may not pretend to be numbered among the true faithful.

"If the race or the people, if the State or one determinate form of government, if the representatives of government power or other fundamental elements of human society——hold in the natural order an essential place worthy of respect; whoever, nevertheless, detaches them from this scale of earthly values and exalts them to the position of constituting the norm of everything, deifying them with idolatrous worship, perverts and falsifies the order created and imposed by God, and is far from true faith in God and from the conception of life conforming to it." [1]

It is certain that none of these latter-day monistic and pantheistic philosophies has attained to the intellectual stature of Hegel's system. Those who constructed them lacked the mental capacity required to envision a synthesis like his. Notwithstanding the ridicule heaped upon him by lesser lights, his philosophy was really the parent soil whence all this banal profusion of collectivist and totalitarian ideologies sprang. That was because his conception of a "dialectic movement" whereby the Absolute or the Idea

---

[1] *Acta Apost. Sed.*, An. et vol. XXIX (Ser. II, v. IV)—Num. 5, 10 Aprilis 1937, p. 171.

progresses to higher and higher planes of perfection, lends powerful support to all political and social ideologies that present the "whole" as the greater, the higher, the truer reality. This conception can only be admitted on condition that the dignity of the human individual has been previously suppressed. The one development presupposes the other, or rather both go hand in hand. The individual is conceived as a manifestation or realization of a superior whole, which in the final analysis is the world-spirit, no matter by what name it may be called. The upshot of it all is that the human individual is degraded to the status of a mere element or part. On the other hand, the importance of the larger "wholes" is enhanced, because these appear to be nearer somehow to the all-comprising Absolute, which gathers up all reality into itself and alone is credited with true existence.

Pantheistic philosophies, however, have not always developed into political theories. Spinozism is an instance of one that did not. The XVIII century, which S. H. Mellone describes as "a century of obloquy" for Spinoza,[1] did not take kindly to his pantheism and certainly did not produce any totalitarianism in the strict political sense of the term. The idea of deifying a single nation or State was repellent to the mentality of an age that idolized individual liberty and laid emphasis on the "rights of man."

However, it was this selfsame XVIII century which, by its rationalistic attacks upon the Catholic Church and even upon theism, contributed enormously to the rise of nationalism. Not that nationalism was entirely unknown before this time. History records more than one example of peoples or princes who resented the existence of a supranational whole. Gallicanism, for instance, was an assertion of national particularism in opposition to the universalism of the Holy See. The spread of this movement among French politicians and ecclesiastics reveals the presence of nationalism even at that early date. Protestantism, too, was a distinctly nationalistic movement, at least so far as Luther is concerned. However, a general drift toward nationalism did not set in until the still effective idea of a whole at once supranational and supernatural had crumbled under the attacks of the French Encyclopedists. Thereupon the trend became marked, and was further intensified after the French Revolution had completed its work of destruction.

---

[1] *The Dawn of Modern Thought*, p. 53 (London, 1930).

Much the same may be said of Totalitarianism. Totalitarian ideas were afoot long before the end of the Middle Ages. However, that totalitarianism was dynastic in character, taking the form of an aggrandizement of the royal power at expense of the independence of the feudal lords. Moreover, such totalitarian tendencies had then a check and counterpoise in the Holy Roman Empire, which might be described as a loose federation of powers, headed by the Roman Emperor and under the guidance of the Holy Father; it was not, however, a fully organized State in the modern acceptance of the term. In a few cases attempts were made to construct a totalitarian organization within some of the smaller States, but none of them met with great or lasting success. Perhaps the most striking instance is the absolutist constitution of the Sicilian kingdom of Frederic II (1215-1250). A true totalitarianism was, of course, out of the question so long as the dignity and importance of the human individual or person were preserved intact: spiritual values that were preserved—as they could only have been preserved—by the Church and the teachings of Christianity throughout the Ages of Faith.

"Our God is a personal God, transcendent, omnipotent, infinitely perfect" (Pius XI), and this Christian theism taught by the Catholic Church is the one and only guarantee of the dignity of persons, of their many-sided independence, of the proper balance between individual rights and public duties. Without a God who is in a true, if analogical, sense *personal* and as such the *prototype* of all persons, the term person loses its meaning and free will itself has no longer any reason for existence.

Modern totalitarianism, in short, is the fruit of all the philosophical movements—or heresies—which have worked together, through many ages, for the depersonalization of human nature. For more than one factor has contributed to this wholesale sabotage of individual distinction, and the fateful consequences have become plainer day by day. It is not pantheism only, but other kindred philosophical conceptions as well, that are responsible for this abasement of human personality, for this growing tendency to look on man as a mere element within a whole which alone has the right to exist. Evolutionism, too, misinterpreted and generalized far beyond the limits of a legitimate scientific hypothesis, has played no small part in eliminating differences. In the name of "continuity," it transforms the stairway from "amoeba to man" into an inclined plane of imperceptible ascent. Having eyes for resemblance only and but *blind spots* for distinction, it recognizes no essential difference whatever between the living and the lifeless, the human person and the irrational beast, thereby doing its share to degrade man to the level of impersonal things. "Everything is 'nothing but' something else, probably inferior to it" (Santayana). Hence it comes to pass that intelligence is nothing but sense, and sense is nothing but physiology, and physiology is nothing but "the chemism of the proteids," and chemistry is nothing but mechanics, and mechanics is nothing but mathematics—until "continuity" reaching the end of its tether weeps for want of other differences to obliterate.

It should not be forgotten that, as atomism was a philosophical theory prior to being a chemical one, so evolution was a philosophical speculation before it became a biological hypothesis. It is noteworthy that its great vogue in science and subsequent popularization coincide with the time when materialism and other monistic philosophies were the fashion, that is, with the last third of the nineteenth century. Marx, who (to borrow his own expression) "coquetted with" Hegel's *Dialektik* as a basis for his doctrine of social progress through the class-struggle, also exploited Darwin's *natural selection* for the same purpose.[1] Indeed, one should not fail to note that Hegelian dialectics is closely connected with biological evolution, on the one hand, and with the idea of "progress" or "perfectibility," on the other. In fact, Hegel's philosophy was, in a sense, a theoretical justification of the dogma so dear to the age of *Enlightenment*, namely, that mankind progresses steadily and inevitably to ever higher degrees of perfection. According to the principles of this Hegelian optimism, the coming age is of necessity better than the passing one, and the newest social or political development is necessarily the best to be had for the time being, superior to anything that has gone before. Thus, progressivism or optimism, which is a characteristic element of "liberalism," is likewise part and parcel of the professedly anti-liberal ideology of totalitarianism.

For German totalitarianism, the collective whole in which the individual is submerged is the "community of the people," not the juridical unity of the State, as was the case with Italian totalitarianism. To the eyes of the former, the primary reality and supreme value is the so-called *folkdom* (Volkstum), which has three ingre-

[1] See Marx, *Capital*, transl. of Untermann, 1906, vol. I, p. 25, also *Selected Correspondence of Marx and Engels*, transl. of Dona Torr, 1934, pp. 125, 126.

dients: 1/Soil (*Boden*); 2/Blood (*Blut*); 3/Community of the People (*Volksgemeinschaft*). The "unanalyzable" basis of this *folkdom* is not spiritual but physical, namely, the allegedly superior Nordic blood or stock whence flower all the hereditary potentialities of the German people. These hereditary factors (the blood) interacting with the environmental factors (the soil) give birth to the racial type comprising bodily, mental and social characteristics. In the peasant, who remains in closest contact with the soil, the racial blood-stream retains its greatest purity. National Socialism, therefore, professes a racial optimism at once biological and nationalistic.

For all their anti-intellectualism and loud disclaimers of metaphysics, the doctrinaires of Nazism base their ideology on two metaphysical conceptions—that of the *myth* and that of racism.

The idea of the *myth* is not original with either Hitler or Rosenberg; it was first conceived by Sorel, who defines it as an emotional rather than intellectual construction "in which the most powerful tendencies of a people, a party or a class, find their expression"; in his previously mentioned *Refléxions sur la violence* he stresses the necessity of the myth as an indispensable element in popular movements. Certainly, post-war Germany had need of a powerful myth if the nation was to recover a belief in itself, and accordingly "the myth of the blood" was launched, less apparently as a theoretical dogma than as a political device to reinforce the German people's assertion of itself as a historical community.

The most official expression of this conception is Alfred Rosenberg's work, *The Myth of the 20th Century,* which has been rightly styled the bible of Nazism. According to Rosenberg, former Head of the National Socialist Party's Department of Foreign Affairs, who is now a "National Leader" (*Reichsleiter*) or "National Culture Leader" (*Reichskulturleiter*), this modern revival of the ancient solar myth of Odin is the "organic German truth"; its present symbol is "the black swastika." [1] He tells the German people:

"To-day this inner voice demands that the Myth of the Blood and the Myth of the Soul, race and I, people and personality, blood and honor must alone, to the exclusion of all else, be uncompromisingly upheld and affirmed as long as we have life in us." [2]

[1] Rosenberg, *Der Mythus des 20. Jahrhunderts,* 61-62. Auflage, S. 689.
[2] *Op. cit.,* S. 698, 699.

Plato had recourse to myths in order to throw light upon the changeable world of sense; for he regarded whatever was subject to becoming as unamenable to rational explanation. For Rosenberg, the German "blood" is an unanalyzable *ne plus ultra* whence all blessings flow. He, too, formulates in terms of a myth the secret of this "blood" that lurks in depths impenetrable to reason.

> *"The life of a race, of a people, is not a philosophy that develops itself logically, neither is it an occurrence that unfolds itself according to a law of nature, but rather the working out of a mystical synthesis* (italics his), of a flowering of the soul, which can neither be clarified by rational deduction nor made conceivable as the effect of cause and action." [1]

The historic myth which Rosenberg exploits as best calculated to depict the stock virtues and national genius of the German people is the pantheistic solar myth of the one-eyed Raven-god *Odin* (Wodan, Woden), who dwells in Valhöl ("the hall of the slain"), in the company of dead warriors brought to his abode by the Vakyrjur ("choosers of the slain") ; god of the sky and roving air, who rides the winds astride his horse Sleipner.

"Odin," the Scandinavian name of this ancient Teutonic god, is said to come from the verb *vada,* to walk, of which the imperfect tense is *od.* To the Norsemen of old Odin was "the infinite wanderer," the all-pervading spirit of the world who, though he does not create nature, yet shapes and governs it; who permeates matter, nay the whole universe; who engenders life and spirit; who as Allfather begets gods and fashions men. He is god of magic, inspirer of poetry and creative art, the "dispenser of victory," the "god of the dead," the guardian of justice, the protector of social organization, the tutelary genius of kings.

Odin's one eye is the sun, which the myth describes him as pawning at eventide to Mimer (Memory), the watcher of Odin's fountain. This fountain is the ocean whereinto the sun sinks each evening to search the secrets of the deep. So, too, the human spirit (Odin) sinks down into the depths of the past and brings back golden thoughts, the knowledge garnered from those secret depths beneath the sea of the race's past experience and bygone history. Says Rosenberg:

> "One form of Odin has died, *i.e.,* Odin, the highest of many gods, as the embodiment of a nature-symbolism of a kind already unreservedly abandoned.

[1] *Op. cit.,* S. 117.

But Odin as the eternal mirror-image of the spiritual primordial powers of the Nordic men lives to-day as much as he did 5,000 years ago. He sums up in himself: honor and heroism, creation of poetry, *i.e.*, of art, guardianship of right and eternal search after wisdom." [1]

The other leading idea of Nazi ideology is *racism*. To race or nation it assigns a value absolute and supreme, making this the measure, test and goal of everything. Man's highest function is to serve the race, to contribute to the grandeur of the German people. In Rosenberg's words:

"If Spann, belying the ancient wisdom of the Greeks, asserts that God should be the measure of all things, that this religion is only to be found in the (Catholic) Church, since there is 'no other,' such a view amounts to pretending that priests should be the measure of all things. In opposition thereto, the new-born world-view declares: the people's soul, which is bound up with the race, is the measure of all our thoughts, aspirations and actions—the ultimate yardstick by which we evaluate." [2]

At the end [3] of his *The Myth of the 20th Century*, Rosenberg points this moral:

"The God that we worship, would not exist, if our soul and blood did not exist, this for our times would be the purport of Master Eckehart's avowal. Therefore, whatever safeguards, strengthens, purifies, effectuates the honor and freedom of this soul and of this blood is for us a matter of religion. On this account holy are all places where German heroes died for these ideas; holy is every place where tombstones and monuments remind us of them and holy are the days on which they fought most gallantly for this cause. And the holy hours of the German will then be at hand when the symbol of awakening, the banner with the sign of resurgent life, shall have become the solely dominant confession of the Reich."

Rosenberg rejects the notion of a personal God, [4] but whether the naturalism of Nazidom's official philosopher is pitched in a pantheistic or an atheistic key is a point he fails to make clear. J. Wilhelm Hauer, the theologian of the movement, is less reticent, or at any rate plainer. The author of *Deutsche Gottschau* (1934), who is professor of the history of religions in the Protestant Theological Faculty of Tübingen, was a missionary in India prior to 1914. He was thus able to enrich his German pantheism with a dash of the Hindu variety.

[1] *Op. cit.*, S. 678, 679.
[2] *Op. cit.*, S. 697.
[3] See *op. cit.*, S. 701.
[4] *Op. cit.*, S. 395-397.

"For us the earth is blest of God. 'The heart of the earth reposes in the highest heaven,' sings an ancient Aryan lay and thereby gives apt expression to primitive Indo-Germanic belief." [1]

"The blood is holy. In it runs the enshrined mystery of the families, the stocks and peoples from of old. Whence germinates this wonderful life? Is it not creation out of the will of the Godhead, emanation from the eternal ground that is actively present in it." [2]

"In the blood flows the source of the Spirit. A divine must lives therein, which forms human beings for the future marked out by fate. . . . The Spirit works itself in the mystery of the blood which runs from generation to generation and determines the spiritual essence of the human being." [3]

"Thus according to the German belief what the people do is done by God. The transformation of the people (Volkwerdung) is the shaping of the will of God. . . .

"Hence, blood and space, soil and Fatherland, the history of our people and their battles are things we love ardently and venerate with profound faith so long as God makes use of our bodily presence here." [4]

To those who object to this "German faith" as being pantheistic Hauer replies:

"The opponents of German faith think to dispose of our kind of piety by decrying it as pantheism—that old fighting word by means of which a creed cherished the world over has been ostracized. If we desire to apprehend God's presence in the sea, in the tree, in the maternal function, that does not mean we submerge God in the being of the world. The world-wide mark of pantheism is an esthetic and intellectual abolition of the Indo-Germanic world-faith. For us God does not terminate with the world, nor begin where it begins. For he is eternal and the eternal Being is infinite. A God submerged in the being of the world would be no God. He is the world and he is in the world and, nonetheless, other than it. . . . World remains world, even if it is Divine. And God is God, even if he hides himself in the world." [5]

Here Hauer, like Paulsen before him, rids himself of the difficulty by resorting to the fallacy of equivocation. A corporeal whole (*e.g.*, a man's body) may be said to be *other* than its part (*e.g.*, a man's head) in the sense that said whole is *not coextensive with* said part, but *extends beyond* it. However, it takes the most crass-minded sort of a picture-thinking corporealist to mistake *extension*

---

[1] J. Wilhelm Hauer, *Deutsche Gottschau*, 3te Auflage, S. 71 (Gutbrod, Stuttgart, 1935).

[2] *Op. cit.*, S. 45; proposition (3), arraigned April 13, 1931, by the S. Congr. of Seminaries and Universities, reads: "From the blood, wherein the genius of the race resides, spring all the intellectual and moral qualities of man, as from their principal source."

[3] *Op. cit.*, S. 45.

[4] *Op. cit.*, S. 65.

[5] *Op. cit.*, S. 78.

beyond (in the *spatial* order) for *transcension* of finite by Infinite (in the *intelligible* order). By this crude subterfuge the immanentist, far from saving, utterly destroys the *transcendence* of the Infinite.

As already remarked, this latter-day pantheism of the National Socialists is a truncated Hegelianism, in which the Universal Spirit (*Geist*) has shrunk to the narrow dimensions of a National Spirit (*Volksgeist*) or Racial Soul (*Rassenseele*) supposed to animate all members of the Popular Collectivity (*Volkstum*, lit. "Folkdom") making them think socially, not individually. Rosenberg tells us:

"The Racial Soul is not to be grasped with hands, but is present in the blood-related Popular Collectivity, crowned and like a symbol, working to engender a culture-cycle that, in its turn, will be supported by the Race and the Racial Soul. This Totality is not only "Spirit," but Spirit and Will, consequently the whole of Life." [1]

The Nazi racists, like many of our own biologically-minded sociologists here in the United States,[2] have allowed themselves to be duped by a *metaphor*. We often speak of human *society* as an *organism*, just as we speak of "laughing water." But in reality society is no more an organism than the gurgling sound of water is real laughter. These are metaphors and, being metaphors, may be used by poets but not by scientific men.

Assuredly there is analogy—imperfect parallelism—between social integration and division of labor on the one hand and functional integration and specialization in organisms on the other. But the organism is a *unity* of physically continuous *cells*, whereas society is a *union* of discontinuous, spatially-separate, self-determining *persons*. In the light of these evident differences, to equate society to a living organism is puerile.

We, too, like these racists and biological sociologists, use such expressions as *national consciousness, social consciousness*, etc., but in speaking thus we do not mean that the nation, the State, or society is the *subject* of said consciousness. On the contrary, we mean that the nation, the State, or society is the *object* of a multi-

[1] *Der Mythus des 20. Jahrhunderts*, S. 697.
[2] See Symposium on "The Biological Basis of Social Problems," held Dec. 20, 1939, in honor of Professor Wm. E. Ritter of California University, *Biological Symposia*, Lancaster, Pa., 1941, vol. II, pp. 165-208.

ple consciousness whose *subjects* are conscious human persons focusing their separate minds and wills upon the common social good.

A nation or State is not integrated by a *national soul* or a *national spirit*. It is a harmony of intelligent individuals, each of which has his own personal consciousness and his own will, independent of all the others. What holds society together is nothing *absolute,* such as a *National Soul,* but *human relations* based on the intercommunication of conceptual thought by means of man's exclusive prerogative, *rational speech.* The thoughts and actions by which each single human person recognizes and contributes to the common good are the real bases of these *social relations* that unite men in society, but a *social relation* is no more an absolute reality like a soul than the spatial relation of *distance* or *apartness* between bodies is an absolute thing like a stick, interposed to keep them apart.

But the exponents of racism are too sensistic to emerge from metaphor into the domain of pure thought. Their "religion of blood and soil" is a frankly materialistic belief. The affectation of lofty pantheistic ideals, with which they seek to gloss over its grossness, degenerates all too soon into materialism pure and simple. Only the idea of a *personal God* can give to men the assurance of values higher than those of the material order. The impersonal deity of pantheism could never, in the nature of things, appeal to the average mind. So of two things one: either pantheism remains an esoteric speculation confined to a few "elect" minds, or else it suffers ere long the transformation into materialism that one notes in its offspring, modern totalitarianism. For no high-sounding phraseology avails to hide from observant and critical minds the fundamentally materialistic character of totalitarianism, be it of the fascist or of the communist variety.

It is an idea too widely and too frequently entertained, that the vagaries of philosophers have no importance for real life—for social development, for political history. The contrary is really the case. It is invariably with the philosophers that revolutions start, whether they be of an abrupt and violent or of a slow and insidious nature. Pantheism may indeed be a philosophical conviction of the comparatively few; but it becomes a force for destruction the moment it is associated with other ideas and infiltrates along with these into the minds of the masses. Hence the close attention the Church pays to such philosophical heresies is motivated not solely by a desire to keep free of error the theoretical convictions of the Catholic people, but also by a provident solicitude for the welfare of mankind in general. Recent historical events have shown all too plainly the way mankind is forced to travel once it ceases to believe in one, personal, eternal God to whom every individual person is strictly accountable. To the impersonal One, to the Hegelian Absolute, there can be no such thing as accountability. The distortion of the idea of right and wrong which we behold to-day in totalitarian ideology and practice is the direct outcome of thinking which began by replacing the personal God with a vague and impersonal intramundane deity and this, in the logic of things, has led with an inexorable and inescapable necessity to that flagrant disregard of human dignity and that deeply ingrained materialism of which the totalitarians of our day have given such overwhelming evidence.

IX

CATHOLIC PERSONALISM FACES OUR TIMES

By ———————

CATHOLIC PERSONALISM FACES OUR TIMES

The tendencies which for the past several years have ranged themselves under the banner of "personalism" lie open to the reproach of showing a diversity and want of precision that run the risk of making the metaphysics of *person* responsible for strange deductions. In fact, it is a matter of every-day experience to see an impenitent individualism refinding its peace of conscience in the formulas of "personalism." Only a short time ago, the writer had occasion to behold in a German review the aforesaid indefatigable "person" pop up as a complacent devil; there, at the time which Communism deemed ripe for proposing to Catholics a non-aggression pact upon its own terms, the pen of a communist intellectual, wielded "in the service of the Spirit," informed us that person was the first step towards race consciousness.

But why should what has come to be known as "the personalist idea" be spared the common fate of all living ideas; why should it, of all others, be exempt from the ordinary handicap of misinterpretations, approximations, simplifications and errors that attends on every achievement of nascent consciousness? Newman[1] tells us:

"It (an idea) necessarily rises out of an existing state of things, and for a time savours of the soil. Its vital element needs disengaging from what is foreign and temporary, and is employed in efforts after freedom which become more vigorous and hopeful as its years increase. Its beginnings are no measure of its capabilities, nor of its scope. At first no one knows what it is, or what it is worth. It remains perhaps for a time quiescent; it tries, as it were, its limbs and proves the ground under it, and feels its way. From time to time it makes essays which fail, and are in consequence abandoned. It seems in suspense which way to go; it wavers, and at length strikes out in one definite direction. In time it enters upon strange territory; points of controversy alter their bearing; parties rise and fall around it; dangers and hopes appear in new relations; and old principles reappear under new forms. It changes with them in order to remain the same. In a higher world it is otherwise, but

[1] *The Development of Christian Doctrine*, P. I, ch. ii, sect. 1, p. 40.

here below to live is to change, and to be perfect is to have changed often."

If this is true of a single idea isolated by reflection, it is even more true of those concrete historical movements which, at certain times, draw after them in one dominant direction a whole train of thoughts and forces that remain confused. There are movements of this sort that find their virtual unity in some urgent, though but dimly felt need which looms upon the consciousness of an age; but in most cases this does not rise above the level of mere presentiments and inefficacious wishes, and, upon contact with former habits, dissolves into so many substitutes for the original inspiration or modifications of it. In such a contingency, it becomes advisable to employ filtration in order to separate the headwaters from those contaminated with impurities, and to point out the proportion of each and their incompatibilities.

Would Catholicism, then, have to reckon with a novelty (if novelty it really be, in contrast to emphasis laid upon an extremely urgent need of the times)? That must depend, some will think, on whether it is something really belonging to Catholicism's own riches, or something in the nature of a perversion. To think thus is to forget that this absolute (*viz.*, person) is a living absolute—a permanent historical probation. There will never come a time when it will be dispensed from the task of finding its answer to the enigmas of history, to the initiatives of profane origin, to the creations and errors of civilizations. Such is the actuality we face with especial immediacy here.

I

The Good News

One need not go beyond the first rough outlines of a preliminary sketch of *person*—for example, the affirmation of a certain absolute of existence, of a certain value to singularity, of a certain inalienable independence as opposed to every collectivity—in order to see one of a number of Christianity's distinctive contributions to the thought and the spiritual life of the West.

To the soul of a Greek, the appearance of the singular in the harmonious course of universal reason was a calamity, something akin to a flaw in the universe.

Plato barely glimpses a "good chance" in favor of the man who, on the brink of death, questions himself concerning his personal destiny. But no sooner has he emerged from Socrates' prison and from that passion of youth for its vast contemplative dream, than he will guarantee no immortality except for the Ideas, or for the Soul that continues, in Hades, to depersonalize itself progressively in order to assimilate itself to its divine models. Could such a soul be credited with the substantial force to resist time and dissolution? The demiurge has compounded it of the different residues of his primitive doughs, it is part of nature as man is a part of the City; it reflects, despite its virtual unity, the compositeness of the real and the compositeness of the City; it has nothing private about it.

Aristotle purges the universe even more rigorously of every personal value. His God is an infinite God that cannot even know singular essences nor will particular volitions. He knows nothing, therefore, for itself, exercises no providence; he would be signing his own abdication, should he condescend to shed "this drop of blood for me," in one corner of Judea. Of what use is it, then, to know that "there is nothing real but the individual," when this individual, as an individual, cannot be either object or subject, be it of full knowledge, be it of the love of predilection?

It is not surprising that Platonism built a City more integrally communistic than a communism having to contend with the resistance of twenty centuries of Christian stuff dared to undertake; or that Aristotelianism, which founded its City upon friendship, ended by justifying slavery.

It is true that this impassive Reason of the philosophers is counter-balanced, in a more dramatic expression of the Greek soul, on the theatrical stage, by the startling decrees of Destiny. But the Destiny of the ancients, compared with immanent reason, is but another impersonal power—a blind power, which if it strikes certain individuals in their individuality, does so purely by accident and without intention.

No more should we allow ourselves to be misled by anything that Plotinian parlance (not altogether insulated from Christian influences) might perhaps suggest. Neoplatonism does, indeed, introduce a history into the world. But what a history? By a sort of defection corresponding to the seductions of matter, the world-soul lets itself totter to a fall that breaks it up into individual souls. But this fall has too little of the voluntary about it and is too temporarily effective; it is too much in the nature of a surrender to blind necessity to give rise to autonomous beings. Plotinus, it is true, has given personal individuality a rational foundation by admitting the existence of as many Ideas as there are singular beings; his inconsistent individuals incarnate in succession many personages, accumulating in this way a multiple memory, from which they cannot but long to be one day delivered by depersonalization, i.e., by divesting themselves of their past experiences and so surmounting the primitive fault which is the source of all individualization. Individual consciousness, and even more profoundly than consciousness, our memory, and our duration, are but so many dilutions of impersonal contemplation. There is no salvation except for him who returns to this contemplation. But since, properly speaking, there is in this transient universe not a single event nor a single act at the origin of the individual being, its return from the exile of sin will not be a conversion, a recollectedness and supreme transfiguration of its whole actual being, but an ecstasy, a trancelike escape from time towards the timeless.[1]

Such were the highest planes reached by the pagan consciousness when Christianity came upon the scene to bring to every man taken singly and separately the message that made him free. We find here and there (Stoicism has still to be taken into account) certain approachings and anticipations which are, as it were, the first glimmers of the new world. But they lack the one thing necessary to burst asunder the chains of thought that bind them; in precise words, they stand in need of the affirmation of an ineffable Person sealing the unforeseeable alliance.

*

* *

The Christian message did not commence, like the moral schools of antiquity, with a philosophy addressed to the learned, but with an appeal directed to each man: Μετανοήσατε—change the core of your heart; *Dii estis,* for thereby each one of you will become a God.

But in the very moment that it was transmitted to a handful of Apostles and Disciples, this appeal came into head-on collision with the turns of thought and the ways of feeling to which six centuries of Greek civilization had so perfectly adjusted the ancient

---

[1] *Cf.* J. Guitton, *Le temps et l'éternité chez Plotin et St. Augustin,* Paris 1933, Boivin.

soul. Specifically, the Greeks would encounter a twofold stumbling-block in facing the problem of man: the first would be the multiplicity of human souls, which would seem to them to break up into fragments dispersed through space the pure essence of thought; the second would be the beginning of souls in time, which in their eyes would seem derogatory to the course of eternity.

The Christian affirmation attacked the pagan soul at both these vulnerable points.

From one little obscure text, over which one solitary people had mounted guard for more than a thousand years, they took out and flung down before the astounded gentile world the affirmation of *creatio ex nihilo*—creation out of nothing. The idea is now so familiar to us that we can only with great difficulty bring ourselves to appreciate the state of stupefaction into which it was bound to cast a mind formed along Hellenic lines. Try, reader, to conjure up the world of such a mind, an uneventful world, unrolling itself with never a stop, without commencement or termination, a necessity without direction, which monotonously reproduced itself; this anthropomorphic, yet inhuman, world whose slightest uncompensated dyssymmetry would forever disrupt its harmony, in which opposites correspond, where mishaps are always retrieved in the return of cycles, even though it might take centuries to bring this about; and then imagine such a universe to be blasted by the thunderbolt of the creative act, contingent and absolute, superseded by the scandal of a created and consequently finite time, by a universal order suspended from a Divine psychology and elevating the individual to a height infinitely above the transitory values of the civic community.

Henceforth how will it be any more possible to express by means of a pure deduction the being that originates by free choice, by an act of love? How uphold any more the supremacy of the timeless Idea, of necessary unrolling in a world sown with essential moments: a Creation, a Fall, an Incarnation; in a world whose explanation will henceforth pivot upon a history of personages? Man is delivered from cosmic destiny. It is because there has been such a thing as an absolute beginning founded upon an act of love that those absolute commencements, like the birth of a soul or a free act, will from now on appear possible.

Later on, when the science of the contingent will develop in sequel to the science of the necessary, the prehistory of the universe, the span that precedes the appearance of man, extending from the crystal to the vertebrate, will throw light on this ontology. It will reveal a vast verging of space-time towards the formation of centers of consciousness and of autonomy more and more independent, the sense of which will not appear until the day when they become the instruments of personal life.

No less inconceivable was it to antiquity that a perfectly simple and unchangeable God could take a part, much less an interest, in the creation of multiple beings. The God of Aristotle ignores a multiplicity for which he is not responsible. The God of Plotinus consents to the emanation from himself of but one single image, and even that has to be as perfect an imitation as possible. As late as the height of the Middle Ages, Averroës had not yet succeeded in justifying the plurality of souls before the bar of reason: since the world was eternal, that, he thought, would involve the admission of an actual infinity of souls. This would be absurd. Hence, he imagined one single soul common to the human species. Why was it, then, that individuals succeeded one another instead of there being only one man existent throughout eternity? It was because the species could not realize itself in one throw. And so, each individual exists only in view of this global realization; it is nothing but an ephemeral consequence of this sort of miserliness of being.

The Christian God, on the contrary, is a God that is lavish and prodigal of His love. If His superabundance has multiplied the universe indefinitely, far more essentially does it delight in multiplying indefinitely and in an indefinitely varied manner this more perfect image of the Divinity which is the human soul. That is the answer St. Bonaventure already makes to the somewhat haughty and miserly spirituality of an Averroës. The Logos of the Johannine tradition is fecundity and generation. Though He has integrally expressed Himself in the Word from all eternity, God has not thus at a single throw exhausted, as it were, His power of creation. Rejoining His Goodness, this Power bestows Himself again in an infinity of images, each one of which will be not a mere broken fragment of the universal mirror, but a unique and total image of His Divinity. The more souls He has to receive the inexhaustibly new forms of His grace, the more will His Goodness glorify itself and rejoice in communicating itself. This multiplicity of persons, called to divine life, which found no justification in a world given over to the impassible eternity of an impersonal God, is now justified through Love. It is to this charity in union with the grace of a sort of Divine exuberance that the Catholic doctors and poets, from the Greek Fathers down to Péguy and Claudel, have appealed every time a species of intellectual miserliness threatened to impoverish the Christian vision.

*

* *

Behold then a world in which not only the existence of centers of free and autonomous action becomes plausible but their multiplication is demanded by the very nature of the creative act. Let no one imagine that this all too brief historical outline is sketched here simply for form's sake. The fact is that whenever we come across an epoch or a school in the process of accepting a too sordid conception of the Divinity, Jansenism for example, or of handing over the universe to some idol of the necessary and the impersonal, e.g., rationalism and the present-day collectivisms, there we shall find a corresponding degree of degeneration in the sense of being persons and in the morals of a humanity with whom person should be paramount.

It is all the more important to put in bold relief the value of this cosmology of generosity implied by Christian personalism in that the most marked forms of irreligion (for example, the one that characterizes the mentality of the worker class today) are prejudiced in precisely the opposite sense. The foundation of all religion, says Proudhon, is "the downfall of personality in the name of divinity"; its essence, Bakunin will add, is "the impoverishment, the annihilation and the systematic, absolute enslavement of humanity for the benefit of Divinity." God is the "absolute despoiler." For these theorizers of the anarchistic tradition the sum of realizable perfections is strictly measured, in such wise that the infinity bestowed upon God by the Christians is taken away from man, whom it reduces to zero. The same perspective exists for Feuerbach and Marx when they describe religion as an alienation which pumps the reality out of man, in order to dissolve it into a world of clouds over his head, leaving him impotent and resigned in the face of his destiny.

Did these men, who spoke sincerely of the "eminent dignity" of man, have any inkling of the supereminent dignity that Catholic life and teaching have conferred upon him? It is no longer a chance result or a refinement of evolution. Image of God, individually conceived and willed by Him, individually redeemed by Him, each person is over and above this called to receive through the life of grace an intimate and effective participation in the Divine life itself. Unlike all other created "natures," it is created immediately by God, *nulla interposita natura* (St. Augustine). No ancient philosophy had dared to imagine this sort of spiritual short-circuit, and Averroës still felt the need of interposing a sort of buffer between the soul and God—the *intellectus agens*. Though He is the primal agent of each operation of every creature, God has nevertheless given to every person a power of acting that warrants his being declared the author of his own action. Theologians differ in their estimation of the limits of this power. St. Thomas assigns to it the maximum scope. But we see the Augustinians themselves, who tend to minimize the activity proper to man, staunchly upholding it in all essential points. St. Bonaventure refuses to write that God Himself is the light of our intelligence—our *intellectus agens;* his meaning is that the activity of the intelligence, no less than its passivity, belongs to it as its very own. In fine, by its virtualities which are, so to speak, a *similitudo luminis creati,*[1] the human soul [2] loses itself in the infinite, it is capable of becoming all things, of ranging to wherever any form of being reaches, of assimilating itself thereto in some manner and of thus putting each man in position to possess the infinite:[3] supreme perfection of the created universe.[4]

*

* *

Minds accustomed to another approach to the problems may be astonished that reflections dealing principally with the problems of civilization should start here—that we should go so far back for our point of departure. It is, I should say, because the temporal demands of personalism are a peremptory matter only if person is

[1] St. Thomas, *Sum. Th.* Ia p., q.84, a. 5.

[2] The *intellect*, says St. Thomas: but we know that by this he designates the mode of being intrinsic to the soul, and not *reason* in the different and more or less particularized and truncated senses that the word takes in modern parlance. The *mens* (Ia p.,q.76, a.3, ad 4; q. 77, a.1, ad 7; Ia IIae, q. 110, a. 4, ad 4; IIIa, q. 8, a. 1) is the essence of the soul, its spiritual principle. Furthermore, it is organically connected with the other "parts" of the soul (vegetative, sensitive) and informs them. This intelligence, therefore, is not separated; it involves the whole "concrete," the whole stuff of the person.

[3] *De Veritate*, q. 2, a. 2; *Sum. Th.,* Ia p., q. 14, a.1; IIa IIae, q. 66, a.1 sq.; *Sum. cont. Gent.,* 1, III, c. 112, a. 114.

[4] "Persona significat id quod est perfectissimum in tota natura, scilicet subsistens in rationali natura." (*Sum. Th.,* Ia p., q. 29, a. 3.)

something ontologically transcendent to the biological and the social, and, to our mind, only a Christian metaphysics gives assurance of this transcendence.

Accordingly, we must delve further into the subject of Christian personalism.

We do not expect the study of it to net us the privilege of a direct and intuitive identification, of which other philosophies would not be capable. Quite the contrary. What confirms, more than anything else, the transcendence of *person* not only over the material universe, but also over any objective awareness I could possibly have, is the fact that it embodies a mystery. All personalism involves a criticism of the philosophies that accept only the testimony of consciousness on the real. If the person of a Christian is constituted by way of a singular Divine intention prolonged in an inexpressible dialogue of advances and responses made between a free will and the unfathomable course of Providence, then its gist will be by definition inaccessible, and its essence incapable of expression. This is what moral theology expresses by putting in the innermost being of each of us a "secret of the heart" to which no one has access, neither man nor angel, but only God. The conscience of the interested person can, blind to its own spiritual good, shroud that secret in an impenetrable murk until the full light that follows immediately upon death. It is the mystery that the Gospel bids us not to "judge" beforehand. The Church herself respects it, even in the case of Judas. In our century of analysis, this comes more especially to mean that the most subtle psychological experiences can expand indefinitely our empirical knowledge of the manifestations of person, and yet its inexpressible focus, whence issue the only decisions that infallibly commit it, will, nevertheless, continue to elude us. This secret belongs to each one, no matter who he is, to the unbeliever as well as to the saint. Indeed, an excellent test for the Christian's sense of *person* is the attitude taken by him in the face of the unbeliever: a scandal to those religious people who speak of the infinite variety of sanctity, who are always on the watch for the slightest movements of grace or of religious sensibility in the life of pious souls, yet who, whenever they confront the mystery of unbelief, satisfy themselves by citing ponderous moral maxims and making certain puerile resolutions.

How, then, shall we be able to know *person,* if it eludes all definite formulation in terms of sensibility and consciousness?

By way, precisely, of a knowledge unrelated to the register of objective data and external signs which right away hand us over to the world of sense. Personal existence belongs to the type of realities which we apprehend only in an act of assent that has been lived, through stages wherein we bestow on them little by little an increasing existence within ourselves. Where is the problem of death if it is not the pressing problem of *my* death, or the problem of "my deaths," in cases of the death of beings who are dear to me? Where is the problem of evil, so long as it is not *I* who have suffered, or sinned? Like all that which "is not of this world," the transcendent reality of each of our persons escapes us so far as its essence is concerned; but we can know it "through a mirror in an obscure manner," by the proof of a life lived in conformity with its appeals, by irradiation from those near us who bear witness thereto.

Let none picture to himself a wholly quiescent knowledge! The Cartesian notion of "obscure knowledge" leads us to believe that the knowledge we have of realities exceeding the capacity of our experience or the grasp of our understanding differs from intuitive and clear knowledge only by reason of an obscuration—a diminution of light. Even our natural knowledge of the transcendental, however, wends a quite different way: at one moment surprisingly certain, then suddenly troubled with ambiguities and alternative interpretations, interfered with by vertigoes, by cloudings, by wearinesses, by feelings of disgust. Nothing is more irritating than that assurance with which the newcomer makes profession of "personalism." "Man knoweth not whether he be worthy of love, or hatred," says Ecclesiastes. Nobody will claim to know offhand what it is that nerves a person to withstand with holy vehemence the threats of tyrants. No one was more innocent than Jeanne d'Arc and yet she prayed: "If I am so, God keep me so, if I am not so, God make me so." It is significant that *persona,* the word for person in Latin, designates at the same time an actor's mask, that mask which can quite as readily dissimulate the personage as it can faithfully portray the same. Let me but try to grasp myself, and I escape from myself; the matter which I imagine myself to clutch in my hands, slips through my fingers, and presently the formless veils of the deceptive interior interpose themselves, not to be drawn aside. In these days, we know where our most intimate monologues become radically suspect due to a yet more secret urge: It is in the frame of reference of these troubles of self-knowledge that the bringing in of transcendence must be judged.

II

Adsum

The most immediate requisite of a personal life, one which concerns the unbeliever no less than the believer, the atheist no less than one of the faithful, is that of committing ourselves: "Say yea, yea, or nay, nay; the rest comes from the devil." When Pascal is minded to begin his apologetic, it is not at the persecutor that he directs his attack, but at the indifferentist, the man who declines to bet, believing that he can hit a balance between yes and no; to bring a man unwilling to say either yes or no to the point of openly avowing his "Non serviam," is without doubt to make him more amenable to the miracles of grace than he was while skulking behind the screen of dodged responsibility. It was a choice that decided for eternity the fate of the angels, another the destiny of man, still another—the one of a Jewish maiden—the Incarnation of the Son. It is their act for all that we are called upon each day to repeat, in yes, and in no. *Adsum,* says the young deacon who receives Orders: "I am here and I am such"; I have struggled against pharisaism, the illusions of self-love, the most subtile forms of cowardice. Verily I have not accepted compromise, I have not held back my gifts; perhaps I can commence to offer a consistent being to the ministry of Christ.

Thus, the first step in Christian life is to narrow within ourselves that zone which Heidegger speaks of as "the world of the indefinite pronoun *one*"—*die Welt des man.* We refer to the world of irresponsibility and of false evasion, which so easily gains a foothold in the mass psychology of vast social bodies, the world of the *one-says-ers* (or "they-say-ers"), and the world of what *one does* (or "people do"). In whatever degree of thoroughness it depersonalizes us through the press, through public conventionalities, through cheap slogans, through accustoming us to irresponsibility, in the same degree it congeals our living communities of unlike and inalienable human beings into those sorts of social concretions that are styled opinion, manners, routine.[1] In

[1] All the contemporary personalist philosophies have described this universe of depersonalization. It is *der man* ("l'on"), the being-cast-into-the-world, which Hei-

Christian parlance, we must inevitably come to speak of a specific and grievous sin against *person*.

I sin against person each time I abandon myself to this anonymity and to this irresponsibility. It would shock a great many "sincere" people who profess to be Marxists, fascists, liberals, if in their presence one were to question, whether in their mouths the verb *to be* had a meaning. Yet, in an affair where their own interests or their most cherished affections were at stake, would they be willing to hazard any decision at all upon such slight grounds of experience, upon such an uncritical assent of thought? A businessman has his point of view on a transaction; he risks his business; if it fails, he loses money; the worker has his idea about his work; if he takes his mind off it, he breaks his machine and is liable to have his wages docked; in all these cases, the sane man is the one who learns to think straight. As much, however, cannot be said for the rough approximations without consequences of which people's opinion for the most part consists—and God knows that democratic freedom of judgment entitles them all to such opinion on every imaginable subject.

I sin against *person* each time that I force a living man into a groove where he becomes identified with one of his functions, or that I behave towards him as if he were in fact reduced to such a fraction of himself. When, for example, I look upon certain men or certain women as though they were "made for" cutting the same iron rods all the days of the life God gives them. When I reduce woman to her function of housekeeping, or to her erotic function, or even to her high function of motherhood, without taking into consideration the spiritual vocation that is appointed for her amid and beyond all her cares and charms; when I consider my workmen as so much implementation or equipment, taking the view that their bodily frailty and family obligations are no concern of mine other than as factor making for waste; when, thrown in by chance with the country people among whom I take my vacation, or with soldier comrades in camp, I resign myself, after a feeble effort at being sociable, to the breaking off of all authentic communication between them and me, merely because they happen to have amongst themselves a set of conventions notably different from those in vogue in my own little cir-

degger contrasts, in the *Dasein*, with the being that confronts the world; it is the *Essein*, the *that*, in contrast to the "I" and the "you" (Buber); the world of *objectivation*, in contrast to the Spirit and Liberty (Berdyaeff); the spatialized world or world of *la morale close*, in contrast to "la morale ouverte" (Bergson).

cle; so, too, with those bad boys, whom the righteous frown upon in their distinguished hearts, but in whom, nevertheless, the preventive grace of Christ will continue to dwell until the last breath they draw. I sin against *person,* in a word, each time that I act as if I despaired of a man, whether I excommunicate him in the name of the highest of human virtualities, or reduce him to the status of a mere thing or tool.

We can also commit the same sin in thought. For example, by thinking about the problems of man where "my all is at stake" in purely objective terms, imitative of the impersonality of scientific problems. One would think that, in view of what anthropology and Christian theology have contributed to Western thought, such an attitude would be impossible, but, thanks to impregnation with the ways of thinking inherited from antiquity, thanks to the polarization, at a later date, of modern thought by scientific techniques, thanks, finally, to the rationalism of the *Illuminati,* spurious offspring of these impersonal gods, solid bastions of resistance to Christian impulse have been established, even in the heart of philosophies nominally Christian. Whether it be "matter" necessitating its inexorable arrangements, or "life" tumbling the species and the individuals into its river without banks, or "economics" secretly determining human wills, or even "the spirit" unrolling its logical processes, "the Ideal" delivering discourses to the event or "the Principles" crushing a restless soul, from every side—from the "spiritualisms" no less than from the "materialisms"—dangers to *person* threaten in the initiatives of modern thought. Nor are these menaces purely ideological. They have given birth to all the dictatorships of modern times: that of the goddess of Reason, in France, in 1793; those more recent ones of Race, of Economics, or of the State. All the weaknesses of the opposing idealist host itself proceed from the selfsame source.

Sin against *person* also comprises a sin of omission. It is at the root of every evasion, however highminded, that diverts me from pursuing my concrete destiny to follow will-o'-the-wisps. Marx, treading in the steps of Feuerbach, reproaches religion with having for its essence just such an evasion, with draining man of his powers for future achievement only to plunge him into an otherworldly mirage, thus alienating him from himself and leaving him a helpless puppet at the mercy of the forces of the day. His criticism holds good against a caricature of Christianity which, though frequently met with on the paths of experience, is, nonetheless, the precise negation thereof. But his dialectic of alienation, if it had not set out from presuppositions equally impersonal, such as economics, matter, value, could with a slight turn of the key be changed into a personalist critique. It is very easy to see this when he describes economic alienation: how the world of money transforms into "things" first the living merchandise and then, by means of the latter, the men who handle it. Quite as much, at least, as it does in threats of oppression, modern life abounds in beautiful seductions and mystifications—in "opiums," e.g., the cinemas by way of overdose, the societies, the clubs and the parties, the collective myths, the eroticism, all the light intoxicants of urban and social life.

One of the most dangerous, especially in a period of trouble, is the temptation to purity. The quest of purity of means in the service of the absolute purity of the last end is one of the elements of the tragic in human kind. But this element is never separable, and that purity is never realizable, for the Kingdom is not of this world. Absolute purity dreamt of as an actual possibility is a murderous idol; either it raises up fanatics, sons of Savanarola or sons of Robespierre, who forge for it the instruments of the worst spiritual imperialism; or else it begets defeatists who retire bag and baggage from their world in order to protect an "interior life" or a studied affectation of integrity. They fail to see that they thereby do a thing which positively aggravates the very disorder from which they pretend to dissociate themselves, and, at the same time, they deny by implication the dramatic rôle and impact of our action, outside of which there is nothing to life but dreaming.

Adsum. Present! The Christian is a being who takes upon himself. The last caution of Christ before His death was to be on guard against denial, and He gave that warning to the head of the Church: *I know not this man*—"I know not this act," words of voluntary death; God's image renounces, along with his responsibility, his privilege. The deeper we plumb the essence of Christian morality the surer we are to find, at the bottom of every sin, this primordial pharisaism whereby the individual sinner in thousands of ways unloads his burden upon his neighbor, upon the collectivity, upon certain myths, in order to secure for himself without exertion the happiness of a satisfied conscience. The Christian is a being who accuses himself, and that in the double sense of confessing the deed and accepting the blame: he feels himself at fault in every sin, and he is not haunted by the terror of of standing out, of not being "like the rest of men." He commits himself. Not only up to this or that point, but whole-heartedly in his each and every action, since in very truth each of his acts is, as it were, a recapitulation of his whole life, while his life tends to resemble the dash of a single act. His "sincerity" is not the sentimental, blind, passive, changing assurance which has caused certain of our contemporaries to mistake for the authentic voice of conscience what in fact is but the clamoring of their most immediate preferences. It is that unity at once difficult and taken for granted; less sought after than it ought to be by the man who is always saying *I* while thinking *me* as seldom as possible; for this self-committing and self-affirming *I* is so intimately bound up with the reality to which it gives itself that it effaces itself with a self-effacement in this case supreme, after the manner of a mediator, of an answerer who wholly identifies himself with his answer. What the *I* thus transfigured receives from Christian life is the reward of a response itself likewise more and more personal, which is not the despotic concession of a collectivism, nor yet the dispassionate answer of a logic or of a Principle, out of sympathy with its own sufferings, but a unique word tendering a unique gift: "this drop of blood which I have shed for you. . . ."

III

Nihil Habentes et Omnia Possidentes

Here we touch upon what may be called the fundamental point of ambiguity in the Christian person. Ambiguity, we have said, which is but one of the external signs of the inexpressibleness of its transcendence, and yet fundamental in that it puts our feet on the track not of confusion, but of a certain understanding of this transcendence.

Person, in the Christian perspective, is presence, affirmation, but it is not presence *to self* nor affirmation *of self;* it is *response.* In Bergsonian language, this perspective puts forward a closed personalism in contrast to an open personalism. While it tones up and energizes person, it at the same time disarms it. It moderates its desires in order to free it for Abandon. It disavows its projects in order to throw it into the arms of Hope.

Abandon and Hope, that is to say the gift of oneself to a transcendent and good Being does *not* consist (as Nietzsche believed

on the strength of certain empirical behaviors) in a masked resignation, presenting a sort of feminine passivity in the face of life's
combats and contradictions. This smiling religiosity, this benedic-
tory optimism, and this effacement without fighting a battle—
closely akin to liberal concordism and so altogether characteristic
of the XIX century—gave rise to systematic but sane reactions,
which Christian anthropology would not be able to reject *in toto*.
I think, for instance, of Heidegger's criticism of that daily banality
(the "one's world"—*die Welt des man*) which he regards as a
flight from the essential anguish of a life confronting death and
having its whole point in this confrontment. I think, in the
same light, of that stern personalism which a young French
philosopher[1] blocked out by means of a series of characteristic
valuations: the irrevocable act, which is opposed to the dissolving
march of time; lucidity; a certain form of hardness and ruthlessness which is opposed to all confusion; horror of compromises, of
self-complacency. This morality of confrontment is at the core of
Malraux's work. It has been the conspicuous mark of one wing
of young French personalism.[2]

The decadence which provoked these vital reactions and these
stiffenings of defense, far from leaving the Catholic world intact,
has flooded it with certain vague and surreptitious romancings.

One might unearth by the kilo the pseudo-pious literature that
wrought this havoc; the listener might surprise on the tongues of
each of us complaisances of language (often indicating complaisances of the heart) towards spiritual comfort, towards utter in-
sipidities, towards facile eloquence. A certain religion of good
fellowship tends to blot out from the Christian memory the irrevocable solitude, the continual presence of suffering and death
(which, contrariwise, rasped on human sensibility during the
Middle Ages) —the smart of pain and struggle that is at the heart
not only of all life but also of all love. By its theology, by its sensibility, Catholicism is the precise antithesis of such a softening of
the religious sense. The very severity of its climate, so closely
allied to its tenderness, also brings it up to an ethic of struggle
and of facing things. Man hovers on the brink of a nothingness no

---

[1] Claude Chevalley, in *l'Ordre nouveau*, July 15, 1938: "The Time of Sternness."
[2] The one expressing itself between 1932 and 1938 in the movement whose organ
is the Bulletin of *l'Ordre nouveau*. The review and the movement *Esprit,* although
open to very diverse expressions, are more strongly imbued with the perspectives of
Christian personalism.

longer mythical but real; annihilation before the Infinite, which is the prophetic substance of the message of St. John of the Cross. There he faces the daily presence of death, which exposes him to the anguish of perdition more terrible than the anguish of destruction; there he faces, too, the weight of a Destiny fed from the springs of God's unfathomable designs, there he is driven to incessant despair of his calculated hopes, to the unaccountable experience of conflicts that constitute the tragic deadlock of his situation.

Nevertheless, the Christian's combat differs doubly from the one that the Heideggerian hero fights. The latter is taut and tense in his struggle, his struggle defines his being, inasmuch as without it he would lapse into temporal death; furthermore, his struggle is really one of desperation; the only transcendence he knows is the transcendence of a menace, that of the annihilation and of the death of being in time, forever prone to sap the defenses of Life. The Christian, however hard the struggle, keeps that great stimulus which inheres in the morals of Charity, and—akin to health— an essential resiliency of soul. The struggle is not for him the mode of being essential to existence, it does not close upon itself, it goes beyond itself, it rises above itself in Hope and acceptance.

This is only a particular aspect of the second step in Christian personalism: dispossession—the spur to availability.

Formulas like these have a strange sound for the ears of a pseudo-personalism which presents itself as a revindication of autonomy or a painless fulfilment of all vital cravings.

It is needless to recall how a dispossession and, to say it all, a sort of total expropriation of self by self under the increasing urge of grace is at the very heart of Christian spirituality. Let it suffice to cite here a few formulas of the prophet of *Nada,* who has traced in lines of fire this ideal of Christian life—St. John of the Cross:

MEANS OF KEEPING THE WHOLE

To come to the knowledge of all,
Will to know naught of anything.

To come to the tasting of all,
Will to taste naught of anything.

To come to the possession of all,
Will to possess naught of anything.

To come to the being of all,
Will to be naught of anything.

MEANS OF NOT OBSTRUCTING THE WHOLE

When thou tarriest in anything,
Thou ceasest to plunge into the whole.

For to arrive at all in all,
Thou must wholly leave all.

And when thou comest to hold the whole,
Thou must guard it without wishing for anything.

For if thou wishest for anything in this whole,
Thou keepest not purely in God thy treasure.

Naught, naught, naught, naught. St. John repeats this refrain with passionate insistence, as if he were smashing an idol. He thrusts into that devouring fire of love not only the sensible attachments of the erring soul, but the spiritual pleasures and appropriations of the soul that seeks creature satisfactions among the goods of heaven. He gives over to be consumed the very substance of his spiritual being to the end that it may emerge from this inferno of agony entirely purified from the sin of appropriation. It would be deceiving oneself to see in this austerity any sublimation of "the instinct of death," so dear to the Freudians —any desperate masochism. All this asceticism is but an aspiration after Being in its fulness, after that state whereof St. Paul already said that in it we would be "as having nothing, yet possessing all things." Thereupon St. John exults: "Mine are the heavens, and mine the earth. Mine are men, the just are mine and mine the sinners, the angels are mine, and the Mother of God, and all things are mine; and God Himself is mine and for me; for Christ is mine and all for me. Well, then, my soul, what more dost thou ask and seek? All this is thine and it is all for thee." [1]

Between the first *Mine* and the second there yawns the infinite of a crucifying transfiguration. *Cupio dissolvi et esse tecum,* says St. John of the Cross to Christ. To be completely dissolved, and then *to be,* but in that higher world, *to be with* a Being to whom we say *thou*—ontological participation, as St. Paul already intimated by using a single compound verb.[2]

It is the resistance and the fundamental opposition in its very

---

[1] *Avisos y sentencias* quoted by J. Maritain, *Degrés du savoir,* p. 726.
[2] συνζήσομεν αὐτῷ (*Rom.* VI, 8).

essence of the bourgeois mind (born of the world of money) to this basic Christianity that the young French personalists have resented most keenly in their criticism of morals. The Antichrist of the modern world, Peguy told them when he was twenty, in a jest—which coming from him is more serious than a formal pronouncement—is not the pornographic book; that is not so evil— the real Antichrist of the modern world is the bank-book for savings accounts. This bank-book, offered to the children of France with a mysticism of economy, which is held up to them as being morality itself, this to his eyes is the first mark of the Beast upon innocence, the direct weapon of attack upon the Evangelical law of the "lilies that labour not, neither do they spin." He regards it as the Tempter giving the child a hand to help it take its first step on the path of this avarice "wasteful and prodigal of its soul, which it sells for nothing, for money," of that "morality of weaklings," which is an ownership, a regime and certain relish of property, "it makes us proprietors of our own poor virtues," of this "honesty" which is a door closed to grace. "The most honest people, or simply the honest people, or in fine those who have the name of being such, and who love to give themselves credit for being so . . . have no chinks in their armor . . . their moral hide, always intact, forms for them a flawless rind and cuirass. . . . What they call morality is an integument that renders man impervious to grace." [1]

Christian prophetism has always risen up in protest against the sociological crystallization of this appropriation of moral life, against the foundation of sects of the pure, and more generally, of any institution pervaded by a sort of collective conscience of the "good people." "Why dost thou call me good?" said Christ Himself to the rich young man. "None is good but God alone." (*Luke,* XVIII, 19.) The Christian keynote is to accentuate the thinness of the partition dividing the sinner from the "normal" man, the profound superiority even of the former's situation as compared with the latter's, not indeed by reason of his sin, but by reason of the greater availability he keeps at that time in the bosom of one of those sins which Peguy calls the *péchés graciés* (the "par-

---

[1] The difference between the prophetic language of the writer and the technical language of the theologian is fertile soil for misunderstandings. It is well to remind the reader here, in order that Peguy may be understood in the proper sense, that his latest work, like all he has written previously, is a defense of the living rule and order.

doned sins"), contrasting them with the sins of callousness. It sometimes falls to the task of the Christian novelist to bring out this line of secret demarcation between availability and unavailability to grace that, while in no way effacing it, does not coincide with the border-line between innocence and sin. In such a case, he can accuse unavailability alone of complacency towards evil. Should one or the other of these distinctions ever trade places, however plausible the reason for it may seem, this should not cause us to forget the essential point of his testimony: That the sin of weakness may close the heart less irrevocably than a haughty virtue, that certain evil inclinations are but generous impulses shriveled up, while as regards certain virtues puffed up with pride, it is well to recall yet another saying of Peguy's: "A man may not save his soul as he would save a treasure. It therefore behooves one to save it as he would lose a treasure—by expending it."[1]

Next to Peguy, no one has better marked out this antithesis between the world and the Christian order than Gabriel Marcel.[2]

The moment I transform something of the living Being into an inert datum which I posit, which I present to myself as a despiritualized or devitalized thing, a specimen capable in its exteriority of being tagged and card-indexed, therefore *at my disposal,* manipulatable and controllable by me, that moment I depart from the luminous realm of Being, and place myself, by a responsible act of spiritual defection, in the blind realm of Having.

The being which I thus debase may be one of the manifold sensible goods that entice me; it may be a person whom I treat like an object, "in the third person," at my mercy; it may be any spiritual wealth whatever. (Jacques Rivière once described magnificently, in his "Carnets," this sort of shame that pursues the writer in consequence of a certain way of capitalizing all "literary matter," of laying hands, for his art's profit, upon all the riches of simplicity). It may be, too, my whole self and each of the acts which proceed from me, if so be that this *me* interposes itself between my being and the Being like an opaque screen, that my deeds tarnish my conscience with an ineffaceable smudge, that my

---

[1] Jacques Rivière, in his notes on war "A la trace de Dieu" (Paris, Gallimard, 1926), lays emphasis on the opposition in the *Confiteor* of placing the sinner in the presence of the totality of the universe, and the repeated possessive laying claim to the fault: *mea culpa*—the only act that is truly my own. For the Greeks, on the contrary, fault was a sort of exterior fatality.

[2] *Etre et Avoir* (Edit. Montaigne), Paris 1935 *Journal métaphysique,* Paris 1923, and *Du refus a l'invocation,* Paris 1940 (Gallimard); several theatrical pieces.

desires obscure the whole significance of an event and all under-standing of it.

Hence it is not enough to speak of *"the expansion"* of one's per-son when we desire to combat the sordid obduracies of the mod-ern world. Certainly, Catholicism holds no brief whatever for a certain Jansenistic bad humor that often adopts this formula in milieus nominally Christian. Transported to the farther side of the carrefour of the Cross, all these expansive, superabundant, and feebly triumphant formulas of naturalism find a new meaning—the canticles of St. John of the Cross, of St. Francis of Assisi—and are more representative of Christian truth than a certain type of dour and righteous niggardliness. But we see how ambiguous the image of expansion is; it can signify the sovereign superabundance which lies beyond *having,* but also—and here we swerve radically from the Christian way—an increase of *having* covering the soul with that profusion of brambles which Christ tells His Apostles choke the word of God every bit as effectively as stony ground.

He who is thus all covered up, all protected with his *havings,* with his precious "person," becomes increasingly unavailable, im-pervious to grace. He no longer strives *to be* that which is worth being realized, but only *to have the reputation* of being, or the illusory appearance of being whatever enjoys esteem socially. So-cial reference that no longer allows of an absolute standard, but only of a relative one; concurrence, and not aspiration; a certain equalitarianism, more petty bourgeois than popular, whose re-quirements would be by preference mediocre provided nobody raised the ante; a certain passion for social climbing, which is the desire not so much for a new state as for a new level; a certain demon of discernment where the desire to accumulate and the desire to equal come into question; the restlessness of greed and the torment of embracing the most unheard of and contradictory experiences; a certain ideological or spiritual fanaticism—all mani-fest this fever for possession quite as much as does the bourgeois sense of property. Under brave appearances, they all rush madly onward to the selfsame void; the lust for power loses itself in a sort of disease in which *having* becomes self-devouring, or else the pos-sessor becomes possessed by his own goods; fain to be rich and free, he becomes the prisoner of the enormous *me.*[1]

[1] The translator cannot resist quoting, in illustration of the point the author makes here an anecdote of the Gold Rush days related by John Ruskin in *Unto this Last:*
"As thus: lately in a wreck of a Californian ship, one of the passengers fastened

Gabriel Marcel was quite right in recognizing that, regardless of appearances to the contrary, the modern assertion of claim to moral or political *autonomy* spells yet another defeat for personalism, if, in the final count, the autonomy claimed is nothing more than the right to have one's own way without control, that is to say, the right to isolate oneself as something apart among alien interests and to concentrate on the management of one's holdings by accentuating this isolation. Indeed, *unavailability* is positively furthered by every social impulse that has its deepest roots in a sense of *claim*. Or again by *anarchism* whose vehement refusal to belong to anyone else amounts to a brutal claim of absolute possession of oneself (often coupled with the kind of "expansion" to which we paid our respects above).

We behold converging from all horizons of the modern world aberrations that, politically speaking, fall into quite different classifications, some borne along by the democratic currents, others by the world of the Possessors and the Strong, others by the autocracies, all nonetheless blood-brothers in that they stem from the selfsame corruption of the Christian man. The type of behavior common to possessor and claimant, to anarchist and dictator, is the practice of monopolizing, backed up by an infatuation. The type of behavior natural to the Christian person is a distraction from self that makes for *availability* in the twofold sense of one who welcomes and of one who perpetually offers himself. Infatuated faces, men who are "full of themselves," as the expression so aptly puts it, puffed up with mere nothing, atrociously absent and inscrutable—detached faces, open faces, far-off looks, which, for all that they are not displayed, never suffer themselves to be forgotten: here we have the true antithesis of ugliness and beauty. Or if you prefer another picture of the same fundamental import, compare the pedantic personality of the man of meager talent, of the deviser of systems or mental games, of the fanatic, of the man of principle, of the sententious preacher, with the absolute self-effacement of the true creature in his creation, of the witness in his testimony, of the spiritual man in the light that transfigures him.

That is why every situation that starts the confiscation of *having* in order to liberate the fecundity of *being* is a momentous situa-

a belt about him with two hundred pounds of gold in it, with which he was found afterwards at the bottom. Now as he was sinking—had he the gold? or had the gold him?" (*Op. cit.,* Essay IV *Ad Valorem,* §62.)

tion for Christian personalism: suffering, risk, exposure, insecurity, which take the props from under our sufficiency; sacrifice which immolates a *having* to open self to an increase of *being;* death which signifies the definitive expoliation of all *having*—the definitive nudation of our real being—and which delivers us from "the temptation of thinking that no longer to have anything is no longer to be anything" (G. Marcel) ; humility, finally, which sums up all the rest. All of them have been accounted values of loss by such as confound true riches with false (and the appreciation of them, it is true, has given rise to as many morbid aberrations, in which the marginal history of Christianity abounds). Understood in their Christian sense, they are rays of the values of "expansion," or better still of accomplishment, in that they dishabituate us to ourselves, and pry loose by dint of the heavy, pitiless blows of their chisel the carapace which shuts us off from Life. The absolute Being defines Himself as He that IS, in all entirety, the only one that essentially is—*Sum qui sum. Adsum,* the saint answers Him: I *am,* I *have* nothing any more, I am but a prayer *to* Thee.

· IV

Intimius Intimo Meo

Today it is the fashion to represent as out of fashion the old distinction of the person from the individual—a custom in vogue for some time. It remains, nevertheless, a pivotal point of view on the problem engaging our attention, upon condition of not materializing into a spatial split a distinction that seeks rather to describe a pair of forces in the same field—an internal distortion. There is no separating what belongs to the "individual" and what to the "person," but, in the same elements, there is a degrading process of individuation, which is a deterioration, and an enriching process of personalization, which is in response to a transcendent appeal. The crassly dualistic aberration that has to be avoided here reaches the maximum of its harmfulness when it straddles the classic cleft of idealism, allotting to the "individual" whatever is bodily, particular, temporal, mundane. It makes of person a sort of abstract power or sublime angelic existence scarcely incarnate at all, which sets one foot upon the peak of our soul, attaching "the individual" to itself as a lackey assigned to menial services. We shall see further on that Christian anthropology rules out any such disjunction. The whole man, "individual" and "person," is present and active in each of his operations.[1] But no sooner is it dissociated from the principle of unity that ensures all its coherence and unification than there develops within it a sort of atrophy of being which decomposes, separates and disperses. We have already described two effects of this degradation. For the living paradox of a presence so much the richer the more thoroughgoing has been its renunciation of all imposition of self, it substitutes the inert paradox of a *me* which is so much the more pretentious the more it sinks to the level of the impersonal elements of the "one's" world. Under this first aspect, individuation appears as a process of (camouflaged) leveling and hardening. Its inconsistency, which is its very being, enables it to wear various other faces, the contradictory character of which manifests its instability.

It goes quite readily with a certain brilliancy, with a certain picturesqueness which affords a good illustration of the misuse of the word "originality," and which parades itself as a piece of pageantry staged in order to mask the real poverty of the elements actually brought into play, with an eye to captivating us by a flashy imitation of genuine riches. The spirituality of the Saints in harsh language casts out this abuse of reliance upon the seductions of sense, so prone to invoke the prestige of the spiritual. For the Christian there is no spirituality other than spirituality in the harsh sense of the word—the kind that the Holy Spirit bestows; this is accordant and only accordant with whatever is in organic alignment with charity. Inasmuch as the whole universe is called to salvation—thought and things, nature and art, bodily grace, scientific research—nothing is excluded *a priori* from this assumption into Heaven, barring evil—the refuse of being. It must be added, too, that very often we know nothing of the indirect ways of this consecration which invariably finds its starting-point where an incorruptible quality prevails. From century to century Catholic humanism repudiates Manichaean temptations and that miserly zeal which tends to put bounds to the advance of grace, to put outside its pale the charm of art, or the beauty of the sensible world, or enthusiasm for knowledge. But everything, including

---

[1] Activity is ascribed to subsisting wholes or "selves"—*actiones sunt suppositorum* —and not to the parts or the powers; it should not, in fact, be said that the hand acts, but rather that the man acts by means of his hand. (*Cf.* St. Thomas, *Sum Th.*, I p., q. 3, a. 8, ad 2.)

the very tokens of sanctity itself, are liable to be affected by a minus-sign that shunts them away from the unity of love. Then all of them—joys, thoughts, virtues—tumble into the circle of that "animal man," of that "flesh" which St. Paul and the whole tradition of mysticism after him oppose collectively to "the spiritual man."

Again, individuation presents itself as a dispersion, whereas personalization is a movement of concentration and recollection. The man that is no longer in the hands of God is precisely the one that "no longer has his own life in hand," the one whose being is split up into a profusion of divergent forces. If I know, however, that a unique drop of blood, and none other, flowed for me on Golgotha from out the bosom of the Trinity, I know, too, that this gift from God's being must have His Word for me, a unique and transcendent message which Christ tries intimately to whisper to me in the midst of the body of the faithful, athwart the babel of words here below: my vocation.

The word is greatly abused in current usage. What goes by the name of a professional "vocation" may enter, like every portion of my destiny, into the general plan of my vocation, but it then assumes a quite altered meaning from happy adaptation of my aptitudes, which is the sense it commonly has in people's mouths. All my traits—to tell them off from the coarsest to the finest: temperament, aptitudes, components of my psychic constitution, character—are objects of fine adaptation; none of them defines a vocation. They comprise an order amenable to rules of greater or lesser generalization; the vocation never allows of generalization. It was *Abraham's* vocation to lead his son Isaac to the slaughter in testimony of his faith. No general commandment has been given to the effect: "Thou shalt immolate thy children for the good pleasure of *God.*" It was *Job's* vocation to endure vermin on his dunghill in arriving at perfect detachment of the heart. The endurance of vermin on a dung-hill is not recommended for everyone as a way to become a good Christian. Every worthy vocation is inimitable. Nevertheless it realizes its unique expression only in the exclusion of all pursuance of singularity. Each Saint differs immeasurably from every other, and nevertheless all of them have sought but one goal—to imitate a single model: Jesus.

Solidabor in te, Deus meus, exclaims St. Augustine: in Thee shall I consolidate myself interiorly, and St. Ildephonse of Toledo, simply echoing him, invites us to confirm what we are in the unity of the Church, *in unitate ipsius Ecclesiae solidari.* This confirmation by and in the Church distinguishes the Catholic notion of a vocation from the Liberal Protestant conception. But this integration does not detract one whit from the infinite diversity which moves St. Peter, in his first Epistle, to speak of the "manifold grace of God." The Church is one, and yet we can speak of a "Paulinism" and a "Johannism," and we have the Benedictine, Franciscan, Dominican, Oratorian and other religious families. This multiplicity will be sanctioned by the final Assumption which, the Apocalypse tells us, will integrate all that comes "out of every tribe, and tongue, and people, and nation."

My vocation may be the development of my natural talents, of my spiritual initiatives themselves; it may also lie in their total temporal frustration, and to tell the truth, a vocation is conceivable in the Christian perspective that would not integrate anything of the grandeur of frustration, not being compensated by verbal heroics and interior lyricism, but yet organically transfigured into oblation. It is not like a ready-made idea that I would only have to decipher and realize. It transcends my existence as the eternal transcends the temporal, and yet, bound up with the mystery of liberty, it is in a very real sense worked out by ourselves in collaboration with the Divine intention; it undergoes sundry setbacks, warpings, accelerations according to the way I respond to the events—to the Divine advances. The finishing touch will only be given by the act of my death.

The permanent call of one's vocation demands an outright break with whatever can hush the voice or alter the sense thereof; clamorings of the world, selfishness of families, public conformances, encroachments of the collectivities—all that would arrogate to itself a right of ward or direction over this untouchable. But this is as yet but a negative condition of freedom of vocation; it calls for more than mere protection: this attentiveness of the heart, this habit of recollectedness which elicits the natural and supernatural virtue of silence, to the end that, passing from one mirage to another, I may come closer to that *intimius intimo meo,* that inaccessible heart of my heart where it has "pleased God, who segregated me from my mother's womb, and called me by his grace, *to reveal his Son in me*" (*Gal.,* I, 15, 16).

If this saying of St. Paul is taken in its full significance, it gives a boundless meaning to that "eminent dignity," indeed, the only one truly eminent, the only one indisputably emancipated from nature; the dignity of that secret of the soul[1] which henceforth, not God's image and likeness alone, but the intimate life of the Trinity comes to occupy when we respond to its advances. At the same instant it bursts asunder the bounds of the sanctuary; along with the presence of God, the whole universe is encompassed, commencing with the total presence of the Church, of her tradition, of her saints, of her Body. The concentration of the "interior life" is in no sense a separation, a retreat from combat and danger, or a refined complacency; in Christian life recollectedness and openness go hand in hand. An exteriorized soul is a hardened and closed soul, a recollected being knows and carries within himself "the breadth, and length, and height, and depth."

V

Non estis sub lege

This disclosure of the person to himself, or what comes to the same, this revelation to the person of his vocation, is not the outcome of any more or less necessary phenomenon—after the analogy of a photographic negative that life would gradually develop —but of a free *act*.

This word need barely be uttered, in order to find ourselves ushered right into the heart of the contemporary drama. Maritain remarked not long ago that in modern times the myth of liberty has been substituted for the medieval myth of force at the service of right. At the present moment the nations have come to grips with one another for or against it. Disregarding the surface facts, we ought to ask ourselves whether the face of Christian liberty has not been badly slashed in the combat by certain disloyalties that are really in accord with each other, even if they do not happen to strike a balance.

Liberalism, which little by little has impregnated to the core the minds, institutions and morals of the modern age, seethes with the impatience of a liberty intolerant of any limits; it lacks the remotest conception not only of the possibility of choosing our lines of action without undergoing the pressure of external constraint, but even of the radical absence of internal necessity that springs from a vocation transcending the individual, or from cer-

[1] *Cf.* Gardeil, *La Structure de l'âme et l'expérience mystique,* Paris (Gabalda).

tain loyalties whereby one might become more and more bound. There are in the liberal aspiration for liberty two quite different elements. In the first place, and we do well not to ignore it, there is a nostalgia for the etherealness and absolute independence of the pure Spirit, a perverted homage to the appeals of the Divine life within us. The drive of person as such is directed towards the absolute *from-selfness* (aseity) of God, and this it is that impels the person on to higher and higher degrees of spontaneousness and independence; the blind awareness of the Absolute is as much alive in the poetry as it is in the thought and the politics of the present day; it is, in this sense, not so relativistic as is commonly believed to be the case. But if God is sufficient to Himself because He is the Being, and if He detaches Himself from all dependence in that He is pure interiority, man can liberate himself from all things else except the Real—the Being. Such a liberation is, nevertheless, the titan-like aspiration of Liberalism; it is so strongly attached to the values of emancipation pure and simple, which is for it a goal in itself, that it rates refusal higher than choice, indetermination higher than adhesion, caprice higher than constancy, the unmotivated act higher than an act as full of freedom in the true sense as a ripe fruit is with its juice. We are acquainted with those learned gatherings in which intellectual superiority is thought to consist in coming to no conclusions; with that generalization, in the social and political jargon, which lays claim to freedom; with that condescending pity of the *grand seigneur* which certain distinguished minds affect to feel for a living faith, for an orthodoxy, for thought that is polemical. The reaction to this intemperance, which volatized the meaning of liberty in the very act of exalting its dignity, was bound to be a brutal one. It is now at hand and is far from being something simple. The sarcasms which the totalitarian regimes pour out unstintedly upon the liberty of the Liberals (not to speak of the injuries to which they daily subject liberty, understood in the proper sense of the word), have awakened coincidently a lively sense of responsibility and the duty of service. They say with truth that liberty has not been given to us in order that we might remain in suspense, but in order that we might commit ourselves: we say that liberty is nothing if it is not an open field for liberation. Commitment liberates only when it is made to a reality in which the person by losing himself finds himself again; while the totalitarians throw person away on various regimentations where it alienates its very being in certain powers that are subordinate to itself, be it that of the race, or of the State, or of production.

What light does Christian ethics shed on this debate?

All Christian confessions agree in picturing the final destiny of the children of God. It is not the infinite, unlimited and absolutely sovereign liberty of liberalism, which is the prerogative of the perfect Being alone. It does, on the other hand, in the Beatific Vision, participate somehow in that imponderable etherealness of the Spirit whereof no one knows "whence he cometh, and whither he goeth."

In the case of the man who is still living in time, this liberty is turned to God like a flower to the sun. Directed towards something other than itself, it can say of itself in so far as it gravitates: *Amor meus, pondus meum.* In the state of beatitude, it will go to God by an intimate necessity, without, however, ceasing to be free. Hence, Christianity provides an outlet, beyond the bourn of time, for that desire of freeness which agitates the world today.

Nevertheless, our action unfurls itself in time. So long as we are in time, our heart desires God with a desire that is enthralling, indeed, but partially blind; that no longer knows how to tell its object infallibly. One man will seek it in solitude, another in excitement, a third in art, or in love, or in combats. If in interpreting liberty supreme, liberty "of spontaneity," "of exaltation," and even "of autonomy," we substitute the Pauline for the Kantian sense of the word,[1] this indigence—and not perfection—adjoins a liberty of choice, which must needs, in an act prepared by a habit of the soul and promoted by grace, discover the relation of each possible form of conduct to the infinite and inefficacious desire of our heart. This act, whenever we place it, commits our whole person; more exactly speaking, it is in and by such acts that the person reveals himself and makes himself. But the choice and, less still, the indetermination are not ends in themselves; the first is nothing but a remedy for the second and the instrument of a dignity which has its ultimate reason solely in its adhesion to the source of all life.

Here again the Christian treads on the brink of a paradox. The

---

[1] Maritain, "L'idée Thomiste de la liberté," *Revue Thomiste,* July-September, 1939.

spontaneity, the freeness, the availability of the children of God are our terminal vocation, and yet it is true that its ways are neither the most voluntary nor the most deliberate. "For by grace you are saved through faith, and that not of yourselves, for it is the gift of God; not by works, that no man may glory" (*Ephes.*, II, 8). But these foreshortenings are not even meant to be willed: "Do we, then, destroy the law through faith? God forbid: but we establish the law." (*Rom.*, III, 31). The reign of the law, therefore, must prepare the reign of liberty and assure it, without destroying itself, but by causing itself to be forgotten through a sort of internal transfiguration. So long as I follow the solicitations of my empirical and discordant wishes, I have the sense of being free, though in reality I act as a slave, because I turn my back upon the truth that sets free. My heart is then made in the image of my desires; and, by the same token, whenever I follow the law out of fear I feel it weighing like a yoke of slavery upon the inclinations of my corrupt nature. "But presently the Holy Spirit inclines the will through love towards the true good; through love He brings it about that the will, whole and entire, gravitates straight towards the center that is deepest in its line of dip. It then throws off at one stroke this twofold yoke of slavery: the slavery wherein, serf of passion and sin, man acts against the natural ordination of his will; and the slavery wherein, serf of the law, and not its friend, he acts according to the law against the movement of his will. *Where the Spirit of the Lord is,* says the Apostle Paul, *there is liberty;* and *If you are led by the Spirit, you are not under the law.*" [1] The freeness and independence have been won by the renunciation prerequisite to the freeness and independence claimed.

*

*   *

This theology of liberty, like liberal and totalitarian ethics, is not without its practical consequences. In the very bosom of the Christian adventure there is set the hard task of eliminating two opposite dangers that constantly come back, under new forms, to threaten it from the flanks.

The first is that of a religious pessimism which regards human liberty as nonexistent in the condition of sin. We recognize here

---

[1] Jacques Maritain, "Du Régime temporel et de la liberté"; and St. Thomas, *Contr. Gent.*, IV, 22.

the position of Luther.[1] The only liberty possible for man is the liberty borrowed from Christ, purely interior and yet externally put on rather than assimilated, entirely inefficacious in the mass of perdition which are the works of men.[2] Consequently, there is no place for liberty in the temporal order. Only a strict and rigorous authority can preserve some cohesion in a humanity corrupt to its very root. All authority, even the most tyrannical, is legitimate and divine, and the Christian must be altogether submissive thereto. No insurrection is legitimate. If their Prince is a tyrant, it is because the people have deserved this by their sins. At the same time that he disarmed the individual in the face of the civil power, Luther removed the counterpoise of the Church's power. The priesthood—that is to say, in the mind of the period, the spiritual power—is conferred upon all the Christians, but inasmuch as the mass of these (so Luther thinks) is stupid and passive, there is nothing suited to collect this power except a very strong organization: the temporal power of the State. By thus conferring upon them all power together with its spiritual consecration, Luther renders the civil governments materially and interiorly sovereign over the corrupt body of Christianity. He tends to give the State a direct competence even in what concerns the sacerdotal organization and religious life of the faithful. He affirms, indeed, that the Prince is not there to christianize society, for liberty cannot be created by means of servitude, but, that notwithstanding, he consigns to the civil rulers the function of repressing the evil propensities of their peoples and of getting out of them works that are *exteriorly* good, which same, in the hands of the astute politician, leads just as directly to Caesaropapism. Calvin in the same vein will affirm that the rôle of civil authority is to organize society and facilitate its ascension towards God, and he, in turn, will inspire Zwingli, the reformer of Zurich, to conceive the service of God after the manner of a warlike epic. The connection, we see, is quite tenuous that allows Protestantism to be bracketed along with individualism as an interchangeable term. Luther is the founder of a veritable religious totalitarianism. Pessimism, skepticism regarding the masses, political providentialism: it will suffice simply to secularize his formulas, in order to de-

[1] On the origin of the politics in question see Pierre Mesnard, "l'Évolution des idées politiques au XVIe Siècle," Paris 1936 (Boivin).

[2] One finds recurring in Kant this same disjunction between interior liberty and exterior servitudes, along with the same indifference to the latter.

rive from them modern totalitarianism, and it is not without reason that the Germans see in him the founder of the *Kulturstaat*—
the State that has spiritual ends for its proper function.[1]

Against these aberrations Catholicism has been protected in the
line of its central orthodoxy by the affirmation of a positive personal liberty which brands with the mark of unlawfulness certain impieties of the State and by the balance that the indirect
power of the Church affords to the expansive might of the temporal powers. Nevertheless, this synthesis was not formed in a day,
neither is its efficacy such as to eliminate from Catholicity all infiltration of the contrary spirit. To that history bears abundant
testimony.

One is justified in speaking of an "Augustinian politics," for
which, however, St. Augustine himself is less responsible than a
sociological crystallization, so to speak, of his teaching that comes
of an interpolation of theology into politics and consists in "a
tendency to absorb the natural law in supernatural justice, the law
of the State in that of the Church." [2] The Augustinian tradition
is known to be characterized by so lively a sense of all things being
encompassed by the grace of God that it tends to consume nature
in the devouring fire of supernature, the whole of reality in the
aspiration for *heaven,* without the possibility of anything being
withheld. If the person no longer has any immediate interest or
any mode of reality other than his aspiration after God, there is
no further place at all for the profane and its government. The
State is directly subordinate to the ends of the contemplative life
and dedicated to the salvation of its subjects, for the advancement
of good and the suppression of evil. It becomes an appendage of
the Church—force at the service of the spiritual power. This min-
isterial conception of the secular power was foreign, as M. Arquilliere rightly remarks, to the Apostolic age, which, preoccupied
exclusively with supernatural justice, did not dream of applying
this to public life, and did not, even after Constantine, know the
State from the spiritual point of view otherwise than as something
to be resisted whenever it sought to impose its own official worship, though preaching, on the other hand, absolute respect for it

[1] In pointing out this kinship, I fully realize what caution should be exercised in
assigning historical filiations in the case of over-mastering thoughts. No doubt ten
thoughts vied with this one in the mind of the stormy Luther. Nevertheless, there
are certain ponderables that even in the simplification of a doctrine precipitate
something of its essence.

[2] Arquilliere, *L'Augustinisme politique* (Paris, Vrin, 1934).

within its proper domain, after the example of St. Paul. It is to Gregory the Great, towards the end of the VI century, that we owe a conception that was to dominate supremely the early Middle Ages. It is he who conceived and set up the Christian Empire, in which the Emperor is charged with the duty of protecting the Church and of propagating the faith;[1] the temporal power, Isidore of Seville will write in the next century, would not be necessary "if it did not impose by the fear of its discipline what the priests are powerless to make prevail by means of the word." [2] The institution of *anointing* will incorporate into the Church the institution of royalty towards the end of the VII century. Soon after Charlemagne comes to make trial of the two powers in his capacity of faithful minister of the Papacy, absorbing the State in his sacred functions and preparing the way for the great era of theocracy, from the IX to the XI century.

Dammed up by the Thomistic synthesis and checked, likewise, by the rising powers (feudalism, later on, the States and the communes), the theocratic current will subside in the course of subsequent centuries and the Catholic doctrine of power will be established definitively upon different bases. But this past is of such weighty significance and is fraught with so much that is redolent of rude grandeur in the memory of the Church that, even to the present day, it has by no means sunk to the level of a simple matter of history. It is quite evident, on the other hand, that if, even up to the XIX century, a certain theocratic temptation, an excessive confidence in the mass salvation of the faithful through the authority of the State, still survived as living currents in the political mentality of Catholics, the heritage of Caesaropapism is claimed nowadays by that very secular power which but yesterday was clamoring for liberation. And it becomes plain that the Church, maintaining the permanence of her message through all the vicissitudes of historical Christian cultures and of the various entanglements of its faithful, now stands out in bold relief before the whole world as a bulwark of spiritual liberty against arbitrary power.

At the opposite pole, a fanatical conception of the sovereign

---

[1] He writes to the Emperor Mauritius *"Ad hoc potestas super omnes homines dominorum nostrorum pietati coelitus data est,* ut qui bona appetunt, adiuventur, et coelorum via largius pateat: ut terrestre regnum coelesti regno famuletur." (Lib. II. *ep.* 11.)

[2] Quoted by Arquilliere, *op. cit.,* 194.

liberty of redeemed man can devour the social contract and the
authority of the sovereign for the profit of a sort of religious anarchism. This may have been a tendency arising from a certain
Erastianism, which would explain the force of the Erastian tradition with a people of temperament so anarchistic as that of the
Spanish people. In any case, this antisocial prophetism, which has
more than once thrust its point into religious history, failed to
dominate Europe in the aftermath of its spread among the Be-
guards in the XIV century and among the Anabaptists in the XVI
century.[1] The Moravian Brethren, who blazed trails for the latter,
saw in the State "the prince of this world" anathematized by
Christ. They professed that it was unlawful for a Christian to exercise the office of the sword under any form whatever, whether
military or even administrative. To satirize it, they wore at their
sides a tiny saber made of wood. "The faithful are a people elect,
separated from the world," says one of their Polish disciples. For
them to participate in the government was to go back into the
world which despised and hated them. At the same time, for the
sake of ensuring this obligatory liberty, they hastened to set up,
wherever they were in control, an authority more despotic than
the one they opposed.

By force of their very spirit, these sects, along the road of religious history, have separated from a Church they looked upon as
having committed the sin of society and reinforced the temporal
power by her connivance and, at times, by her participation. On
the other hand, there are even in our times, especially in these
troubled latter years, certain Catholics addicted to this virtual
heresy. We note, at the end of the count, that not a few young
people of the present day, especially in the so-called democratic
countries, have been brought up on a species of political Jansenism which is now producing its unfortunate results. Does the reason for.this lie in the fact that the new powers were born in a sort
of persecution of established prerogatives of the Church, and that
this has had the effect of alienating from the State the sympathies
of Christian educators? May it not also be due to a romantic and
individualistic seepage into our idea of the "interior life," conceived as though it ought to be scrupulously shielded from the
defiling contact of works that are too practical? The fact of the
matter is that in these more recent years succeeding the First

[1] Regarding the political incidence of these movements, see MESNARD, *op. cit.*

World War the Catholic spiritual revival has only too often been characterized by the sentiment of non-politism, if not positive antipolitism, given overmuch to solitary and inefficacious protests of the individual or to the resignation of the catacombs, and that in the very hour of trial when it is a Christian's duty to be on the spot, to take up pick and shovel, to go to work upon whatever is actual with all the sound forces available in his day.

Catholic theology is just as far removed from this religious anarchism as it is from a spiritual totalitarianism. It has, as we shall see later, too keen a sense of man's condition, of his attachments and limitations, to let itself be seduced thereby.

Its definitive doctrine on political authority was formed in sequel to the long debates of the XVI century concerning insurrection and tyrannicide. We shall view it in connection with its most characteristic synthesis—that of Suarez.

The State is not an artificial corporation but a *communitas,* later one will say (Rommen) a "moral organism." From certain passages of St. Augustine it had been thought necessary to conclude that the institution of political power was included under original sin, even though it belonged to the condition of man only exteriorly and by accident. Suarez rejects this thesis. He admits solely that if there had been no original fall, political authority, which is from nature, would have been purely directive and not coërcitive. Much less was it suppressed by the New Law, as the "spirituals" believed; "civil authority remains the same under the law of grace." [1]

Neverthless Suarez is at great pains not to "objectivate" this natural community to the point where it would jeopardize the margin of inalienable independence of the person. He is loath to use the word *corpus* to describe it, for the term does not comport, says he, with a manifold of autonomous individuals endowed with free will. All political monism from the time of Plato onward (the imperialism of Alexander reputed to be the first of racist imperialisms, the Roman myth about the unity of *potestas* in the known world) is founded upon this primary aberration which posits perfect unity in a collective whole, seen as the object of man's strongest aspirations. Suarez prefers, when referring to political society, to speak of *persona ficta.* Moreover, this community is not a sort of exterior nature which came to be imposed upon

---

[1] *De Legibus,* c. V, 5—See MESNARD, *op. cit.*

man from without. To be formed, it requires a moral act, the
active intervention of united human wills. Let no one characterize this as voluntarism. The consensus in question is not, as
with Rousseau, a contract emanating exclusively from the individual wills and creating a collective being *ex nihilo;* it is a free
and creative adhesion to a natural necessity having a structure
already marked out prior to said act, but waiting upon it for a
consecration and efficiency it could not otherwise possess. In short,
this "adhesion" is wholly out of accord with alienation and regi-
mentation; it is given on the model of the personal act dealing
with certain realities or with certain prerequired conditions. We
come across a quite similar perspective in the researches currently
conducted with a view to substituting an institutional conception
of public law for the contractual conception, and (in a less fixed
perspective) for the purpose of determining the origin of "social
law" (Gurvitch) which remains the law of a world of free wills
without being grounded upon their arbitrary caprice.

The person finds himself protected thereby on three sides, in his
relations with the public power.

The assignment of the State's purpose is for him a first guarantee. This is due to the recognition by Thomistic humanism, now
renascent, of a "nature" at once individual and collective which,
though intimately subordinated to the supernatural (that is the
inalienable legacy of Augustinianism) has, nevertheless, a value
of its own and constitutes a sort of determinable order, even if
unachieved and open.

Anent the philosophical formulation of this notion and anent
the objections purporting to invalidate it, more than one reservation may be made. Since the vital articulation of the natural
with the supernatural order is so much the less rigid the more we
forget God's image or traces in the "natural" order to see there
one object among the rest, we are implicating ourselves in plant-
ing that naturalism which led, by way of a progressive lowering
of level, from the Christian jurinaturalists to the completely secularized vision of the XVIII century. But we may not materialize
this reasonable "nature" into a universe existing for itself. It behooves us rather to see in it an intermediate sphere—a universe
of union between animality and spirituality. This is the domain
proper of law.

It is to its order that the State and purpose of the State are
relevant. The State is not a minister of God. It is a natural society

destined to ensure a common temporal good. In all things else its power is illegitimate. Its end is not the supernatural happiness of persons but their political happiness; for spiritual perfectioning is an interior action that cannot be assured from without.[1] No more does its end absorb the all of human persons. And so we may point out two sources of totalitarianism. The State can only remain autonomous while leaving persons transcendentally free upon condition that it pursues an end of its own, albeit subordinate to the absolutely last end of persons: the conservation of exterior peace and legal justice, meaning thereby the justice that concerns the realization of the common good. "It does not directly make good men, but good citizens." [2] And if the "good citizen" is liable to smother the Christian, if he tends to mistake utility for justice, tranquillity for order, and a sort of inherited conformism for the spirit of obedience, that is only by way of a lapse, which however easy it be to make, is not in the nature of a fatal necessity.

If the Church, at certain times, has not been proof against abusing its temporal and even its indirect spiritual power, it is only fair to point out how well the control and moderation she has always exercised over the spiritual—through the indirect power she claims over the activities of State—have served the cause of human liberty. Against the arbitrariness of Princes and their legists who in later times turned this to good account in the service of their respective nationalisms, then, at a still later date, against the arbitrariness of the masses, the Church will struggle at once for the liberty of the individuals and for the religious and spiritual cohesion of the nations, in default of a Christian culture which has disappeared. The latest testimony thereto is the farsightedness with which Pius XI pronounced, within the same week, his anathema against Nazism and against Communism.

Medieval Christendom was only a first approximation of this universalism. New historical realizations are possible after the disorder of four or five past centuries which has marked the enfranchisement of the modern nations and of the citizens in the bosom of those nations. All personalism implies a certain institutional pluralism whose task it is to preserve the cohesion necessary

[1] St. Thomas, *S. Th.*, Ia IIae, q. 3, a. 2 ad 3, and *Comm. Eth.*, N. 13. "The public power not only does not have in view as its particular end their supernatural happiness in the future life, but it does not even pursue directly the spiritual happiness of its members in this life"—SUAREZ, *De Legibus*.

[2] "Lex ergo civilis facit bonum civem sed non simpliciter bonum virum" (*De Legibus*).

to the City through a flexible adaptation to the single families of the spirit that goes to constitute said City. Our epoch stands in need of a new St. Thomas or a new Suarez to solve the difficulties which the theology of this new City raises. We do no more here than point the way and designate its place.[1]

In fine, though Catholicism does indeed profess that the liberty of the person is at once limited in its nature and wounded in its exercise by original sin, it cannot but be solicitous for whatever can heal and raise up that stricken dignity. Every time we hear a man nominally Catholic reacting skeptically to any mention of the word liberty, we scent a trace of that Jansenism (still far from dead in France, for example) which lurks in the outskirts of Catholic sensibility, like a dilute but chronic touch of Lutheran contamination. On the same order of a miserly view of God's work in human hearts are the false prudences, the pusillanimities and the steps taken out of time. The Christian view of the development of civilization sees in it at bottom a progressive apprenticeship for liberty in an unremitting effort to enlarge the conditions of its exercise. All real advances in this direction (as distinguished from accommodating shams like the liberal "liberties") are so many spiritual achievements. St. Thomas describes and condemns under the name of "servitude," a state not far removed from Marx's "alienation," in which the one who is in control turns to his own account the authority he wields, treating the man under him like a chattel or

---

[1] Jacques Maritain, in his *Humanisme Intégral*, has made a first attempt. The unity of such a City, according to him, will be real, in contrast to the liberal City, but "minimal," in the sense that it is situated in the life of the person on the plane of the temporal and not at the level of his spiritual interests. Hence, it does not require *of itself* unity of faith or of religion, and may incorporate non-Christians. Dogmatic tolerance is a contradiction in terms, but it is not to be confounded with civil tolerance, which will be inserted into the setup of such a City. Nevertheless, it has an ethically and definitively religious specification "inasmuch as the religious element impregnates the political specification itself," from within, and not by way of dogmatic conformism. But it differs from the medieval City or from a City decoratively Christian, in that it admits of certain internal heterogeneities and aims at giving only "a general sense or direction, an orientation of the ensemble." It is impossible to unite men upon a philosophical minimum. Hence, to seek the unity of the social body in a profession of faith is a project that will have to be abandoned.

On the other hand, the simple unity of friendship does not suffice to give it a form. This form must be *vitally* Christian, understanding by this "a City intrinsically vivified and impregnated by Christianity," but with different strata impregnated in differing degrees of intensity, some of them, it may be, rather slightly, the non-Christian families enjoying a just liberty.—Certain of M. Maritain's critiques have further extended the frontiers of pluralism.

tool designed for his own special use.[1] Between the XIII and the XVI century Catholic theology brought to the stage of precise formulation a doctrine now classic on the right of insurrection and the licitness of tyrannicide under urgent circumstances and with all the safeguards taken: that is to say, authority, not having for its proper end the final vocation of persons, automatically destroys itself whenever it attempts such control. And thus, in determining the relations between the private Christian man and the public powers, we come back again to the tradition of the Apostolic age, made precise as the result of fifteen centuries of vicissitudes and reflection. If the "democratic liberties" have aroused a strong suspicion in the minds of not a few theologians—be that because of the political or ideological affiliations of certain of them, or because of the questionable philosophies and the shaky institutions to which they traditionally adhered—the great dramas of Western civilization enacted during the last several years have shown clearly enough on which side the mind of the Church is ranged when questions are raised regarding the fundamentals underneath the surface of an epoch, irrespective of the political preferences of the individual.

It is doubtless superfluous to recall, in conclusion, what an invaluable interior safeguard an authentic Christian formation opposes to the idolatries of the tribe, the embroilments, the organized violences that pave the way for totalitarian enterprises. Where he does subordinate himself, the Christian does not yield himself up to an impersonal something or to a non-entity—to that "totalization of nothingness" in which Bakunin sees the sole reality of God. He yields himself up to a Person who has said to those who accept His service: "He that is the greatest among you shall be your servant," and: "I will not now call you servants . . . but I have called you friends." He devotes himself to a Person who addresses to him the call to develop within himself, beyond anything human hope might expect, a participation in God's own liberty, and who in the course of history gradually educates him by a pedagogy of preparations, of advances, of developments, exactly opposite to the issuance of a behest.

To liberalism and the totalitarian spirit Catholicism opposes an attitude made up of two constituents, of whose need and solidarity

[1] See Maritain, *Humanisme Intégral.*

historical consciousness may not have taken simultaneous cognizance, but which are nonetheless inseparable: a total commitment
in a continual liberation.

VI

A man went down from Jerusalem to Jericho

All the foregoing analyses go to make us associate with the idea
of person the image of openness, of acceptance. They radically
conflict with all the imitations of personalism under cover of which
an individualism, amended but not transformed, might re-establish
itself. They thereby lead us to where a new fundamental perspective of the Gospel opens: the revelation of our neighbor.

Let us start out once more from the world of the impersonal
"one," to which previous reference has been made, but this time in
a new direction. In that world men are shorn of their personal
being and degenerate into so many objects. It would seem as
though all nature were sapped by this deadening temptation to
dissolution, by this discouragement of the drive impelling life to
meet a divine idea.[1] The effort by which I free myself from this
death and make headway against the drag of its inertia may seem
to some as nothing more than a singlehanded and desperate resistance. Antiquity knew of it only as something that was itself
offspring of spiritual death—the aristocratic knowledge of self or
stoic staunchness in the face of Destiny; it does not disclose itself
as a foretaste of the New Law except in the extremely pure note
of friendship that from time to time breaks in upon its solitude
in the form of forgiveness.

Is that all there is to the Christian message? A first glance might
lead one to believe so. After the passing of a primitive Christianity,
of whose profound reality we still do not always discern the appearances, the Christian tide has largely ebbed from the modern world,
leaving behind a situation worse in many respects than the one
preceding its advent, denial involving so much more malice than
ignorance. On the one side, there has been set up in its kingdom
—in consequence of liberalism, of legalism, of the pitilessness of

[1] A young essayist, René Caillois (*Le Mythe et l'Homme,* Gallimard 1938),
has even wished to see a first glimpse of this temptation in animal mimicry, which
so interpreted would not be a fact of adaptation, but an expression of "the instinct
of death," a tendency of life to be re-absorbed in uniform space.

the economic struggle, of the multiplication of intermediaries between man and man—indifference, blindness on so many points in
the beings that compete with one another, in the dramas that pivot
upon its import. Along side of this and perhaps on account of it, by
way of a resentment of love in dry souls unconscious of their own
thirst, we have: the proliferation of hate—hatred of one's neighbor,
class hatred, party hatreds, national hatreds, ideological hatreds.
The mechanisms of alienation and of self-mystification, described
by Marx, Freud, Scheler, go hand in hand here with the diagnosis
given by Christian ethics. The sinner, burdened with his own
guilt but unaware of it, feels an obscure need to acquit himself of
it and to lay the blame on somebody else, flattering himself the
while on being personally innocent. He then proceeds to saddle
accountability for it upon his neighbor, his father, his son, a social
class, a nation, a myth, and happy at being able to attribute his
misfortunes to a fault in which he himself has no share, he spues
forth his hate (hatred born of sheer bad humor) against this
bloated visage of the masks that clutter up his inner self.

A theorist of National Socialism, Karl Schmidt, speaks of the
ability to detect one's enemies as the fundamental factor in the political instinct. Reversing this formula, we may say that the ability
to discover one's neighbor is the fundamental factor in Christian
life. Oh dangerous banality of the worldly formula! Is there need
to recall this other as the former in reverse? "And one of them,
a doctor of the law, asked him tempting him: Master, which is the
great commandment in the law? Jesus said to him: Thou shalt love
the Lord thy God with thy whole heart, and with thy whole soul,
and with thy whole mind. This is the greatest and the first commandment. And the second *is like unto this:* Thou shalt love thy
neighbor as thyself." This means that the man who crosses my path
is nevermore to figure as the opaque movable nonentity to which
the man of indifference reduces him, neither is he to serve as that
receptacle of my spites and butt of my disappointments which he
becomes for the man of hatred—but he is, to speak properly, a
sacramental host, a wayside miracle, an incognito presence of God,
a "temple of Jesus Christ." Nay, even to define him thus as a separate reality outside of me, no matter how lofty that reality may
be, is to picture badly the revelation of one's neighbor. His reality
is not merely himself, face to face with me, it is *we two;* it comprises the bond uniting us in one single spiritual flesh within the

mystical Body of Christ and that unique relation which I hold with a being of whom I no longer speak in the third person, as I would of a thing, but to whom I begin to say: *you*.

Hence it is not in any proud isolation, but in the discovery of this *you* that I come to know person and my own person too. The solitary quest of self, in that, on the very face of things, it deprives my spiritual life of a vital dimension, leads me but so much the farther away therefrom—towards the most deceiving aspects of my individuality. What is wanting to my search is the fruitful yet hard ascesis of understanding someone else, the apprenticeship of love, the acquaintance with liberty experienced no longer as vague spontaneity, or as joyous amplitude, but in the form of resistance and appeal.

It is no longer sufficient to say that experience of one's neighbor is a fundamental factor in Christian life; it is its prerequisite condition. And it is the principal domain of the life of the person which it discloses to us. It is none other, too, than the domain of religion. Religion, writes Gabriel Marcel, begins wherever I transform a *him* into a *you*. He adds: "If an empirical *you* can be converted into a *him*, God is the absolute *you* who can never be converted into a *him*." [1] If the supreme vocation of the person is to make himself divine by making the world divine, to personalize himself supernaturally by making the world personal, his daily bread henceforth is not to give pain, not to divert himself, or to accumulate external goods, but hourly to make neighbors on every side. His everyday demeanor may nevermore wear the semblance of refusal, of irritation, of assertiveness, of hostility, or even of coldness and reserve; it must be one of availability, acceptance, presence, responsiveness, understanding, of welcoming. We have seen that overdevelopment of self is the cause of unavailability; Christian charity is "presence, absolute availability" (G. Marcel), a never-ending crusade against indifference and hate.

VII

The Condition of Man

Crusade, awareness of the absolute. Does Christian personalism resolve itself into quixotism? One of the most intoxicating temptations for men on their first contact with the Christian impetus, so

[1] This dialectic of the *you*, as is well known, is common to several contemporary thinkers, such as Scheler, Buber, Gabriel Marcel.

completely have they misunderstood it, is to lose sight of the concrete condition which assigns to this impetus its measure, its field
of action, its tempo, which invests it with fleshly presence. The
Middle Ages gave birth periodically to sects of illuminati who
believed in the imminence of the Parousia or of the advent of the
reign of the Holy Spirit, a third age of history, which to tell the
truth won ascendancy over the time in which the New Law reigned
supreme in hearts and in States. Doubtless it is better to be intoxi-
cated with hope than to content oneself with indifference. But
such enthusiasms generally go wrong for want of a point of application; charity gets mixed up with all the sinister motivations of
the spirit and the flesh, and this double tumult upsets the equilibrium of the spiritual organism.

Between this illuminism and certain less turbulent temptations,
there is no essential difference. It is significant that by the very
force of things we have already written nearly everything that it
remained for us to say. We could not have blocked out what I
would call the person in expansion, the exertion entailed by its
transcendence and its impetus towards the eternal, without determining *at the same time* the situations which fetter it and weigh
it down. This is what has already led us to take account of the
havoc wrought by a certain temptation of purity to desert at the
moment when, misunderstanding the condition of man, the human person ventures out into the *no man's land* that lies between
man and God, and from which man is absent, without any way
to meet Him of whom we have been told that He dwells in the
most intimate depths of our flesh and in the tabernacle of our
neighbor.

The word "absolute" is liable to mislead us here.

The person is, by God's creative will, an absolute in the sense
that, because of the model it is expected to imitate and the
ontological perfection it is thereby called to realize, it is "that
which is most perfect in the whole of nature"—perfection that the
life of grace will further elevate to the infinite. Person is such that
not only is nothing in nature able to prevail against it, but even
God Himself, once He has invested it with its supereminent perfection and power, as something akin to Himself, binds Himself
by the very fact of creating and redeeming it, with the result that
He cannot either annihilate it or treat it any other way than as a
person.

But it is not an absolute in the sense of its being emancipated by

virtue of this supereminence from all servitudes—from the fetters
of time and place—and called to realize its capabilities instanta-
neously and independently of all conditions. The human person
is placed, ontologically and historically, in a certain situation that
forms part and parcel of its very definition as well as of its ultimate
capabilities. A personalist ethics, a personalist politics and their
corollary, a personalist anthropology, cannot be formulated otherwise than in terms of this situation, apart from which we lose contact with the real and in so doing frustrate our effectiveness.

Thus the concrete existence of the person is particularized on
two scores: on the score of its ontological status and on that of its
historical status.

*

*   *

What is the first thing that Christian anthropology tells us?

It begins by affirming, in virtue of man's free creation and election by God, the transcendence of person as regards its empirical
conditions. Nevertheless, its condition as creature subjects the
person to an infinite reality that transcends it, upon whom it depends, by whom it is sustained. Concerning the relations of the
twain, Christian thought is not unanimous but varies between
certain limits, as the divergence between the Augustinian and
Suarezian traditions bears witness. The fact remains that all Christian philosophy must needs recognize the utterly miserable condition of our intelligence and our sensibility—of our action.[1]

To this primary dependence is added, thanks to the tearing apart
of my personal life by the tug-of-war between its transcendence
and its concrete attachments, an element of discomfort and of
ontological anguish that constitutes one of the essential themes of
religious reflection, from the time of Pascal down to that of philosophers like Kierkergaard, Heidegger and Jasper. Such are the
ontological limits that obstruct the indefinite expression of the
person's aspirations. To endure God without being able to be God,
that perhaps is the first acceptance demanded of man.

This flaw is accentuated in the situation created for man by

---

[1] St. Thomas, although he is, among all Christian philosophers, the one who takes
the most optimistic view of our natural powers, when he comes to assign the human
intelligence its place in the immaterial universe, says that it only participates in
intellectual nature "infimo et debilissimo modo" (*De An.*, a. 15), that its condition
of being in a state of total privation as regards its object, gives it in said immaterial
universe a position comparable to that of prime matter in corporeal nature. (A. 7.)

original sin. One might say to those who are most shocked about this question: Tell me what is your conception of sin, and I will tell you what your politics are. The doctrines that ignore sin base upon an immoderate optimism their politics of unlimited confidence in the free play of human activity. Condorcet is the prototype of such schools of thought, and we all know what influence the myth of infallible and indefinite Progress has exercised for the past two centuries upon the development of liberalism and of socialism, both blood-brothers upon this point. On the other hand, the doctrines that take as their starting-point a thorough-going pessimism regarding man, such as Lutheranism, the philosophy of Hobbes, and the systems of most political authoritarians, seek in the iron-handed might of a ruthless authority the antidote for this constant danger from the anarchy that seethes within the human animal. In the Christian's private life, Lutheran pessimism severs the bond connecting piety with morality, handing over to the devil the entire domain of moral activity and works. In like manner, it anathematizes any work of Christian society that might be, if not the established realization of a "temporal Christian order," at least the effort to ingraft the Christian spiritual in the temporal: the Evangelical ignores the law of man even as he ignores the works of man; he leaves it to the will of the mighty.

Catholic anthropology is not, as the attempt is sometimes made to present it, a synthesis, a sort of middle ground between these two utopias. To be explicit, it is by way of opposite perversions of what it really contemplates that social optimism and social pessimism have arisen. The man whom it presents to us is a being whose nature has not been so radically vitiated as not to be capable of sound and meritorious acts. He does, nevertheless, suffer from a deep ontological wound that affects his inmost nature, that strips him of the supernatural gifts which were intimately ingrafted in him before the fall and leaves him stricken even in his natural attributes with a weakness only grace can heal.

This theology rules out all the utopias of moral and social optimism, and the Church's opposition to the democratic currents, in the course of the XIX century, was due in part to their having been bound up with these utopias. On the other hand, it does not envision a sad and morose civilization. It establishes a political humanism never complacent, but always open, for nothing of whatever belongs to man redeemed can rest content with the progress it has made along the way; it earns a credit for its activity to which we must beware of too hastily assigning limits. In each succeeding generation, along this slender dividing-line (whose concrete position is seldom apparent), we assist at a debate forever renewed between those who are more keenly alive to the really inexhaustible generosities of a nature made in the image and likeness of God as well as to the incalculable possibilities realizable through the working of the Christian leaven, and those who, prone to dwell upon the crippling of human nature and the small number of the elect in this world, remain painfully aware of the fragility of the structures we build, of the enormous power of evil, of the chronic weakness of man apart from God. The life of Catholicism, in so far as it is the leaven of civilization, consists without doubt in this tension between two temperaments, each of which must limit itself to that place in the system to which the living truth entitles it.

This practical debate is grounded on a theoretical debate concerning the idea of nature.[1]

"Nature is in the right," wrote Ramuz on one occasion. At least, a certain static conception of nature conceived as a definitive datum in which there is a strong temptation to include the too human and provisory features of acquired states, while rejecting as the heresy of "supernaturalism" any attempt to reassert the right of the Christian absolute to be uncomfortable.

The Thomistic notion of nature could lend itself to this too curtailed view, even though it is ultimately exonerated from responsibility for it. Thomistic nature has nothing, it is true, but what it receives from God, but once it is constituted and assisted by God, it contains in itself the sufficient reason of its own aspirations; for but one form can be united to but one matter, in such wise that when they are united, the matter "satisfies completely the appetite of the form, the form achieves fully all the possibilities of this matter," and that there results therefrom a "being complete, fulfilled, which no longer holds in reserve any further possibility of development" (Gilson): from here the transition to a thoroughgoing conservatism will be easy. That transition will be made by many theorists of "natural law" which, let us not forget, was in the sequel construed by the men of the XVIII century as being

---

[1] Apropos of this, see É. Gilson, *Le thomisme*; P. Vigneaux, *La philosophie au Moyen age*, Paris 1938; Labrousse, *Essai sur la philosophie politique de l'ancien Espagne*, Paris, 1938, and the recent work of P. Lachance, *L'Humanisme politique de St. Thomas* (2 vols.), Paris, Sirey, and Ottawa, Lévrier, 1939.

partially contrary to the revealed law. Separated from the God of *Abraham* and of *Jacob*, nature tends soon to spell itself with a capital *N* and to set itself up as a justification of the established order.

But this conception is not the only one to be found in Catholic tradition. As St. Bonaventure sees it, for example, nature has not received a *mise de fond* such that simply the general influence of God suffices thereafter to account for its operations. Therefore, it is far more open to the illuminations and the unforeseeable intervention of God than in the conception of St. Thomas. Its state, moreover, facilitates such things. In the eyes of St. Bonaventure, the union of matter with a form puts into play a dynamic composite, inasmuch as the form in question has in reserve certain virtualities—the seminal reasons—which the matters whereof it is possessed have prevented from developing and which are possible matter of a higher organization. St. Thomas, we should not forget, had to contend with the potent force of a pantheizing Aristotelianism, and in his case a somewhat heavy accentuation is, in more than one instance, to be explained by the necessity of delimitating for the creature a being, a domain that would suppress once for all its pretensions to be divine. St. Bonaventure, more concerned to prevent nature from ascribing to itself complete self-sufficiency, makes it to teem with shadows, with vestiges, with symbols and images of God, whereof God knows which are the inexhaustible and unforeseeable gems.

Two families of spirit, two families of thought, two families of politics, both of them Christian and Catholic, will stem from these two mother notions. According to the vicissitudes of their times, the theologians will erect barriers, at times against naturalism, at other times against supernaturalism. And each age will take up again on its own account, apropos of new data, the same bifid research, the selfsame unstable synthesis.

What the Church will always uphold of St. Thomas' "naturalism" is primarily the affirmation of Christian humanism, which is its soul, and she will maintain this against Lutheranism for which nature is a mass of perdition, against the Orthodoxy for which nature is, in itself, a process of corruption, as also against the "realist" politicians. It is a corollary of the idea that man's most daring constructions must rest upon a primordial soil, upon what is native. The rationalist anthropology of the XVIII century, which reduced man to a faculty of reason productive of concepts and machines, gave to that whole age a sort of spontaneous conviction that man's creative activity, whether of thought, of art, of technology or of action, is capable of an infinity of groundless combinations and that consequently no limit is assignable to its dynamism. Christian anthropology, even when it quibbles about the idea of nature and the content thereof, always retains something of St. Thomas' formula that "the voluntary has its foundation in the natural"[1] and that "it is necessary that something of the mode proper to nature should be participated by the will, as that which characterizes the prior ground (causa) is participated by what is posterior." Social institutions have always started with a nucleus of initiatives upon the plane of morals; explicit law with certain spontaneous customs; reflection with a conditioned experience. It is in this sense that a Catholic politics will keep on reminding the utopias, whether evangelical or rationalist, of the value of roots, of the importance of permanence, of the limits to dreaming.

Does this mean that it will always throw its weight into the scales against the side of imagination and generosity, that, in the march of history, it will content itself with discharging the functions of a brake? St. Thomas, of whom we too often forget that he was away ahead of his time, would be the first to repudiate such an idea—it is he who puts us on our guard against that "natural" and that "spontaneous" which is already a by-product of free-will, or at least of a nature previously degraded thereby. The innovators generally find their path blocked by those vehement apostles of "nature" and of "common sense" who baptize with these respectable names the ingrained habits of their age. We must never forget that, though it was able to incorporate in its altogether new perspective something of the Greek notion of nature, to a far greater degree did Christianity itself blaze the trails for the notions of creative liberty and progress (which in the aftermath were diverted and turned against it) and of which Antiquity had no inkling whatever; that it endowed the human intelligence with an unlimited range—with a capacity that extends to the whole of the knowable; that along with the power of love it introduced into the human soul a force for renovation and creation that, aided by faith, avails to cure disease and to move mountains. How shall we be able to assign offhand the human—too human limits—of the activity of those whom the First Letter to the Corinthians calls *Dei adjutores*, (θεοῦ συνεργοί) and St. Dennis *Dei cooperatores*—the

---

[1] *Sum. Th.*, Ia IIae, q. 10, a. 1, ad 1.

coworkers with God? Even the most "static" of the Christian anthropologies, the one of St. Thomas, is really far less such than would at first sight appear to be the case. We find him teaching that from the unity of a "nature" it is impossible to determine by a simple analysis the measure of its activity. Inasmuch as natures depend upon matter for their dynamism, it is not enough to consider what they are; we must view them in action in order to guage all their possibilities. How is one to set bounds beforehand to what such observation may reveal?[1] We do not know whether, before time gives place to eternity, it is in the designs of Providence to give his chance to a "superman" who would still be a man, and to make trial of us amid abundance, peace and the disappearance of all temporal terrors, or rather to allow the consequences of sin to gravitate towards some apocalypse. Nothing in the present warrants either the catastrophism expected by some or the millennium expected by others. Both are possible (and both might become the matter of experience), provided certain fundamental conditions of human action are kept intact.

To speak of the *condition* rather than the *nature* of man leaves, perhaps, more latitude for the indeterminable virtualities of man while affirming at the same time the permanence of a frame of action. Having defined the ontological data, it remains for us to determine the empirical data.

*
* *

Et incarnatus est. All Catholic theology, all Catholic daily life is solely intelligible in the light of continuation of the Incarnation. The Incarnation is not a myth exterior to history. A mystery transcending history, it nevertheless unfurls itself in the full blaze of history. The Incarnation is not a date, not a point, but the focus itself of the world's history, without limits in either space or time. Each day the Church extends it in time by her continued existence. Each of our acts is called upon to prolong its effects—more than that, even to collaborate with it after a certain manner. That the condition of man should be the condition of an incarnate being, nowhere does this result of reflexive analysis receive so solid a support from such possibilities of extrapolation as in the religion of the Incarnate Word.

The carnal condition of the human person, which not a few

[1] *In Boet.,* q. 6, a. 1; pars 2a, ad 4.

Christian theologians have misunderstood, is the dominant theme of Catholic thought and feeling. These are not only at variance with the Platonism of the Phaedo, for which the soul is accidentally present in this body as the helmsman in his ship, a corpse in its tomb, a prisoner in his prison; they posit that the only complete substance is the soul-body composite, a union as intimate as the inseparable commingling of water with wine—the soul and body taken separately being nothing more than what in Thomistic terminology are called "incomplete substances," from the point of view of the unity of the composite. All the realism of the Middle Ages, ranging from philosophy to that art rife with symbols and with truculence, has its root in this. We know how it was driven out of the modern world by that one of the currents of Cartesian thought which finally outdid the others in historical proliferation:[1] the distinction without any possible elasticity of a pure spirit and a matter reduced to spatial determinations—ruination of the realism of the Incarnation—came in the course of the following centuries to lose itself in two abortive adventures: (1) the adventure of a matter made exclusively subservient to technology and blindly developing an aimless potency, soon after made subservient by the passions calm or obstreperous, but equally ferocious, of comfort and of power; (2) the career of a discarnate spirit, without object, without memory, punctilious about its own independence, puffed up by the successes of science and technology and making itself over by mimicry to the image and likeness of a machine for turning out objectless concepts of a more and more subtle character; or else giving itself up to dreams originating at the level of the subconscious from the murk of the flesh it has disavowed; or just indulging in rhetoric.

The day that Maine de Brian wrote: "The 'I' is not an abstract substance which has thought for its attribute, but the complete individual of whom the body is an essentially constituent part," he was only reviving, unbeknown to all, the Christian tradition lost to everybody in the modern world.

[1] When one speaks of Descartes, let us forget neither the decisive and existential character of the *Cogito,* nor the *Lettres à Elizabeth* in which he writes that the distinction of soul and body does not suppress "the notion of the union that each one always experiences in himself without philosophizing: to wit that he is one single person, that he has together a body and a thought." It is proper, too, to distinguish the authentic descent of a great philosophy from the proliferation of its systematic elements for which nevertheless it remains responsible with a sort of secret responsibility, which seems to result from the moral responsibility.

"Brother body" (*Frate corpo*), St. Francis was wont to say of that which St. Paul calls the *temple of the Holy Spirit*. What Catholicism teaches me about my body—it is needful to repeat, so stubbornly resistant to the notion are certain unsound survivals —does not countenance the least trace of puritanism. The notion of "body," for the rest, in the current sense, in which one says, "my body," is not a primary notion of Catholic anthropology and spirituality. The primary idea has to do with the indissoluble soul-and-body composite; it is the secondary one that connotes under the name "flesh" that force of inertia which comprises no less the complacencies of "the spirit" or of the "interior life" than those of sense. My body can be borne with or even managed, but as an object, a means-of, an apparatus-for, and in that rôle it becomes the most unwieldy, the most opaque among my properties— the factor that darkens at one and the same time my perception of the things of God, my understanding of my fellow man, my knowledge of myself and my taste for the "personal." Or else I choose to keep it under control in the capacity of a helper in my effort at deliverance through an act which saves it and causes it to share in every dignity that I achieve. It is then no longer a slave; it then becomes wholly identified with myself advancing or falling back on the path of holiness. The dogma of the resurrection has no other sense. It is often thought of as a vague extra gift; it is pictured as the reanimation of an image; in simple fact, the resurrection of the body is the resurrection of the whole man, who as a whole has participated in the acts of salvation, and that salvation is not complete until it has attained to this culmination.

It is not only my immediate body that I employ in the activity of my person, but the entire universe which, as an annex of my body, I, so far as in me lies, enlist in the work of Redemption, or which I make use of against this. Just as I can betray my proximate body, by abandoning to the automatisms of matter that modest cross-roads of the world which it is my duty to save, so I can betray the whole universe by taking it for mere scenery shifted by mechanical laws—for an objective and indifferent spectacle. A good many Christians have become calloused to this betrayal, so docile are they, with the modern way of feeling, to the influence of scientific objectivism and to idealism. Let us, however, call back to our memory the cathedrals and the image-makers, that assumption of the vegetal world into an edifice of stone, from the decoration to the construction of the master members, those animal sarabands,

those ages of the earth in confrontation with the ages of life: they
proclaim a cosmic perspective of Catholicism that our theological
literature has not constantly improved upon, and to which we have
become all but insensible.[1] Just as an emergency or a turning-point
in our personal life often furnishes us with the key to our whole
past, so the knowledge of man permits us to invent as regards his
origin an interpretative hypothesis that gives insight into the
progressive concentration of the indetermination of matter in vital
spontaneity, followed by the power of choice, with a final emergence in the transcendence received from the Person. Let us
ponder upon that vast body which the universe presents to us.
With it, too, we are intimately mingled, from the influences of the
elements on our humors to the rhythms of life that throb beneath
our skin in unison therewith—to that film of organized matter
which we put to use in our own service. It was not by mere co-
incidence that Middle Ages in their flower produced St. Francis,
or that the century of social atomism was likewise the century of
physical atomism, or that Marxism gained a footing in a world
where the Cartesian matter, having absorbed back into itself all
divinity, reigned like a tyrant.

Tethered to a universe, I am also a being living in time. In time
baptized by Christ, to be sure, which is no longer comparable to
any other. Eternity, having inundated it through the breach
opened by the Incarnation, galvanizes it with a transcendent Presence that summons it from the four corners of history and focuses
it whole and entire, together with the individual span of each one
of us, upon Golgotha's act of salvation—the center of radiation for
the whole human universe. But this transfiguration, which it devolves upon us to maintain, does not warp time from its progressive nature. The Incarnation, which has given it an infinite elevation, simultaneously confirms time in its earthly reality. Certain
sects grow impatient at this flesh of duration just as others—and
very often they are the same people—grow impatient over our
bodily servitudes. They have wished the Incarnation and the
Parousia to be as instantaneous as a thunderclap, pulverizing history and its laggardly delays; and, in the belief that end of time
was at hand, they have gone forth into the fields to install little
earthly paradises, which they ingenuously made ready for them-

---

[1] It is now on the point of being rediscovered. Is it necessary to recall the poetry
of Claudel? Less familiarly known are the suggestions, still loosely-knit, but highly
significant, of a great anthropologist, Father Teilhard du Chardin.

selves. Certain others were not quite so oblivious to the accustomed condition of man, yet they were bent upon having their standing with the Divinity settled, not from time to time, but with proud forthrightness, through the medium of violent and infallible illuminations. For Luther, in the same vein, justification is a favor out of time, entire and instantaneous, with which duration has no more to do than works.

Catholic theology, on the contrary, as Peguy said in a phrase which has all his characteristic ring, is a theology of temporal salvation—*une theologie du salut temporel.* Therein time is not simply a support as foreign to what it holds as the lines he jots down in his manuscript are to a writer's creation. It is not a form of evil which it is the aim of spiritual asceticism to escape (Plotinus) or the duty of the act of freedom to deny with violence (Heidegger). It is, like all flesh, possibility of death and possibility of salvation. When it is saved from this earth, it is saved in the substance of the days and the hours.

This salvation, which takes away time's weariness and drag, causes us to love with a new tenderness that copes directly with the pangs of development, on the same plane and not in some imaginary world. This incarnate duration assumes its full meaning in the moral world: time, seen from below is a spiritual effort, the persevering adherence of man to his data, the fidelity which, from one deed to another, binds man to himself and to the unity of the universe; seen from above, it is God's patience, the mobile image of Charity, the divine act of confidence in liberty, or more correctly still, the substance of liberty; and seen from in-between, it is the longing of the world and of man for God, the vast process of conversion at which the mills of the universe are slowly grinding away. Until the day when it shall be definitively imported into eternity, time like all flesh enters as an ingredient into the upbuilding of the Universe of persons, and eventually, like all flesh, it will be assumed. From now till then, its servitudes engage me no less than its promises. "Be in the world as if you were not in it," but be in it.

We ought not to allow ourselves to be misled by these generalities. When we say that Catholic ethics attaches us inescapably to the universe and to time, we do not mean that it rivets our attention upon certain abstractions, but rather upon *this* corner of the universe whence I have derived my blood, my language, my parents, my condition, upon *this* epoch which has fashioned me,

upon this very date at which, the world not having ceased to revolve, nothing is precisely the same as it was a year ago or even
yesterday. *Adsum*—I am present. The ethics of the Incarnation
do not lead me to these data in order to anchor me in them as in
a goal realizing the ultimate meaning of my life; from viewing
things that way, it is a hundred leagues away, in defiance of all the
clogs of language, racialism, nationalism, provincialism, class consciousness, clannishness, or parochialism. It brings me back to the
here and now as to a starting-point, so to speak—as to a base for
revictualing and refreshment, cut off from which I would be as
one who has lost his way in a hostile country. It puts me back in
the general movement of the Incarnation: God Himself has
chosen, for the sake of saving us, to wear this individual body of this
particular species created by Himself, among all the legions of
spiritual beings existing and possible, in this corner of Judea; nay,
He asks for nothing more, in order to communicate Himself, than
this tiny fragment of bread. And you are reluctant to take your
post, here, now!

*

* *

Finally, society is a component of this flesh considered from
every point of view. We speak of it here as flesh, because it is no
longer a question of the spiritual relationship expressed in the *you*
or in the *we*, but of the temporal reality which stands to those
values in the same relation as my body does to the transcendence of
my person. The Thomists have frequently expressed the force of
this relation by saying of the individual that he is "a part" of society.[1] Is not the very use of such an expression shocking after all
we have said about the incommensurable destiny of a redeemed
person? We have seen how careful Suarez was to refrain from using
any expression suggestive of organicism when he spoke of the
relation of the person to the collectivity, out of fear to encourage
the coagulation of massive idols: is not this the direction that an
authentically Christian view should take?

The Thomistic formulas concerning the condition of man

---

[1] St. Thomas, IIa IIae, q. 64, a. 5: "Every part, for what it is, belongs to the whole.
But every man is part of the community: and thus, *for what he is, belongs to the
community* (homo est communitatis: et ita quod est, est communitatis)." See also
ibidem, q. 65, a. 1: "ipse totus homo ordinatur, ut ad finem, ad totam communitatem, cujus est pars." See also Ia IIae, q. 96, a. 4. Cajetan will even say (*De Monte
Pietatis*): "Partes civitatis sunt singulares personae."

cannot be correctly understood otherwise than by constantly pro-
jecting them upon the perspective of the Thomistic distinction
between nature and supernature: in another passage which takes
both these "orders" into account in this connection, St. Thomas
says that "the supernatural good of one single man is greater than
the natural good of the entire whole." This in contrast to the
fact that he has just remarked: "The good of the whole is greater
than the particular good of one, provided both be taken in the same
order." [1] The latter formula is inapplicable to the interior of the
supernatural save on condition of certain qualifications that radically transform it, for it is made perfectly clear that the image of
whole and part is wholly inadequate to express the relationship
between the Mystical Body and the persons who compose it, except in so far as it implies with respect to these last a certain limitation of condition. St. Thomas, on the other hand, does not hesitate
to subordinate the natural person and his individual good to the
natural City and the common good. If, in effect, the person, in the
absolute, is that which cannot be a part, let us not forget that man
participates in person under conditions much too needy for him
to be able to hold his own without the help of social life. In this
sense society belongs to his flesh, like the senses and the body apart
from whose mediation he would have no access to spiritual truths.
And in the former case the "part-whole" terminology accentuates
a helplessness more marked even than that of the latter.

Nevertheless, it too easily conjures up the image of crude spatial
inclusion to pass muster as the best possible expression. We have
already adverted to the perpetual danger that exists of materializing the nature-supernature distinction, unless one is careful to keep
before his eyes what is, perhaps, more fully presented in the theology than in the philosophy of St. Thomas, namely, the unity of
the Christian man. The indications given in this theology enable
us in more than one instance to unite organically what analysis has
distinguished almost to the point of separation. The "natural person," we have seen, is "that which is most perfect in the whole of
nature": is it, therefore, possible to include it statically in the social
organism as a unit is included in a number? Moreover, this "temporal common good," of which the good of the person is supposed
to be part, is itself no more than an intermediate end subordinated

---

[1] "Bonum universi est majus quam bonum particulare unius, si accipiatur utrum-
que in eodem genere. Sed bonum gratiae unius majus est quam bonum naturae
totius universi." (Ia IIae, q. 113, a. 9, ad 2.) See also IIa IIae, q. 152, a. 4, ad 3.

to the eternal interests of the person; [1] wherefore, it is no longer
a closed sum of persons, but a necessary taking-off place (hence
their dependence upon it) from which they launch themselves towards their sole and incommensurable end. That is why St.
Thomas writes that man (*homo*, it is no longer a question of the
redeemed soul) is not ordained for the political community "according to his whole self and all that is his." [2] Something, therefore, even of the "natural person" escapes social subordination
from an angle that St. Thomas does not as yet define, because in
his day Christian thought had not developed a sharpened consciousness in this regard, a state it did not reach till the time of
Vitoria, who will say that, even in the Church, the particular good
is not principally ordained for the good of the whole. [3] In this restored perspective, in this living organization of nature for supernature, that which was rigid became flexible, that which fore-
boded corruption became sound truth.

*

* *

This last example, if indeed we are minded to tie it up with
several previously considered points, enables us to lay our finger
on one of the cardinal difficulties of Catholic personalism, as well
as of all politics inspired by Christianity, and more generally, of all
politics laying stress on the philosophical or the spiritual. [4] The
administration of Cities is an art, which has its rules and must decide its acts from moment to moment upon the indication of a
ready reckoner of forces, of influences, of determinisms and empirical wills. A politics on the order of the one we advocate runs the
risk of furnishing for action only a set of extremely general and
consequently inefficacious principles, whose very generality will
serve as an alibi for all the realist politicians: what tyrant, what
conqueror has failed to advertise himself as representing "nature,"

---

[1] St. Thomas, *Q. Disp. de Virtutibus Card.*, a. 4, ad 3; *Sum. Th.*, Ia IIae, q. 65, a. 2.
Maritain, *Humanisme intégral*, p. 146; *Science et Sagesse*, pp. 245, 299, 304, 346-56.
[2] "Homo non ordinatur ad communitatem politicam secundum se totum, et secundum omnia sua." (*Sum. Th.*, Ia IIae, q. 21, a. 4, ad 3.)
[3] "In the Church, each one exists for God and for himself, and the particular
good is not ordained, at least not expressly and principally, for that of the whole."
(*Relect. secunda de potestate Ecclesiae*, n. 5. Lyon, 1587, p. 121.)
[4] Let us reserve the expression "ideological politics" for the politics that subserve
systems, and not give it to politics animated by an inspiration that transcends cal-
culating interests. The problem, posed by recent events, is to know whether it exists
for any purpose other than to serve as a front for practical politics.

good sense, or the rights of the people? Or else, should it desire to go farther, the politics in question will run the risk of indiscreetly intruding its normative elements upon the domain proper to the rules of political art, and of thereby bringing about a dangerous short-circuit between the authentic spiritual and the sincere temporal. The latter temptation has ever been that of the politics inspired by Christianity, and the reaction, perfectly sound and legitimate, against the positivism of *Action Français,* has taught as much to the most up-to-date of these movements, which interests us particularly by reason of its personalist intentions—the "Christian-Democratic" movement. Its one formula is typical: One is not democratic and Christian on the same plane. This is true, and certain polemics have quite unfairly ignored the fact that, after various initial confusions, this movement, or rather these movements have for the most part drawn, on the doctrinal plane, a sharp line of demarcation between the two orders. But this does not preclude that the sentiment of the majority among them was formed in an atmosphere somewhat vexed by the Augustinian reaction, and the Bondelian one at the beginning of this century, at the moment when certain unauthorized controversialists were quite free about fastening on men who did not deserve it the suspicion of being *modernists.* And these same democrats, who no longer say they are democrats because they are Christians, but whose political reactions adhere closely to the Christian life, are under constant temptation to tackle directly and to resolve a little hastily temporal problems by means of moral and religious considerations, instead of first making the necessary balance sheet of the forces in play, of the possible techniques, of political needs—a brief of the sum total of the data pertaining to the temporal order.

The generation which began to think once more in terms of Christian politics about the year 1930 is especially alive to this confusion. It does not believe that it goes wrong at the outset in abandoning that "eternal Augustinism" in which the Christian is always relearning the unitary existence of his faith and his resources against every form of naturalism. But it feels that, here as elsewhere, the thing to do is, by ruling out at one and the same time the two facile extremisms and the middle-of-the-road compromise, to re-establish the tension which universally conditions Christian existence. To restore and deepen in a thorough-going manner anthropology and theology which alone will give us the fundamental rule and last word concerning all action in the field of civilization; and then—without premature harmonizings, without unseasonable intrusion of the sacred, eschewing moralism, or any resort to mere verbalism for the sake of camouflaging an evasion of a difficulty—to learn one's trade as a man of action, a syndicalist, a representative, in the same way as any other trade is learnt, honestly and in tune with what is real. To seek to extract from what is thus historically given the maximum of Christian service whereof it is capable, but to set out with a clear vision and with truly angelic patience. Such is our realism. Let us not, however, present it as an evidence, as something we have; in the face of the questioning of this world, which already reverberates with dull rumblings, there is still nearly everything to do, both in theology and in technique.

X

THE STATE AND OCCUPATIONAL GROUPS
By LUIGI STURZO, PH.D., S.T.D.

THE STATE AND OCCUPATIONAL GROUPS

I

In dealing with the problem of the relationship between the State and occupational groups, we start from a firm principle concerning the natural right of man to form particular societies. This principle Leo XIII authoritatively applied to worker's unions in his celebrated encyclical *Rerum novarum*, when he said, "To enter into a society of this kind (particular society) is the natural right of man. . . . The State must protect natural rights, not destroy them." The demonstration which the Pope gave of this tenet sounded novel to contemporary ears, nor is there even today any lack of sociologists and philosophers who contradict it—but in its logical evidence the Pope's conclusion is incontrovertible. "If it (the State) forbids its citizens to form associations, it contradicts the very principle of its own existence, for both they and it exist in virtue of the same principle: namely, the natural propensity of men to live in society."

Indeed, there is no room for any doubt about it: both the State and professional groups, like all other societies having legitimate and useful ends, have the same natural source, that is, man's own nature, which is sociable and which needs, in order fully to realize itself, the reciprocal aid of individuals grouped together. It is passing strange, then, that nearly half a century later another Pope, Pius XII, should have found it necessary to repeat this teaching, which, though so evident in itself, is frequently misunderstood and flouted. He wrote in his letter to the Church in the United States on November 1, 1939: "Since man is naturally sociable . . . it is not possible, without injustice, to deny or limit the freedom to form associations in the case of workers any more than in the case of employers."

We now point out that this right flows from human personality, because it is this that realizes itself in society. Human personality, laid down as the source or principle of every human right, leads us to the true root thereof: reason, unfolding itself in understanding,

383

will and work—claiming for itself the complex and organic activity of social life.

Pope Leo XIII's thesis, belonging as it does to the best Christian tradition, was especially directed against two theories prevalent fifty years ago: (a) that the State was the source of all rights, and (b) that the State ought not to allow labor associations, as being opposed to economic freedom and individual initiative.

The two errors were not new; for they had sprung from the false conception identifying the State with human society as constituting a totality of wills and interests. Strange as it may seem, we perceive—going to the bottom of things—that both democratic-liberal individualism and totalitarian pantheism (Bolshevist, Nazi, or Fascist) have, as a common root, the identification of the State with human society.

For nearly two centuries Catholic thought has been free from this error. True, the infection of "étatisme" (stateism) has touched certain groups of scholars and politicians. That was only to be expected, for the prevailing atmosphere was bound to exert its deleterious influence, notwithstanding the wholesome currents of air and light that emanated occasionally at first and then more frequently from the Vatican.

The theory of natural law has saved some thinkers, even non-Catholic, from falling into the errors of individualism, or of State pantheism. But political experimentation has followed prevalent philosophical currents (which were not those of Christianity) and the historical process has been enormously influenced thereby.

Fortunately the practice of social life does not revolve undeviatingly within the logical circle of ideas, and the oscillation between the two extremes often leads to a historical resultant very different from the theoretical premises. Thus it came to pass that, although theoretically the State was conceived as identical with society, this identity was in point of fact never realized; for intensively no less than extensively, the forces of opposition to the State let loose during this period transcended the limits of the State itself.

To say nothing of the moral and religious forces that have played a rôle antagonistic not to the State as civil power, but to the ethical content of the modern State, the forces that have borne the brunt of the conflict with the so-called "bourgeois" State have been the economic and social ones; everywhere the working masses, be it under the banner of socialism, or of communism, or of anarchism destructive of all society, or of anti-State syndicalism, or of Christian-democratic leadership exhorting them to claim their just rights, have engaged in a struggle against the State. All this signifies that within the bosom of modern society a dualism has been born in view of which it has become impossible any longer to regard the State as the social whole, as certain theorists of yesterday pretended and some few still continue to do.

This fact in its concrete reality paves the way to a better understanding of that equivocal acceptation of the term State which has tormented modern society. The State represents the political moment of society but is not society itself; it controls public power but is not the whole of social power; it deals with economic interests but not with the whole of economic life; it formulates laws but does not create them; it is charged with the defense of the country but the duty of fighting for the latter is not incumbent upon it alone. The State is to be regarded as the political juridical organism of society, but must never be confounded with society itself. Were the State a perfect organism, no social factor could elude the consequences of the State's organicity and functionality. But since nothing in this world is perfect, though everything is perfectible, the State is never wholly efficient, but like every other social activity develops historically according to the dynamism of the forces operative within society.

Among these forces, fundamental—so far as the individuals and the social groups are concerned—is the accumulation of wealth and of power, the one of these generating, influencing, or limiting the other. It is indisputable, however, that the lust for power and the lust for riches keep society in turmoil influencing the governmental policies of all countries whatever their governmental structure may be.

Wealth and power are often, not to say always, united in the same class or in kindred classes, which sociologists speak of under such various names as the governing classes, the political classes, the ruling elite and so forth. As a corollary, the middle and working classes are, so far as possible, either excluded from power (in non-democratic regimes) or nominally included but really shut out (in regimes based on individualist and capitalist democracy). Simultaneously, and at every step, they are hampered either by State action or by economic competition in their effort to attain to a just participation in wealth proportioned to their needs and abilities.

Hence, the State, which ought to be the supreme political expression of all classes, is often controlled by powerful families, by aristocratic classes, by big business, by financial concerns, by profit-seeking bourgeoisie, becoming at times a veritable monopoly in the hands of these privileged classes. The theories that help to entrench privilege are well received. When Louis XIV originated the saying: *L'État c'est moi,* monarchist writers celebrated the divine right of kings. Napoleon and the members of his family found warrant for their prerogatives now in the rights of man, now in the rights of victory. The French bourgeoisie of the Restoration framed their own principle of liberty with a view to denying to workers the right to organize, though at that very time they themselves were organizing on a capitalistic basis, bringing pressure to bear on governments for the enactment of protective tariffs and the granting of bounties and privileges.[1]

Therefore, in any regime, so long as the working classes have no voice, direct or indirect, they will have no choice but that between economic oppression and revolutionary agitation.

This dilemma, historically, is only resolved through political organization with economic purposes. This, in fact, has been the

[1] In his *Quadragesimo anno* Pius XI has a very trenchant passage on the accumulation of capital in the hands of a few in a regime of free competition and of uncontrolled power. It is not out of place to quote him here at length:

"It is patent that in our days not wealth alone is accumulated, but immense power and despotic economic domination are concentrated in the hands of the few, who for the most part are not the owners, but only the trustees and directors of invested funds, which they administer at their own good pleasure.

"This domination is most powerfully exercised by those who, because they hold and control money, also govern credit and determine its allotment, for that reason supplying, so to speak, the lifeblood to the entire economic body, and grasping in their hands, as it were, the very soul of production, so that no one can breathe against their will.

"This accumulation of power, the characteristic note of the modern economic order, is a natural result of limitless free competition, which permits the survival only of those who are the strongest, and this often means those who fight most relentlessly, who pay least heed to the dictates of conscience.

"This concentration of power has, in its turn, led to a threefold struggle: First, there is the struggle for economic supremacy itself; then the fierce battle to acquire control of the State, so that its resources and authority may be abused in economic struggles; finally the clash between States themselves. This latter arises from two causes: because the nations apply their power and political influence to promote the economic advantages of their citizens; and because economic forces and economic domination are used to decide political controversies between nations."

On this question, see ch. I: "Possession and Power," of *Politics and Morality* by Luigi Sturzo (Burns, Oates & Washbourne, London 1938).

most salient development of the past century, having reached an acute phase when Leo XIII intervened with his *Rerum novarum*.

The economic organization of a country is not something that can be isolated, since it is inextricably intertwined with the political system. The two social factors—economic and political—are inter-related and reciprocally influenced. It is a costly mistake to believe that one can be dealt with and the other disregarded. Some Christian social theoricians have let themselves be ensnared by this error. Such are the so-called "pure" organizers of professional groups, conceived as entities existing "outside of time and space," with politics wholly left aside.

In the periods of the Communes of the Middle Ages, guilds of artisans not only had a corporate personality of their own (corporation), but participated through their representatives in the government of a free city or City-State, or of a Municipality subject to a feudal lord.

When the monarchs of the *ancien régime* narrowed the guilds to closed privileged groups, without any political significance, this entailed their inevitable sterilization and atrophy. Indeed, public and private economy developed without them and therefore against them. In the sequel, mercantilism, which was a necessary phase in the economic transformation of modern times, superseded the corporate system. The reason is clear: While political life, following its impulses, was broadening, surmounting class barriers and making room for the Third Estate—the bourgeoisie of capital, trade, and of small property-holders—it was impossible for economic life to be hampered by duties and tolls levied at every city or castle, by the privileges of guilds and their component families which excluded the masses of people anxious for work, by the feudal rights of landed aristocracies, by tremendous royal and ecclesiastical mortmain. Economic life in its turn had to be molded according to a new pattern and the forces resisting the change had to yield. This is the law of the historical process.

The guilds were accused of being what they had never been in their great past: a defunct institution obstructing life. But the accusation was true only of the emasculated form to which they had been reduced. The reformed monarchies of the eighteenth century, instead of rebuilding the guilds according to the needs of economic life and the development of political life, deprived them of governmental help. Thereupon they fell as a dead tree falls. But shortly afterwards the paternalistic and absolute State of the *ancien régime* in continental Europe collapsed, because the drive towards economic evolution had not been met with the measures required to free property from feudal ties and from the domination of primogeniture and mortmain.

Thus the divorce of economics from politics (and vice versa) created one of the greatest crises in history; a crisis which under different aspects dragged on into the nineteenth century because of persistent failure to recognize the law of solidarity between economy and politics, either within the State or in international relations.

For this second or XIX-century crisis economic liberalism is accused of being responsible, though it was rather a consequence than a cause. The actual cause is to be found in the disequilibrium between economic transformation and political conceptions. While international and intercontinental markets were being enlarged, contacts made easier and more frequent, production augmented, supply rendered more abundant and circulation more intensive, the political structure continued to be monopolized by one class—the bourgeoisie. To the aristocratic feudal landed régime there had only succeeded the bourgeois mercantilistic industrial one. The former, based on privilege, had regulated participation of the various social nuclei in this privileged system according to rank in a hierarchically-ordered society. The latter aimed at freedom (for itself) in order to produce trade and gain.

In this way political liberalism was born out of economic liberalism, and the two systems, present in variable measure, formed the social complex of the past century; not to the extent, however, of bringing about the total extinction of the past. In some countries, such as England, Germany, Austro-Hungary, Scandinavia and Switzerland (we are not here discussing Russia), many vestiges of the old regimes survived, while elsewhere, as in Italy, France, Belgium and Holland, almost every trace was obliterated. In Spain, impoverished by the loss of colonies and civil wars, there remained, as heritage from the past, social sentiments and resentments which were, and are even today, very strong.

When statesmen, sociologists, economists or ecclesiastics of the past century deplored the misdeeds of liberalism, sacrificing as it did the welfare of the then cruelly exploited working classes to the principle of liberty, they could see the consequences, but were not aware of the causes (so clearly analyzed since then by Leo XIII from the moral point of view), foremost among which was the divorce of economics from politics. The bourgeoisie, entrenched in its position as the dominant political class, was using liberal theories in order to forward its own advantage, and so created not the "liberal State"—which in fact has never existed—but properly speaking, the "bourgeois State." Freedom was for the bourgeoisie a one-way street, to be extolled, that is, whenever freedom was useful to itself; when, on the other hand, freedom was demanded in favor of other classes or, in some countries, in favor of the Church, it denied freedom, invoking the celebrated maxim: "The State must defend itself!"

No wonder the Marxian myth of the bourgeoisie and the proletariat as two struggling forces spread so quickly, and the theory of historic materialism was so readily accepted as the key to social dynamism. What was merely a transitory phase, caused by the industrial transformation, became with Marx and the Marxists the fundamental scheme of society. According to Marx, the way to overcome the division of classes was to foment the class struggle which would eventuate in a classless communistic society. The capitalistic bourgeois State and the proletarian communistic State became for many the opposing camps engaged in a fight for victory.

*
* *

Neither of these conceptions represented the real state of affairs; both were theoretical and polemical exaggerations of a reality that was gradually ripening toward a climactic crisis. To this process, Catholic elements did not remain extraneous. Pius XI underscores this fact when he writes in *Quadragesimo anno:* "In fact the Encyclical *Rerum novarum* completely overthrew those tottering tenets of liberalism which had long hampered effective interference by the government. It prevailed upon the peoples themselves to develop their social policy more intensively on sounder lines and encouraged the élite among Catholics to give such efficacious help and assistance to rulers of the State that in legislative assemblies they were not infrequently the foremost advocates of the new policy. Furthermore, not a few recent laws dealing with social questions were originally proposed to the suffrage of the people's representatives by ecclesiastics thoroughly imbued with Leo's teaching, who afterwards with watchful care proposed and fostered their execution."

The enactment of so-called "social" laws favoring Labor,

whereby European and American States, abandoning the "liberalist" economy, accepted partially the interventionist thesis, was not due, as some might think, to economic motives, but rather to a political fact of great significance. The formation of workers' parties in Europe, alongside of trade unions, of worker's syndicates and leagues organized under various banners—socialist, syndicalist, communist and lastly, the Christian-Democratic—had an important bearing: the workers were beginning to participate in political life in a constitutional régime and to act no longer as revolutionists and anarchists but in the political and legal arena of the State. The bourgeois parties deemed it well to subject their stand and their theories to a new examination; the very conservative groups themselves, whether for the sake of votes or out of mere snobbishness, posed in certain cases as upholders of the interests of the working class. At the same time there were not wanting disinterested men, humanitarian and Christian, who recoiled in horror before the conditions of the workers of that time and attempted to find a remedy.

Despite all that, however, professional workers' groups, whatever their name and shade, were looked upon with suspicion and barely tolerated. Social laws were thought desirable, but only if granted by the State (*viz.,* the bourgeoisie) and not if pushed through by proletarian associations. Consequently, the unjust laws against which Leo XIII had raised his voice, remained in force. Workers' unions were considered as *de facto* associations, not *de jure,* and as such they were subject to police supervision without civil and economic rights.

Gradually a new legal status developed whereby certain rights and duties of members and officers were regulated. The elaboration of this status has been a long, uncertain process, with unequal development in different countries, until with the end of the First World War and the institution of the International Labor Office there came recognition having international validity. Another notable forward step was that of giving a certain legal validity to collective labor agreements negotiated by unions.

It is not our task to write a country-by-country history of this development which lasted nearly three quarters of a century. It is enough to observe here that the help of the Church and the contributions of Catholics have played an important rôle in removing from the workers' movement the old anti-social and anarchical stigma, in tempering the Marxist revolutionary tendency, in piloting a section of the working masses of certain European countries into Christian trade unionism, in dissipating class prejudices and the false notion that class struggle was a real social necessity.

Thus the theories of economic liberalism and of political individualism, which had been used by the bourgeoisie to exploit their advantageous position in the mechanism of big industry, received mortal wounds when they proclaimed State intervention in social matters. At the same time, too, the "bourgeois State" itself was mortally wounded, and the workers made their first appearance in popular assemblies in the person of representatives or deputies acting in their name.

II

Between the end of the last century and our own day—a period which, roughly speaking, began with the issuance of the *Rerum novarum* and ended with the publication of the *Quadragesimo anno*—three problems were debated with reference to the relationship between the State and professional groups. Of these, (a) one was a juridical problem concerning the nature, character and extension of such groups; (b) the second was an economic problem: how to reconcile free initiative with the intervention of such groups and of the State in economic life; and finally, (c) the third —a technical issue: how to organize these groups within each nation and in the international sphere.

Catholic pioneers in this field and Leo XIII himself had great difficulty in making themselves understood either by the bourgeoisie, or by the working class. They were accused of wanting to resuscitate the past with its guilds and corporations, without taking into account industrial changes and the formation of great proletarian masses. The masses themselves, politically organized in powerful parties with socialist tendencies (some of them with an uncompromising Marxian creed), represented an international power and were not at all anxious to lose their autonomy by yielding ground to local guilds and mixed corporations. They had at their disposal the weapon of the general strike and of mass demonstrations (let us recall what May Day once meant in Europe and how the bourgeoisie trembled at its approach). Theirs was a revolutionary idea.

Two schools were then developed within workers' organizations: the *socialist* which made use of the electoral or parliamentary sys-

tems of constitutional regimes in order to come into power and set
up so-called State socialism; the *Christian-social,* aiming at a State
reform which would permit legal recognition of professional
unions or groups as autonomous class organs with a function intermediate between public and private economy.

The socialists for a long time opposed legal recognition of
unions because they did not want them to be subject to juridical
discipline that would fix their moral and economic responsibilities,
thereby eliminating the revolutionary influence of political parties.
On the other hand the Christian Democrats wanted their recognition and the granting to them of a juridical status so as to achieve
a peaceful and gradual evolution from liberal economy to what
they called "organic economy."

Facts are more convincing than theories. European socialists and
laborites had been gradually organizing unions, workers' co-opera-
tives, mutual assistance societies, and had been devoting hard
work and money to such enterprises, creating new instruments of
welfare such as housing projects, credit institutions, retail commis-
saries, obtaining for these purposes agreements with banks, municipalities, the State itself, for financial commitments and legal and
fiscal privileges. From then on they began to develop on an increasing scale a sense of responsibility for these enterprises, a desire
of capitalistic gain, a petit-bourgeois spirit of accumulation and
even a bureaucratic formalism.

It is enough to look at what the socialists had achieved in Germany, Austria, Holland and Belgium, Scandinavia, Italy and elsewhere to realize how many economic interests of the working
classes had been placed in their hands. A good many socialists continued to act as revolutionaries at party meetings and in the press,
but were careful to avoid acting in that rôle when appearing before administrative bodies which they sought to penetrate in
every conceivable way in order to gain as many advantages as possible; claiming for themselves, at the same time, the privilege and
exclusive right of representing the working classes and their
interests.

As the number and practical interests of workers' organizations
increased—even the Christian Democrats had organized throughout Europe a close-knit network of mutual aid associations, co-
operatives and leagues—the revolutionary flame subsided and belief in the class war declined. And while left-wing communists
and syndicalists continued to be a nucleus of notable strength, the

bulk of workers' groups were tending toward a "reformist" and "possibilist" outlook. The revolution was in the "creed" but not in the "practice."

After the war the International Labor Office was created near the League of Nations, but with an autonomous character. Among the many advantages which it brought to the workers' cause and to social order we must list first of all the legalization of workers' representatives from every country, meeting with delegates of the employers, through the intervention of a third party—the representative of the State. The manner in which the workers' representatives were selected is not above criticism, but we are interested, at this point, mainly in the ethical and juridical principle of a workers' delegation sitting at the same meeting on a par with an employers' delegation. During its twenty-four years' existence, the State-representatives of the International Labor Office have often joined the employers' representatives, thus putting the workers in the minority. At times, this was doubtless the part of wisdom, but one cannot help feeling that, on other occasions, such action represented a defense of class interest, to which the States acceded because of their solidarity with capitalism and their distrust of laborism. But, apart from the fact that no social organism is always able to overcome or evade the warping stress of personal interests, since perfection is not of this world, it can be said that on the whole the International Labor Office has performed functions of information, education, technical and social assistance of a high order.

Whether in consequence of events at Geneva, of previous initiatives, or subsequent developments, it is a fact that workers in every country obtained legal recognition, varying in degree according to the country. At the same time industrialists and landowners were reorganizing their associations and legalizing their delegations. When compared with the time when workers did not have the right of forming associations, the advance represented by the International Labor Office is striking, although, as we shall see, that development was, and still is, incomplete.

*

* *

The problem which came to the fore in many countries both before and after the International Labor Office was established—and which still remains unsolved—is that of a unified workers movement. In free countries not all workers are unionized. Unions

are voluntary organizations and there can be different unions because of political contrasts, technical reasons, or grouping of related professions. Geneva solved the problem by admitting as first
workers' delegate the representative of the organization having
the largest number of members. He alone had the right to vote,
the others being admitted simply as technical experts without
voting rights. In practice the socialist delegates had almost the totality of votes, whereas the Christian Democrats and independent
delegates were decidedly in the minority (the latter coming from
Holland, Ireland and in some cases from Czechoslovakia and Poland). Where workers' representatives from many countries were
admitted in public committees or councils, the same rule was
adopted, as for example in France, pre-Fascist Italy and elsewhere
in Europe.

Here again the socialist unions were nearly always placed in a
more advantageous position. This caused resentment on the part of
workers affiliated with Christian-Democratic unions, which after
the war promoted their own international federation with headquarters in Utrecht—with a membership of not less than 3 million
Christian workers in its flourishing period. The number would
have been greater had Germany, which had then an organization
of more than 3 million Christian workers, participated; but in
point of fact only 1,142,956 German workers were represented at
Utrecht and at Geneva. The same was true of Yugoslavia, which
in 1928 had 200,000 organized peasants; also of France with about
450,000 organized workers in 1938.[2]

---

[2] For the benefit of the many who are unaware of the importance of the Utrecht
confederation (dissolved by the Nazis after Holland was occupied by the latter), I
subjoin here the data for the year 1922. It was then that Fascism started the totalitarian movement which, among other consequences, had the effect of abolishing in
Italy all free unions, including the Catholic ones.

1922 MEMBERSHIP IN THE UTRECHT CONFEDERATION

Country	Number of Adherents
Austria	78,561
Belgium	200,202
Czechoslovakia	15,000
France	125,000
Germany	1,142,956
Italy	1,052,694
Yugoslavia	9,990
Luxemburg	500
Holland	199,095
Spain	42,319

Once Fascism came into power in Italy, it organized its own syndicates, suppressing all others, and then it went to Geneva sustaining the legitimacy of its own workers' delegation. The workers' representatives in the International Labor Office voted against the Fascist claim, but the State representatives and those representing employers voted in favor of it. This had the effect of focusing attention upon the limits of State intervention in the formation of occupational groups and upon the representative capacity of the latter in the political field.

State totalitarianism was bound to bring into the labor field the same revolution of principle and practice that it brought into the other fields of politics, economics and morality. It could not leave to the workers, after having denied them to all the other organisms of social life, either liberty or initiative. We shall return to this point later; suffice it to say now that the problem of a united workers movement was by no means solved through a law compelling everybody to pay his tribute to privileged Fascist unions. The socialists of continental Europe had always and everywhere aimed at a *de facto* monopoly. The Italian Fascists established a *de jure* monopoly.

In Anglo-Saxon countries a different situation exists. In England the trade unions are in fact the only workers organizations morally entitled to represent all the interests of the workers, and in the great majority they adhere to the Labor Party as being their own organization. The small group of four Independent Labor Party men in the House of Commons and the lone Communist member do not enjoy any real following among the masses; that, at any rate, was the situation before the outbreak of the war. In England, however, trade unionism, never a Marxist movement, has always been tolerant and respectful in religious matters, so that Catholic workers, too, participate in it and occupy responsible directorial positions.[3]

| Switzerland | 14,959 |
| Hungary | 113,855 |

The workers' organization of Ireland never affiliated with Utrecht; the British Trade Union Council (including Catholics), on the other hand, affiliated with the socialist Amsterdam International. As for the United States, there never have been organized Christian unions in that country.

[3] Catholic workers in England have a cultural organization of their own—the *Catholic Social Guild*, and their own newspaper, *The Catholic Worker*. This paper is not the organ of said Guild, but stemmed from *The* (American) *Catholic Worker* founded at New York in May of 1933. The Catholic Social Guild, however, does publish a monthly bulletin, namely *The Christian Democrat*.

In France and other European countries, even in free Germany and Italy of the past, where the Socialist unions were not only Marxian in creed but frequently anti-religious in morals and anti-clerical in politics, such a thing would have been inconceivable.

In the United States the first important workers association was known as The Knights of Labor, founded in 1869 at Philadelphia, with the characteristics of a secret and mystical association. This organization gave occasion to a well-known controversy and was saved from Rome's condemnation (demanded by the Canadian hierarchy) through Cardinal Gibbons' intervention with Pope Leo XIII. Nevertheless, the Knights of Labor went into a decline. The American Federation of Labor was formed at Pittsburgh in 1881. That was the era of craft unionism rather than of the industrial union, when the jealous preservation of the "absolute" rights of private enterprise, the frequent publication of black-lists, together with the *blackleg* abuses, were the order of the day. It was not until the beginning of the present century and even later—in the period of the First World War—that unions developed in big industry, strong in numbers and sympathies, so that the existing Administration was compelled to come to terms with them in order to step up war production.

The split in the labor movement is of recent date: the Committee for (now Congress of) Industrial Organizations has been growing into a powerful force antagonistic to the American Federation of Labor. Agreements between unions are difficult when, above and beyond professional interests, personal ambitions come into play. Anti-unionism in industry, too, was another factor making for discord; ever active, it tended to repress the labor movement which, on the other hand, was gaining in favor with the Federal Government and which, particularly after the *Quadragesimo anno,* succeeded in enlisting the support of a large section of Catholic opinion.

The American bishops as early as 1919 had reasserted the right of the workers to organize, stating that "it is to be hoped that this right will never again be called into question by any considerable number of employers." This stand was reaffirmed in 1933. The following year the Secretary of the Conference of American Bishops addressed a letter to the Chairman of the Senate Committee on Education and Labor in support of the bill "to diminish the cause of labor disputes" (which later became the National Labor Relations Act) stating, among other things: "From a practical standpoint, the workers' free choice of representatives must be safeguarded in order to secure for him equality of contractual power in the wage contract. Undue interference with this choice is an unfair labor practice, unjust alike to workers and the general public."

The strongest opposition to labor unions in the past has always come from employers, either in the form of discrimination, espionage, the yellow-dog contract or—what was still worse—by way of maintaining so-called "company towns" which placed the workers wholly at the mercy of the management owning all the houses, shops and public halls in the community. A certain section of the press, too, by seeking to arouse hostile public opinion, fostered this opposition to unionism. Thus, at the present day, in spite of prolonged efforts to organize labor in the United States, the total membership of the unions hardly exceeds 20% of the country's working class.

In 1935 the position of American unions was strengthened by the Wagner Act which guaranteed the workers the right to organize and bargain collectively through representatives of their own choosing and which described as unfair labor practices such actions of employers as tended to interfere with the workers' freedom in the above matters. The Wagner Act must be viewed rather as a defense of the right of the workers to organize than as a clarification of the juridical status of their unions. On the other hand, since the working class in the United States does not enjoy the backing of a powerful labor party as in England (or of a socialist or a Christian-Democratic party as in continental Europe before the advent of the totalitarian regimes, or of the war), the struggle for the protection of the workers' rights takes place not in the legislative assemblies but in the workshops. Hence those numerous strikes for the acquisition of elementary rights of association that have so troubled American economy. At present the workers have gained only a part of what must be theirs in an organic conception of the State.[4]

[4] American Catholic workers are members of national unions. They have their own association—the A.C.T.U. (Association of Christian Trade Unionists) founded in 1938 "to foster and spread in the American labor movement sound trade unionism based on Christian principles, first by bringing to Catholic workers in particular, and all workers in general, a knowledge of these principles, and second, by training leaders and supplying an organization to put these principles into practice." The present development of the A.C.T.U., whose New York branch publishes a paper called *The Labor Leader*, is very promising, and it may be added that the

*

*   *

The technical problem, given its national and international repercussions, the complexities of modern industrialism and the political nature of workers organizations themselves, was not one that could be solved *a priori*. Experimentation was the best way, but so long as the unions failed to attain a legal status, they continued their agitation on the margins of the law and political life, undergoing defeats which involved heavy losses to society. At length the moment arrived when, having obtained a *de facto* recognition and while still awaiting the *de jure* recognition, their character and functions came in for a great deal of discussion.

1. *Class representation.* As long as the union is a free one and does not represent a majority of the workers, can it be recognized by law as the legitimate representative of the workers in its field? Here the unions have met with opposition on the part of both the employers and the State (legislatures and courts), although exercising in fact, at least in particular cases, the function of total representation. But even today headway is not made without a struggle.

2. *Collective agreements.* If the unions represent the entire class, they can not only negotiate labor contracts with employers but validly sign them and see to their recognition, even before the courts, as binding and applicable to all the workers.

3. *Hiring of workers.* If the unions represent the professional interests of the workers and stipulate labor contracts, they must be

interest taken by the N.C.W.C. (National Catholic Welfare Conference) in social questions is very great and appreciated for its equilibrium and practical approach.

The fact that a good many workers are interested in union affairs tends to give union leaders a too powerful control over the unions and prompts them to demand real privileges, such as *the closed shop*. On the other hand, it cannot be denied that the closed shop is, in many cases, the only defense against employers' hostility. The question of the closed shop is a very difficult one from the moral, social and political points of view. This is not the place to deal with it. Rev. Jerome L. Toner, O.S.B., M.A., has written a dissertation on it entitled *The Closed Shop in the American Labor Movement*, published by The American Council on Public Affairs, Washington, D. C., in 1942 and previously (in 1941) by The Catholic University of America Press, Washington, D. C. It is very interesting and well done, though I do not agree with the author in certain instances. What is of fundamental importance is to combine the right to free association with the right to work. The present situation shows the necessity of better legislation giving the unions a well-established legal status together with a definition of their rights and responsibilities. The Smith-Connally Anti-strike Law, passed on June 25, 1943, is a wartime measure that does not meet the needs of unionism in America; indeed, some of its provisions show an anti-labor feeling.

heard in the establishment of regulations for the hiring and firing of workers and apropos of the conditions of employment.

As a result of these three fundamental claims, we witness, on the one hand, the disappearance of the free individual worker (who, in point of fact, had not been so very free) and the appearance of a collective bargaining organization. In order to temper its monopolistic effects, the *Social Catholic* school advocates a plurality of free unions rather than one single union. On the other hand, it becomes necessary to assert the rights of the employer regarding the choice of the workers, the establishment of working conditions and the application of the contract. Hence the necessity of mixed shop committees to effect a real collaboration for the protection of rights on both sides and to ensure the observance of reciprocal duties.

Gradually the common interests of both employers and employees in production has been acknowledged, and two practical consequences have followed: (a) the collective and permanent representation of both in organizations, having local or national jurisdiction, to protect the common interest of a given branch of production; (b) the growth of profit-sharing plans. The particular form of profit-sharing that the Christian Democrats have advocated has been stock-holding on the part of the workers.[5]

If economics could be divorced from politics, we might stop at this point. But politics and economics go hand in hand. If capital and labor were left to manage by themselves, the first consequence would be the creation of an intolerable monopoly, both in the sphere of production, where all competition would be suppressed, and in the sphere of consumption, where monopolistic prices would be exacted. Such a thing can happen even in a liberal regime in which we have capital monopolies with trusts and horizontal as well as vertical cartels. Inevitably society reacts—a crisis is precipitated; all political crises have in some degree an economic substratum.

The State is obliged to intervene in order to protect just economic freedom and the consumer. The mode of intervention in every country is related to the political and juridical system; the main thing is to assert the general interest of the community to

[5] The Italian Workers Confederation (Christian-Democratic) offered to the Giolitti government in 1920 a bill on workers' stock-holding, the bill being printed in the *Parliamentary Acts*.

which the particular interests of classes must be subordinated, thus putting a stop to selfish overstepping of social boundaries by any particular group.

On the basis of these principles, both Pius XI and Pius XII have outlined an ideal scheme intended to serve as groundwork for the solution of the technical problem of labor organization. Of relevance here is the following passage taken from Pius XII's allocution of June 1, 1941, in commemoration of the 50th anniversary of the *Rerum novarum*:

"He (Leo XIII) had no intention of laying down guiding principles anent the purely practical, we might say the technical, side of the social structure; for he was well aware—as our immediate predecessor of saintly memory, Pius XI, pointed out ten years ago in his commemorative encyclical *Quadragesimo anno*—that the Church lays claim to no such mission.

"In the general framework of labor, to stimulate the sane and responsible development of all the energies, physical and spiritual, of individuals in their free organization a wide field of action opens up, where public authority enters with its integrating and co-ordinating activity, exercised first through local and professional corporations and finally in the activity of the State itself, whose higher moderating social authority has the important duty of forestalling the dislocations of economic balance arising from plurality and divergence of clashing interests, individual and collective."

It is interesting to hear this restatement in 1941, in the full flowering of social and political totalitarianism, of Leo XIII's theory of free workers' organizations through the voice of his successor, the present Pope Pius XII. Leo XIII lived in an era of State liberalism when the rights of free workers organizations had to be upheld in the face of a theory that forbade them in the name of economic freedom. Today the selfsame fight is being waged against the totalitarianism of the State, which itself organizes unions or workers "syndicates" granting to these monopolistic rights. The Popes extend freedom of organization to the enterprises thus deprived of freedom in the totalitarian States. Hence, this affirmation takes on a cardinal importance transcending the contingent motivations of the times (whether of Leo or of the two Piuses) because it bears upon the sacred right of human personality.

In order to co-ordinate these free associations among themselves and in the general interest of production and consumption, there is need of a higher body. The Popes have named it, in the parlance of Latin countries, a "professional corporation." In English-speaking countries "corporation" would be termed a "corporate body." According to the Papal conception, the representatives of employees and of employers, plus the local or national representatives of public authority, would constitute such a "corporate body" which, for the rest, might very well be called even in English a "professional corporation." In fact, the Whitley councils in England bear a certain resemblance to the body in question. Such bodies or councils decide questions of a professional and economic nature as between labor and management, or producers and consumers. The function of representatives of public authority in such corporations must be—according to Pope Pius XII, who is repeating what Pope Pius XI had written—that of "integrating and co-ordinating activity," such activity to take place within the "local and professional corporations" (meaning both local and nation-wide corporations of each profession or branch).

We ascend in this way to the level of the State, the character of whose intervention Pius XII describes in these clear words: " (The State's) higher moderating social authority has the important duty of forestalling the dislocation of economic balance arising from plurality and divergence of clashing interests, individual and collective." Is this a defense of the principle of intervention as exemplified, for instance, in the American New Deal? Leaving open the question of whether the New Deal has been, in the concrete, erroneous, or incomplete, or too particularistic, the State's right, in the abstract, to intervene (actually exercised in the United States since 1933) is something that cannot be questioned.

*
* *

Thus it is evident that the teachings which uninterruptedly for over half a century have come from the Vatican have been directed against: (a) individualistic liberalism, denying to workers the right to associate; (b) the unorganic system of class struggle between capital and labor proclaimed by Marxian Socialism; (c) totalitarianism, which has created a syndicalist monopoly and a bureaucratic corporativism of the State.

The first of these three has today been left behind by the facts. The few theoricians that still uphold it are negligible. The diehards who weep over the past do so in the name of private initiative and just competition, which indeed should be safeguarded not

by economic liberalism, but by the social organic system as propounded by the *Social Catholic* school.

The second still exists in an endemic state occasioning social
convulsions, although nowadays the general feeling is that class
struggle represented a stage of transition leading to vanquishing
individualism as an obstacle to adequate organization of the forces
of production.

The third is the really dangerous evil threatening us today. Its
fate is now bound up with the outcome of the war and with the
fate of the totalitarian States, representing a conception of the
whole ethical and structural complex of society. But since ideas
germinate beyond the sphere of historical facts and since war never
kills an ideal, it is advisable to look into the facts as they developed
in totalitarian countries before the war.

We cannot analyze here the Russian system. In Russia the State
is at once the capitalist, management and master. All private initiative and competition having ceased, the class struggle has ceased
too. Workers associations have only the task of watching over the
working conditions (not the rights) which they discharge through
adjustments, petitions, protests—provided these do not, as is likely,
lead to harsh repressions. The reports we have on the position of
the working classes in Russia vary from a bland optimism to a
dark pessimism. A factual judgment appears impossible; from the
theoretical point of view, the problem must perforce be discussed
on the basis of the State system founded upon totalitarianism and
the abolition of all real liberty.

In Italy the Fascist government granted its syndicates a monopolistic position, barring every other syndicate from legally representing the workers—from the right to bargain with the employer
and to supervise the hiring of workers. Before that time there were
in Italy two great labor confederations: the socialists and the
Christian Democrats, not to mention a third of local import—the
syndicalists.[6]

These confederations fell under Fascist attack, although theoretically the law allowed their survival as private associations. In
1927, when Catholic Action promoted a social institute that classified its members according to their professions, the Fascist government protested, fearing lest in this way—as a study association

[6] The Socialists had 1,500,000 members, the Christian Democrats 1,200,000 the
Syndicalists 300,000.

—the White Confederation (this being the nickname for Christian Democracy) might be reborn. The Catholic Actionists were, of course, obliged to yield.

Pius XI referred briefly to the matter in the *Quadragesimo anno,* where he said: "The State here (in Italy) grants legal recognition to the syndicate or union and thereby confers on it some features of a monopoly; for, in virtue of this recognition, it alone can represent workingmen and employers respectively and it alone can conclude labor contracts and labor agreements. Affiliation with the syndicate is optional to everyone; but in this sense only can the syndical organization be said to be free, since the contribution to the union and other special taxes are obligatory for all who belong to a given branch, be they workingmen or employers. The labor contracts drawn up by the legal syndicate are likewise obligatory. It is true that it has been authoritatively declared that the legal syndicate does not exclude the existence of unrecognized trade associations."

This text is in reality a criticism of the Fascist syndicalist monopoly. The last sentence beginning with the words "It is true," was added not to omit the technical point the Fascist government advanced in its own defense, which made it appear a concession to the Catholics, but a worthless concession that in fact was meaningless. Coincidentally with the publication of the *Quadragesimo anno* there convened in Rome on May 15, 1931, a great congress of representatives of workers unions from many European countries. This meeting, which took place at the monument to the Catholic worker in the Lateran, as a tribute to the memory of Leo XIII, so irritated the Fascists that it precipitated the struggle to do away with the last trace of Catholic unionism.

Pope Pius XI himself did not fail to stress certain other criticisms which had been advanced against the Fascist labor system. In almost immediate sequence to the aforesaid passage he wrote: "But in order to overlook nothing in a matter of such importance, and in the light of the general principles stated above as well as of what We are now about to formulate, We feel bound to add that to Our knowledge there are some who fear the State is substituting itself in the place of private initiative, instead of limiting itself to necessary and sufficient help and assistance. It is feared that the new syndical and corporative institution possesses an excessively bureaucratic and political character and that, notwithstanding the general advantages referred to above, it risks serving political aims rather than contributing to the initiation of a better social order."

It would be difficult indeed in such a dignified document as a papal encyclical to pronounce a more serene, objective and measured criticism than this one by Pius XI. The full significance of his observations on the Italian *corporative State* did not dawn upon the public mind until today; but now, in the lurid light of the Second World War, men readily come to see how regulated planning and autarchy were the substratum underlying State corporativism, a system that had been acclaimed as the social system of the future, a system that some naïve Catholics had hailed as a return to medieval tradition—an application of the *guild system* to modern economy.

The situation in Italy was in brief as follows: The workers syndicate was a monopoly of the Fascist party, whose head was the head of the government; the corporation (a bureaucratic body, set up for every field of production and representing employers, employees and the State) and the National Council of Corporations were party and governmental monopolies. The technical functioning of the corporation and of the Council were subject to the political directions of the party and the political decisions of the government. Hence one single individual had the complete and sole responsibility for the country's economic life: the head of the party and the head of the government—one and the same person.

Discussion of the Italian "Corporative State" has gone on at great length without any attempt to understand fully its true meaning. We must bear in mind that in the course of the past century continental *Social Catholics,* in their opposition to the individualistic parliamentary system, had contended often that one branch of parliament ought to be representative of social bodies like the municipalities, the provinces, the universities and the corporations.[7] But it is evident that the invariable presupposition was that such bodies were to have their own autonomous directive councils, freely elected, and that they should be free also in the nomination of their representatives in parliament. The situation in Italy was entirely different. The corporations had

---

[7] In its 1919 program the Italian Popular Party favored the creation of an elected Senate (the Senate in Italy being at that time composed of royal appointees nominated for life) to represent local and professional bodies, the universities and other cultural associations.

neither free choice in the selection of their councils nor freedom in the nomination of their representatives in Parliament. Moreover, Parliament had no vitality of its own nor had it any legislative autonomy. Consequently, the whole elaborate façade of the so-called corporative State falls to the ground, unmasking the stark reality of the totalitarian State.[8]

In Germany Nazism similarly suppressed the trade unions that were in the hands of Socialists, Catholics and Protestants[9] and in May of 1933 confiscated the assets both of workers' unions and employers' associations. The system of collective bargaining was abolished as well as that of the labor councils—in brief, every form of social and economic representation.

With the National Labor Act of January 1934 every relationship between workers and management was put under the control of the State; the representatives of the State, the so-called "labor trustees," decide all points at issue. They must hear both sides, but under the "leadership principle" they are free to fix the collective regulations which have superseded the abolished collective agreements. On the other hand, both the regulation of labor exchanges and the fixing of wages is a State function. The State is empowered to dictate any shift of workers from one working place

[8] The opinion of certain writers that all political representation should be based upon economic bodies cannot be accepted, for the economic aspect must not be deemed the only factor of social life nor the sole exponent of the State's political life.

[9] In Germany there was a Christian trade union movement and also Catholic and Protestant workers associations, both collaborating very closely with the *Volksverein für das katholische Deutschland,* founded by Windhorst. The union of the *"Angestellte"* (white collar workers and higher employees) and the *Deutschnationale Handlungsgehilfenverband,* together with the Christian trade unions and certain associations of railroad workers, were united in the so-called *Deutscher Arbeiterkongress.* After the war, the *Arbeiterkongress* was supplanted by a permanent national organization, the *Deutsche Gewerkschaftsbund,* which in certain sections of private business had a majority, nay, totality of members and had succeeded in driving the Socialists out of many important positions they had held before. Its membership was over 3,000,000. Furthermore, there was a co-operative movement which was very successful, especially among peasants and workers of the Rhineland, Bavaria and Westphalia. During the revolution of November 1918 a central voluntary organization was founded to maintain constant close collaboration between the two trade union movements and the top organizations of German industry and agriculture. This was the *Zentralarbeitsgemeinschaft,* which was extraordinarily successful. That agency nominated the members of the *Reichswirtschaftsrat,* the corporative advisory parliament provided for in the Weimar constitution. What weakened the effort of the *Social Catholics* in Germany before 1933 was firstly, the misunderstanding between Catholic and Protestant groups as to how to meet Marxist and Communist penetration, and secondly, Nazi infiltration in conservative quarters.

to another and to decree compulsory labor. Labor was regimented, for all the etiquette of the "Labor Front," to subserve political motives which soon revealed themselves as aiming at the setting up of a war economy.

Other countries before and after the war have followed the Italian and German systems, mitigating some of their rigidities, and they have done so in the mistaken belief that they were applying papal teachings. But given the fundamental mistake of denying freedom of association to the workers, while monopolistic groups under State tutelage were organized, the foundation stone of a system inspired by the teachings of the *Social Catholic* school was missing.

III

The war has affected world economy and the whole of our social life. It could not be otherwise since this is a total war from which not even neutral and non-belligerent countries are immune. The relationships between State and professional groups during such a war are modified both in intensity and extension. The difference between democratic and totalitarian States is that in the former, workers, maintaining their free associations and guarantees, voluntarily submit themselves to war discipline and co-operate politically in the common effort while accepting such restrictions as necessity imposes. In the latter, it may well be that a national sentiment developed among the working classes will likewise accept the harsh discipline of war. But the lack of liberty, the social restrictions, the exploitation of energies, the absence of all juridical and moral guarantees will weigh heavily on the working classes, realizing as they must that their status is one of slavery from which they have no prospect of emerging, even if their own country should be victorious.

It has been claimed that Russian workers, artisans and peasants fight with a courage and an ardor they never showed in the same degree under the czars. However difficult it may be to understand the psychology of peoples detached from our civilization, it must be noted first of all that Russia has been attacked and her territory invaded; consequently, these workers and peasants are defending their own fatherland. Furthermore it cannot be denied that the working classes, deprived under the czars of all participation in civic and political life,[10] inadequately provided with schools for vocational training, had no party spirit comparable to that which the Soviets have been careful to foster.

With this prefaced in the interest of an exact diagnosis, we cannot accept the view which places Soviet and democratic labor unions on the same level. This matter was often debated at international workers congresses after the First World War where, on the basis of a false appreciation of realities, British labor fought for several years in favor of admitting the Russian unions, which German and French workers representatives, among others, opposed for the reason that the unions in question were not free.

As a rule, all totalitarian systems, including the Russian, stifle that free breathing possible only in the air of liberty. Hence they have no alternative but to recur to the repressive devices of stricter bureaucratic and police organization. War accelerates the rhythm of human activities by means of general restrictions. In totalitarian countries these restrictions have not eliminated liberty, which did not exist, but have taken away from the workers even the possibility of adapting themselves to the system of slavery—an adaptation that might slowly have become, as it did for the slaves of antiquity, a kind of pseudo-liberty—the only sort that mankind knew for thousands of years.

For this reason, the situation of workers groups in the democratic State during a war like the present one is completely different from their situation in the totalitarian State both as regards the factual condition brought about by the war and as relates to the reconstruction period after the war.[11] The former can talk of rights, can make their voice heard, can debate their interests even while making allowance for the difficulties of a crisis affecting the whole of economic life; the latter, if they aspire to break the servile bonds that bind them, can only look forward to the possibility of exploiting some revolutionary crisis as a means of regaining their freedom.

[10] The old local organization of peasants and artisans in Russia was confined to the economic and domestic spheres and had no political bearing.

[11] In the steel industries, the *labor-management* committees, where established, have proved to be a "tremendous contribution" to the war effort according to the statement of Gordon Lefebvre, vice-president and general manager of the Cooper-Bessemer Corporation, who remarks that said committees "had the effect of educating management—and I hope labor—to the other fellow's viewpoint." (See *The Commonweal*, March 5, 1943, pp. 484, 485.)

And this brings us back once more to the question at the root of the workers problem in the modern world (a question we have repeatedly touched upon in the course of this study) : How is it possible to induce the working class to abandon its position of antagonism to the State and to reverse this into one of co-operation with the State? Upon this point we must focus our attention if we would arrive at a solution of the post-war problem. For if the working class has no freedom to organize along occupational lines and no voice in political life, as is the case in totalitarian countries, then, notwithstanding the pseudo-system of political representation, it will be impossible to give labor effective parity with other classes, in a broader scheme of social co-operation. Only the workers of democratic countries will be able to attain this goal, provided the voluntary and effective understanding reached during the war is continued, developed and consolidated during the period of peace.

*

*   *

In England and the United States not a few important initiatives have been started for the study and preparation of a better world after the war, both from the economic and the financial points of view: studies, some under private auspices, others conducted by government agencies, still others by universities. Problems of peace will be as formidable as those of war, with the difference that the pressure of war developments and preoccupation with victory having ceased, there will be a psychological bewilderment and relaxation of activities that might easily lead to chaotic situations. Hence, the preparation for the new order must be made with infinite foresight and the greatest possible care, with sound criteria and long-range vision in order to preclude hasty stopgap measures that often impede true and radical solutions. Consequently, we must welcome such forward-looking work as that of the conference of the International Labor organization held in New York in October, 1941, in which no less than 34 governments participated. The conference was promoted by the International Labor Office, whose present headquarters are in Montreal with branch bureaus in Geneva and elsewhere.

The International Labor Office continues even today, although with reduced means, its work for the protection and betterment of social and economic conditions of laboring groups, comprising exchange of information, technical and statistical research and whatever else tends to assure the vast problems of labor their place in the economic and political field.

It is of the utmost importance now not to be content with standing firm upon the ground already won by labor, whether nationally or internationally, but—anticipating other crises which the future is sure to bring—to prepare and establish clearly, here and now, the essential data for a new social policy. Taking this into account, the employers, workers and governmental delegates of the United States offered to the assembly in New York a resolution[12] which was unanimously adopted.

[12] . . . . WHEREAS the close of the war must be followed by immediate action, previously planned and arranged, for the feeding of peoples in need, for the reconstruction of the devastated countries, for the provision and transportation of raw materials and capital equipment necessary for the restoration of economic activity, for the reopening of trade outlets, for the resettlement of workers and their families under circumstances in which they can work in freedom and security and hope, for the changing over of industry to the needs of peace, for the maintenance of employment, and for the raising of standards of living throughout the world; and. . . . :

The Conference of the International Labour Organization Requests the Governing Body:

(a) to transmit this resolution forthwith to the governments of all Member States, to call to their attention the desirability of associating the International Labour Organization with the planning and application of measures of reconstruction, and to ask that the International Labour Organization be represented in any Peace or Reconstruction Conference following the war;

(b) to suggest to the Governments of the Member States that they should, if they have not already done so, set up representative agencies for the study of the social and economic needs of the post-war world and that such agencies should consult with the appropriate organs of the International Labour Organization;

(c) to set up from its own membership a small tripartite committee, instructed to study and prepare (i) measures of reconstruction and (ii) emergency measures to deal with unemployment, which should be empowered to enlist the assistance of technically qualified experts, authorized to co-operate with the governmental, intergovernmental and private agencies engaged in similar studies and with those agencies whose present activities in the social and economic field affect the conditions under which post-war programs will be carried out;

(d) to make full use of such existing organs of the I.L.O. as the International Public Works Committee, the Permanent Agricultural Committee, the Permanent Committee on Migration for Settlement, and the Joint Maritime Commission, and from time to time to make such modifications in the composition of these agencies, and to set up such new agencies, as may be needed to meet the responsibilities implied in this resolution;

(e) to direct the programme of work of the International Labour Office to fulfill the purposes of this resolution; and

(f) to report on the subject matter of this resolution to the next and subsequent meetings of the International Labour Conference so that the International Labour Organization shall be in a position to give authoritative expression to the social objectives confided to it, in the rebuilding of a peaceful world upon the basis of "improved labour standards, economic adjustments and social security."

The fact that the American government has taken the initiative in ensuring that the I.L.O. will be represented in the future conference for peace and reconstruction is an event of great historical significance. It represents the fulfilment of more than fifty years of persistent and assiduous effort to free the masses from the grip of the anti-social and revolutionary vise and to allow of their entrance into collective life not merely as individual citizens (this had already been accomplished by democracy through universal suffrage) , but as organs of the principal social factor which is labor, on a footing of equality with the other social factor which is capital, for the peaceful discussion of the general interests of society.

While labor should have its legitimate place in the agencies of reconstruction and at the peace conference, it would be intolerable were the system of representation heretofore in force in the I.L.O. to be maintained without the changes which justice dictates. As previously mentioned, the present system confines representation exclusively to the unions having the largest membership, all other unions being deprived of voting powers.

Today, in continental Europe, old rivalries between Christian and socialist trade unions have ceased. No longer, either, can the opposition of industrialists to free and federated trade unionism lay claim to justification. The working class itself must feel compelled by the logic of facts to unite in professional groups. The freedom that makes possible a multiplicity of groups must be assured, but it must not be such as to harm the solidarity of the

---

The Acting Director of the I.L.O. in his report to the New York conference summarized as follows the lines of a program for an international social policy:

(a) The elimination of unemployment,
(b) The establishment of machinery for placing, vocational training and retraining,
(c) The improvement of social insurance in all its fields and in particular its extension to all classes of workers,
(d) The institution of a wage policy aimed at securing a just share of the fruits of progress for the workers,
(e) A minimum living wage for those too weak to secure it for themselves,
(f) Measures to promote better nutrition, and to provide adequate housing and facilities for recreation and culture,
(g) Greater equality and occupational opportunity,
(h) An international public works policy for the development of the world's resources,
(i) The organization of migration for employment and settlement under adequate guarantees for all concerned.
(j) The collaboration of employers and workers in the initiation and application of economic and social measures.

workers, or disrupt the harmony of the various initiatives. At this point the governments must intervene in order to help both labor and the community. They must give to unions that juridical status which is theirs by right in a society organically constructed and, along with it, that economic and public responsibility which is necessary to ensure their stability and the fulfilment of their functions.

Among the Christian Democrats in Europe there were some who took the view that the enrolment of workers in their respective unions should be made compulsory by law. This view, raising as it did delicate issues, was counterbalanced by the affirmation (fundamental in papal teachings) that syndicates and groups must be free in order to avoid the unfairness of arbitrarily giving to any one union a monopolistic privilege over all workers in the same trade. According to this point of view there should be, even within the same profession, as many unions as the workers are disposed to support, provided the legal conditions for their recognition are satisfied. Accordingly, once the organizational problem within each State is solved, it will be necessary to modify the system of the representation of the workers at the assemblies and conferences of the International Labor Office.

We desire to stress here not only an organic principle—the just and effective representation of labor—but also a principle of liberty and autonomy. The worker is not to be the slave of the State, nor of the political parties, or even of the occupational groups, but is to have real freedom of choice and action. And if so be the obligation to enroll in one of the unions of his trade should be imposed upon the worker *with all due caution*—we say "with all due caution" in order to avoid all real curtailment of freedom—the initiative to organize on the basis he thinks best must be left to him in the interest both of his class and of society. This will leave some scope, however limited, for competition, a moderate degree of which is useful in all fields of social life.

Another step in the reconstruction of the future must be taken: both in theory and practice the principle of class struggle must be liquidated and replaced by the principle of co-operation of classes. Of late years Marxism has receded considerably; but it still pervades the social atmosphere like an infection which under favorable circumstances might again become virulent and spread. The post-war period may easily be conducive to the revival of Marxism,[13] whether as a consequence of extremely difficult social conditions, or as a result of the influence of Russian bolshevism.

If instead of 8 or 10 million organized workers in the United States there were 20 or 30 million, the Marxist or bolshevist danger would be proportionately lessened by the existence of large unions and labor organizations which of their very nature tend rather to collaboration than to revolution. Moreover, the idea of co-operation between the classes must cease to be confined to the realm of labor problems. It will have to be extended to the wider domain of universal social economy (of which labor, though forming a large part, is not the whole) and consequently of politics which by its nature influences all social problems.

Thus we arrive at an organic conception of democracy (which might well be called "social democracy" were the name not reminiscent of the old German socialist conception) according to which public power would no longer take the form of a *de facto* monopoly of the bourgeoisie nor of a "tendential exploitation" in the interest of the capitalistic system but of a *de jure* and *de facto* co-operation on the part of all classes.

In order to make such co-operation not only effective but harmonious, we must bring to the fore a vital matter that has been expressed in various ways: the *right to a job*, the *right to the necessities of life, just participation in the economic resources, the right to earn a family-wage, etc.* In all civilized countries social legislation has made notable progress during the last 50 years, but it still requires new provisions and numerous changes.[14]

---

[13] I say *Marxism*, not *Socialism*, because, for many, the word *Socialism* does not imply class-war or abolition of property. I know that, in America, Marxism is currently used for Socialism, and that some "Marxists" here are not interested in the theory of the class-war, the materialistic interpretation of history and other Marxian tenets. I use the term *Marxism*, however, in its full acceptance.

[14] Among these changes we must look for what Pius XII urges in his Christmas Message of 1942. "These exigencies," he says, "include, besides a just wage which covers the needs of the worker and his family, the conservation and perfection of a social order which will make possible an assured, even if modest, private property for all classes of society; which will promote higher education for the children of the working class who are especially endowed with intelligence and goodwill; which will promote the care and the practice of the social spirit in one's immediate neighborhood, in the district, the province, the people and the nation, a spirit which, by smoothing over friction arising from privileges or class interests, removes from the workers the sense of isolation through the assuring experience of a genuinely human and fraternally Christian solidarity."— In his address to the Italian workers, June 13, 1943, Pius XII has further stressed these social achievements, warning all that "salvation and justice are not to be found in revolution, but in an evolution through concord."

The post-war situation will be difficult due chiefly to the unemployment destined to follow demobilization of the armed forces, to the large number of men wounded or otherwise disabled in the war, to epidemics and famines which will ravage the earth, especially the poorer countries where medical supplies are scarce. When that time comes, a gigantic effort will be necessary—a union of all countries, primarily of the United States and England—to save the situation with adequate means and with a feeling of solidarity among all classes as well as among all nations.

Sacrifices will be demanded from all for the sake of the common good, but all must be assigned their proper part and place in the world-wide task of reconstruction. The worker must have his rightful place in the single States and in the society of States. In this way he will not be left outside to agitate and to promote revolts, but will be called upon to participate, together with the other classes represented, in the councils and deliberations. The world that must then be saved—the world of all—is his world, too, and all the more his in that as the worker he is peculiarly exposed to physical sufferings and moral deceits.

When this stage shall have been reached, the historic cycle of two centuries will be complete: from the time when labor was economically and politically disorganized, its social nature unrecognized, and only a private character attributed to it—to the period when it began to be organized into outlawed societies conspiring against the State—to the era when it became a tolerated association, but still kept outside of the State—down to the culminating epoch when, integrated into the State and into the community of States, it will be fully recognized as a factor at once economic, political and social.

Index of Names

Abelard, 289, 292
Abraham, 347, 369
Adam, 261
Adler, Mortimer J., V, IXn, 73, 84, 84n, 85n, 88n, 89
Alexander, S., 300
Alexander the Great, 357
Alsberg, Paul, 132, 132n
Amalric (Amaury) of Bène, 298, 305
Anaxagoras, 248
Anaximander, 274
Anaximenes, 274, 275
Andrieu, Pierre-Paulin Cardinal, Archb. of Bordeaux, 188
d'Annunzio, Gabriele, 180, 185, 189
Antigone, 252
Aquinas, St. Thomas, V, 77, 85, 85n, 86, 87, 88, 88n, 91, 92, 124, 220, 222, 233, 234, 239, 240, 250, 250n, 264n, 289, 289n, 291, 296, 330, 330n, 346n, 352n, 359, 360, 366, 366n, 369, 371, 376n, 377, 378, 378n
Aristotle, 72n, 74, 76, 81, 82, 85, 86, 87, 88, 88n, 230, 266, 266n, 273, 274, 278, 278n, 279, 290, 291, 307, 325, 328
Arquilliere, R., 354, 354n, 355n
Augustine, St., 91, 124, 211, 236, 283, 330, 347, 354, 357
Augustus, Emperor, 283
Aurelius, Marcus, Emperor, 283
Averroës, 307, 328, 330

Bakunin, M. A., 250, 329, 361
Barres, Maurice, 185
Baudrillart, Henrico Cardinal, 29
Baumann, Émile, 188
Bellarmine, Robert Cardinal, St., 253, 254
Benedict XV, 188, 202
Bergson, Henri, 27, 306
Bernard of Chartres, 288
Bernard of Clairvaux, St., 293
Bernouille, Gaetan, 188
Bernstein, F., 9
Bilfinger, Carl, 21n
Billot, Cardinal Louis, 256
von Bismarck, Otto E. L., Prince, 178, 180
Blondel, Maurice, 185

Bonaventure, St., 328, 330, 369
Bonnard, Roger, 3n, 6n, 7n, 11n, 13n, 66n
Bosanquet, Bernard, 296
Bossuet, Jacques B., 106
Bradley, F. H., 296
de Brian, Maine, 372
de la Brière, Yves, S.J., XI, 95
Bristler, Edouard, 3n, 21n
Brown, W. A., 85, 85n, 86
Brunetière, Ferdinand, 30
Bruno, Giordano, 291, 292
Brutzkus, J., 92
Buber, Martin, 364n
Buckner, Ludwig, 133, 134
Budge, E. A. Wallis, 269n
Burnet, John, 273, 275
Bury, R. G., 260

Caesar, Julius, 189
Caillois, René, 362n
Cajetan, Thomas de Vio, 376n
Calmettes, A., 5
Calvin, John, 353
Carneades, 260
Cathrein, Viktor, S. J., 174
Cavagnis, Felice Cardinal, 250
Cesalpinus, 292
Chalybäus, Heinrich Moritz, 301
Chamberlain, Houston Stewart, 4, 130, 178
Chamberlain, Joseph, 180, 181
Chamberlain, Neville, 18
du Chardin, Pierre Teilhard, 374n
Chesterton, Gilbert, 261
Chevalier, Jacques, 27n
Chevalley, Claude, 338n
Christ, 27, 106, 117, 120, 121, 125, 129, 139, 140, 143, 144, 154, 335, 340, 347, 353, 363, 364, 374
Claudel, Paul, 329
Chaptal, Emmanuel A., Bishop, 187
Charlemagne, 355
Chrysippus, 281
Clermont, Ferrand, 234
Comte, Auguste, 184, 193, 226, 298
Constantine, Emperor, 354
Copernicus, Nicholas, 73

415

INDEX OF SUBJECTS